SONGS IN DARK TIMES

SONGS IN DARK TIMES

YIDDISH POETRY OF STRUGGLE FROM
SCOTTSBORO TO PALESTINE

AMELIA M. GLASER

HARVARD UNIVERSITY PRESS

Cambridge, Massachusetts, and London, England

2020

Publication of this book has been supported through the generous
provisions of the Maurice and Lula Bradley Smith Memorial Fund.

Second printing

LIBRARY OF CONGRESS CATALOGING-IN-PUBLICATION DATA

Names: Glaser, Amelia, author.
Title: Songs in dark times : Yiddish poetry of struggle from Scottsboro
to Palestine / Amelia M. Glaser.
Description: Cambridge, Massachusetts : Harvard University
Press, 2020. | Includes index. | In English; poems in Yiddish
with English translations.
Identifiers: LCCN 2020015150 | ISBN 9780674248458 (cloth)
Subjects: LCSH: Yiddish poetry—20th century. | Yiddish poetry—Social
aspects—History—20th century. | Poets, Yiddish—Political and
social views—History—20th century. | Jews—Intellectual life. |
Communist literature—20th century.
Classification: LCC PJ5122 .G59 2020 | DDC 839/.11309—dc23
LC record available at https://lccn.loc.gov/2020015150

For my parents, Carol Boone Glaser and John Philip Glaser,
who taught me to be an optimist.

CONTENTS

Preface
The Optimists   ix

Introduction
Yiddish Passwords in the Age of Internationalism   1

1   FROM THE YANGTZE TO THE BLACK SEA:
Esther Shumiatcher's Travels   39

2   ANGRY WINDS: Jewish Leftists and the Challenge of Palestine   72

3   SCOTTSBORO CROSS: Translating Pogroms to Lynchings   107

4   *NO PASARÁN:* Jewish Collective Memory in the
Spanish Civil War   139

5   MY SONGS, MY *DUMAS:* Rewriting Ukraine   174

6   *TESHUVAH:* Moishe Nadir's Relocated Passwords   211

Afterword
Kaddish   243

APPENDIX: Poems from the Age of Internationalism   251

H. Leivick, "A Sacco-Vanzetti Year"   251
Esther Shumiatcher, "At the Border of China"   252
Moyshe Teyf, "Sing, Desert Wind"   253
Shifre Vays, "Accusations"   255
Malka Lee, "God's Black Lamb"   256
Peretz Markish, "Spain"   257
Aaron Kurtz, "Kol Nidre"   261
Dovid Hofshteyn, "Ukraine" (1944)   262
Moishe Nadir, "Closer"   263
Aaron Kurtz, "Kaddish"   264

NOTES   269
ACKNOWLEDGMENTS   333
INDEX   337

PREFACE

The Optimists

AARON KURTZ (1891–1964) was a teenager when he left his Lubavitcher Hassidic family to join the circus. Neither an acrobat nor a magician, Kurtz traveled as a circus and theater hairdresser and at twenty made his way to the United States, where he joined the Communist Party and eventually became, by some accounts, the leading proletarian Yiddish poet.[1] Kurtz breathlessly embraced varying forms and broad political content, combining the fragmentation and declarations of the Russian futurists with the self-reflective empathy of the American Yiddish Introspectivists.[2] In one poem, he imagines a Soviet blacksmith's torrid love affair in his smithy. In another, he retells the contents of a letter from a young nurse in the Spanish Civil War. Kurtz's poems, laced with fragments of prayers and Party shibboleths, do not neatly fit into an American Jewish narrative of shtetl memory. Similarly, Kurtz's ethos remains an enigma: his poems of justice and tolerance belie his rigid adherence to the Communist Party line (he wrote a birthday poem to Stalin in December 1949—when rumors about the imprisonment of the leading Soviet Yiddish writers were already circulating). This book is an attempt to make sense of Kurtz, and his fellow Party-aligned Yiddish poets, in North America as well as in the Soviet Union. These poets, to varying degrees, put their faith in a future, liberating, world revolution at a time of rising nationalist movements.

Itche Goldberg (1904–2006), the editor of the last of the interwar American Yiddish literary journals, *Yidishe Kultur,* once attempted to explain his generation of leftist Yiddish writers to me through a self-deprecating description of his own faith: "I am an optimist because I'm not smart enough to be a pessimist." This conversation took place in 1998 in Itche's office off Union Square in New York City. I was a student of Yiddish, beginning what would become a master's thesis on the poets affiliated with the proletarian Yiddish writer's union Proletpen. Goldberg's self-proclaimed naïve optimism constituted its own belief system. The left-wing Yiddish poets with whom Goldberg came of age in the interwar years aligned themselves with the enormous, nebulous category of the workers of the world, sometimes naively and sometimes strategically. The tragedy of the Holocaust, together with the Cold War, meant that the few Yiddish writers who made it into English excluded most of these Party-aligned writers. Those who continued writing and editing after World War II focused on preserving Yiddish and its literature, not the complex politics that often came with it. Goldberg edited *Yidishe Kultur* until 2003, when he retired at the age of one hundred. By then, the journal—no longer part of a radical movement of writers working to spawn world revolution—largely republished earlier Yiddish literature. Nonetheless, its existence, and the fact that Goldberg worked to keep it alive longer than anyone could have imagined, provided a bridge between my own generation and the Yiddish writers who, in the 1930s, wanted to build a more just world.

In approaching the Party-aligned Yiddish poets of the interwar period, I could have concentrated on themes of labor, gender, and immigration or on their odes to the nascent Soviet Union. I leave these topics for future scholarship. My choice to focus on portrayals of non-Jewish ethnic minorities reflects what I believe is the most formally complex Party-aligned poetry and the most relevant to the twenty-first century. As Nariman Skakov has recently suggested, Soviet representations of national minorities continued a modernist practice of formal experimentation even as Socialist Realism officially replaced modernism. According to Skakov, "national form was the last sanctuary of modernist *strangeness.*"[3] The portrayal of ethnic minorities cuts to the core of these writers' efforts to build communist internationalism. If these efforts involved a degree of cultural appropriation, the poets at the center of this book were exploring the ways Jewishness fit into this new world of workers. Without ignoring the shortcomings of the communist / anticommunist binary model to which many of these writers subscribed, I aim to explain how the Soviet-centered project of deparochializing Jewish culture extended well beyond the Soviet Union and influenced conversations in the United States. These little-studied writers witnessed others' struggles in an attempt to overcome the condition of Otherness. If they did not manage to create the just world they envisioned, they did leave us a legacy of imagining one.

In the interest of making this book accessible to the English-language reader, I have opted to transliterate the original Yiddish in the text and appendix. I have standardized my original citations to match the YIVO transliteration guidelines, as modified by Isaac L. Bleaman in "Guidelines for Yiddish in Bibliographies: A Supplement to YIVO Transliteration," *In Geveb: A Journal of Yiddish Studies,* July 2, 2019. Occasional exceptions include alternate pronunciations (for example, Galitzianer or Litvak) that are necessary to understand the use of rhyme, rhythm, or alliteration in a poem. Wherever possible, I have used the most common English spelling of writers' names. I have included several lines by the Hebrew-language poet Chaim Nachman Bialik, and have offered these in a transliterated Ashkenazi Hebrew, with thanks to Dovid Katz. Not only would Bialik have used an Ashkenazi pronunciation when he wrote these lines in 1903, but the East European poets who cited him would have used this pronunciation to read him. In my transliteration of Russian and Ukrainian, I use the modified Library of Congress system, except for the names of writers who are better known by a traditional English spelling. I use the current *New York Times* standard spelling of cities (for example, Kyiv, Vilnius), except in cases where a title, name, or phrase demands a different transliteration (for example, the Yiddish Kiev-grupe or the Vilna Ghetto). In my translations, I have made an effort to render the verse as literally as possible, while also giving a sense of the poets' alliteration and rhythm. This is particularly challenging in my occasional translations of translations. My hope is that the transliterated originals will give more readers access to these poets' choices and innovations.

SONGS IN DARK TIMES

INTRODUCTION

Yiddish Passwords in the Age of Internationalism

"In the dark times / Will there be singing?," Bertolt Brecht asked in 1939.[1] The 1930s were dark times. It was a decade marked by the rise of fascism and imperialist violence on a global scale; isolationism and "America First" were at the center of American discourse. And yet this was also the moment when a wave of young Yiddish poets, born into traditional Jewish families but identifying with world revolution, chose to write about the struggles of other groups, from African Americans to ethnic Ukrainians. The revolutionary Yiddish poets who, facing rising nationalism, turned their pens to ethnic minorities is an important, and overlooked, chapter in Jewish history. The enormity of the Holocaust meant that Jewish conversations in the post–World War II period in the United States centered on Jewish specificity. Meanwhile, in the postwar Soviet Union, Yiddish was largely suppressed. In the United States of the Cold War, Revolutionary poets across languages fell into obscurity. Nearly a century later, new conversations about solidarity in the face of tyranny have emerged. It is time to tell the story of the Yiddish internationalist poets.

What do Jews have to offer an ongoing discussion about the struggles of ethnic groups around the world against racism, imperialism, and economic disenfranchisement, from Honduran refugees to Palestinian Arabs? The Yiddish poets whose verse filled Communist Party journals during the long 1930s offer a counternarrative to the story of Jewish religious and ethnic insularity. These revolutionary writers were proposing a radically new understanding of community: if their parents and grandparents had identified as Jews, they chose instead to identify as workers of the world. And yet their vocabulary for describing group belonging came from Jewish tradition and Jewish collective memory. Writers did *teshuvah* (penance) to return to the Party; Chinese workers were described in similar terms to pogrom victims; volunteers from around the world in the Spanish Civil War were described as reciting the Kol Nidre prayer in the trenches. The poets I consider in this book were not merely describing other struggling peoples; they were bringing other peoples into the fold, making them metaphorically Jewish.

Most of the young women and men who are the subject of this book were based in the United States or Soviet Union. They were well educated in Jewish religious tradition and found in religious practice metaphors that could easily be applied to their newly discovered revolutionary struggle. Increasingly, throughout the 1930s, these writers also applied culturally marked *non*-Jewish passwords to Jews. In effect, the figures at the center of this study were using poetry to build a new religious tradition, modeled on Judaism and consecrated through its affiliation with the Communist Party. It is my goal, in this book, to help decode the shibboleths and aspirations of a group of understudied poets. These poets offer a case study in how poetry can inform and reinscribe group identity.

At midnight on August 23, 1927, the Italian American anarchists Nicola Sacco and Bartolomeo Vanzetti were executed in Boston, Massachusetts, for suspected murder. When the Yiddish poet H. Leivick (born Leyvik Halpern, 1888–1962) wrote about Sacco and Vanzetti a year later, he identified the perpetrator as "the same evil from accuser to accuser" (Dos zelbe shlekhts fun kateyger tsu kateyger). Sacco and Vanzetti's "accusers" were the unjust US courts of law and the Massachusetts governor, Alvin Fuller. For Leivick, as for many Yiddish poets of his generation, the evil that oppressed Jews in Europe and anarchist immigrants in the United States was one and the same.

Haynt, azoy vi farayorn,	Today, like last year,
tsharlstonen iber der erd dem talyens	the hangman's feet dance the
fis;	Charleston the world over;
s'iz nokh afile nit fartsoygn gevorn	Fuller's bite hasn't even been covered
mit keyn haytl der fulerisher bis.	with a scab.
Dos zelbe shlekhts fun kateyger tsu	The same evil from accuser to
kateyger,	accuser,
der zelber foyst, di zelbe makht;	the same fist, the same power;
o, mir fargesn nit di vayzers fun	oh, we won't forget how the clock
zeyger	hands
vi zey hobn getrift mit blut in	dripped with blood that August night.
oygust-nakht.[2]	

Leivick's "A yor Sako Vanzeti" (A Sacco-Vanzetti year) mourns the Italian anarchists and calls upon fellow Jewish immigrants to fight the cycle of injustice perpetuated against innocent victims. In Leivick's original, the "accusers" are *kateygers*: the classical rabbinic term for "prosecutor," a *kateyger* in Yiddish is a "prosecuting angel" who delivers a heavenly verdict.[3] Whereas a legal prosecutor, or *prokuror,* might be found in a court of law, the *kateyger* in Yiddish had become a moral prosecutor, and sometimes a synonym for Satan.[4] The ultimate devil's advocate in Jewish folk and religious tradition has passed judgment on the Italian political victims. For Leivick's left-wing Yiddish reader, *kateyger* was a password, admitting the non-Jewish, Italian anarchists into Jewish collective memory in the context of a humanitarian Yiddish poem.

For the purposes of this book, I use the term password to refer to a culturally coded word, name, or phrase that conveys group identity. As a password, *kateyger* referenced both Jewish law and a beloved work of Yiddish literature. The classic Yiddish writer Y. L. Peretz had described a *kateyger* in the heavenly trial of "Bontshe Shvayg" (Bontshe Silent), hero of his 1894 eponymous story and a quintessential Jewish victim, a man so humble that he has never attempted to defend himself. When even the *kateyger* judges Bontshe worthy of all the heavens, the honored guest can only think to ask for a warm roll with butter every morning. In response, "the judges and angels hung their heads in shame; the *kateyger* started to laugh."[5] Peretz's ending is legible to those who are familiar with the Talmudic Hebrew proverb "Eyn kategor naaseh sanegor" (The prosecutor is not made the advocate).[6] Like Bontshe Shvayg, who epitomizes the perpetually accused, irreparably weakened eastern European Jew, the Italian anarchists and other victims of discriminatory law faced *kateygers* who would never become their advocates. If, as Anita Norich has asserted, Peretz's line is "a call to arms, or at least to action," then Leivick's attention to non-Jewish victims is a call to his American Yiddish readers to stand up on behalf of others.[7] The extension of such marked Jewish terms as *kateyger* to a multiethnic community is a poetic hallmark of the turbulent and politically charged period. "There will be singing," Brecht reassured his readers in 1939, "Of the dark times."[8] To the poets committed to combating the rising threats of fascism and xenophobia, singing in their dark time meant rejecting the marginal condition of Otherness by forging an age of internationalism.

How poets developed and merged a vocabulary of collective Jewish identity with a poetics of internationalism is the subject of this book. As I shall argue, they did this by applying Jewish passwords—terms like *kateyger* that were specific to Jewish practice and collective memory— to the contemporary struggles of non-Jewish minorities. In the chapters that follow, I address the semantic slippage between Jewish collective identity and the broader, multinational, workers' identity that characterized leftist internationalism from the late 1920s through World War II. This slippage was linguistic in nature and took the form of shifting terms—passwords, as I refer to them here—ordinarily applicable to a specific ethnic group or context and applied to a cross-section of national or ethnic minorities with the goal of analogizing these groups' current or historical suffering. Like all words, passwords change, shifting to take on new ideological meanings over time. This book analyzes how Yiddish poets applied these passwords to admit non-Jewish "Others" into a Jewish fold.

This is the story of a generation of left-wing, eastern-European-born, Yiddish poets who came of age in the long decade of proletarian internationalism—a decade that began around 1927, with the execution of Sacco and Vanzetti in the United States and the hard-left turn known as the "Third Period" that began with the Sixth Comintern Congress in 1928.[9] Whereas the years immediately following the Bolshevik Revolution saw Lenin, Trotsky, and others emphasizing the need for socialism on a world scale, by the time Stalin had established power in the late 1920s, the doctrine of "socialism in one country" had taken hold. The proletarian internationalism that characterized the long 1930s was centered in Moscow and demanded loyalty to the Soviet Union. Most of the poets I discuss were born in small towns in eastern Europe and migrated, on their own or with their families, to one of the many metropolises that became Yiddish cultural centers in the 1920s, including Kiev, Warsaw, Moscow, New York, and Mexico City. A few traveled briefly to Palestine, where Zionists sought political legitimacy for a Jewish nation state.[10] Others sought a hybrid form of Jewish cultural autonomy and Soviet Communism by joining the Soviet Jewish farming colonies established in Crimea in the 1920s, or migrating to the far-eastern Soviet Jewish autonomous region of Birobidjan. But the majority of the Party-aligned writers discussed here were ready to lend their own experience as perennial Others to the utopian process of dissolving national boundaries. Yuri Slezkine has usefully identified Jews in the diaspora as a "Mercurian" people—outsiders who, unlike their rooted "Apollonian" counterparts, are "as vulnerable as they are foreign."[11] This is a story about Jewish revolutionaries who believed that their experience as vulnerable outsiders could inspire workers to welcome a new, proletarian, order—a replacement for religion and ethnic allegiance. They believed in shifting the us / them binary of Jew / gentile to the proletarian binary of worker / oppressor.

Leftist Yiddish writers used the term "international" broadly, often applying it to ethnic minorities like African Americans, Rroma, or Arabs in Mandate Palestine. I therefore occasionally use the terms "nation" and "ethnicity" interchangeably.[12] To understand the internationalist turn in Yiddish literature, I consider Yiddish writers who, at any point in the 1920s, '30s, or '40s, published in Party-aligned venues. This includes writers who, like Leivick, eventually changed their views to align themselves with the anti-Stalinist Left. The many clusters of Jewish writers on the left worked to expand group identity from the category of nation to a broader category of class. There were many political op-tions at the time: secular Jews could align themselves with various forms of Zionism, socialism, communism, or anarchism. That individuals often moved between political groups meant that Party discourse extended beyond Party politics. The long decade of internationalism ended, for the writers I discuss, with World War II, when the utopian ideals of the prewar Left succumbed to a changing global order. In the years following World War II, the Soviet authorities mounted an anticosmopolitan campaign that targeted the historically rootless Soviet Jewish population as potential spies. The passwords these poets developed would remain integral to modern Jewish literature, both inside and outside the Soviet Union, long after the Communist International had ended in 1943. This is, then, also a story of how Soviet communism in its most orthodox period—the late 1920s through World War II—exerted a lasting influence on ideas of empathy and internationalism.

Leivick's poetic commemoration of Sacco and Vanzetti provides us with a sampling of the themes explored throughout this book. In this introduction, following a brief overview of the book, I address three manifestations of the internationalist password. I first discuss how lexical passwords—shibboleths like *kateyger*—merged Jewish tradition with the experience of other national minorities. I then turn to passwords that refer explicitly to a wound, as a marker of shared trauma. Passwords were intimately tied to the wounds of modernity. Governor Fuller's "bite," Leivick asserts, is still open a year later, marking its victims and their mourners as comrades in a common struggle. Finally, I turn to the way the internationalist poets mark time, inscribing historical events on the collective memory. Like Leivick, for whom the clock hands "dripped with blood that August night," the other poets I discuss immortalize watershed historical moments that united and divided groups. These dates and time stamps allow politically like-minded individuals to align multiple groups' distinct suffering under the banner of a common cause.

The case studies that make up this book highlight Yiddish poetic representations of politically polarizing struggles facing distinct national or ethnic groups. In each chapter, I address a highly charged word or words that became passwords for the proletarian internationalist poets and their readers. I first discuss Esther Shumiatcher's poems about East Asia of 1926–1928, which she places in dialogue with poems about Russian Jews. Shumiatcher's peripatetic path, naiveté, and desire to communicate with communities beyond her own can be read as a metaphor for her generation. The final stop in Shumiatcher's travels was Soviet Crimea, in 1928–1929. There, she and her husband—the well-known playwright Peretz Hirschbein—lived on a Jewish farming colony, becoming strong supporters of the OZET (the Soviet Jewish coloniza-tion aid organization).[13] Shumiatcher's gaze was at once Orientalizing and self-exoticizing, exposing the extent to which Jewish writers self-identified as Asiatic. Indeed, Soviet Crimea in the late 1920s offered poets a metaphorical, as well as a real, point of encounter, where Soviet ideology, Jews seeking a version of autonomy, and Asian figures coexisted.

The wave of violence in Mandatory Palestine in autumn 1929 divided the Jewish Left throughout the world. Jewish poets who remained with the Party defended the Comintern's position that the Arab riots in Pal-estine were a revolutionary uprising, but many poets rejected commu-nism, unwilling to ignore what looked like an all-too-familiar eastern European anti-Jewish pogrom, albeit in Palestine. This included Leivick, who had considered immigration to the Soviet Union just a few years earlier. Chapter 2 examines the rift between the Soviet-identified Left and the anti-Stalinist Left over the issue of identification with Palestinian Arabs. Chapter 3 turns to Scottsboro, Alabama, where, in 1931, nine young African American men were framed for a crime they did not commit. The Party mobilized on behalf of the defense. As Robin Kelley has formulated, "For most African Americans, as well as black people all over the world, the Party was best known for its defense of the Scottsboro Nine and the International Labor Defense's (ILD) unremitting challenge to a racist criminal justice system."[14] "Scottsboro" became a password for racial injustice in the United States, and the lengthy trial inspired a series of Yiddish "Scottsboro" poems, many echoing pogrom poems.

Spanish Civil War slogans frequently appeared in Yiddish poetry in the late 1930s. Phrases such as "¡No pasarán!" (They shall not pass), a ral-lying cry that signified the necessity of the Spanish struggle against the monarchists, took on added meaning when used in a Yiddish poem about the rise of fascism across Europe. In the mid-1930s, the rift that opened over Palestine in 1929 relaxed slightly when the rise of fascism prompted the Party to collaborate with the noncommunist Left in the Popular Front, a strategic alliance, as Helen Graham and Paul Preston have put it, for "linking worker and bourgeois across barriers of social class."[15] The Popular Front, which drew writers together to speak out against fascism, represented a widespread cultural movement during the Spanish Civil War. Chapter 4 analyzes three book-length poetic cycles about Spain by the Soviet poet Peretz Markish, the American poet Aaron Kurtz, and the Mexican poet Jacobo Glantz. Markish, Kurtz, and Glantz merge collective Jewish memory of the Spanish Inquisition with descriptions of the Spanish Civil War, to yield visions of a collective future for Spain that Jews were participating in creating.

The final two chapters center on the uneasy year 1939 in the Soviet Union and the United States, respectively. Chapter 5 describes the boundaries of accepted discourse around nation by focusing on Yiddish translations and discussions of Ukrainian literature in the 1930s. Translation in the Soviet 1930s was both a means of identifying with the other and a Trojan horse for smuggling concerns about one's own ethnic group into a public sphere that had rejected ethno-nationalism. At the center of this chapter is the Yiddish modernist poet Dovid Hofshteyn, whose translations of the celebrated Ukrainian Romantic poet Taras Shevchenko suggest a kinship between the Ukrainian bard, born into serfdom, and the Jews of Soviet Ukraine. A comparison of Hofshteyn's Yiddish translations to contemporaneous translations of Shevchenko into Russian reveals the flexibility of Yiddish to allow the poet to comment, in the language of translation, on the value of cultural tradition.

Chapter 6 addresses the spread of Nazism, culminating in the Hitler-Stalin pact, which led many internationalist Yiddish writers back to Jewish tradition. This final chapter focuses on the *teshuvah* (return, or penance) of Moishe Nadir—the only former Yunge poet to have remained with the US communist daily *Frayhayt* following the 1929 split over Palestine—in the late 1930s. The term *teshuvah*, meaning a return to Judaism, had gained the alternative connotation of a return to the Communist Party. Nadir had been rehearsing the existential process of penance (for his bourgeois modernism) in his Party-aligned poetry of the 1920s and '30s. He reinscribed this practice of doing *teshuvah* with Jewish meaning at the end of his life, turning away from the Party and publicly reevaluating his allegiances. Despite this final rejection of the Party, each chapter in Nadir's life bears a trace of the one before. So, too, the Yid-

dish poetry of internationalism left its mark on later generations, sharp-
ening and nuancing portrayals of Jewish culture.

The dates writers use to mark the end of the 1930s function as passwords in their own right, signaling the boundaries of their relationship to the political Left. Those writers who place the end of the 1930s in
1939—with the Moscow trials, Hitler-Stalin pact, and beginning of
World War II—are, for Michael Denning, individuals for whom "the
thirties tell a cautionary tale: a story of impetuous youthful radicalism,
of seduction and betrayal, of a 'god that failed.'"[16] Denning suggests
that for most of the Popular Front writers, the onset of the Cold War
around 1948 marked the end of an era of optimism. The Yiddish era of
leftist internationalism grinds to a similarly somber pause and an even
more tragic Cold War terror at the end of the 1940s. The rise of McCarthyism and execution of the Rosenbergs in the United States coincided
with the murder of the Yiddish actor and director Solomon Mikhoels
in 1948 and the arrest of the most celebrated Soviet Yiddish writers and
cultural figures, including Peretz Markish, Dovid Hofshteyn, Leib
Kvitko, Itzik Fefer, and Dovid Bergelson. If Yiddish had helped to unite
Soviet Jews during World War II, then Yiddish, one chillingly recognizes, was no longer needed after the war. Along with the tragic loss of
millions of Jewish lives, World War II marked the end of the age of
internationalism.

And yet there is an after story. The passwords that gave Yiddish poets
and readers entrée—imagined or real—into the experiences of other
marginalized groups established a precedent for translating Jewish
trauma into empathy. If, in the wake of World War II, Jewish writers
turned inward to a Jewish community, the proletarian internationalism
of the 1930s had nonetheless established a vocabulary for speaking across
national boundaries. As I discuss in the afterword, the poetics of internationalism outlived the decade of internationalism, and having established a tradition of sharing passwords, Jewish writers continued to seek
points of comparison with other minority groups. The language, for
many, had by then shifted away from Yiddish.

Party-aligned Yiddish poets have been largely absent from an American canon of Jewish literature for the past century. This omission is part
of the wider phenomenon of Cold War scholarship, which often excluded

Party affiliates due to a justifiable distaste for Stalin's institutionalizing of totalitarianism and antisemitism. There is only so much room for Yiddish in an American canon that privileges English-language texts. However, ignoring Party-aligned writers means losing the connections between the conversations they inspired and the concerns about equality that inspired them. This book, as a project of salvage literary history, aims to tread a delicate balance: to redeem the Soviet-aligned literary institutions that encouraged a movement toward internationalism without overlooking the shadow cast by the purges.

THE SHIBBOLETH

The modern human, in the twenty-first century, has been burdened by a plethora of personal passwords designed to verify one's identity. If passwords have become highly individualized—cryptographic sequences in a digital era—the literary password remains a social utterance: it is designed to be shared. A verbal key to an otherwise restricted space, a password lets people in, allows us to cross thresholds, borders, boundaries. Passwords are signifiers, in the Saussurean sense; however, their meaning is not only lexical but performative: they are, as Jean Baudrillard has remarked, "'passers' or vehicles of ideas."[17] Since ancient times, passwords could also bar entry, lock doors, and discriminate against those who cannot transmit or pronounce them. Passwords are by definition untranslatable. The Hebrew word *shibboleth* (literally an ear of corn in ancient Hebrew, Phoenician, Judeo-Aramaic, and Syriac) appears in Judges (Mishpatim) 12:6. The tribe of Gilead, following its defeat of the Ephraimites, asked suspected enemies, who were known to mispronounce *shi* as *si,* to say the word *shibboleth* aloud. The enemy Ephraimites were thus apprehended and killed. The word *shibboleth,* writes Jacques Derrida, "is traversed by a multiplicity of meanings: river, stream, ear of grain, olive twig. But beyond these meanings, it has acquired the value of a password."[18] Yiddish is a language of passwords. The German Jewish language has coexisted with the languages of many host countries and with biblical Hebrew since it emerged in Alsace close to a millennium ago.[19] The multilayered, multilingual vocabulary of

Yiddish can be used to test group affinity and collective memory. Jewish subcultures, moreover, developed marked argots such as the well-documented *ganovim-loshn* (thieves' language), *klezmer-loshn* (musician-speak), *Balagole-loshn* (coachman language), and even *katsoves-loshn* (ritual slaughterer language) to communicate within the profession. In a 1923 study of Yiddish dialects, Avrom-Yitskhak Trivaks observed the tendency of thieves' dialects to borrow words from other language groups (usually Hebrew and Slavic languages) to make their speech less comprehensible to the general public.[20] Left-wing Yiddish speakers, of course, developed political argots to distinguish allies from enemies. At a moment when secular Jews were rapidly joining political movements on the left, from Labor Zionism to the Communist Party, passwords could differentiate between political factions and redraw lines that cut across political parties. Poetry helped to generate the terms that united or divided ideologies.

Passwords exclude and include. Yiddish poets on the left used internationalist passwords to admit their poetry to a leftist international canon. "¡No pasarán!" (they shall not pass) demonstrated a poet's desire to be included among those leftists fighting fascism in the Spanish Civil War; "Scottsboro" aligned Yiddish writers with the Party's struggle on behalf of African Americans; "Sacco-Vanzetti" signaled an American Yiddish poet's commitment to fighting systemic injustice. Similarly, Jewish passwords admitted non-Jewish oppressed peoples into a Jewish collective. Thus, Leivick, using the Jewish term *kateyger* to describe Sacco and Vanzetti's accusers, admits the Italian anarchists into the Jewish fold. This sharing of passwords allows slippages in meaning that combine and conflate Leivick's (and his readers') identities as Jews and workers.

As Raymond Williams writes in his preface to his *Keywords: A Vocabulary of Culture and Society,* "The original meanings of words are always interesting. But what is often most interesting is the subsequent variation."[21] In the poem cited above, Leivick's *kateyger,* a word deriving, via the Hebrew, from the Greek *kategor,* is etymologically bound to the English "category." As Adam Seligman and Robert Weller articulate in their study of cultural ambiguity, "Laws and categories are interwoven. Both attempt to disambiguate in the most critical realm we inhabit, that of human relations."[22] The left-wing discourse of the 1920s and '30s produced a productive ambiguity that destabilized the accepted categories, including categories of the national and the ethnic. Leivick, offering the mythical *kateyger* (whose legal title is at once Jewish and foreign) as a password to admit the Italian anarchists into modern Jewish collective concern, is working against standard categorization and the accusing angels who enforce it. He is using Yiddish poetry to encourage left-wing cultural ambiguity.

Leivick was well equipped to make a case for fighting for a new, international, revolutionary order, for he had come into contact with his own "*kateyger* after *kateyger*." Born and raised in the Belarusian shtetl of Igumen, Leivick left his yeshiva to join the Bund, was arrested in 1906 for revolutionary activity, and was sentenced to four years in a labor camp followed by exile to Siberia. At the trial, Leivick refused to defend his actions: "I am a member of the Jewish revolutionary party, the Bund, and I will do everything in my power to overthrow the tsarist autocracy, its bloody henchmen, and you as well."[23] Leivick escaped with the help of a revolutionary aid organization, immigrating in 1913 to the United States, where he made a living as a wallpaper hanger while becoming one of the world's most respected Yiddish modernists. The passwords that Leivick and other leftist Yiddish poets used to demonstrate their internationalist commitment in the interwar period were at once Jewish and leftist. At the time of the anarchists' execution, Leivick was sympathetic to the Party, though he was not a member. He traveled to the Soviet Union in 1925 and regularly published in the American communist daily *Frayhayt* and monthly *Der Hamer* as well as the Soviet *Royte Velt* until his decisive break with Party politics in 1929.

Sacco-Vanzetti, the hyphenated formula that evoked the persecuted Italian anarchists, constituted what may have been the first leftist-internationalist password. The anarchists Emma Goldman and Alexander Berkman, marking the second anniversary of Sacco and Vanzetti's death, wrote in August 1929, "Throughout the civilized world Sacco and Vanzetti have become a symbol, the shibboleth of Justice crushed by Might. That is the great historic significance of this 20th century crucifixion, and truly prophetic, were the words of Vanzetti when he declared, 'The last moment belongs to us—that agony is our triumph.'"[24]

Sacco and Vanzetti were commemorated in writing by Yiddish poets across the political Left, from the Introspectivist journal *In Zikh* to card-carrying communist poets. An anarchist cause quickly became a symbol for fighting oppression in the United States more generally. As Jordan Finkin has written, "The ideological pedestal on which these groups placed Sacco and Vanzetti serves ultimately to universalize both the alleged criminals and the Yiddish poets' participation in this American genre."[25] Leivick included two Sacco-Vanzetti poems in the *Altmodish* (old-fashioned) section of his collected works—a sign, in Finkin's reading, that Sacco-Vanzetti figured into "a critical framework . . . to understand how to refashion oneself in America when haunted both by the afterlives of one's European experiences *and* by the social problems of America."[26] Passwords were a means of sharing experiences across cultural divides.

TRANSLOCATING CULTURE

Literary passwords allow for a form of poetic adaptation that I refer to as *translocation*—the rewriting of a culturally specific text, event, or concept to fit a different cultural context, in the process likening two cultural experiences and shifting the established categories of group identity. Anthony Pym has discussed the paradigm of broad cultural adaptation as integral to the internationalizing of a text or product, from the Bible to film and software. The Yiddish internationalist poets of the 1930s were similarly engaged in localization from a Jewish to a non-Jewish context, adapting Jewish narratives—particularly narratives of struggle—to non-Jewish groups. Thus, writers would pattern a poem about lynching in the US South on familiar poems about pogroms, in the process drawing an explicit connection between Jewish and African American suffering. This poetic translocation is closer to cultural adaptation than to translation proper but is more intimately connected to textual translation than to the commerce-oriented world of localization.

If the displacements that lead to migrancy render all culture transnational, as Homi Bhabha has suggested, then culture becomes *translational* thanks to the complexities of global media.[27] The left-wing Yiddish poets in this book were not writing for a multilingual global community. However, faced with the post–World War I reality of new national formations in Europe, of political migration and rising fascism, the writers I consider chose, to varying degrees, to align themselves with an international workers' movement committed to fighting global capitalism and imperialism. To translate this movement to a Yiddish readership meant translocating Jews' historical struggles onto non-Jewish groups. This process was both literary and revolutionary: the goal was to use the medium of Yiddish-language poetry, a body of work that was appreciated almost exclusively by Jews, to shift its readers' primary affinity from "Jewish" to "international worker."

Many of the Yiddish internationalist poets were also translators in the most classical sense of the term, rendering poems from Ukrainian, Arabic, Russian, or English into Yiddish. Others produced what John Dryden termed "imitations" in his seventeenth-century taxonomy of translation styles: "where the Translator (if now he has not lost that Name) assumes the liberty not only to vary from the words and sense, but to forsake them both as he sees occasion."[28] The Yiddish internationalist poets, engaging with what Walter Benjamin has called the "afterlife" of the texts that influence them, effected change on the originals. By introducing passwords to their translations, they rendered past works more international.[29] Thus, in Dovid Hofshteyn's Soviet Yiddish translation, the Ukrainian poet Taras Shevchenko's biblical Maria becomes Miriam; in a more radical gesture, the Soviet poet Moyshe Teyf rewrote Chaim Nachman Bialik's Hebrew-language 1903 pogrom poem as an anti-Zionist poem replete with proletarian slogans. Even Y. L. Peretz, who in essence invented a Yiddish high modernism, asserted, at the 1908 Czernowitz conference, "The Jewish proletariat modernizes the Yiddish language."[30] Poetic translocation transcended lexical translation and shaped the aesthetics of proletarian internationalism.

In a politically charged moment like the 1930s, in a transnational language like Yiddish, poetry established the tone of certain highly charged words. Party-aligned Yiddish poets in the interwar period suggested that modern literature was inseparable from politics. If, for Jacques Rancière, the difference between literature's "regime of signification" and the "democratic political stage" is that "the latter deliberately sets itself up in fact by hijacking the words, phrases and figures of founding texts and of the dominant rhetoric," then the leftist Yiddish poets were self-consciously merging these two regimes, willingly helping to mobilize words and phrases for use in political rhetoric.[31] These words would reshape a poetics of Jewish trauma into a poetics of proletarian and international trauma. They would also engender creative and often performative practices of adaptation, translocation, and imitation.

The Party-aligned venues that published the Yiddish internationalists, from the US daily *Frayhayt* to the Soviet literary journal *Royte Velt,* regularly published translations into Yiddish, and translators tested the limits of Yiddish to convey experiences utterly foreign to Ashkenazi Jews. Moishe Nadir published a cycle of translations from multiple languages, including Arabic, Latin, and Greek, in the *Frayhayt,* titled "Fun fremde kvaln" (From foreign wellsprings). The poems should more appropriately be termed "imitations," for Nadir includes no originals, and the bibliographic details are spotty at best. One of these poems includes a note: "Arabic—written around the year 1000." The poem begins with the ancient speaker, longing for the desert wilderness:

Deresn mir tsu zayn in dorf, un shtot	I'm sick of being in the town, and city
benk ikh nokh a tselt in midber,	I long for a tent in the desert,
der duft fun lavender, zol mikh ton derfrishn,	for the waft of lavender to freshen me,
un der kiler shteyn zol zayn mayn kishn.[32]	and the cool stone to cushion me.

Nadir, with his characteristic wordplay, rhymes the verb "derfrishn" (freshen) with the noun "kishn" (pillow)—favorably comparing, in what Jonathan Culler has called a "felicitous" rhyme, the desert scent to the city comfort of bedding.[33] Whereas Zionists were reclaiming Palestine as a historic Jewish homeland, Nadir rejected the idea of a Jewish nation state. By translating an Arabic poem about longing for the desert, he engages the word "midber" (desert), shifting a password from its Zionist context to an Arabic context, albeit in Yiddish. That the poem was published amid the 1929 rift in the Yiddish-speaking community over Palestine is significant. Nadir counters a fundamental Zionist argument—that the desert of Palestine historically belongs to the Jews. The poem ends with images of regrowth:

Fun dr'erd es blit alts yung aroys:	Everything young blossoms from the earth:
Der mentsh, der keml un di royz	The man, the camel and the rose
un fun toyte knokhn in di heyse shtoybn	and from dead bones in the hot dust
bliyen henglakh lakhendike troybn.[34]	flourish clusters of laughing grapes.

Nadir's use of the contraction "dr'erd" (the earth) offers multiple interpretive possibilities: *der erd,* depending on the context, can connote "the soil," "the ground," and—more ominously—"the grave" or even "hell." The choice of "dr'erd" contains an element of undecidability: the simultaneous possibility of life-bearing soil and a land rendered a graveyard by contemporary political strife produces what Derrida has termed "différance"—a play of temporal and contextual differences that exposes the impossibility of exact meaning.[35] The idea that life might spring from the earth is also a Zionist cliché. Early Zionist rhetoric would often cite a passage in Isaiah, where it is prophesied that "the desert shall rejoice, and blossom as the rose" (35:1). The "rose"—a biblical metaphor for the people of Israel—is here transferred from the Jew to the Arab. In the reference to "dr'erd," Nadir parodies this Zionist idea in two ways: the earth is compared to hell, and, moreover, what should really blossom from it is an Arab community, not a Jewish one. The claiming and reclaiming of passwords, in keeping with the modernist tradition of displacing signified with signifier, was fodder for both political play and wordplay.

The reclamation of a password on behalf of a non-Jewish group was, of course, itself a vexed act of representation. Even in those cases where a Yiddish poet brought an Arabic-language (or Ukrainian, English, or Russian) writer into a Jewish cultural conversation through traditional (lexical) translation, the foreignness of that text often became the operative password for the Marxist Yiddish reader. As Bhabha articulates, linguistic signifiers and cultural signs are all too often elided in favor of conveying a simplified version of a message: "The 'foreignness' of language is the nucleus of the untranslatable that goes beyond the transferal of subject matter between cultural texts or practices."[36] The fact of an Arabic poem appearing in a Yiddish newspaper in the midst of the 1929 Palestine debates means more than its content.

Naomi Seidman has used the term "translator culture" to describe the "foreignness" that modern Jewish writers were perceived as bringing to non-Jewish European cultures, through translation and their own writing.[37] The Yiddish poets who make up this book, like the many Jewish translators into non-Jewish languages, smuggled foreignness across cultural boundaries. In this case, the goal was to diversify a conversation in a Jewish (rather than a non-Jewish) language. The poets who attempted to merge Jewish collective memory with the experiences of Palestinian Arabs, Chinese Marxists, Spanish Loyalists, Italian anarchists, or African Americans were hoping to bring Others' experience to bear on a Jewish collective consciousness; they were also attempting to represent these groups in a closed conversation among Yiddish readers and writers. With few exceptions, these poems were rarely translated for the groups they described. This conversation would remain closed for decades to come. To be sure, by describing groups that were not part of their closed conversation, the internationalist Yiddish poets were denying the Other a voice.[38] What is more, despite the poets' universalist goals, many of the poems discussed in this book exploit stereotypes, generalizations, and racial type-casting. We must recall that although internationalists sought to forge a new meaning of "us," they were products of an earlier age—the age of nationalism.

THE WOUND: TRANSLOCATING THE MODERNIST POGROM POEM

"In this most Christian of worlds / Poets are Jews" (V sem khristianeishem iz mirov / poety zhidy), the Russian poet Marina Tsvetaeva famously wrote, in her 1924 "Poema kontsa" (Poem of the end).[39] With this axiom, a Christian Symbolist suggests that the eternally marginalized, physically endangered condition of Jews in eastern Europe is also the condition of the modern poet. In fact, for Tsvetaeva, all decent humans are susceptible to the pogrom:

Zhizn', eto mesto, gde zhit' nel'zia:	Life is a place where you can't live:
Evreiskii kvartal . . .	A Jewish quarter . . .

Tak ne dostoinee l' vo sto krat	Wouldn't it be a hundred times better
Stat' vechnym zhidom?	To become the eternal Jew?
Ibo dlia kazhdogo, kto ne gad,	For there's a Jewish pogrom
Evreiskii pogrom—[40]	For everyone who's not a scoundrel—

Tsvetaeva uses "pogrom" as a password, marking solidarity with Jews and absorbing the wounds of the modern world. A wound inscribes its bearers with a trace of a shared history. For Derrida, Tsvetaeva's poet/Jew bears a wound, scar, or scab, epitomized by circumcision—the wound that seals Jews' covenant with God. The circumcision, the *bris*—literally, a bond—is a sign of belonging.[41] The violent cut, like the ritual wound of circumcision—whether the result of pogrom violence or state violence—marks its recipients as kindred victims of modern oppressive ideologies. Internationalist Yiddish poems that translocated the pogrom into poems about other marginalized groups' experiences, then, marked these others as recipients of a Jewish wound—indeed, as members of a common tribe.

H. Leivick opens "A yor Sako Vanzeti" with a cut:

Ir hot zikh ayngeshnitn in unzer zikorn,	You've cut into our memory
vi an ongegliter meser in a vund;	like a hot knife in a wound;
o, vemen nokh azoy hot der toyt gekent portn	oh, who else could Death have taken
in aza farzigltn bund?[42]	in such a sealed bond?

The ultimate wound, the sealed bond with Death, marks the victim as a martyr. Leivick's Sacco and Vanzetti, like Tsvetaeva's "poets," bear wounds that, in turn, inflict new wounds ("like a hot knife in a wound") on the already marked community that mourns them. Leivick, calling attention to the wound shared with Sacco-Vanzetti, makes clear how much is at stake in a shared password: the Jewish community, already wounded by the antisemitic violence of the early twentieth century, has been newly scarred by the injustice against others. By commemorating the *yortsayt* of the convicted Italian anarchists ("Fuller's bite / hasn't even been covered / with a scab"), Leivick calls Jews to action on behalf of one of their own.

The national and international outrage at the execution of Sacco and Vanzetti radicalized many American Jewish writers.[43] However, several decades of Jewish culture in Europe and the United States had already compelled Yiddish writers to take an active role in the broader struggle for social justice. The Jewish political movements from the 1880s through 1905 were premised on a need for Jewish liberation from institutionalized antisemitism and from the recurring threat of pogroms. Despite the failure of the 1905 revolution in Russia, the 1905 constitution promised new rights for Russia's Jews. As Jonathan Frankel has noted, however, the pogroms against Russian Jewish communities in the early twentieth century became a call to political action. Whereas Russian Jews responded to the 1881–1882 pogroms primarily with mass emigration, by the 1903–1906 wave of pogroms, "the issue was in what form the Jewish people should participate in the Russian insurrection."[44] The Jewish Enlightenment (Haskalah) in its western and eastern European manifestations had inspired Jewish intellectuals to promote Jewish secularizing art, literature, and journalism in Hebrew and Yiddish.[45] The Revolutionary Jewish Bund, formed in 1897 as a Russian-language organization, strove for national-cultural autonomy in Russia and eventually adopted Yiddish as its official language in the early twentieth century. Many of the writers who later aligned themselves with the Communist Party had initially embraced the idea of revolution through the Bund and had shifted toward Bolshevism, convinced by Lenin's arguments for the necessity of unity between Russian and non-Russian workers in the territory of Russia.[46] The Bund inspired major Yiddish literary figures, including Y. L. Peretz, to take up the cause of Jewish workers in their writing.[47] Young Bundist poets like Avrom Reyzen (1876–1953) captured a spirit of positive and terrifying social change for a young generation of Jewish revolutionaries. "Hulyet, hulyet beyze vintn" (Revel, revel angry winds) went one popular song by Reyzen, and the line simultaneously embodied the rising spirit of antisemitism threatening the Jewish community and the rising revolutionary spirit driving Jews to demand change from within. The late nineteenth century was a time of political idealism, and language played a key role in these utopian visions. Ludwik

Zamenhof, who had once worked to develop Yiddish for use in a future Jewish state, abandoned his Zionist dreams in favor of universalism, and published his first pamphlets promoting his newly developed international language, Esperanto, in the 1880s.[48]

As Socialist Jews were forming the Bund in Europe in the late 1890s, the American "sweatshop poets" were publishing songs and stories of New York's factories. Morris Winchevsky's translation of Thomas Hood's "Song of the Shirt" into Yiddish and his own poems of labor unionism, like "Unfurl the Red Flag" and "To the Worker," helped introduce a rhythm of shop labor to American Yiddish poetry. At the turn of the twentieth century, socialist and Zionist ethics often coexisted, particularly in the United States: Morris Rosenfeld, a founding figure in American sweatshop poetry, was a vocal Zionist.[49] David Fishman has observed the cross-pollination between the American and European revolutionary poets, noting that "the proletarian and revolutionary poems of Morris Winchevsky, Dovid Edelshtadt, Morris Rosenfeld, and Avrom Reyzen were extremely popular among organized workers and youth, and secret meetings of Bundist cells and trade unions usually concluded with the recitation or communal singing of their poems."[50] The Bund, which after 1905 advocated a policy of "radical Yiddishism" that included the rejection of religion and the Modern Hebrew revival alike, viewed itself as an internationalist organization.[51] By then, Bundists rejected Zionist territorial politics, although the Bund, which believed in group self-determinacy, would part ways with the radically internationalist communists as well.[52] Those Yiddish writers who identified with Bundist politics at the turn of the twentieth century would, by 1917, have to choose between a national sensitivity and an internationalist rejection of any form of Jewish cultural autonomy. The early Bundist and sweatshop poets would serve as parental figures for the generally younger and more radical Party-affiliated poets. Some of these older writers, including Morris Winchevsky, would join the Party.

It is difficult to overstate the role the pogroms played in Jewish politics and Jewish literature at the turn of the twentieth century. Eastern European Jewish modernism arose and spread in large part in response to pogrom violence. The pogroms, which had become the subject of folk poems after the 1881–1882 wave of violence in the tsarist empire's Pale of

Settlement, inspired modern manifestations of medieval lamentations by the turn of the century.[53] As David Roskies has shown, "when it came to moments of national crisis—to pogroms—the oldest liturgical strategies came to the fore to reorder the outrage into fixed phrases and stock images."[54] The pogroms thus engendered a series of Jewish liberationist passwords that could mourn a collective loss and inspire solidarity. The 1903 Kishinev pogrom reignited the Jewish community's outrage over eastern European violence. According to the historian Steven Zipperstein, "just weeks after the pogrom's end, it was commonplace to liken Kishinev to the worst of Jewish history's catastrophes, including the destruction of the temples of Jerusalem. Special liturgies highlighting the tragedy were introduced into American synagogues."[55] Chaim Nachman Bialik's Hebrew-language poem "B'ir haHaregah" (In the city of slaughter), written in the wake of the Kishinev pogrom, was among the first modernist Jewish poems. Bialik (1873–1934), using a grotesque form of documentary reportage, describes the "spattered blood and dried brains of the dead," simultaneously exalting human victims to the level of liturgy, undermining Jewish prayer through graphic depictions of dead bodies, and giving birth to a modernist Jewish national poetry.[56] The poem, based on a series of interviews with survivors of the pogrom, reproaches Jews for their passivity. The mixture of glowing praise and harsh criticism that the poem received attests to its centrality, as a document from Kishinev and as a new kind of poem. "In the City of Slaughter" changed the way Jews thought about collective trauma, creating a modern text about the ugliness of violence and the need for immediate action. Dan Miron has called the narrator "at certain moments half-demented."[57] The Hebrew critic Joseph Klausner called the poem "a greater achievement than Ecclesiastes."[58] The modernist pogrom poet was using what Maurice Halbwachs had called "recent collective memory" to augment, and in some cases to replace, "historical memory."[59] However, Bialik went a step further: he called for a Jewish national awakening in the wake of Kishinev. Pogroms were central to both Jewish political thought and Jewish modern literary experimentation from 1881 through World War I.

The modernist period saw dramatic, even violent, experimentation with subject matter and form. This was the era when Filippo Tommaso

Marinetti and his fellow Italian futurists glorified speed and war, "the world's only hygiene."[60] Early twentieth-century European modernists across languages were testing the rigidity of literary traditions and semiotic law, as Saussure had defined it, which holds that a signifier always corresponds to a signified. Tristan Tzara's insistence that "Dada doesn't mean anything!" provocatively sums up the radical efforts to question the necessity of meaning in the early twentieth century.[61] For Jews, the quest for linguistic meaning was inextricable from the quest for a modern group identity. For Zionists in the wake of World War I, Modern Hebrew constituted its own semiotic innovation, reflecting, as Benjamin Harshav has articulated, "domains of life entirely new both to them and to the Hebrew language."[62] Yiddish modernist poets, too, tested the limits of their transnational, fusion language.

The Bolshevik Revolution ushered in an especially fertile period of Yiddish literary experimentation. Kenneth Moss has identified the chaotic period of 1917–1919 as a "history in miniature of how the cultural project was violently altered by the most extreme forms of twentieth-century sociopolitics and revolutionary socialism."[63] The eastern European Yiddish poets of the expressionist "Khalyastre" group ("The Gang")—including Uri Tzvi Grinberg and Peretz Markish—who had experienced World War I firsthand, sought to represent the chaos of war and violence in language.[64] Peretz Markish (1895–1952), in his 1921–1922 *Di kupe* (The mound), considered the Jewish deaths to be comparable not only to the founding myths of Jewish religious practice but to all religions:

Alla! Khristos! Shaday! Ver nokh?　　　Allah! Christ! El Shaday! Who else?
　Aher, —　　　　　　　　　　　　　　　Come here,—
farbaygeyer, farfirte piligrimen!　　　Passerby, lost pilgrim!
Aher, o, yunglingen farblandzhete,　　Come here, o young wanderer, it's a
　s'iz a beyszoyne! . . .　　　　　　　　whorehouse! . . .
Fun gor der velt, fun erdn un fun　　　From everywhere, from earths and
　himlen,　　　　　　　　　　　　　　from heavens,
Far malke iber ale berg vel ikh dikh,　　I'll crown you, mound, queen of all
　kupe, kroynen. . . .[65]　　　　　　　　mountains. . . .

Seth Wolitz has called *Di kupe* a dirge (*kine*) for the modern era.[66] However, following Markish's 1926 return to the Soviet Union, he was among the Yiddish poets charged with writing a poetry that was, if

Jewish in form, then at least internationalist in content. Markish, whose verse was translated and printed across the Soviet Union, took seriously his role as a Soviet writer and worked to demonstrate the relevance of the Jewish condition to the human condition.

The New York "In Zikh" (Introspectivist) poets responded to the violence of their generation by examining its effects on the psyche. The Introspectivists looked down on overtly political poetry, yet they too strove to depict the global interconnectedness of their epoch. As Aaron Glantz-Leyeles (1889–1966), one of the founders of the In Zikh movement, put it, the poet "is simultaneously at the Ganges and at the Hudson, in the year 1922 and in the year when Tiglathpileser conquered and terrorized a world. Therefore, the Introspectivist is chaotic and kaleidoscopic."[67] By the 1920s, when it became impossible to think about one's place in the world without thinking about the changes taking place throughout the rest of the world, Yiddish poetry gave a modernizing Jewish readership a poetic language to embody recent violence, and texts, that competed with liturgy.

The Jewish literary renaissance—in its Yiddishist and its Hebraist manifestations—was dispersed and diasporic in its essence and thus cannot be simplistically combined with the more general national impulse in European modernism. Whereas in England and in France, the geographically defined nation emerged as a new unifying force in the post-Nietzschean world, Jewish modernists wrote within a tradition of diaspora.[68] As Chana Kronfeld has observed, "The development of modern Yiddish literature involves the construction of a collective identity that cannot be reduced to the Eurocentric model of the nation-state."[69] European Jews of the interwar period appear to escape Ernst Gellner's definition of nationalism, a problem that "does not arise when there is no state."[70] Nevertheless, a rapidly secularizing, geographically dispersed Jewish population of writers, many from observant families, often viewed literature as a replacement for religion. The fragile "diaspora nationalism" championed by the Bund relied not on the idea of a state but on the uniting powers of a textual tradition, including folklore, literature, and language.[71] The language-centered Yiddishist movement was closely tied to diaspora nationalism, but, as Cecile Kuznitz has put it in her study of the academic institute YIVO, "Yiddishists such as [the Socialist Revolutionary] Chaim Zhitlowsky went one step further, viewing the language itself as the basis of Jewish identity."[72] The Jewish communists who synthesized Yiddishist values with revolutionary internationalism would sharpen this textual tradition into a language of passwords that could broaden the horizons of Jewish texts.

Kenneth Moss has discussed the debates among Jewish culturists in the early twentieth century over the relative merits of authentic and "deparochialized" Jewish culture. Translation was an essential tool for advocates of such deparochialization, and "the goal was to reorient Hebrew or Yiddish literatures as institutions toward an ever-more universal European literary culture by infusing them with a compensatory European literary tradition."[73] Jewish literature in the Revolutionary period flourished—in both Yiddish and Hebrew. The Kultur-Lige, which Moss has called "the most expansive and economically successful Yiddishist organization of the day," was the site of an experimental, revolutionary Yiddish modernism before its eventual absorption into the centralized network of Soviet publishing houses.[74] This universalizing tendency in Jewish literature before and during the Bolshevik Revolution transformed, in the Soviet Union, into a carefully curated literature of proletarian internationalism in the 1920s.

Wounds, one's own and others', were the ties that bound Jewish leftist writers to the non-Jewish proletariat. When, following the Bolshevik Revolution, international workers' organizations emerged, writers strove to describe, and inspire empathy with, the pain of others. Many did so on the pages of new proletarian journals that were being formed in eastern Europe and North America. The short-lived Soviet organization of proletarian culture Proletkult emerged in 1918, and under its auspices, major Russian modernist writers and artists, including Alexander Blok and Vladimir Mayakovsky, visited factories with the goal of teaching workers to write.[75] In the early years of the Soviet Union, the concept of "proletarian internationalism" put class before nation, while still valuing the experience of oppressed and formerly colonized peoples.[76] The simultaneous value placed on workers and oppressed nations in the 1920s could be seen in the two Soviet Kharkiv-based Yiddish journals from the 1920s: the proletarian *Prolit,* which emphasized factory work, and the more internationalist *Royte Velt,* which emphasized questions of nationhood. The two journals published over-lapping authors and jokingly poked fun at each other, but as Gennady Estraikh has noted, "*Di royte velt* was a highbrow periodical, following the example of Russian 'thick journals,' whereas the *Prolit* was not ashamed to publish novice writers—the literary yield of the worker correspondent movement."[77] These two tendencies, the proletarian and the more literary internationalist, were in dialogue with each other. Those Yiddish writers who emphasized internationalism—the focus of this book—were consciously adapting modernist poems of Jewish nationhood (including poems of collective trauma) to other, non-Jewish, oppressed groups.

Avant-garde literature thrived in the 1920s outside the Soviet Union, and many leading writers were sympathetic to the nascent Soviet Union. In Warsaw, Peretz Markish, a founding member of the Kiev-grupe, helped Uri Tzvi Grinberg to found *Albatros* in 1922 and helped Melech Ravitch, I. I. Singer, and Nakhman Mayzel to found *Literarish Bleter* in Warsaw in 1924 before he moved permanently to Moscow in 1926. From Berlin, Dovid Bergelson, Markish's fellow Kiev-grupe member and life-long rival, edited the short-lived leftist journal *In Shpan* in 1926.[78] American proletarian writers' movements were gaining momentum at the same moment when Soviet publishing was becoming more centralized and Soviet proletarian writers movements were disappearing. Several short-lived Yiddish proletarian journals emerged in the 1920s, including *Yung Kuznye* (Young Smith) and *Union Square,* where American Yiddish writers could integrate their respect for the Soviet Union with uniquely American concerns. The Russian futurist Mayakovsky's 1925 visit to New York found the celebrated Soviet poet amid the Yiddish literary circle. Mayakovsky (1893–1930) contributed a poem to the New York experimental trilingual proletarian journal titled *Spartak.* One issue, appearing in October 1925, featured poetry and prose in Russian, English, and Yiddish. "We aren't immigrants," wrote the editors in the preface. "We live the life of the American Proletariat. We fight along with them. We permeate American daily life."[79] Langston Hughes (1901–1967) and the Yiddish proletarian poet Alexander Pomerantz (1901–1965) also appeared in the issue. This trilingual journal remains frozen in its one 1925 issue, a momentary merging of three worlds.

The synthesis of earlier traditions emphasizing Jewish collective trauma (in particular the pogrom poem) and proletarian internationalism in the long 1930s is the subject of this book. The literary experimentation that led Jewish leftists to apply Jewish themes to non-Jewish struggles, however, demonstrates the interconnectedness of ethnic identity and interethnic politics. The Gordian knot of Jewish leftism in the 1930s remains unresolved in the twenty-first century, as Jewish activists facing multiple prejudices struggle to make a case for inclusion in Kimberlé Crenshaw's groundbreaking model of intersectionality, conceived to make visible the dangerous legal intersections of racism and sexism in the United States.[80] Michael Rothberg has proposed the concept of "multidirectional memory" as a solution to bringing together post-Holocaust and postcolonial memory. Rothberg's assessment of the potential for the long-irreconcilable fields of postcolonial and Holocaust trauma studies is optimistic: "While still in a nascent state, the comparative study of genocide—and especially of genocide in colonial contexts and its relationship to the Holocaust—is developing rapidly."[81] Critical cultural studies often precede paradigm shifts among activists. It is my hope that this study of seldom-translated leftist Yiddish poetry will offer a precedent for those looking to complicate the historical role of Jews as a disaggregated European minority, in anti-imperialist and antiracist activism. Jews on the left in the age of internationalism wrote in a national language for a national group, exalted racial and national minority struggles, and yet did not constitute a territorial nation. They rejected the idea of Zionism, denouncing the notion of a Jewish state for its irreparable ties to British imperialism. What, then, does it mean to write as members of a Jewish nation when one has rejected the concept of nationhood? The writers of the 1930s attempted to substitute a universalist peoplehood for Jewish peoplehood. The passwords they used to make a case for universalism constituted a language of Jewish internationalism. If Yiddish writers in the age of internationalism were unable to agree about what it meant to be a Jewish internationalist, perhaps we can use their discussions as a starting point a century later.

As Harriet Murav has written of Peretz Markish's postwar struggle between the universality of suffering and specifically Jewish suffering,

"Where, indeed, is the boundary between pain and pain?"[82] Poems describing the struggles of Chinese workers, African Americans, Ukrainian peasants, Spanish antifascists, and Crimean Roma filled the pages of Soviet and Soviet-aligned Yiddish journals in the 1930s. These poems of other Others all recognizably borrow from the pogrom poems that had flourished in the early twentieth century in eastern Europe. The passage from collective Jewish suffering to others' suffering was a direct response to Soviet views on nationality and nationhood, originating with Lenin's acknowledgment that "national differences will remain for a very long time after the realization of the dictatorship of the proletariat on a world scale."[83] There was, however, more at stake for Jewish poets than Party alignment: the choice to describe other nations' struggles also affirmed and demonstrated Jews' successful modernization. Survivors of pogroms and tsarist strictures, Soviet Jews were now part of a nation-building effort. Eastern European Jewish immigrants to North and South America, while still facing rampant antisemitism, nonetheless sometimes passed for members of a privileged white majority. As recently as 1920, Henry Ford had published a translation of the antisemitic forgery "The Protocols of the Elders of Zion" in his newspaper, and in the 1930s, opponents of the New Deal spread rumors about Franklin Roosevelt's Jewish ties.[84] Partly in response to these growing concerns, Jewish Party-aligned writers sought to make social justice an international issue and not only a Jewish issue. To make Yiddish into a language of internationalism, leftist poets sought to make it a language of passwords—words that could pass from a Jewish to a non-Jewish context, granting the writer (and reader) entrance into other territories, other homes. I briefly turn now to the political and literary developments in the United States and Soviet Union that led up to the age of internationalism.

NATIONAL IN FORM, INTERNATIONALIST IN CONTENT

Leivick's "A yor Sako Vanzeti" not only applies Jewish language to the executed Italian anarchists. It commemorates the event of Sacco and Vanzetti's midnight execution as a precise historical moment:

O, mir fargesn nit di vayzers fun zeyger	Oh, we won't forget how the clock hands
vi zey hobn getrift mit blut in oygust-nakht.	dripped with blood that August night.
In yener nakht, oyf ongeglite shteyner,	That night, on the glowing stones,
hobn mir ale gevoyet vi mide velf,	we all howled like tired wolves,
ven es zaynen gefaln oyf unz, vi s'faln beyner,	when they fell on us, like falling bones,
di letste rege's fun der shtunde tsvelf.[85]	the last moments of the twelfth hour.

Leivick wrote this poem for the anarchists' *yortsayt*—the year anniversary of their death—a date when the community recites the *yortsayt* version of the mourner's Kaddish. Just as the hour is the subject of the poem, the date, in Leivick's poem, functions as a password, marking the historical moment of Sacco and Vanzetti's death and, a year following the execution, calling those who recognize and remember that date to action once more.[86]

Remembered moments of revolutionary struggle united the internationalist generation. Lenin, speaking at the Sixth All-Russian Congress of Soviets, referred to the revolutionary spark, now "a conflagration that has spread to many countries": "We were never so close to an international proletarian revolution as at this very moment."[87] In 1919, Lenin founded the Communist International with the goal of creating a Moscow-centered network of toilers of the world. The nascent Soviet Union offered an institutionalized departure from the national focus of post–World War I Europe that came with the founding of the League of Nations and Paris Peace Treaties of 1919.[88] After Stalin—the former nationalities commissar—seized power in 1925 and began to implement Nikolai Bukharin's doctrine of "socialism in one country," Lenin's vision of internationalism gave way to a Soviet Russian hegemony that made Moscow an even stronger center of world communism. Stalin would dissolve the Comintern in 1943. However, it was Stalin's Third Period, which arose around the 1928 Sixth Comintern Congress, that opened the long decade of proletarian internationalism.[89] The Sixth Comintern Congress included the thesis that "the achievement of a fraternal, combative alliance with the laboring masses of the colonies is one of the principal objectives of the industrial proletariat of the world which exercises the hegemony and the leadership in the struggle against imperialism."[90] Many who privately expressed concern over Stalin and his policies remained with communism out of a firm conviction that the Party was an agent of global good in an age of rising fascism and imperialist violence. There is, even today, no more divisive a time in communist history than the Third Period, with its mixed legacy of anti-imperialism and Stalinist purges. Most significantly for global revolutionary movements, the Third Period of the Comintern formally recognized colonized peoples as part of the international proletariat. However, the new doctrine also implemented a zero-tolerance policy for noncommunist left-wing parties, which helped the Party to justify its purging of purported political adversaries. The long decade between Stalin's 1928–1934 Third Period and the dissolution of the Comintern in 1943 constituted, then, a period when communist sympathizers around the world struggled to reconcile the concerns of national groups with those of the Soviet state.

Throughout the twenty-four years of the Comintern's existence and especially in the late 1920s, left-wing activists and advocates throughout the world were in dialogue with Soviet ideas of internationalism. This included prominent philosophers of American multiculturalism, like Horace Kallen, who developed a philosophy of cultural pluralism in the United States in the 1920s. Steven Lee, in his study of Soviet multinationalism and American multiculturalism, has observed, "Kallen and Stalin both allowed for the fixedness of descent based identities ('natio' and 'ethnos,' respectively), and both stressed the persistence of language."[91] The American Yiddish poets aligned with the Comintern were advocates of a pluralist ideology that was compatible with both American multiculturalism and Soviet multinationalism. They were advocates of an assimilationist ethos, but as Yiddish writers, they drew liberally from Jewish cultural signposts and worked to describe other ethnicities with respect to cultural difference.

Within the Soviet Union, literature became the mechanism for establishing a unified socialist ideology and for offering a controlled voice to minority groups writing in minority languages. The Soviet cultural leadership valued literary discourse, but took it seriously to a fault, seeking writers' absolute loyalty to the state. Within the Party, Soviet-identified passwords became a means of convincing the censors of such loyalty, while ethnically specific passwords could be a means of subtly undermining this loyalty among the initiated. Literature occupied a highly visible place in the early Soviet Union: it was viewed as a means of proving the ethical and intellectual authority of the Party. As Katerina Clark has observed, literature penetrated the very landscape of Soviet cities: "the early 1930s were a moment when literature, architecture, and ideology came together in the one 'city,' a moment when as Gorky and Marx 'met' at that city's center, disparate biographies, disparate subjec-tivities, came together in one narrative."[92] Russian was not the only So-viet literary language; during the 1920s and '30s even Yiddish, a language of diaspora for its millennium of existence, suddenly had a home—if a brief one. Yiddish, in Lenin's Soviet Union, became a national Jewish lan-guage, and the Jewish section of the Party strove to populate it with the world's most respected literary figures. Soviet Yiddish writers worked hard to build their country as the center of Yiddish literature interna-tionally. As Gennady Estraikh has discussed, in April 1926, forty-eight Soviet Yiddish writers signed an open letter published in *Der Emes* and addressed "to all the Yiddish writers in Europe and America," appealing to their colleagues to come help build socialism in the Soviet Union: "For our very best, Mendele, for Sholem-Aleichem, for Peretz—this was but a dream: the transformation of a people made up of market-venders and Menachem-Mendels into builders and workers."[93] That year, the Amer-ican Yiddish writer Moishe Nadir traveled to the Soviet Union on what he would later call "a holy pilgrimage to the land of the Soviets." The sweatshop poet Morris Winchevsky had made the trip in 1924, H. Leivick in 1925, and Avrom Reyzen in early 1929. The well-known modernists Peretz Markish, Der Nister, and Dovid Hofshteyn moved permanently to Moscow in the 1920s. "People here love a writer," wrote Peretz Markish, having made Moscow his home in 1926.[94] At the same time, the risk of transgressing the state ideology was already becoming apparent. Leivick, in a letter to Shmuel Niger-Charney from the Soviet Union, wrote that the most famous Yiddish writers were abroad and that those writers who lived in the Soviet Union lived in "deep-seated fear of being interpreted as nationalists."[95] Leivick, in the wake of his 1925 visit, wrote admiringly of the Yiddish institutions that had sprung up in Russia, while noting the irony that few were ready to sign on to the regime: "Yiddish became a *government* project, but here there is no one to place at the head of the departments."[96] As leading Soviet writers migrated to the Soviet Union they were tasked with molding Yiddish to a Marxist-Leninist ideology. The transnational passwords that helped identify like-minded leftist Yiddish readers and writers was the currency that gave Soviet internationalist Yiddish literature its value in the 1920s and 1930s.

Lenin and Stalin were opposed to the concept of the nation-state.[97] Nonetheless, the early Soviet leaders saw the necessity of harnessing national consciousness as a means of engendering class consciousness. For early Soviet thinkers including both Lenin and Stalin, national consciousness was necessary to develop a modern, rational sensibility. As Terry Martin has put it in *The Affirmative Action Empire,* "national consciousness was an unavoidable historic phase that all peoples must pass through on the way to internationalism."[98] Writers worked to distill proletarian passwords from historical national struggles. Nation, understood as ethnic identity, was simultaneously retrograde and necessary in the nascent Soviet Union. As a result, non-Russian-language writers who wished to discuss the condition of Soviet national minorities found they could do so if they discussed nations other than their own. Jewish writers debated Azerbaijani poetic form, and Georgian translators celebrated the tradition of Ukrainian folk poetry.

Stalin famously asserted that art could be "national in form" so long as it was "socialist in content."[99] In his 1925 lecture "The Political Tasks of the University of the Peoples of the East," Stalin declared that "Proletarian culture does not abolish national culture; it fills it with content. And vice versa, national culture does not abolish proletarian culture. It gives it form. . . . The slogan of national culture became proletarian when power came into the hands of the proletariat and when the consolidation of nations began to take its course under the aegis of Soviet government."[100] These national slogans functioned in two ways. They simultaneously helped to win members of national minorities over to a proletarian cause and allowed individual nations to preserve an element of cultural particularism even as the state attempted to replace national beliefs with a proletarian ethos. The Communist University of the Toilers of the East

(KUTV) was founded in 1921 and was dedicated to educating revolutionary leaders and potential leaders from Central Asia, East Asia, and the Middle East in Marxist-Leninism. The core Marxist principle of supporting former oppressed peoples, while gradually moving from a national and toward a workers' aesthetic, informed and inspired all of those who identified with the Party, whether in or outside the Soviet Union.

Among American Yiddish writers, proletarian literature began gaining a foothold in the late 1920s. In 1929, the legal Workers Party of America officially merged with the theretofore underground Communist Party USA.[101] Although American Jewish communists never faced the same imperative as their Soviet counterparts to reject all forms of nationalism, they sought to describe the suffering of others—particularly African Americans, who were threatened by a resurgence in lynch violence, but also Italians following the Sacco and Vanzetti trial, Spanish Republicans during the Spanish Civil War, and Native Americans. The events and beliefs that united American Party members and fellow travelers were not always the same as those used in the Soviet Union. Robin Kelley has demonstrated in his study of Alabama communists that "Party work was determined less by Communist internal machinations than by the conditions on the ground."[102] The same can be said of the many American Jewish communists and fellow travelers whose concerns were grounded in their own, American, reality. Americans engendered their own brand of communism with its own signposts. Those American writers who remained close to Moscow throughout the '30s were not necessarily of uniform opinion. Some believed firmly in the Party's declared Third Period support of the colonized peoples of the world. Others were assimilationists whose support of the Soviet Union came from a more general support of the worker.[103]

Considering the plight of the Other was part of the Jewish process of modernization, one that included Soviet communism but with branches throughout the world. Each chapter in this book takes up a nationally specific historical event between 1927 and 1939—the rise of the Chinese communist movement; the Arab rebellions against Jews in Palestine that split the leftist Jewish community; the Scottsboro trial in the US South; the Spanish Civil War; the Soviet creation of a Ukrainian national literature; and the rejection of communism and turn back toward the Jewish community by American fellow travelers following the Hitler-Stalin pact in 1939. Writing about other groups' experiences at the time meant adapting untranslatable terms and place-names, whether from China, Spain, or the US South, to Yiddish poetry. Culturally specific untranslatables gathered from Jewish tradition ("pogrom," "Inquisition," "teshuvah"), as well as from non-Jewish traditions ("Scottsboro," "Ukraina," "¡No pasarán!") assume new significance as passwords, becoming objects that, as Baudrillard observes, "in that world of signs, very quickly broke away from their use-value to enter into play and correspondence with one another."[104] This also meant adapting a modern Yiddish poetics of trauma to accommodate non-Jewish struggles. The most obvious and immediate goal of this translation of trauma was the sublation of nationally defined collective memory, without abandoning a sensitivity to the struggles of individual nations. These poets were offering their own version of Stalin's "national in form, socialist in content" mandate: they were attempting to write literature that was national in form but internationalist in content. Everything changed with World War II—the Jewish internationalist moment was lost when the Nazi Party imposed, with the help of collaborators, its final solution to exterminate the Jews as a nation. And yet it remains instructive—even essential—to recall Yiddish writers' attempts in the 1930s to renounce their own group interests in an effort to foster an international workers' identity. If one lesson of the internationalist 1930s is that it is politically dangerous to renounce one's own national identity and history, another lesson, I shall attempt to demonstrate, is that the efforts to draw comparisons and find commonalities between ethnic groups can lead to greater empathy and understanding. The writers explored in these pages were attempting to use culturally specific untranslatables to approach an understanding of the significance of a nation.

As Michael Denning reminds us, "The 'proletarian' movement in culture was in fact one of the few important avant-gardes in US culture, and it attracted many of the artists whose careers had begun under the sign of an oppositional European modernism, the 'exiles' who returned."[105] Leftist Yiddish writers signaled their allegiance to the Party by publishing their work in left-wing venues. It is telling that in the age of proletarian internationalism, Party-aligned poets increasingly published their work not in experimentalist avant-garde journals but in newspapers, alongside current events. The Moscow-based Yiddish daily *Der Emes* was published from 1921 and 1939 and edited by Moyshe Litvakov, a Party apparatchik whose criticism could make or break a Soviet Yiddish writer. *Emes* only occasionally published poetry, but its affiliated publishing houses published Yiddish literature. In 1922, the American communist Yiddish-language daily newspaper was founded. Partially funded by the Communist International, *Di Frayhayt* (formally redubbed the *Morgn Frayhayt,* "Morning freedom," in 1929) had a circulation of fourteen thousand readers at its peak in the late 1920s. The editors were two former Bundists-turned-communists, Moyshe Olgin and Shakhne Epshteyn, and, unlike most of its counterparts, it regularly featured poems by American and Soviet poets.[106] The *Frayhayt*'s editors managed to convince leading American modernists to join their ranks upon its founding, including Moyshe Leyb Halpern, H. Leivick, and Moishe Nadir. The paper ran poems in each issue, illustrating current events, from the 1929 Arab riots in Palestine to the Scottsboro trial in the US South, the Spanish Civil War, and the creation of a Jewish autonomous region (Birobidjan) in the Soviet Union.[107] As Tony Michels observes, the *Frayhayt* sought to differentiate itself from the socialist *Forverts* (Forward), which, the *Frayhayt* editors suggested, catered to the masses: "Rather than indulge the 'backward tastes' and 'primitive inclinations' of the 'rabble,' *Di Frayhayt* promised to offer 'true revolutionary enlightenment, true education.'"[108] The paper announced Party events alongside advertisements for practical home products, progressive summer camps, and trips to the Soviet Union. Correspondents cast a critical eye on the bourgeois values of mainstream America and the foreign policy of the British Empire, expressing solidarity with the Soviet side in its conflict with China and alarm at the rise of fascism in Europe. The socialist daily *Forverts,* by contrast, published more prose than poetry, and the Soviet *Der Emes* published less literature in general. Leading European modernists like Peretz Markish and Dovid Hofshteyn often published in the *Frayhayt,* making the American communist press an important forum for Yiddish proletarian art.[109]

Dovid Bergelson, then still in Berlin, resigned from the socialist *Forverts* and began publishing pro-Soviet writing in the *Frayhayt* in 1926, which many took to be a public assertion of his own Party alignment and preceded his move to the Soviet Union by eight years.[110] Bergelson's enigmatic relationship to the Party is an instructive sign of the times. The most famous Revolutionary fiction writer, Bergelson had long stood between the Soviet and fellow-traveler camps. The poet Chaim Nachman Bialik, making a toast at the Yiddish writer Dovid Bergelson's wedding, had purportedly turned to Bergelson's wife, Tsipora, and said, "Tsipele, don't let the Bolsheviks have him."[111] Bergelson's shift to the *Frayhayt* in 1926 was a sign to many people that the Bolsheviks definitively "had him." And yet poets from across the political and literary spectrum wrote for the *Frayhayt* and the proletarian journals in the 1920s, even as they privately voiced uncertainty about Stalin's 1927 denunciation of German Social Democrats as "fascists." The New York–based communist *Frayhayt,* with its investment in poetry and its commitment to internationalism, was seen as a venue that spoke truth to power. Comintern-identified Yiddish writers' movements had been emerging in several major centers outside the Soviet Union, from Uruguay to Canada, South Africa, and throughout Europe, and the *Frayhayt* published like-minded poets from around the world, especially in the 1930s, when writers were forced to choose whether to look toward Moscow.[112]

Moments of historical rupture are critical to understanding the American Yiddish Left. At key points, what began as political debates quickly became firewalls, and lines were redrawn according to the extent to which individuals accepted the Party line. The first significant break in the American Jewish Left occurred in August 1929, when a wave of anti-Jewish violence in Palestine forced leftist poets to choose between their Jewish or worker identities. The *Frayhayt,* which declared its support of the Arab rioters, was labeled traitorous by most centrist American Jewish organizations, and the poets who continued to publish there were thrown out of the Y. L. Peretz writers' trade union—the workers' union and advocacy organization for Yiddish journalists and writers. In the months following the August uprising and September stock-market crash, Party-aligned poets formed a new writers' union in the autumn of 1929, Proletpen.[113] Most of the Party-aligned Proletpen writers were younger and less established than the poets who left the Party over the Palestine crisis. If their writing was more tendentious, and generally less aesthetically oriented, than that of their political rivals, they led the way in identifying the key social concerns of the 1930s, raising public concern among their Jewish readers around the Scottsboro trial and Spanish Civil War. A second significant exodus from the Party occurred only in 1939, with the Molotov-Ribbentrop pact. The left-wing literary networks that existed from the late 1920s to World War II were, of course, fluid. For this reason, this book is not only about those poets who remained true to the Party until 1939 or later but also about those who became disillusioned along the way, some leaving as early as 1929, following the violence in Palestine. The historian Joshua Karlip provocatively observes in his study of Jewish diaspora nationalism, "in the first half of the twentieth century, people who cared passionately about the survival of the Jewish people often sought answers to Jewish identity consecutively in differing and often opposing camps."[114] The passwords that translocated texts from Jewish tradition to non-Jewish minorities and back were not the sole property of the Left. However, given the institutionalized effort by the Left to foster internationalism, this book focuses on writers who identified with the Party or the Soviet Union. Although many of them have been excluded from the Yiddish literary canon, their focus on ethnic minorities left a lasting mark on the identity of Jewish culture.

While acknowledging the disastrous effects of Stalinism on Soviet citizenry in general and Soviet Jewish culture in particular, I aim to revise the Cold War view that communist ideology around nationality only benefited a repressive state. As Alan Wald has cautioned, "Too often a preoccupation with Communist affiliations leads to the deductive fallacy of making presumptions about the artistic process according to supposed political loyalties of authors."[115] Even Hannah Arendt, who was skeptical of Party-aligned art, acknowledged that the Party brought Bertolt Brecht "into daily contact with what his compassion had already told him was reality: the darkness and the great cold in this valley of tears."[116] The imperative of empathizing with those who had been historically silenced, of empathizing with workers across cultures, helped to shape the ethics of a generation of poets, regardless of whether they remained with the Party. In the 1930s, American Yiddish writers asked the same question that many American Jews are asking nearly a century later: Can an individual support a Jewish community while simultaneously supporting the left-wing networks that have undermined Jewish cultural practices and, in some cases, taken Jewish lives? The Yiddish poets at the center of this book were young, idealistic writers, mostly from traditional backgrounds, who migrated to urban settings in the Soviet Union or the West. They moved in and out of far-left politics. During and after World War II, many of these poets shifted their gaze back to the Jewish community. However, the internationalist language they developed left a lasting mark on the way Jewish writers imagined their role.

A point often ignored in the discussion of communist literature is that Party-aligned internationalist writers, sometimes in spite of themselves, developed tools that celebrated, rather than rejected, nation as a defining category. This point has been identified by historians who, upon the fall of the Soviet Union, observed that the Soviet formation of nation-states prepared a national resurgence in the post-Soviet period. As Ronald Suny has observed, "Rather than a melting pot, the Soviet Union became the incubator of new nations."[117] That is to say, the center of communist internationalism gave birth to nation-states that would fortify their borders after the fall of the Soviet Union. As Rossen Djagalov has recently pointed out, even as the Soviet international ideals were eroding, the "tropes and narratives of transnational solidarity" that were important to Third-Worldist writers and filmmakers remained strong outside the Soviet sphere.[118] Internationalist Yiddish writers, too, by acknowledging the boundaries between ethnicities, were appraising their own cultural traditions. Yiddish writers' translocation between Jewish and non-Jewish trauma helped them to build a utopian vision of a collective where Jews, too, had a place.

How does a writer move between the self and the other? Might the experience of one's own trauma become more acute when contemplating the trauma of one's neighbor? H. Leivick, who moved in and out of Party politics throughout the 1920s and '30s, lived until 1962, experiencing the intense emotional trauma of one who saw European Jewry disappear. Leivick also faced physical pain, spending months in a tuberculosis sanatorium in the 1930s and suffering a debilitating stroke in 1958. Writing in the sanatorium in Denver, he described the terror following a neighbor's death:

Dervayle—biz vanen—vos—ven—
mayn shokhen—er iz shoyn in shtibl;
un ikh shrayb nokh alts mit mayn pen,
gram shtibl—faribl—mit ibl.
Baginen. Di velt iz farshneyt.
Di velt iz in vinter farkrokhn;
mikh shrekt nit mayn eygener toyt,
nor di leydike bet fun mayn shokhn.[119]

And before we can think—what—and when—
My neighbor is in that room;
And I am still writing with my pen,
Rhyming: room—gloom—doom.
Dawn. The world snowed in.
The world in winter's labor;
I am not afraid of my death,
But of the empty bed of my neighbor.

It is, Leivick suggests, through the experience of others' suffering that we understand our own. Viewing another life from the outside allows individuals, as Mikhail Bakhtin has formulated, to sympathetically *coexperience,* that is, to better know themselves.[120] Might turning to other nations' pain similarly heighten a poet's ability to see the trauma facing their own community?

The Soviet-aligned 1930s offer a prehistory for the question that has become paramount in memory studies: How does one compare group experiences of pain? Michael Rothberg has attempted to answer this question through his multidirectional memory model, which "acknowlededges how remembrance both cuts across and binds together diverse spatial, temporal, and cultural sites."[121] The Yiddish poets who translated the trauma of pogroms into the trauma of racism and colonialism, worldwide, attempted an act of multidirectional memory *avant la lettre.* Their story is a story of political extremes, of disputed realities, of a tense but seductive relationship between the Soviet Union and the United States. The idealism of this generation of poets, as well as the polarization that undermined it, remains instructive a century later.

1

FROM THE YANGTZE TO THE BLACK SEA

Esther Shumiatcher's Travels

IN JULY 1928, the Kharkov-based Soviet Yiddish literary journal *Royte Velt* published five poems by the young Canadian Yiddish poet Esther Shumiatcher (1899–1985).[1] "May lid" (May song) characterizes the workers' celebration in Moscow:

Ver yomtevt do, ver yomtevt do, ba aykh	Who is celebrating, who is celebrating with you
mit fonen nonte in yeder fester hant?	With familiar flags in that sturdy hand?
O, es geyen do di reyen. Vi der friling af ayer taykh!	Oh, the columns advance. Like spring on your river!
—S'iz May, s'iz ershter May, o do in land![2]	Oh it's May, it's May First, here in this land!

Moscow's 1928 May Day celebration was by all accounts a sight to behold. More than a holiday, it was a demonstration of Moscow as the center of world communism, the governing body of, and example for, the Communist International. Shumiatcher, who had recently arrived in the Soviet Union after two years in Asia and the Middle East, marveled

at the spectacle. "And here it is, and here it is, Red Square!" the poem
continues. "It breathes with victory and the joy of millions" (Un do iz
shoyn, un do iz shoyn, der royter plats; / Er otemt mit nitsokhn un mi-
lyonendiker freyd).

Esther Shumiatcher and her husband, the well-known Yiddish playwright Peretz Hirschbein (1880–1948), were, in the 1920s, fellow travelers
in both senses of the term. Though never members of the Communist
Party, they supported the Soviet Union and shared a particular interest
in the Soviet territorialist plans for a Jewish Soviet home.[3] They were also
travelers: having met and married in Canada in 1918, the couple visited
six continents together between 1920 and 1929, ending their decade-long
sojourn with ten months in the nascent Soviet Union before departing,
first to spend time with their close literary colleagues in Warsaw and
finally for the United States. Hirschbein, nineteen years older than his
spouse and already a celebrated playwright, theater director, and writer
for Yiddish newspapers in several countries, had the means to fund the
couple's world tour—an unprecedented experience for a poet of Shumiatcher's age and social class. Born in Homel (now Belarus), Shumiatcher
had emigrated with her family at the age of ten to Calgary, where she at-
tended secondary school and, before meeting Hirschbein, worked at a
music store and in a meat-packing factory.[4] The family was highly educated and well integrated into Montreal's Yiddish-speaking community
(some of the Shumiatchers were quickly becoming important entrepre-
neurs in their adopted Calgary), but in her poems about the Soviet
Union, she emphasizes her family's proletarian credentials, first as victims of pre-Revolutionary antisemitism and later in the Canadian work-
force as new immigrants.

Shumiatcher's travels with Hirschbein were as significant to her en-
thusiasm for the Soviet project as her immigrant childhood was: isolated
from any one community of writers but suddenly exposed to literary
communities (Jewish and non-Jewish) in multiple countries, Shumiatcher found a poetic voice that was internationalist in spirit—her
poems from the 1920s reflect a desire for world revolution, with new
rights for historically oppressed nations. While in the Soviet Union, the
couple lived in Crimea, where Hirschbein wrote the novel *Royte felder*
(Red fields) and Shumiatcher edited her travel poems. During this time,

Shumiatcher published poetic cycles in the Soviet journal *Royte Velt* (Red world), a journal that, David Shneer has observed, published the works of sympathetic foreigners who made pilgrimages to the Soviet Union.[5] She also sent the Party-aligned New York journal *Hamer* several poems that highlight a connection between her travels in East Asia and her support of the Soviet Union. She published her travel poems in her 1930 book *In shoen fun libshaft* (In the hours of love) shortly after returning to North America.

In the 1920s, Shumiatcher was breathlessly excited about her own mobility. In Tahiti in 1921, she had written "Albatros" (Albatross), a poem about wandering:

Un ven likht	And when light
vert in tunkl dertrunken—	Drowns in darkness
zenen khvalyes	The waves are
dayn heym,	your home,
zenen khvalyes	The waves are
dayn bet.[6]	Your bed.

Shumiatcher was in Warsaw in 1922, when this poem appeared in the first issue of *Albatros,* and as Faith Jones surmises, the poem probably gave the journal its name. This poem of wandering and artistic homelessness, Jones observes, "may have meshed with European sensibilities to create the kind of murky, mythological image that embodied the dislocations and contingency of life for the group of Yiddish writers, the *Khalyastre,* gathered then in Warsaw."[7] Shumiatcher's anomalous travels and her poems of wandering symbolized the youthful moment that eastern European poetry was experiencing in the 1920s. Still in her twenties when she wrote most of her travel poems, she embodied the Russian poet Osip Mandelstam's 1913 assertion that "a twenty-year old American girl / ought to make it to Egypt" (Amerikanka v dvadtsat' let / Dolzhna dobrat'sia do Egipta).[8] If all eastern European cosmopolitan writers were, to some extent, like the young American tourist, Shumiatcher *was* the young American tourist.

The 1920s was a time of travel. Soviet-aligned poets moved in and out of the Soviet Union, sharing impressions, often laced with proletarian passwords, in poems they published during and after their visits. In 1925,

H. Leivick traveled to the Soviet Union and published poems in the So-viet Yiddish journal *Royte Velt* until his split with the Party following the Palestine uprisings of August 1929. In July 1929, Leivick wrote a three-page poem in the form of a letter to a comrade and lover. The poem is followed by a glossary of Americanisms: "Grinhorn," "Boarders," "Boss," "Hurry Up," and so forth.[9] Moyshe Nadir, Avrom Reyzen, and Morris Winchevsky made similar pilgrimages.[10] These writers served as left-wing cultural ambassadors from the United States and were toasted by young writers in the nascent Soviet Union who indulged their American guests' curiosity about the new state. The American writer Theodore Dreiser and the philosopher Horace Kallen visited the Soviet Union in 1926 and 1927.[11] Walter Benjamin, who visited Moscow in 1926, wrote to Jula Radt, "Everything is being built or rebuilt and every moment poses very critical questions."[12] The world was changing rapidly, and young in-tellectuals sought their proper place in it. The Russian futurist Vladimir Mayakovsky visited Mexico, Cuba, and the United States in 1925, paying a visit to (and writing a poem in honor of) the communist Yiddish summer camp Nit Gedayget (Don't worry), and spent the bulk of his time in New York among the Russian-speaking, Russian Jewish émigré community. "Brooklyn Bridge!" he wrote. "Now that's quite the thing!" The Ukrainian-born Kiev-grupe poet Dovid Hofshteyn spent the year 1925–1926 in Palestine, returning in 1926 to make his permanent home in the Soviet Union.[13] Hofshteyn's two fellow Kiev-grupe poets, Leyb Kvitko and Peretz Markish, moved permanently to the Soviet Union in 1925 and 1926. Others were emigrating to North America: in 1925, a young Jewish dentist named Jacobo Glantz emigrated from Ukraine to Mexico City, where he became a celebrated Yiddish poet who, in the 1930s, welcomed the transformative potential of the Communist International. The world was becoming smaller, and for left-wing writers, the Soviet Union was the axis of its orbit. Esther Shumiatcher and Peretz Hirschbein spent the 1920s traveling the world, where Shumiatcher recorded her impressions of the inequality they witnessed between locals and the empires that oppressed them. The couple left eastern Europe amid the disillusionment that came with the rift among left-wing writers over the 1929 violence in Palestine.

A US passport was issued to Peretz Hirschbein on August 24, 1920, for travel with "his wife Ethel." Alongside the image of the couple is a

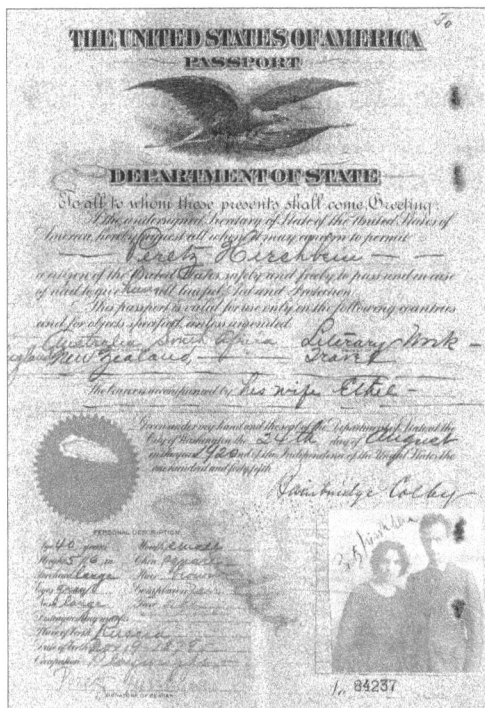

Fig 1.1 Peretz Hirschbein's US Passport, 1920, for travel with "his wife Ethel." *Credit:* YIVO Institute

personal description of Hirschbein: "Age 40 years; height 5 ft. 6 in.; forehead large; eyes gray; nose large; place of birth Russia." The space for distinguishing marks (for recording scars, birthmarks, tattoos) is left blank.[14] The American passport, in its early twentieth-century manifestation and its current streamlined version, documents a citizen's identity, while legitimizing their movement between spaces. The passwords that Shumiatcher employed in her poetry during her stay in the Soviet Union functioned as verbal passports, legitimizing her presence in the nascent Soviet Union and documenting her past itinerary.[15] Shumiatcher, a poet who crossed multiple borders in the 1920s, in the process developed an internationalist poetics that allowed her to translocate her own experience as a Russian-born Jewish worker to the experience of workers internationally. Her travel writing has been underappreciated since it was first published in the late 1920s, but she was an early innovator who used translocation to hone a poetics of internationalism. She did so through a combination of self-exoticism and adaptation: by adapting themes and terms from pogrom poetry to the poverty she witnessed in Asia, she developed a poetics of empathy that connected the Jewish and Chinese worker. She further creates this connection between the Jewish and Asiatic Other in the poems she writes about Crimea.

Arriving in the Soviet Union after two years in East Asia and the Middle East, Shumiatcher found the May 1 holiday a stark contrast to East Asia, where Chinese communists had been the victims of a brutal massacre the previous year. Shumiatcher's aforementioned "May lid" continues,

Ikh hob in vandernishn mayne teg gezeyt,	I have sown my days in wanderings,
fun Yangtses fule breges bizn Gang.	from the broad shores of the Yangtze to the Ganges.
Ikh hob in oygn tunkele gezukht a nontn basheyd,	I have sought in dark eyes a familiar interpretation,
un hob in yeder oyg derkent dem serp-un hamer-klang.[16]	and recognized in those eyes the sound of the hammer and sickle.

It is tempting to read into Shumiatcher's search for familiarity in the "dark eyes" of the Asian figure an Orientalist naiveté.[17] And indeed, when Shumiatcher's book of poems appeared in 1930, the Yiddish press accused her of sentimentalism and generalizations—criticism that was often leveraged against female poets in a male-dominated milieu. Shmuel Niger-Charney, writing for the *Tsukunft,* called the poems "amateurish lyricism,"[18] and Melech Ravitch titled a review of the book, "A Woman Writer Travels the World behind a Veil."[19] These critics fault Shumiatcher with simplification, with surface-level portrayals of East Asia. Faith Jones has noted, "Particularly irritating to many critics were the exotic locales evoked in the poetry: they complained that the writer appeared too detached from her subject matter."[20] Read in tandem with the verse she wrote in the Soviet Union, however, Shumiatcher's poems of East Asia emerge as innovative experiments in merging the exoticized Other with the exoticized Jew. In this sense, her poetry is redolent of earlier European Jewish writers like Eugénie Foa (1796–1853), whom Maurice Samuels credits with using the figure of the Orientalized Jew to help place Jewish culture within an international context.[21] Shumiatcher's explicit and metaphorical identification with her subject bespeaks a desire to cultivate her own internationalist identity. Her impressionistic accounts of Asia appear through the lens of her own experience: struggling Asian workers are described in terms familiar from Yiddish poems about pre-Revolutionary antisemitism. As a fellow traveler, Shumiatcher was independent of the Communist Party line. Nonetheless, during the ten months she spent in the Soviet Union, she adapted her own version of internationalism to that of her Soviet colleagues. Her East Asian motifs from the late 1920s represent a form of specifically communist Orientalism—an empathetic identification with the Asian Other as a means of depicting an international community.[22] Shumiatcher, publishing her impressions of China in a Soviet journal in 1928, modeled poetic translocation: by applying Jewish passwords that evoked Jewish collective memory of tsarist pogroms within a discussion of Chinese workers, she demonstrates the potential of a Jewish poetic tradition to promote empathy and solidarity across ethnic boundaries.

Shumiatcher's trip to East Asia had coincided with a series of suppressed uprisings in China, culminating (following Shumiatcher's departure from China) in the April 1927 Shanghai massacre of Chinese communists by the Party's former allies—the nationalist Kuomintang. In the poems she published from the Soviet Union, Shumiatcher presents the ongoing struggle of Asian communists to achieve a workers' society. The couple arrived in Japan in the summer of 1926, traveled to China, followed by India, Egypt, and Palestine, and arrived in the Soviet Union in early 1928.[23] Her time in Asia also gave her a language to decipher Jews' relationship to the Soviet Union. Shumiatcher's portrayal of the Asian revolutionary project is inextricable from her vision of a communist internationalism—one that is centered in Moscow, will liberate the oppressed of China, has already liberated the Jews, and will soon include a Soviet Jewish homeland.

Shumiatcher's communist internationalism—and communist Orientalism—reveals some ideological gaps, as well as important alignments, between her identity as a North American Jewish fellow traveler and the Party line in the late 1920s. Her 1930 book of poems appeared as the Soviet Union was moving further from internationalism and toward Stalin's notion of socialism in one country. Her poems then are a poignant souvenir of the dreams of the fellow traveler. In the pages that follow, I first discuss how Shumiatcher's incorporation of East Asia into her internationalist poetics borrowed from a trend in Soviet letters. I then turn specifically to Shumiatcher's incorporation of motifs from a national Jewish poetics into her portrayals of China. Finally, turning to Crimea, I show how East Asia figured into Shumiatcher and others' visions of a Jewish space within the nascent Soviet Union.

INTERNATIONAL CHINA

China in the 1920s was a multiethnic republic. At the beginning of the twentieth century, Japan and Britain controlled significant territories across China, and the United States pursued business ventures on the continent. Japanese, Indian, and Korean communities had settled in China, and German, Russian, and Iraqi Jewish populations were concentrated in Shanghai. The cosmopolitan northeastern city of Harbin was under Japanese control until 1922 and had become home to a sizable Russian-speaking community following World War I, which included a large Jewish population.[24] Shumiatcher and Hirschbein arrived in China at a time when Chinese writers were experimenting with revolutionary forms and Soviet intellectuals were describing the Chinese revolutionary movement.[25] The couple, who did not speak any Asian languages, formed their impressions of East Asia in large part through the Russians, Americans, and other Westerners they met there. Russian writers had long viewed their own country in Orientalized terms. Moreover, Marx's prophecy that "revolution would come from the East" led Revolutionary Russia to turn to Asia as a kindred territory. "We're Scythians, yes! With Asiatic mien," wrote Alexander Blok in 1918. "We watch you, gloating, through our slit-squint eyelids."[26] The futurist Velimir Khlebnikov included Russia in a proposed utopian "Asiaunion."[27] The filmmaker Sergei Eisenstein compared his filmic montage methods to what he called Japanese "hieroglyphs."[28] The playwright and journalist Sergei Tretiakov worked as a Russian teacher and reporter in Beijing from 1924 until 1926 and wrote his 1926 play *Roar China* about what he hoped China's nascent Marxist revolutionaries would achieve in their country. Western writers' interests in China ranged, Steven Lee has shown, from the emphasis on Chinese "backwardness" that interested Soviet artists like Sergei Eisenstein as well as Western writers like Ezra Pound to Sergei Tret'iakov's factographic approach.[29]

Shumiatcher, a Yiddish writer who developed her voice in the absence of a stable literary group (apart from her husband), resembles the Russian writer Boris Pilniak in her approach to East Asia, for both viewed East Asia through a pre-Revolutionary Russian lens and both tended to veil the East in a sleepy, mystical haze that raised the ire of Pilniak's Soviet critics and Shumiatcher's non-Soviet critics alike. In the mid-1920s, Pilniak sojourned to Japan and China under the auspices of VOKS, the Soviet Society for Cultural Relations with Foreign Countries.[30] As Katerina Clark has noted, Pilniak may have been selected for this trip in part "because as a noncommunist and maverick figure he could not be accused of being a purveyor of communist propaganda."[31] For Pilniak, a visit to China is a visit to the past—where revolution was still fomenting. Pilniak writes of waking one morning to memories of his grandmother's home in Saratov and immediately going out to "wander around [his] childhood, because the view is exactly the same."[32] Alexander Bukh observes of Pilniak's *Chinese Diary* that "the China that emerges from the narrative is familiar and understandable."[33] A literary celebrity before 1917, Pilniak viewed the Revolution as a means of redeeming the Russian peasant nation.[34] His writings about the East, which strike a hazier, more exotic tone than his descriptions of Russia, also describe the struggles of the poor.[35]

Shumiatcher and Hirschbein's trip and itinerary coincided with Pilniak's travels to Japan and China, and soon after arriving in Nara, Japan, the couple met and befriended the celebrated Russian writer. Pilniak wrote warmly of them: "And my three days in Nara will always be connected in my memory with these two wonderful individuals, with husband and wife H., people dear to me, with a mixture of sorrow and tenderness. It doesn't matter that they are both writers, that she looked like a Frenchwoman, and he—like a Swede: what matters to me is their humanity."[36] Pilniak devoted a chapter of his 1927 memoir to the couple, remarking with wonder at the couple's solitary travels. He describes

Hirschbein as a father figure and Shumiatcher as a "young, beautiful, black-haired woman, raised in the American way, liberated and dignified [svobodnaia i dostoinaia],"[37] who preferred to speak in Yiddish, English, and French but who could occasionally conjure Russian words: "Mrs. H., giving birth once more to words, spoke, glancing at the moon, of nights in Africa, in Australia, on the oceans."[38] Pilniak, who had written passionately against pogroms, takes pride in having mistaken Shumiatcher and Hirschbein's identity, exposing his internationalist ethos: Jews and Slavs were close relatives against the backdrop of East Asia.

Shumiatcher, like Pilniak, sought the recognizable in the foreign. Both describe the simultaneously life-giving and deadly Yangtze River. Pilniak opens his "Chinese Story" with a description of a village on the bank of the Yangtze, which he compares to Russia's Volga: "The other bank of the Yangtze is almost lost to sight; this river is about five times as broad as the Volga."[39] The narrator then turns his gaze to the surface of the "yellow water, which looks more like stewed tea than anything else," where he sees a floating corpse. "His face is down, his brown back and dark-blue trousers are exposed; the corpse is swollen, and the water carries it along in the most leisurely way, rocking it gently from side to side."[40] With this description, Pilniak launches a narrative about the rot and decay that pervades the Chinese landscape, culture, and religious traditions. China, in Pilniak's description, is overripe for revolution: "What limitless heights might the peasants of China gain if they were really marching forward instead of marking time on the spot as they do, pumping water from the canals to the rice fields and from one rice field to another?!"[41] By removing a discussion of revolution from Russia, Pilniak sheds new light on the proletarian utopianism that had drastically altered his homeland.

Shumiatcher, in her impressions of East Asia, also combines a defamiliarized portrait of foreign cities with the revolutionary urgency of pre–Civil War Russia. In April 1927, she published a cycle of East Asia poems in the New York communist journal *Hamer*, including "Saygon" (Saigon), a poem dated 1926 that begins with bells ringing on high and sparkling sails on the river, then swiftly moves to a description of poverty: the sails have been badly damaged, and stray dogs howl.

Bay di breges fun taykh Saygon	By the banks of the river Saigon
zingen kloystershe gleker a frumen gezang.	church bells sing a pious song.
Blanken zeglen, gedikht vi a vald,	Sails sparkle, dense as a forest,
blinde, tseflikte fun shturm un vint,	blindly tattered by storm and wind,
un s'fargeyt zikh a voyen fun heym- loze hint.[42]	and the howling of homeless dogs passes.

The architectural contrast between towering buildings and misery below is a familiar trope in avant-garde East European poetry. Vladimir May-akovsky, in his 1913 "Ia" (I), famously moves from the towers, frozen in cloud nooses (v petle oblaka / zastyli bashen) to the intersection "that has crucified policemen" (perekrestkom / raspiaty gorodovye).[43] The Yiddish revolutionary poet Peretz Markish, in his 1921 pogrom poem *Di kupe* (The mound), describes a church beside a mound of murdered po-grom victims as sitting "like a skunk by a pile of strangled chickens" (vi a tkhoyr, bay a kupe oysgeshtikte oyfes).[44] Shumiatcher deepens the spa-tial and social contrast in her second stanza, which illuminates the in-equality between "children's bellies, swollen with hunger and need" (kindershe bakhlekh, geshvoln fun hunger un noyt) and "granaries, full from floor to ceiling with bread" (shpaykhler, farfulte fun dil biz der stele mit broyt). Here, the well-worn rhyme broyt / noyt (bread / need) is softened by Shumiatcher's careful, documentary description. This leads to the final, gruesome stanza, where the poet's gaze stops at corpses floating on the surface of the water:

Af dem eyberflakh fun taykh Saygon	On the surface of the river Saigon
shvimt der toyt mitn ponem arop,	swims death with its face down,
un es trogt zikh a krrra-a in der hoykh,	and a krrrra-a carries aloft,
tsirklen foygl mit dershtikter freyd:	birds circle with suppressed joy:
—toyt hot unz moltsayt gegreyt!	—Death has prepared a meal for us!
Toyt hot unz moltsayt gegreyt![45]	Death has prepared a meal for us!

The poem, which began with a promise of the picturesque, ends with the horrific, defiled corpse—made less human by the gulls that prey on it. In the span of the poem, the people are not only denied bread: they become bread. Pilniak, in his description of the corpse on the Yangtze, similarly belabors the grotesque view by reflecting on his response to the dead: "Silly, but, I must admit, it is less disturbing to see the corpse floating head forward."[46] Both writers force the reader to look closely at death and, in Shumiatcher's poem, to taste it.

Both writers, moreover, evoke East Asia in immediate contrast to Russia. Pilniak observes, in the paragraph following his description of the corpse, that "at midnight when the tide begins to rise, all at once the Chinese start shouting—it is then, in the midst of all this strangeness, in this dark night—darker than any Russian night—that terror comes."[47] Shumiatcher published "Saygon" in *Hamer* alongside a poem titled "A betler" (A beggar), in which the poetic persona encounters a Russian beggar on the streets of Mukden (now Shenyang). The poem begins and ends with a quotation in Russian: "Barishnya, pomogitie bednomu na khleb" (Madam, help a poor man for bread). The poetic persona is out-raged and ashamed:

Vifl broyt trogt in shoys Ruslands erd!	How much bread is in the womb of Russia's earth!
Shtrekstu betlerhant in vayter fremd	You stretch out your beggar-hand in a distant land,
un s'traybt blut in mayne bakn di shand,	and the shame drives the blood to my cheeks,
far zikh, far dir	for myself, for you
un far mame erd.	and for Mother Earth.
Mayn shotn, aza brekele vigt zikh in der vayter fremd	My scrap of shadow sways in this distant land
antkegn bloyoygiker, braytpleytsiker geshtalt.[48]	facing this blue-eyed, broad-shouldered figure.

We do not know the Russian beggar's backstory, but he plausibly has re-mained in the city following the 1905 battle of Mukden—the last battle of the Russo-Japanese War and the episode that led to Russia's humiliating defeat. He is a figure from Russia's past—left in the wake of the Revolution and symbolic of the difference between Bolshevik Russia's advanced so-ciety and the as-yet-unsuccessful revolution in East Asia. East Asia is, for Shumiatcher as for Pilniak, temporally inferior to the Soviet Union.[49] Their comparison between the post-Revolutionary Soviet Union and the exploitation in East Asia promotes an international revolutionary cause, while exalting the Soviet Union as leader and center.[50]

Peretz Hirschbein later described Pilniak in an article he wrote for the New York Yiddish daily *Der Tog* in January 1929, shortly after returning from the Soviet Union. "I befriended Pilniak in Japan. His restlessness wouldn't let him sit still." In a racially and geopolitically Orientalizing metaphor, Hirschbein describes the revolutionary Japanese poets who gathered around Pilniak as blinded by their Soviet model: "A circle of Japanese poets surrounded him and they looked to him as one looks at an eclipse through squinted eyes."[51] Hirschbein, observing the formation of multiple revolutionary literary circles from the outside, places Soviet Moscow at the center of a new orbit—a bright light and model for "backward nations." Hirschbein, writing for the liberal-left *Der Tog*, presented contemporary Soviet literature in an unmistakably positive light. However, Hirschbein and Pilniak present the new Soviet society with more skepticism than Shumiatcher in the late 1920s. Hirschbein remarks that Pilniak "is convinced that the Russian population is no longer Asiatic, but Slavic," and yet the Russian writer declares, while showing Hirschbein around the Kremlin portion of Moscow, "Well, Mister Hirschbein, didn't I tell you that you would come to us in Moscow and feel like you're in Asia?"[52]

Asia offered Hirschbein, too, a contrast with the West, and he attempted to describe the inequality he witnessed in his private correspondences. In a letter from Asia to H. Leivick, Peretz Hirschbein described the poverty of China and India: "Now we return to China and the Oriental nightmare that lies upon life and attempts to rip bloody tears from my eyes. . . . A lot of our unappreciated advantages are coming to the fore. And how sadly it shouts in blood; the west. West is west!" In China, Hirschbein muses, "the uncleannest fall on our heads and on our consciences." Hirschbein may be drawing the concept of "the unclean" from Maykovsky, whose 1922 play *Mystery Bouffe* pitted the world's workers, the "Unclean," against the "Clean," the capitalists. Hirschbein was, after all, a playwright, writing to Leivick, a fellow playwright. He concludes his reflection on inequality by telling Leivick of his plans to suspend judgment during his forthcoming visit to the Soviet Union: "I'll go with my face toward them."[53] Hirschbein's open mind about the Soviet Union sheds light on Shumiatcher's similar desire to find an answer to world poverty in the Soviet project. Shumiatcher further personalizes the relationship between East Asian suffering and the revolutionary potential of the workers by referencing—albeit subtly—the Jewish experience of violence in pre-Revolutionary Russia.

THE TRASH HEAP OF HISTORY

Shumiatcher's poetic innovation lay in her translocation of a Jewish poetics to the context of another nation. She did so by identifying passwords from a modern Jewish language of trauma and applying them to the peoples she observed in her travels. Shumiatcher, like most of the Jewish intellectuals of her generation, was steeped in the Jewish modernism of the early twentieth century—a genre that emerged in large part as a means of grappling with eastern European pogroms. If for some writers, including Chaim Nakhman Bialik and Uri Tzvi Grinberg, the pogroms were a pretext for nationalism, for others they necessitated internationalism. Trauma, as Cathy Caruth has observed, "may lead . . . to the encounter with another, through the very possibility and surprise of listening to another's wound."[54] Shumiatcher's descriptions of human refuse in China and the violence wrought on the body recall the gruesome portrayals of victims in the pogrom poetry of Bialik and those who followed him. But whereas the modernism of the aughts focused on Jewish trauma, Shumiatcher used similar imagery to focus on other groups, in particular Chinese workers sants and peasants. Moreover, whereas Bialik's pogrom poems locate violence in a male Jewish subject, Shumiatcher highlights the physical suffering of women. Shumiatcher published "Baym rand fun Khine" (At the border of China) alongside "May lid" in *Royte Velt* in 1928. She opens with a description of impoverished women of the East:

Froy un muter	Wife and mother
baym rand fun Khine un Ind!	at the border of China and India!
Es hengen di korbn fun ayere akslen	Baskets hang from your shoulders,
gelodn mit umet un mi.	loaded with toil and sadness.
Es hengen di trukene brustn, vi	Your barren breasts hang, like dry
fartriknte loglen	vessels

In blend funem dorshtikn vist.	in the dazzle of the thirsty void.
Un s'viklen trantes farfoylte ayer faroremtn guf—	And the rotten wreckage swaddles your destitute body—
Af ayere lipn glit a fariglter flukh.[55]	A sealed curse burns on your lips.

The exhausted shoulders and barren breasts recall the sacrificed bodies of pogrom victims. In Shumiatcher's poem, human body parts merge with cast-off objects in a trash heap. The women's baskets (*korbn*) are "loaded with pain and sadness." *Korbn,* however, spelled in the Soviet orthography, is a homonym, meaning both "baskets" and "sacrifice." The women are carrying not only basketsful of pain but sacrifices. Further in the poem, Shumiatcher writes,

Royen zikh lebns af bergele mist.	Lives swarm on a pile of trash.
Fayf. Fayfl, a lid mir, in vind un in vist.	Whistle me a song in the wind, in the void.
Rinshtok iz heym far heymloze hent,	Homeless hands find a home in the gutter,
brekele guf hot hunger farlendt.	hunger has ruined a crumb of a body.
Hot zikh der vey afn mistbarg gemert—	Here on the trash heap, the sorrow has grown—
Emitsns lebn-iz oysgeyn bashert.	Somebody's life is bound to expire.
Ver s'hot gezindikt antkegn di hent,	Whoever has sinned against these hands,
der hot dos lebn geflikt un geshendt.[56]	he has plucked and dishonored this life.

I have tried, with my translation, to replicate Shumiatcher's dactylic, waltz-like lines, the rhythm and rhyming couplets suggesting a relentless dance of time.

Shumiatcher's "bergele mist" (pile of trash), witnessed by the poetic persona and the wind, is a password with leftist, as well as Jewish, precedents. For leftists, it recalls Leon Trotsky, who in 1917 allegedly relegated the anti-Bolsheviks to the "trash heap of history" (Svalka istorii).[57] Shumiatcher also dramatizes the basic premise of China's movement toward Marxism in the 1920s: the combined forces of foreign imperialism and the tradition of Chinese feudalism had betrayed China's proletarian and agrarian populations.[58] It is, of course, crucial to note that Shumiatcher, informed as she was by what Katerina Clark has termed "'scientific socialist' internationalism," was as vulnerable to abstractions as her Russian counterparts were, occasionally devolving into what Clark calls "utopian generalizations or a set of abstractions, that presuppose a common humanity or a truly international proletariat, . . . or it will purvey essentialist notions, such as the 'sleepy' East."[59] However, we must observe that Asia played a unique role for Jewish writers like Shumiatcher, who sought parallels for the long-exoticized figure of the European Jew.

Shumiatcher was clearly reading Russian revolutionary writers, like Trotsky and Tretiakov, closely and synthesizing their Marxist rhetoric with the Hebrew and Yiddish poets who had reshaped Jewish poetry with their descriptions of the early twentieth century in eastern Europe. A "mistbarg"—trash heap—of human body parts had by the 1920s also become a password for early twentieth-century anti-Jewish pogrom violence. References to trash heaps appear in two significant pogrom poems, both Chaim Nachman Bialik's Hebrew-language 1903 "B'ir haHaregah" (B'ir haHaréygo, in its Ashkenazi pronunciation) and Peretz Markish's 1921–1922 Yiddish-language pogrom poem *Di kupe* (The mound). Bialik's description of the 1903 Kishinev pogrom includes a mound of trash that includes human and animal corpses:

Uvorákhto uvóso el-khótseyr,
  vəhekhatser gál bòy—
Al hagál hazè nérfu shnáyim: Yehúdi
  vekhál-bòy . . .

Kàrdoym ékhod aròfom vəel-àshpe-
  ákhas hutólù
Uvèyrev-dóm shnéyhem yəkhàtu
  khazèyrim vəyisgoylólù;

Then wilt thou flee to a yard, observe
  its mound.
Upon the mound lie two, and both
  are headless—
A Jew and his hound . . .

The self-same axe struck both, and
  both were flung
Unto the self-same heap where swine
  seek dung;

Bialik's application of artistic fragmentation to a collective tragedy established new images to describe Jewish suffering. His poem ends with the admonishment to "flee to the desert" and, moreover, to "send thy bitter cry into the storm!"[60] Twentieth-century Yiddish and Hebrew poetry arose as a modern means of making sense of Jewish catastrophe, supplanting for modernizing Jews a liturgical textual tradition with artistic expressions of ideology—be it Zionist, diaspora nationalist, socialist, or a combination of the three.[61] It exemplified the late nineteenth-century emphasis on the nation as a force uniting linguistic and cultural communities.[62] If modernist writers tended to emphasize the particular as a case study for the universal, the internationalist poets borrowed passwords and devices developed to describe Jewish communities, and applied them to a pluralistic worldview.[63] Shumiatcher, describing a heap of doomed lives in China, creates a new manifestation of a Jewish literary lineage, translocating Bialik's poem of Jewish national loss to a non-Jewish context.

Markish, in his Yiddish pogrom poem *Di kupe,* published in the wake of the Ukrainian Civil War, evokes mounds of corpses that combine Bialik's mound with Trotsky's historical detritus. Markish, like Bialik, effects a prophetic figure who beholds Jewish corpses, defiled in a pogrom, and defies the wind—a surrogate for God—to do what it wants with the mound:

A kupe koytik gret—fun untn biz aruf iz!	A mound of dirty laundry—from the bottom up!
Na! Vos dir vilt zikh, dul-vint, krats aroys un nem dir!	Here! Take what you want, crazy wind, dig in and take it!
Antkegn zitst der kloyster,	Sitting opposite is the church
vi a tkhoyr, bay kupe oysgeshtikte oyfes.[64]	like a skunk by a heap of strangled fowl.

Markish's poem, which was published by the Kiev-grupe in 1921 and 1922, quickly joined Bialik's as a modernist documentation of a pogrom. Throughout the poem, his mound of bodies becomes, alternately, a deity and a pile of merchandise, strewn across the market where the pogrom took place. The mound, in the language of market-exchange, cries to God, "Na dir, na dir" (Take it, take it), in reference to the pile of desecrated Jewish bodies. Pogrom poems, by the mid-1920s, represented the modern Jewish experience, altering and replacing biblical text.

Shumiatcher was immersed in the literature of the Yiddish avant-garde and knew both Chaim Nachman Bialik and Peretz Markish personally. In a poem she later published alongside "Baym rand fun Khine," Shumiatcher repeats Markish's image of returning bodies to the earth:

O, mame-erd,	O, Mother Earth!
na dir, na dir undzere hent,	Take them, take our hands,
vos zenen keynmol umtray nisht	which were never untrue to hard labor
geven der shverer arbet	
un undzer pratse bet tsu dir:	and our toil begs of you:
Nisht shend!⁶⁵	Don't defile them!

Whereas Markish's mound of bodies speaks to God, Shumiatcher's female hands represent a collective feminized labor force, which can be read to include women workers the world over and which speaks to Mother Earth as opposed to a male God of traditional prayer. Through this desperate relinquishing of body parts, Shumiatcher connects her recent memory of China to the pogrom poem.

It is significant that Shumiatcher, a Canadian fellow traveler living only temporarily in the Soviet Union, may have been the first poet to translocate a motif used in Jewish pogrom poems (the trash heap) to the struggles of Chinese workers, for the Soviet Yiddish readers of *Royte Velt* in the 1920s. Her unlikely mobility afforded her a broad view of social stratification in the many countries that she and Hirschbein visited. She was, moreover, sharply aware of her privilege as a North American tourist in East Asia. Pilniak recounts the embarrassment of his companion, Olga Sergeevna, when, returning from a shopping trip with Shumiatcher, she whispered to him, "Mrs. G [Hirschbein] behaved herself as though she wanted to buy up the entire shop and give it to Olga Sergeevna."⁶⁶ The young North American, certain of her comparative wealth vis-à-vis her Soviet comrades, sought to share her good fortune in a gesture that must have appeared naive and demonstratively bourgeois to her European acquaintances. Shumiatcher's desire, however awkward, to empathize and to equalize is apparent in her poetry and her behavior alike.

The poverty in China conflicts with the pastoral beauty of the bountiful landscape itself:

Froy un muter—	Wife and mother—
Ariber mayn kop hengen himlen in	Over my head hang clear blue
geleytertn bloy,	heavens,
vigt zikh di zatkayt af zangen in feld	the fullness swings on ears of corn
farn shnit.	before the harvest.
Un umetik nidert af lebn, harts	The dew hovers sadly over life, my
mayns, der toy	heart,
bam rand fun Khine un Ind.[67]	at the border of China and India.

The contrast between a picturesque landscape and human suffering is also a familiar pogrom motif. Lamed Shapiro, in his gruesome 1909 pogrom tale "The Cross," has his protagonist stop, on the eve of the pogrom, to observe the beauty of his city: "The sun was just going down, and a light, delicate veil, spun of gold and happiness, lay in soft folds on the streets and the houses. Our city was a beautiful city."[68] Markish includes a section in *Di kupe* that describes a market day following the pogrom, in which "happiness flickers on everyone's faces" (Es flakert freyd af alemens gezikhter).[69] Natural beauty and the possibility for happiness heighten the inequality of human trauma.

Shumiatcher's experience of China is mediated by her memory of pre-Revolutionary antisemitism and her immersion in the Jewish pogrom poems that had formed the sensibility of her generation. Shumiatcher was four years old in 1903, when a pogrom broke out in her native Homel, and she recalls this in a short 1928 homage to her hometown, "Homel, 1905–1928":

Ikh bin avek fun dir nokh nor a	I left you when I was just a sprout
shprotserl	
un shoyn mit broygez in mayn ponem.	And with anger already in my face.
Un s'hot mir nokhgeshirt vi gor a	And it trailed me like a loyal dog
trayer hunt	
s'pakhed tunkele far hak un lom,	This dark fear of axe and crowbar,
un federn pukhike af shteynerdike	And downy feathers on the stony
brukn	cobbles
un dayns an ibldik vort: —*bei zhidov*[70]	And your nauseating word: —*bei zhidov*

The short poem, which opens a cycle dedicated to Homel, establishes the poet's relationship to both pre-Revolutionary pogrom violence and the

Revolutionary eastern European Jewish narrative. The speaker obses-
sively repeats a rallying cry in Russian: "Bei zhidov"—"Kill the Jews,"
which had become a passphrase for describing pogroms.

The 1903–1905 pogroms in the tsarist empire were a reference point
for most of eastern European Jewish literature in the twentieth century.
The Kishinev pogrom, which broke out in April 1903, was the first major
pogrom since the early 1880s and resulted in forty-nine deaths—far
more casualties than all the nineteenth-century pogroms combined.
Shumiatcher's native Homel, where half the population was Jewish, was
the site of the first major pogrom after Kishinev: eight people were killed
in late August–early September 1903, and, having prepared self-defense
units following the spring violence in Kishinev, Jewish community
members armed and defended themselves. They were tried for violent
crimes alongside their Slavic antagonists.[71] Hans Rogger views the
Homel pogrom as "a turning point, less in what was done there to Jews
by pogromists and soldiers than in subsequent interpretations of what
transpired."[72] Shumiatcher's choice to title her poem "Homel, 1905–1928"
could either indicate a lapse in her memory of the date of the 1903 Homel
pogrom or a reference to Homel's role in the first—failed—Russian Revolution of 1905. The title, with its explicit periodization, marks Shumiatcher's development as a poet and Soviet sympathizer from the early
years of the twentieth century, with its pogrom violence and failed revolution, to her return as an adult, a poet, and a traveler.

Writing from the Soviet Union in 1927–1928, Shumiatcher presents
Jewish history and Jewish identity as inextricable from the struggle for
world revolution. In January 1929, *Royte Velt* printed Shumiatcher's "Nito
a freyd aza" (No happiness like this), a long letter-poem from the Soviet
Union to her six siblings in Canada. The poem begins with a response
to the question "Have you, sister, celebrated the Great October?" (Tsi
hostu, shvester, dort geyomtevt dem Oktyaber?), hinting at the poet's Canadian Jewish émigré family's investment in the nascent Soviet Union.
In response, the poet writes, "Every weekday's a holiday here" (Si'z yo-
mtev do a yeder indervokhn), then reminds her siblings that they, too,
"fought for this land / in the ranks of the liberators" (Ir hot aleyn, . . .
gekemft af higer erd do / in reyen fun bafrayer):

Di poyerim un poyertes, in vayse
  laynene khalatn,
fartseyln mir mayses tunkele un
  royte,
In teg fun far oktyaber,
Un az der keyzer iz geven a gornishtl
  a mentsh.
Ugodye iz aykh bakant geven der
  royter troyer;
Ir hot aleyn, dakht mir, gekemft af
  higer erd do
In reyen fun bafrayer.[73]

The peasants and peasant women, in
  white linen robes,
tell me stories, dark and red,

of the days before October,
that the tsar was a nothing of a man.

You are surely familiar with the red
  sadness;
you yourselves, it seems to me,
  fought for this land
in the ranks of the liberators.

Shumiatcher, in addition to hinting at her own revolutionary credentials, extends the Bolshevik revolution to world revolution. She goes on to connect (somewhat improbably) the Bolshevik struggle against the Tsar to British imperialism in Canada:

Vos hert zikh epes in mayn heym?
Zingt men alts nokh dort Britanyes
  lider?
Shoyn tsayt, az alts zol ufgeyn fun
  der nider,
es zol a shayn ton
dos ponem fun derniderikte brider.

Ir meynt avade, az na-venad zayn iz a
  klole.
Mayn na-venad zayn hot mir gegebn a
  dakh:
Di gantse velt gevorn iz mayn khaver,—

fun Yangtses toln
un dursht fun Indies heyse pleynen.[74]

How are things at home?
Do they still sing Britain's songs?

It's time for everything to come up
  from below,
for a light to glow
from the face of the downtrodden
  brother.

You surely think that wandering is a
  curse.
My wandering has given me a roof:

The whole world has become my
  comrade,—
from the Yangtze's valleys
And the thirst of India's hot plains.

In the final lines cited above, Shumiatcher links Asia, the Soviet Union, and her Russian-born, Canadian Jewish family. The Yangtze—a password for those revolutions still to come—has given the poet entry into international communism. In conclusion, she describes her metaphysical transformation—a Soviet baptism of sorts:

Atsindert	Now
iz mayn kop gebentsht	my head is blessed
mit roytn flater.	with the red flutter.
Nito iz nokh a tsveyte freyd aza	There is no other joy
vi do, af erd fun ratn![75]	like here, in the land of the Soviets!

This formulaic ending is significant. Shumiatcher has not merely embraced the Soviet Union. She has substituted a discussion of universalist suffering for a Jewish collective memory of pogrom suffering. Her radical remapping of community evokes a Hegelian model of transubstantiation: without disappearing in substance, the individual transforms, in this case from a Jew to a communist internationalist.[76]

TOWARD AN INTERNATIONALIST IDENTITY

Shumiatcher's transubstantiation of the subject is nowhere more apparent than in her description of her return to her native Homel. In an untitled poem dated "Homel, 1928," Shumiatcher describes an encounter with a figment of her grandmother:

Bist aroysgekumen, Bobe, in dayn sametenem beged,	You came out, Grandma, in your velvet garment,
bagegenen an opklang fun dayn blut,	To greet an echo of your blood,
un s'hot der shvarts fun samet zikh gerunslt	and the black velvet wrinkled
in letstn opglants nokh fun yikhesdikn blut.	in a last reflection of ancestral blood.
Ikh hob azoyfil shifn, bobeshi, af vasern gemitn	Granny, I have missed so many ships on waters
un s'hot ayede shif gelozt a kroyveshaft in blut	and every ship has left a blood kinship.
Ver hot gekent dem opglants fun a vaytn shmeykhl tsu farhitn,	Who could resist a distant smile's reflection?
ven vayte vandlungen hobn durkhgekreytst mayn blut?[77]	When distant wanderings have crossed my blood?

Every second line, in the Yiddish, ends with the word "blood" (blut). Shumiatcher's speaker, encountering her past, describes a change in her group identity. She is still the grandchild of a woman from Homel, but her encounters with other groups have affected her "blood kinship." An internationalist identity has augmented the speaker's loyalty to a Jewish lineage. It has "crossed" (durkhgegreytst) her blood.

East Asia helped Shumiatcher to articulate the need for world revolution; it also helped her to fashion her identity as a Russian Jew in exile. In lines that elide contextual differences, she highlights her identification with those whom she meets in Asia—from the "dark eyes" that long for the "hammer and sickle" to the geishas with whom she identifies in Japan:

Gey ikh mir mit geyshes tsu di vasern,	I go with geishas to the waters,
tsu yogn di levone afn taykh.	to chase the moon on the river.
Ikh tu zey nokh un buk zikh tsu di vasern	I copy them and bow before the waters
un s'kusht levone undz in ponem blaykh.[78]	and the moon kisses us on our pale face.

Contemporaries describe Shumiatcher's playful attempts to embody her fascination with Asia. Pilniak, having met Shumiatcher in Japan, would later describe her poetry, which he asked her to translate for him, as "night-time, moonlit lines" (nochnye, lunnye stikhi).[79] Shumiatcher's friend and colleague Melech Ravitch recalled Shumiatcher's tendency to dress in turbans and robes.[80] Shumiatcher Orientalizes her speaker throughout her 1930 book of poems. In an untitled poem dedicated to her native Homel, Shumiatcher writes, "Your earth did not recognize me, a foreigner" (Dayn erd hot mikh, a vayte, nisht derkent).[81]

Shumiatcher arrived in Soviet Crimea as a poet eager to transcend groups. In "Tsigeyner" (Gypsies), she writes of an encounter with a fortune-teller in Agai, Crimea. The poetic persona and the Gypsy each observe the other, comparing physical features. The Gypsies are identified by their dark skin, "squinting children," and antiquated horse-drawn wagons. But the Jewish persona is also an Other. If, in "May lid," Shumiatcher recognizes a class struggle in the "dark eyes" (oygn tunkele) of

Asian workers, in "Tsigeyner," it is the Gypsy who recognizes longing in
the subject's "black eyes" (shvartse oygn):

Tsigeyner zenen haynt gekumen in mayn dorf Agai,	Gypsies came today to my town Agai,
Tsigeyner broynenke, mit boydn un mit drobne ferdlekh,	tanned-brown Gypsies, with wagons and small horses,
mit kinderlekh farmurzete, mit tseplekh un mit ringen,	with squinting children, with braids and rings,
mit kleydlekh farbike, mit blankndike tseyn un oygn—	with colorful dresses, with sparkling teeth and eyes—
gekumen zenen zey vi harbst-foygl in mayn dorf tsu zingen:	they came like autumn birds to my town to sing:
—Gib, shvartsoygike, gib, krasavitse, gib dayn hant, di shneyike,	—Give, black eyes, give, beautiful girl, give your snowy white hand,
vi a bin af shoybn zhumt aroys dayn mazl fun di oygn . . .	your fortune buzzes from your eyes like a bee in the dust . . .

The fortune-teller sees that the Jewish woman has come "from distant
waters and deep oceans" (fun vayte vasern un tife okeanen) and that she
longs for someone at home.[82]

The Crimean peninsula has a storied, multiethnic history. Once the
site of Greek colonies, the peninsula belonged alternately to the Roman
Empire and the Byzantine Empire, and parts of it were later settled by
Venetians, Genovese, Scythians, Tauri, Hungs, Bulgars, and Khazars,
among others. Slavs controlled parts of Crimea under Kyivan Rus, until
the thirteenth-century Mongol invasion. The Crimean Khanate and Ottoman Empire subsequently controlled the region until Catherine the
Great annexed it in 1783. The Crimean War of 1853–1856, between the
tsarist empire and allied Ottoman Empire and France, devastated Russia.
War again broke out on the peninsula during the Revolution, and a battle
between the White Army and Red Army in 1920 eventually led to the
victory of the Bolsheviks.

The Soviet Crimea that greeted Shumiatcher was eastern European
and Asian—home to Muslim Tatars, as well as eastern European Jews,
Ukrainian Christians, and Roma—a space that Shumiatcher could make
her home alongside other national minorities.[83] In the early 1920s, shtetl
Jews had migrated to the peninsula on their own initiative, forming

farming colonies, including a few Zionist communes.[84] As Jonathan Dekel-Chen has discussed, this colonization happened spontaneously, during the relatively liberal NEP era, with some help from external organizations including the American Jewish Joint Distribution Committee (JDC). "Community leaders and townspeople wagered that colonization, especially at a safe distance from the vulnerable shtetles, could stabilize economic and social life."[85] Shumiatcher dedicates a long poem about the nascent Soviet Union, "Yung iz erd un royt iz blut" (Young is the earth and red is blood), to the "Jewish migrants in the Soviet Union" (Di Yidishe ibervanderer in ratnfarband). The first section describes Jews who have come to work the fields in Crimea and Kherson: "Bearded Jews came, with wives and children:/—Steppe, you have never been close to us" (Gekumen Yidn berdike, mit vayb un kinder in zeyern farmeg:/—noent bistu, step, unz keynmol nisht geven).[86] Shumiatcher's Crimea cycle is an origin tale of Jews who are prepared to sacrifice everything to work the Crimean land, a Revolutionary ode to rival Zionist poems of the period.

Shumiatcher had visited Palestine after leaving East Asia and before coming to the Soviet Union in 1927, and in contrast to the religious practice she observed there, the Jewish Crimean farming colonies were sites of monumental change: religion was giving way to a generation of Marxist-Leninist Jewish workers. Later in the cycle, Shumiatcher writes in the voice of Zionists who have replaced their dreams of Palestine with the reality of the Soviet Union:

Mir hobn in kholem gezen a midber	We saw a desert in a dream
un hobn gefirt dort di benkshaft tsu trinken.	and went there, longing to drink.
Kemlen hobn demerung-lider af horbn getrogn	Camels carried twilight-songs on their humps
un kemlen hobn faygn in koyshn gefirt durkhn midber	and camels carried figs in baskets through the desert
un hobn di benkshaft in kholem gezetikt.	and satisfied this longing in a dream.
Gekumen a dor un avek iz a dor	A generation came and a generation went
un alts iz geven azoy poshet un klor:	and all became so simple and clear:

Mir hobn mirazhn gekukt in di oygn	We looked mirages in the eye
un hobn farnumen dos vorken fun toybn	and replaced the cooing of doves
un alts iz geven azoy klor.[87]	and all became so clear.

Crimea, the site of a new Jewish community, is an attainable solution to the Zionist dream. It is also a bridge between Asia and the Soviet Union. In the 1920s, Jews viewed Crimea as a Soviet promised land, an exotic former-Ottoman peninsula and fertile ground for a new kind of Jewish culture. It was a way of simultaneously embracing aspects of Zionism and the Soviet project.[88] In the 1920s, Jewish Crimea was still in the realm of the artistic imagination. In 1927, Abram Room, with the help of Viktor Shklovsky and Vladimir Mayakovsky, directed the film *Jews on the Land*, based on Viktor Shklovsky's screenplay and with intertitles by Vladimir Mayakovsky. Dovid Bergelson traveled to Crimea to spend time on a Jewish farming colony. In 1926, Chairman Kalinin announced that the northern steppe of Crimea would be devoted to Jewish collective farms.[89] *Royte Velt* filled its pages with poems of Crimea in the late 1920s by Peretz Markish, Dovid Hofshteyn, Khane Levin, and Esther Shumiatcher, among others.

Dovid Hofshteyn (1889–1952), who made his home in the Soviet Union in 1924, published an excerpt from his "Krimer tsikl" (Crimea Cycle) in *Royte Velt* in 1927, opening it with a description of a wine cellar on the road between the city of Alupka and the southern seaside village of Miskhor, with a sign that reads, "In Vino Veritas":

Mir geyen keyn Miskor, mir geyen fun Alupka.	We're going to Miskhor, we're coming from Alupka.
Der hoykher veg iz shtil, es rut der diner shtoyb.	The highway is quiet, the fine dust rests.
Ay-petri shteyt in roykh, der yam fun untn toybt[90]	Ai-Petri stands in smoke, the sea deafens from below

The Crimean landscape, with its mountains and towns with Turkic names, conjures an Eastern exotic. The Soviet Yiddish poet Khane Levin (1900–1969) describes a Crimean landscape of mythical proportions and creates a protagonist who embodies the peninsula's mixed cultural identity. Levin names her hero "Anaki," a name conjuring the biblical Anakim—a Canaanite tribe of mythical giants who lived in the

Judean hills.[91] Anaki, a strapping youth, is "like an oak," an outsider and descendant of the family of Goliath who must overcome the influence of his two fathers—one a Jewish peddler and the other the tsar. Levin's poem mixes biblical mythology, a romantic idealization of the Crimean landscape, and Marxism: Anaki, a strong, young Crimean Jew, recognizes in himself an outsider to the Jewish community with the strength to move mountains:

Iz vos zol ton Anaki	So what should Anaki do
mit hent	with these hands
azoyne yinge,	so young,
az s'zogt im op der tog	As the day joyfully takes its leave
in glik fun last un yokh?	of its weight and yoke?

Anaki, however, must struggle with the sins of past generations:

Hot Anakis tate	Anaki's father
gezungen afn vogn	sang on the wagon
in Krim gebentshtn land	in Crimea the blessed land
fun rozhinkes un mandlen.	of raisins and almonds.
Der kenig in Livadye	The king in Livadia
hot nit gelernt arbet,	didn't learn to work
hot nit gelernt arbet—	didn't learn to work—
iz men gegangen handlen . . .	but went to buy and sell . . .

Unlike Anaki's biological father, who is a merchant, or Tsar-father, who vacations in the Crimean seaside palace of Livadia, Anaki longs to work. He hopes that an alternate father—the "man from Moscow" (Mentsh fun Moskve)—might call him "to be a fisherman." The poem ends with a call from the gulls: "How long can one be a guest?"[92] The quotation derives unmistakably from Yehudah Leib Gordon's 1863 Jewish enlightenment poem "Awake, my people," which pushed Jews to integrate with Russian culture. Levin, by citing Gordon, celebrates simultaneously the transformation of the Crimean landscape into something useful and the transformation of the wandering Jew into a figure rooted in the land. Crimea promised Soviet Jews all that Palestine promised the Zionist, without the burden of past religion.[93]

The connection that Shumiatcher made between Asia, pre-Revolutionary Russian Jewish life, and the Soviet Union is closely related to Levin's vision of Crimea as a landscape of renewal. In this landscape, the subject transforms from weak shtetl Jew to strong Soviet worker. Shumiatcher's poetic rejection of the Jewish past and embrace of the new is especially pronounced in one of her untitled Crimean poems. Here, she applies the word "mistbarg" (trash heap), familiar from "Baym rand fun Khine," to the religious community that refuses to build a new, Soviet, Jewish life.

Der mistbarg iz groys	The trash heap is huge
un der mistbarg iz laybik.	and the trash heap is fleshy.
Un eygener shoys	And its own womb
iz farsamt un iz leydik.	is poisoned and empty.
Ver hot es gelozn,	Who has abandoned it,
az an eydeh zol blaybn	so a religious community can stay
oyf eygenem mistbarg,	on its very own trash heap
oyf mistbarg tsu klaybn?[94]	to gather on this trash heap?

The poem rejects the religious community along with the refuse of history. The assonant close rhyme between "laybik" (fleshy) and "leydik" (empty) suggests a kinship between the retrograde religious community and the useless excesses of the bourgeoisie. Anthologized alongside her China poems, Shumiatcher's "mistbarg" (trash heap) of Jewish history simultaneously conjures Trotsky's "trash heap of history" and recalls the "mistbarg" that she encountered two years earlier, where Chinese workers are destined to die.

Hot zikh der vey afn mistbarg gemert—	Here on the trash heap, the sorrow has grown—
emitsns lebn-iz oysgeyn bashert.[95]	Somebody's life is bound to expire.

Shumiatcher uses a loose dactylic meter for both "mistbarg" poems, along with a tight rhyme scheme. The poems, in addition to resembling one another in their waltzing rhythms and Marxist subject matter, recall the Russian dactylic tradition. Shumiatcher's two trash heaps are closely related—they are grotesque mounds conjuring Bialik's and Markish's pogrom poems and remnants from a former order that must be abandoned.

Shumiatcher captured the excitement of a generation of Soviet Jews who were coming to view Crimea as a mythical territory and a modern-day Babel. A similar connection between Jews, East Asia, and Crimea can be found in Peretz Markish, who by the late 1920s was writing poems celebrating the Revolution. Markish published excerpts from his longer poem in progress, *Brider* (Brothers), in *Royte Velt* in 1927. The hero, Shloyme Ber, is, to cite Harriet Murav, a shtetl Jew, rewritten "as a Bolshevik internationalist."[96] The excerpt published in *Royte Velt* finds Shloyme Ber" together with a Chinese man, who is also fighting the Whites:

Leshn bam Kitaiets zikh gele zayne bakn,	The Chinese man's cheeks are yellow,
un di kleyne oygelekh fibern un glantsn;	and his little eyes are feverish and shine;
—shtendik, ven Kitaiets dermont zikh on Kozakn,	—whenever the Chinese man thinks of Cossacks,
shpilyet zikh zayn hemd oyf, tseveynt zikh im zayn ranets . . .	his shirt pokes out, his satchel makes him cry . . .
S'shrayen zayne bakn, s'shrayen zayne beyner,	His cheeks and bones cry,
s'shmekn zayne hent mit tsimring un mit tey;	his hands smell of cinnamon and tea;
—ay, iz er geven amol a korobeynik,	—oh, he was once a peddler,
itster a Budyonev in der roytinker armey! . . .	now a Budionny soldier in the Red Army! . . .

Markish's Chinese soldier magnifies Shloyme Ber's alienation as a Soviet Jew. Like the prototypical Russian Jew, whose mercantile profession was frequently viewed as the embodiment of capitalism, Markish's Chinese soldier is a former merchant:

Hering hot er lib gehat tsu kokhn in a tshan,	He loved to cook herring in a vat,
er hot dan gehandlt mit zayd un tsheshuta,	he used to trade in silk and baubles,
—an arshin a langer un a langer tsop;	—a long yardstick and a long braid;
tayerer kitayets! Umetiker bruder!	Dear Chinese man! Brooding brother!
—oysfarkoyft dos zeyd af rusishe yaridn,	—they've bought up your silk at Russian fairs,
itster vestu hengen af a boym in Perekop![97]	now you will hang on a tree in Perekop!

Perekop—the site of the Chinese peddler's probable demise—is the Crimean town where the Red Army drove the Whites out of Crimea in 1920. A turning point in the war, the battle led to the Red Army's successful occupation of Crimea. The Chinese man may be fighting for the Red Army, but he is marked by his past and will fall victim to the Revolution.

Markish's Chinese soldier is a pre-Revolutionary holdover. Unable to cleanse himself of his history, he is a stand-in for a past generation of Russian Jews as much as a reminder of the ongoing struggle against imperialism in China. The Asian Other is, for Markish, a foil for the rational aims of revolution, representing an exotic that is at once Asian and Jewish. Jews, Europe's perennial Other, are ever-belated figures, holdovers from a messianic belief system who, as Walter Benjamin formulates, are focused on the past, though they may see in the future messianic possibility.[98] As in Shumiatcher's travel poems, Markish's Chinese vendor is retrograde and utopian: an unstruggled remnant of Russia's past and a reminder of the internationalist goals of revolution. With this tragic embodiment of foreignness and capitalism, Markish demonstrates the vision and the impossibility of a truly internationalist revolution.

Esther Shumiatcher, who would go on to write many poems about Jewish culture and tradition, was eager to replace a traditional Jewish community with international solidarity in her Crimea cycle. The last poem in Shumiatcher's 1930 collection *In shoen fun libshaft* (In the hours of love) is an untitled section of her Crimea cycle, dated "Agai, Crimea, 1928." As in "May lid," she cites the far-flung rivers she has visited, expressing her belief that the wide world she has just seen on her travels will soon recognize a new Jewish community in a new Soviet Union:

Zeyet aykh, yidn tayere, zeyet gezunterheyt! / Sow, dear Jews, sow in good health!
Mir veln kumen esn un derkvikn zikh mit ayer varem broyt. / We will come to eat and revel in your warm bread.
Es zenen brider do baym Vaysl un baym Hodsn-breg, / You have brothers here by the Vistula and by the shores of the Hudson,
un bay Laplata un baym Yardens doyresdikn shteg, / and by the La Plata and by the Jordan's age-old path,
vos zenen aykh mekane ayer mi.[99] / who envy you your labor.

The rejection of history's trash heap and the welcoming of a new era are, for Shumiatcher, a collective, international task, and Crimea, positioned between Europe and Asia, is well placed to become a model for this project.

CODA: BETWEEN UTOPIAS

In Crimea, Shumiatcher merged her affinity for proletarian internation-alism with her belief in Jewish self-determinacy. The months that sepa-rated Shumiatcher and Hirschbein's time in China from their sojourn in the Soviet Union found them exploring the Middle East, including Palestine, where their friend Chaim Nachman Bialik formally welcomed Hirschbein and the Yiddish fiction writer Sholem Asch at an event at the Hebrew Writer's Union in Tel Aviv, despite ongoing polemics sur-rounding Yiddish in Palestine.[100] Hirschbein, purportedly, debated with the Hebrew poet over the efficacy of Palestine as a future Jewish state.[101] There are few references to Shumiatcher's own political opinions of the time, which she appears to have expressed more often in poems than in conversation. What is clear from the writing of both wife and husband is that they were optimistic about the Soviet Jewish settlement project, which, under the auspices of the territorialist organization Ozet, al-lowed Jews for a brief time to be both pro-Soviet and pro-Zionist. This all changed at the end of August 1929, when a week of violence in Pal-estine forced Jews to choose between their sympathy with the Commu-nist Party and their aspiration toward Jewish self-determinacy.

The last week of August 1929 saw a series of violent attacks by Arabs, who were frustrated and disgruntled by the British support of the Zionist project, against Jewish civilians and a violent retaliation by the British against the Arab rebels. Esther Shumiatcher and Peretz Hirschbein were, by then, in Warsaw. As we will see in the next chapter, the violence in Palestine and the Party's subsequent denunciation of those Yiddish writers who failed to welcome the event as a revolutionary uprising drove many Yiddish writers to loudly declare their positions and others to si-lence. In an article published on November 8, 1929, "on the departure of Perets Hirschbein and Esther Shumiatcher from Poland," Nachman

Mayzil wrote that Hirschbein was paralyzed by the rift between two camps that he held dear—the Soviet and the Zionist. "He takes all these matters on himself, he reads every article from the right and from the left, suffers in their aftermath more and more with the recounting and the conversations, and with the attempt to get to the bottom of it all . . . mountains fall on him, which oppress him, which don't let him breath." Hirschbein, according to Mayzil, was devastated by the rift between his close friends in the Soviet and Zionist camps. "He lies beaten on the sofa, and asks like a helpless child: 'Sister-Esther [Ester-shvestern] take me away from all of this . . .' And where to go, to the Soviet Union or to America?"[102] Shumiatcher kept silent alongside her husband. Eventually, the two departed for the United States, buoyed, Mayzil writes, by their friend H. Leivick's literary activity following his own rift with the Party over Palestine.

After August 1929, Esther Shumiatcher ceased to publish in Soviet and Party-aligned venues until she, along with Leivick and others, joined the antifascist Popular Front in the mid-1930s. By then, she was living in California and raising a son. Her interest in the Soviet Union took on a decidedly distant quality. The Soviet Jewish autonomous project had been relocated from Crimea to Birobidjan, a region bordering Mongolia in eastern Siberia. Shumiatcher's "Honik fun Birebidzhan" (Honey from Birobidjan), which she included in her 1939 book *Ale Tog* (All day), suggests continued optimism about an autonomous Soviet Jewish project.

Ikh hob haynt farzukht honik fun Birobidzhan.	Today I tasted honey from Birobidjan.
Der sharfer tam hot a bri geton in gumen.	The sharp taste burned my gums.
S'hot a veye geton fun emer	In a gust from the pail came
der reyekh fun korn-feld,	the scent of corn fields,
mit toy,	with dew,
mit klever,	with clover,
un mit levone-bloy.[103]	and with moon-blue.

A decade after her sojourn in Crimea, Shumiatcher places herself outside the Soviet center—uprooted and "Meyver-leyam" (overseas). The Birobidjan poem, included in the cycle "Mayn gas" (My street), appeared alongside poems about, among other subjects, the Spanish Civil War, the Navajo, and the "Little Chinese Van-pu," which finds a Chinese sage surrounded by old men engaged in a "powerful dispute" (vayakoyekhdikn shtrayt).[104] A decade after her Yangtze poems, Shumiatcher was still mixing Chinese and Jewish passwords to advocate for a renewed world. She had left the Soviet Union, but the Hegelian transubstantiation that had altered Shumiatcher's identity in the 1920s had produced a poet attuned to the Jewish voice within a multi-ethnic context.

Many of the contemporary critics who dismissed Shumiatcher's first book of poems as vague and sentimental preferred her second book.[105] Notably, most of the harsh critiques of Shumiatcher's first book of poems came from writers, including Melech Ravitch and Shmuel Niger-Charney, who were, even before the Palestine disturbances, skeptical of the Soviet project. Appearing a few months after the lines had been drawn between internationalist Party sympathizers and the anticommunist Left, Shumiatcher's poems were distasteful to anti-Soviet literary critics, and the pro-Soviet literary critics would not review a poet who had left their camp to publish with the anti-Stalinist opposition. Lost in the political abyss of 1929 to 1930 was an appreciation for Shumiatcher's contribution to the burgeoning mode of cross-cultural translocation that entered leftist Yiddish poetry in the late 1920s. Shumiatcher's wide-eyed North American naiveté yielded a modern Jewish approach to the Orientalized Other that mixed self-exoticism with depictions of the still oppressed Asiatic worker to create a Jewish narrative of Soviet liberation. Shumiatcher's impressionistic accounts of Asia are filtered through the lens of her own experience: struggling Asian workers are described using imagery familiar from Yiddish poems about pre-Revolutionary Russian antisemitism. The 1920s, more than a time of travel, were a time of considering where in the world to make a home. Shumiatcher, a Yiddish writer born in the tsarist empire who spent her teenage years in Canada, filtered her own perceptions of East Asia through her memories of pre-Revolutionary Russian antisemitism, finding—albeit briefly—an imagined, poetic home in the nascent Soviet state.

2

ANGRY WINDS

Jewish Leftists and the Challenge of Palestine

IN THE IMMEDIATE WAKE of the 1903 Kishinev pogrom, the poet Chaim Nachman Bialik wrote words in Hebrew that would encapsulate anti-Jewish violence for the twentieth century:

Kum lékh ləkhò, el ìr ha-haréygo, uvóso el-hakhatséyroys,	Arise and go now to the city of slaughter, Into its courtyards wind thy way;
Uveynèkho síre, uvyòdkho smásheysh al-hagdéyroys	There with thine own hand touch, and with the eyes of thine head,
Vəal ho-éytsim, vəal-hoavónim, vəal-gàbey tìakh-haksólim	Behold on tree, on stone, on fence, on mural clay,
Es hadòm-hakórush, vəes hamòyakh-haníkshe shèl hakhalólim.¹	The spattered blood and dried brains of the dead.

Bialik's "B'ir haHaregah" (In the city of slaughter) quickly became the quintessential pogrom poem, augmenting sacred text for many eastern European Jews. The Minsk-born Soviet Yiddish writer Moyshe Teyf (1904–1966) offered an unlikely response to this poem of violence and victimhood in 1929. Teyf used Bialik's famous opening line as an epigraph for his own poem "Zing, vint fun midber!" (Sing, desert wind!).

Teyf's poem, however, takes an unexpected turn: here the city of slaughter is not in eastern Europe but in Palestine; and the perpetrators are not Slavic antisemites but the Zionists, who are deemed responsible for a wave of violence in August 1929 that erupted between Arabs and Jews throughout Mandatory Palestine.

Vey tsu der heyliker heym	Woe to the holy home
—a shkhite-shtot!	—a city of slaughter!
Vey tsu dem heylikn nakhtleger	Woe to the holy resting places
—a blutiker mizbeyakh!—	—a bloody sacrificial altar!—
ir—fun keynem gezalbte,	you are no anointed one,
ir—gest nit gebetene,	you are uninvited guests,
vos hot ir gegazlt di bloy-vayse farbn	why have you stolen the blue and white colors
fun undzere erlekhe himlen?	from our honest heavens?
Neyn!	No!
Biz tsentn dor	Even the tenth generation
zey veln shoyn nit opvashn	will not wash away
dos blut umshuldike, vos ir hot do	the innocent blood, you've spilled
fargosn![2]	here!

What led to this poetic reversal of the ultimate poem of Jewish victimhood to a poem of Jewish aggression was a conscious political response to the 1929 violence on the part of the Communist International, and its affiliated newspapers, worldwide. After some uncertainty, the Party formally welcomed the unrest as a revolutionary impulse against what it considered to be the united forces of Zionism and British imperialism in the region. The overwhelming poetic response to the 1929 riots in Palestine, in support of either the Jews or Arabs, demonstrates the symbolic importance of these events to Jewish identity. After Hebron, poets had to choose whether they were willing to stand with Jewish victims regardless of their political and religious beliefs or whether they were willing to give up their identification with victimized Jews, identifying instead with the Arab workers and peasants as the Comintern demanded. As we will see, however, the ideological conflict that took place in the fall of 1929 was less about a specific political event, or even a region, than about how to define the boundaries of a Jewish revolutionary identity.

The clashes in Palestine centered on a confluence of religion, territory, and colonialism and began over a symbol. The Western Wall, which lies at the base of the Temple Mount—the site, since the year 705 of the Common Era, of the al-Aqsa Mosque (one of Islam's holiest sites)—had long held religious significance for Jews as the last vestige of the pre-Rabbinic temple. Religious Jews, desiring autonomy over the Wall as a site of prayer, in September 1928 erected a ritual barrier (*mekhitse*) so that men and women could pray separately. The leading Islamic authority, the Grand Mufti of Jerusalem, Hajj Amin al-Hussayni, demanded restrictions on Jewish infrastructure at the wall; the British authorities responded with a ruling that Muslims own the Western Wall but that Jews could pray there. The following May 1929, when Muslims opened an entrance to the Temple Mount, which was adjacent to the Wall, small clashes with Jews followed. These clashes intensified by mid-August, a period that coincided with the Jewish observance of the ninth of Av on August 15, a fast day commemorating the destruction of the Temple, and the Muslim celebration of the birth of Mohammad on August 16. Religious Jews and Muslims used both holy days as opportunities for protest: Jews staged a protest at the Wall, and Muslims responded by desecrating Jewish books. By August 17, one Jew had been killed, Arab homes were burned, and numerous Arabs and Jews were injured. The violence and protests escalated, reaching a peak with an attack on Jewish families in Hebron, a city located about twenty miles south of Jerusalem, in the West Bank, on August 25, that left 67 Jews dead and 53 wounded. Jewish newspapers throughout the world condemned the uprising and mourned the Jewish victims.[3] In less than a week, the cities of Jerusalem, Hebron, Jaffa, Ramla, Gaza, Majdal (Ashkelon), Haifa, Acre, Nazareth, Nablus, Beisan, and Safed saw 133 Jews and 116 Arabs killed and 241 Jews and 232 Arabs injured in clashes.[4] Jewish civilians were killed largely by Arabs in the uprisings, and Arab civilians were killed largely by British forces and Jewish Haganah members who justified their acts as self-defense. The violence revealed widespread local anxiety about the large influx of Jewish immigrants to Palestine after World War I.[5] These incidents divided the worldwide Jewish Left into those who sympathized with the Arabs and those who condemned the recent violence as a new manifestation of the eastern European anti-Jewish pogrom aimed at the Jews of Palestine.

How did a tragic rift between Jews and Arabs in Palestine lead to a rift among Yiddish poets who chose to identify with either Jewish nationhood or the Communist International? The Yiddish poetry about the 1929 Palestine violence illuminates the imperative that Jewish leftists faced if they were to remain aligned with the Soviet Union to apply the passwords of Jewish collective suffering to non-Jewish workers. As we have seen, Soviet-aligned poets were already shifting from national to internationalist themes in the late 1920s: Esther Shumiatcher drew from Jewish pogrom motifs to express solidarity with East Asian workers and, in turn, from East Asian motifs to describe the burgeoning Jewish Crimean farming project. The 1929 Arab uprisings compelled Soviet-aligned poets not only to place Arabs in the role previously reserved for Jewish victims but to place Zionists in the role of perpetrator. In this chapter, I first describe how the 1929 events divided the Yiddish literary Left. I then turn to poets' debates over the meaning of the terms "pogrom" and "uprising," Jewish and Soviet passwords, respectively. Finally, I discuss how these language discrepancies deepened a rift within the leftist poetic community. The poetic rift over the Palestine events of 1929 illustrates the irreconcilability between Jewish national sentiments and the Soviet-centered Comintern, which had recently shifted toward supporting anticolonial struggles. The poets at the center of this conflict disagreed on how to define Jewish identity.

Even as the events in Palestine were still unfolding, the Comintern-affiliated New York Yiddish daily *Morgn Frayhayt* (Morning freedom) rapidly shifted its position on the violence and on anticolonial struggles more broadly. On August 25, the *Frayhayt* condemned the anti-Jewish violence in Palestine, with a cover story that bore the subheading, "Arab pogroms against Jews turn into battles between Jewish self-defense and Arab assailants—18 Arabs, 11 Jews dead, and 150 wounded from both sides."[6] At this early date, even the communist daily used "pogrom," the eastern European term for antisemitic violence, to describe the Arab uprising. On August 26, a headline in the *Frayhayt* attributed the violence more specifically to wealthy and religious Arabs: "Over 100 dead in battles in Palestine. . . . Efendis and Mulas have inspired religious fanaticism with the help of the English regime."[7] By August 27, however, the Communist International had reconsidered its stance on Palestine, and the *Frayhayt* changed the emphasis from Arab to British guilt. A cover article in the *Frayhayt* asserted that the guilt lay with the Zionists and British Army, whereas "correct are the Palestinian communists, who call for an independent proletarian-peasant Palestine for the Palestinian masses—Arabs and Jews alike."[8] On August 28, the *Frayhayt* editor Moyshe Olgin announced at a meeting in Irving Plaza Hall in New York that "in Palestine there isn't a pogrom, but an uprising." In his article in the *Frayhayt* the following day, Olgin explained the uprising as national-revolutionary.[9] Meanwhile, Jewish venues to the right of the communists (including all major socialist venues, such as the *Forverts* and *Tog*) continued to use the term "pogrom" as a password that emphasized Arab violence against Jews.[10]

To reconsider the concept of a "pogrom," communist poets had to return to the canonical texts about modern antisemitism, including Bialik's 1903 "B'ir haHaregah." Both Bialik and the *Frayhayt* poets were engaged in a Foucauldian practice of *parrhesia*—of speaking truth to power.[11] As Jewish writers and readers of the 1920s shifted their focus from eastern Europe to the violence in Palestine, poets on the left reappraised the modern Jewish canon to fit a new time, with a new balance of powers and new truths. Bialik provided Teyf with what Gerard Genette has called a "paratext"—a text that defines the boundaries of a conversation—in this case, about violence.[12] The memory of the 1903 Kishinev pogrom had once evoked Jewish solidarity against antisemitism in tsarist Russia. Now, grafting his own poem onto Bialik's allowed Teyf to apply a textual tradition of Jewish victimhood to Jews' new situation of empowerment in Palestine under the British Mandate.

Recent Jewish scholarship has reexamined the importance of August 1929 to the region's politics. The Israeli historian Hillel Cohen has aptly called 1929 "year zero" of the Israeli-Palestinian conflict. Matthew Hoffman, writing of the debates that consumed the fall of 1929 in the United States, has called the split the "Red Divide."[13] Two months into the debates, the stock market collapsed, intensifying anticapitalist sentiments and plunging many New York poets into poverty. This was also the year of Stalin's "Great Turn" (*Velikii perelom*), which Sheila Fitzpatrick has described as a social and economic revolution from above that sought "the 'class enemies' of socialism, at home and abroad."[14] Gennady Estraikh places the rift over Palestine into the context of a series of rifts in Soviet-aligned literature during the "Great Turn."[15] Ruth Wisse has discussed the effects of Soviet directives on Jewish adherents in the 1920s, which "limited ever more of their autonomy of mind and spirit the longer they stayed under its ideological influence."[16] To be sure, Jewish communists were manipulated by the Comintern. And yet there is more to the story than that: the poets who remained with the *Frayhayt* had committed to fighting for the underrepresented. Sensing a fundamental injustice against the Arabs, including the loss of land, in Mandatory Palestine and recognizing the rhetorical power they had as Jews, Jewish communists chose to disregard Jewish national interests. If we dismiss communist-aligned poetry as merely ideologically manipulated, we lose the opportunity to closely examine the dialogue that ensued.

The Yiddish conversations far away from Hebron shed light on how these events affected Jewish politics in the United States and Soviet Union.[17] Other poets held even greater stakes in the political moment, most obviously Arab and Zionist poets writing in Palestine. However, the poets witnessing the violence in Palestine from afar were compelled to redefining the boundaries of their own commitment to internationalism. The Yiddish poems about Palestine that were published in the United States in 1929 fell largely into the ephemeral genre of newspaper poetry. In the autumn of 1929, these poems were at the heart of debates over Jewish identity, nationalism, and an international struggle against imperialism. The result was a significant output of poems that applied loaded eastern European terminology to the Arab-Jewish standoff in Palestine. If the Arabs took the place of eastern European Jews—victimized by a corrupt imperial system—then the Jews in Palestine took the place of the Slavs who stood by and let it happen, reinforcing an unfair power dynamic.

Literary modernism had led Jewish poets from across the political spectrum—from the Zionist Chaim Nachman Bialik to the Bundist Avrom Reyzen—to find new forms for expressing collective Jewish trauma. The 1929 events in Palestine drove a wedge between those poets for whom Jewish trauma remained paramount and those, affiliated with the Party, who were no longer primarily concerned with Jewish victimhood. The departure of four renowned writers from the *Frayhayt* at the end of August was at the center of the debates of the fall. September and October 1929 saw vicious attacks between the camp that remained with the Party and those writers who left. On September 2, an article appeared on the cover of the *Morgn Frayhayt:* "Reyzen, Manakhem, Leivick and Raboy are consumed by the murderous-patriotic hysteria." On September 27, the Warsaw Yiddish literary journal *Literarishe Bleter* published statements by the four "runaways." Avrom Reyzen, the oldest of the group, had written Bundist poems at the turn of the century that were set to music and sung in left-wing youth circles. Raboy, Leivick, and Boreysho had all been members of the New York–based modernist group "Di Yunge." Others would follow suit.[18] Moishe Nadir—also a former Yunge member—was the exception who proved the rule: in a September 29 article, "Tsion vakkhanalia" (Zion bacchanalia), Nadir disabused readers of the assumption that he, too, had left the paper. "I am *not* resigning from the *Frayhayt*! To the contrary. I am with the Communist Party—more than ever."[19]

A major boycott followed the exodus of the leading literary figures from the *Frayhayt:* businesses ceased to advertise in the *Frayhayt,* and newspaper stands refused to sell the paper for several days. The remaining *Frayhayt* writers were expelled from the Y. L. Peretz Yiddish Writers' Union for antisemitism.[20] The *Frayhayt*, in turn, lashed out at its opponents, comparing them, as Matthew Hoffman observes, to the "most heinous of antisemites, both past and present, which effectively served to identify the communists with their fellow Jews as perennial victims of antisemitism."[21] From the end of August throughout the fall of 1929, articles, poems, and manifestos in the *Frayhayt* accused the "runaways" of abandonment. Two such "runaways"—Leivick and Boreysho—in October 1929 founded the literary journal *Vokh* (Week), which they edited together with the fiction writer Lamed Shapiro. *Vokh* considered itself nonpartisan, but its contributors tended to espouse a stance that was both left-wing and anti-Stalinist. Their contributors ranged from Trotskyists like Aaron Glantz-Leyeles to recent fellow travelers like H. Leivick and Esther Shumiatcher. The journal carried lengthy editorials addressing the events in Palestine and the communists' responses to them. It continued for twenty weeks, ending when the heated debate around Palestine had subsided.[22] It is impossible to disentangle the Yiddish writers' discussions about Palestine from their discussion of the rift in their own community: by the time *Vokh* was founded far away from the events in Hebron, the two conflicts seemed inextricable, and the collateral damage included the fragmentation of a literary community that stood with either the Jews or the Arabs.

Hillel Cohen, in writing about the chasm that opened between Muslims and Jews in 1929, reminds us that "each nation mourns its own dead, not those of their enemies."[23] Far away from the violence, leftist Jews in the United States and eastern Europe were asking themselves what "their own" meant. The year 1929 changed the way Jewish leftists discussed group identity, forcing them to identify publicly as Jews or internationalist workers first. The Party's identification of the Arab anticolonial movement as a workers' movement complicated this discussion: for the anticommunist Left, the Party's celebration of what was, at least in part, a national and religious Arab uprising was a bridge too far. Predominant in the rift was the use of terms that became litmus tests for where one fell in the Palestine divide. To understand how the poetry of the period reflected this divide, let us examine how writers reassessed and debated two passwords—"pogrom" and "uprising"—in the fall of 1929.

A POGROM IN PALESTINE?

Communists and anti-communists alike blamed the violence on the British, likening them to the tsarist authorities or to the Cossacks who had committed violent acts against Jews in the years before and during the Bolshevik Revolution. Jews on both sides accused the British of reluctance to suppress the rioters. The *Frayhayt* ran a cartoon by William Gropper on September 1, 1929, that pictured the British prime minister, James Ramsay Macdonald, on horseback, holding a sword, his signature mustache lengthened to resemble a Cossack's. The caption reads, "He brings calm and order to Palestine" (figure 2.1).[24] The *Frayhayt*'s opponents also evoked the Cossacks' reputation as pogromists. On August 23, when unrest broke out in Jerusalem, *Der Tog*, a liberal-left paper that

ער שטעלט אײן רו אין ארדינונג אין פאלעסטינע

Fig 2.1 "He brings calm and order to Palestine." William Gropper, *Morgn Frayhayt*, September 1, 1929. *Credit:* Craig Gropper

published opinions from Communist to socialist Zionist, ran a cartoon by Joseph Foshko depicting the English colonial minister, looking in the mirror and seeing an image of Simon Petliura, commander of the Ukrainian army during the Ukrainian Civil War (1918–1920), under whom multiple pogroms had occurred. The caption reads, "He doesn't recognize himself in the mirror" (figure 2.2).[25]

By the end of August, however, the *Frayhayt* shifted from emphasizing British wrongdoing and Jewish victimhood toward an emphasis on Jewish collaboration with the British. It began running caricatured images of Jewish religious figures and Jewish business tycoons whose funding financed an unjust colonial regime (figure 2.3).[26] *Der Tog,* for its part, explicitly equated Arabs with eastern European pogromists. A cartoon on September 4 depicts an English high commissioner unsuccessfully holding onto the enormous arm of a caricatured Muslim, labeled "Arab pogromchik" and wielding a gun and a knife (figure 2.4).[27]

עד דערקענט זיד ניט אין שפיגעל

Fig 2.2 "He doesn't recognize himself in the mirror." Joseph Foshko, *Der Tog,* August 23, 1929. *Credit:* Richard Steinberg

Aaron Glantz-Leyeles, a Trotskyist and founding member of the modernist Introspectivist movement, published an article in *Vokh* titled "Dem Muftis arbl" (The Mufti's sleeve), addressing the role of the Grand Mufti of Jerusalem—Al Hussayni—in stirring anti-Jewish sentiment. "From time to time the 'uprising' will slaughter the occasional Jewish old person on the Jerusalem streets, murder another Jewish boy on a path. This way they'll know in London to fear the Mufti's sorcery." Leyeles explicitly compares the Arab violence to eastern European Cossack violence: "Above and beyond every correct complaint about the relationship to the Arab majority resounds the gruesome call to the Arab 'heroic revolutionaries,' who have flung themselves according to the familiar, tried and true style of the Haidamaks."[28] The Haidamaks, Cossack rebels who left thousands of Jewish casualties in their wars against the Polish magnates, are presented as the original pogromists. Eastern European pogroms were, of course, the most obvious point of comparison for eastern European Jews experiencing or witnessing violence

Fig 2.3 "The mask behind which he shoots," William Gropper, *Morgn Frayhayt*, Sept. 2, 1929. *Credit:* Craig Gropper

Fig 2.4 "I have the 'situation' in hand." Joseph Foshko, *Der Tog*, Sept. 4, 1929. *Credit:* Richard Steinberg

from afar, and writers on the right and left evoked the eastern European pogrom to describe the bloodshed of 1929.[29]

Moyshe Teyf, in his "Zing, vint fun midber!," constantly repeats the phrase "in shkhite shtot" (in the city of slaughter), the title of Bialik's 1903 poem in its Yiddish translation. Although Hebrew-language publishing and teaching were both suppressed in the Soviet Union, Teyf and his readers would have known Bialik's poem well.[30] Hebrew publishing had blossomed between 1916 and 1918, a time of new political freedoms for Russia's Jews.[31] Bialik's pre-Revolutionary Hebrew and Yiddish verse was read in Jewish households throughout eastern Europe.[32] Years later—in the 1960s—Teyf would recall his father reciting the poem to the family on Friday evenings, when "he loved to declaim in a loud voice in Russian his favorite writer Korolenko or read the stories of Sholem Aleichem, Mendele, Peretz. No one at the table was allowed to move an inch, especially when Papa recited, with a melody, Bialik's poem 'In Shkhite Shtot.'"[33] If we trust Teyf's memory, this would have been in the years immediately preceding the Bolshevik Revolution.[34] By 1929, copies of Bialik's poem were no longer in circulation in the Soviet Union, though Bialik's poem certainly remained in private collections and many people still knew it well. Teyf's poem, then, must be read as an ideological re-evaluation of Bialik's Zionist poem. Teyf distorts and dismantles Bialik's Zionist vision, at times employing antisemitic images to make a political point. His strange adaptation is, however, a remarkable artifact of the pathos and emotions of the moment. The poem is both a revision and "re-vision"—as the American poet Adrienne Rich has formulated—an "act of looking back, of seeing with fresh eyes, of entering an old text from a new critical direction."[35] Teyf's re-vision of Bialik's poem tracks the ideological shifts that affected Russia's Jewish community between 1903 and 1929.

Like Bialik, Teyf denounces eastern European Jewish passivity, but whereas Bialik admonishes Jews for not standing up to fight for themselves in Kishinev, Teyf admonishes Jews for their blindness to Arab suffering in their adherence to Zionism. Teyf begins from the assumption that Arab masses in Jerusalem, Hebron, and elsewhere have a legitimate complaint against their Jewish neighbors and the British authorities and challenges his readers to identify with the Palestinian Arabs. Teyf's redrawing of the boundaries of group identity is significant: eastern European Jews should no longer claim allegiance to a traditionally defined Jewish community but rather to Mother Russia, as communists and workers.

Teyf rejects religious Judaism as a force oppressing the colonized people of Palestine. Lest the dangers of Jewish religious tradition be lost on his readers, Teyf imports the vilest of European antisemitic caricatures from Shakespeare:

Mit beyzer nikhterkayt	With the evil sobriety
fun ayer tatn Shaylok	of your father Shylock
hot ir oyf falshe vogsholn	on false scales you have
gevoygn erd baroybte,	weighed stolen land,
—shtiker fleysh fun kinder—	—bits of children's flesh—
to trinkt fun fule krugn	so drink from full tankards
nit keyn vayn fun Karmel-vayntroybn,	not the wine from Carmel-grapes,
nor a getrank fun kraytekher!	but an herbal potion!
Vayl azoy hot bafoyln der vint der gerekhter	For this is how the wind of justice comes
fun midber,	from the desert,
fayer fun oyfshtand,	fire of rebellion,
vos geyt oyf tsu himlen tsu heyse	that goes up to the hot heavens
tsu himlen fun mizrekh!	to the eastern heavens!

Teyf's relation of Zionists to Shylock relies on a long-held European tradition of conflating Jews with corruption, a tradition that includes medieval blood-libel myths and antisemitic conspiracy theories. The connection between Shakespeare's merchant and the Zionists, Teyf suggests, lies in deal-making, in this case with the British. The poetic justice that comes to Shylock in the form of a proposed death sentence, Teyf moreover suggests, comes to the Zionists in the form of the Palestinian "rebellion" (oyfshtand) in the desert, a place that Teyf does not accept as a Jewish ancestral homeland.

Moyshe Teyf, who was born in Minsk, was twenty-five years old when he wrote this poem. A wallpaper-factory worker by day, he became a poet under the auspices of the Moscow Association of Proletarian Writers (MAPP).[36] His first poem described the liberation of Minsk by the Red Army and was titled with the date of the liberation, "July 11, 1920." His poetry might best be described as a hybrid infusing the proletarian themes of the 1920s with elements of the lyrical modernism of the Kiev-grupe poets Dovid Hofshteyn and Leyb Kvitko. In the 1930s, Yehezkel Dobrushin described Teyf's storytelling and wordplay as folkloric—he could portray a construction site or pastoral scene with a similar attention to their lyric qualities.[37] Dovid Bergelson hailed him a few years later as a "most original talent."[38]

Teyf liberally references Jewish religious figures in his poetry of this period, albeit as negative examples. In "Zing, vint fun midber!," Teyf connects two of the Zionists' preferred symbols of Jewish strength—Samson and the Maccabees—with the disaster that has befallen Palestine.

O, ir oreme shimshons,	O, you poor Samsons,
shvindzikhtiie zin fun Makabi,	consumptive sons of Maccabee,
vos knien far shveln fun henker	who kneel at the executioners' thresholds
un lekn a beyn fun groyzamen, blutikn moltsayt.	licking a bone from an atrocious, bloody meal.
Vey tsu der heliker heym	Woe to the holy home
—a shkhite-shtot!—	—a city of slaughter!—
vey tsu dem heylikn nakhtleger	woe to the holy resting places
—a blutiker mizbeyekh!—	—a bloody sacrificial altar!—

Bialik, in his 1903 poem, contrasts the weakness of diaspora Jews with the strength of biblical figures. Bialik sardonically condemns the sons of Hasmoneans and sons of Maccabees for failing to live up to their brave Jewish forefathers, for lying—"with trembling knees / Concealed and cowering."[39] Teyf, by contrast, condemns religious observance and Zionism in one breath, suggesting that Bialik's falsely empowered Zionist Maccabees have forsaken their Soviet homeland. Teyf explicitly states, at the end of his poem, that Zionism has led Jews astray. Those eastern European Jews who find themselves in Palestine, albeit incorrectly, are in a position to reach out to their Arab neighbors, to bring them closer to international communism.

Zol lebn di sho,	May the hour come,
ven oykh unter ayere himlen	when beneath your heavens too
vet oyfgeyn un vimlen	the flag of Moscow's Kremlin
di fon fun Moskver Kreml! . . .	will rise and fill the air! . . .

By suggesting that Moscow could be the spiritual homeland of Arab workers, Teyf reiterates the message of the (primarily Jewish-led) Palestinian Communist Party.[40] Teyf's command to "stretch out your hands" in sympathy with the Arabs corrects Bialik's command, in his Yiddish version of "B'ir haHaregah": "And stretch them out, crooked hands that have learned to beg" (un shtrekn oys, gelernte tsu betlen, krume hent!).[41] Teyf inverts Bialik's pogrom poem, suggesting that the eastern European Jewish diaspora will become holy, and the "Holy Land" will become a mere outskirt of the Moscow-centered Communist International that will hold value only if Jews can work with their Arab neighbors to overcome the colonial condition of Palestine.

The image of a Moscow center recapitulates earlier Russian Orthodox Christian visions of Moscow as a Third Rome. As Katerina Clark has observed, "In the 1930s, Bolshevik messianic proclivities in the cultural sphere were echoed by many intellectuals who were taken by a dream of Moscow's cultural and spiritual dominance in the world."[42] The idea of repatriation to Moscow reverses Bialik's call for Jewish repatriation to Palestine. Let us recall that at the end of Bialik's poem, a heavenly voice commands the poet to flee to the desert: "Rise, to the desert flee! / The cup of affliction thither bear with thee! / Take thou thy soul, rend it in many a shred! [. . .] And send they bitter cry into the storm!"[43] Bialik's poem provides not only a paratext for Teyf; Teyf offers a sequel to Bialik, in whose desert the Jew has allied himself with pogrom perpetrators. Teyf's off-rhyme between "kemlen" (camels) and "Kreml" (Kremlin) further reiterates the idea of a connection between the peoples of the desert (particularly the nomadic ones) and Moscow, the center of international communism. Teyf here uses a traditional pogrom poem to illustrate a new imperial world order where Jews have taken the place of antisemites by aligning themselves with an unjust empire that perpetrates the victimization of local Arabs. The communist Jew is morally obliged to support the oppressed Arab worker by recognizing the need for liberation and revolution through Moscow.

Moyshe Teyf was not alone in repositioning Moscow as a center and Palestine as an unjust and violent diaspora. The American proletarian poet Betsalel Fridman draws from personal experience to convey a similar message in his poem "Palestine," published in the *Frayhayt* on September 27, 1929. Fridman, born in what is now Belarus, had been a member of the Marxist Zionist "Poale Tsion" (Workers of Zion) and had lived in Palestine from 1920 to 1922 before moving permanently to New York.

Palestine!	Palestine!
Vi lang tsurik	How long ago
hob ikh, banand	I, side by side
mit borvise Arabishe Felakhn,	with barefoot Arab Fellahin,
gegrobn land,	dug the land,
gehoybn flakhn	hoisted flats
in der kolonie Rekhovot.[44]	in the colony of Rekhovot.

Fridman's pastoral setting is akin to earlier neo-Romantic Zionist verse. Fridman's orchards (1897–1941), for example, conjure Saul Chernikhovsky's 1923 "Man is nothing but the image of his landscape."[45] And yet the form Fridman's poem takes is decidedly proletarian. Fridman grounds his support of reorganized affinity groups—from nation to class—in his experience working alongside Arabs. The imagined utopia of Palestine does not divide "Jews" from "Arabs" but deepens the partnership between Arabs and their communist allies.

Un oyb es hobn zikh gebrudert,	And if someone has become brothers,
iz dos geven:	this was:
Araber un farfolgter komunist	Arab and persecuted Communist
antkegn tsiunist![46]	against the Zionist!

Fridman's personal shift from left-wing Zionist to communist follows the contours of the Communist Party in Palestine. In 1923, a year after Fridman had left Palestine, the Comintern formally accepted the Palestinian Communist Party (PCP), which was asked to educate Arab sympathizers, to forge "constructive connections with Arab national groups and with peasants; and to help in establishing a Communist party in Lebanon and Syria."[47] The Party's choice to include national interests under the rubric of class interests was institutionalized with the Third Period move to include the anticolonial struggle as part of the urban proletarian cause at the Sixth World Congress of the Comintern in 1928.[48] It is against this political backdrop that Teyf and Fridman celebrated an Arab uprising.

REJECTING THE RUNAWAYS

A second paratext in Teyf's "Zing, vint fun midber!" comes from one of the *Morgn Frayhayt*'s "runaway" poets—Avrom Reyzen. In inciting the "wind" to "sing," Teyf evokes Reyzen's "Vinter-lid" (Winter song), an allegory for the antisemitic atmosphere in eastern Europe that begins with the line, "Revel, revel angry winds" (Hulyet, hulyet, beyze vintn). Reyzen wrote this poem in Warsaw in 1899, and it was later set to music and sung in clandestine Jewish socialist circles in the late tsarist empire.[49]

Hulyet, hulyet, beyze vintn	Revel, revel angry winds!
Fray bahersht di velt!	Take over the world!
Brekht di tsvaygn, varft di beymer,	Break the branches, hurl the trees,
tut vos aykh gefelt![50]	do just as you please!

There is some ambiguity in the Yiddish word *hulyen,* a word of Slavic origin that can be translated as "revel" in the positive sense of merry-making or "carouse" in the sense of "hooliganism." Moreover, *beyze* might mean "angry," "wicked," or "cruel." Reyzen's poem thus simultaneously evokes cruelty and anger, festivity and rioting.

In 1899, the twenty-three-year-old Reyzen was witnessing the onset of new political movements in response to European antisemitism. The late nineteenth century saw the appearance of Herzl's pamphlet *Der Judenstadt* (The Jewish state) in 1896, the First Zionist Congress, which took place in Basel in 1897, and the creation of the revolutionary Bund in 1897.[51] Reyzen would recall, in his 1929 memoir, the heated opposition between Zionists and Bundists in the tsarist empire and the constant fear of arrest among Jewish intellectuals.[52] Reyzen's sympathy was with the socialist Bund, and by the time he arrived in Warsaw in 1899, he threw himself into the "war" raging in Warsaw's cafés between the Zionists and socialists over how best to unite Jews against the social forces still oppressing them.[53] Reyzen's wind quickly become violent:

Traybt di feygl fun di velder	Drive the birds from the woods
un faryogt zey fort;	hunt them further yet;
di vos kenen vayt nisht fliyen,—	those who cannot fly so far,—
teyt zey oyfn ort![54]	kill them on the spot!

For Reyzen, the new century marked a perilous clash between Jewish revolutionaries of diverse stripes and the tsarist empire. Teyf's reference to the desert winds can be read as an assessment of the state of Jewish politics three decades later, having transferred from European antisemitism to bloodshed in Palestine.

In an article in the *Morgn Frayhayt* on September 4, 1929, titled with Reyzen's opening line, "Revel, revel, angry winds!" (Hulyet, hulyet, beyze vintn!), the journalist Dovid Tanievitsh, ironically, used Reyzen's "angry winds" to denounce the poet and his fellow "runaways." Lest his readers miss the reference, Tanievitsh writes, "The angry winds have blown, have surged. Not those 'gentile' angry winds, about which the old Avrom Reyzen wrote his masterful poem, but the *Jewish* angry winds, which have led the current Avrom Reyzen himself into temptation!"[55] This particular angry wind is the mass uprising, Tanievitsh explains, waged by the religious community, along with the Yiddish *Forverts, Tog,* and *Morgn Zhurnal,* against the Jewish working class, represented by the communist *Frayhayt.* Only the *Frayhayt,* Tanievitsh continues, had the strength to tell the truth about "the bloody occurrences in Palestine: that this is an ongoing revolt on the part of the downtrodden Arabs against their oppressors and slaveholders—against the English imperialists and Zionist fascists."[56]

Autumn 1929 was consumed by escalating attacks between the *Frayhayt* and its opponents. In a mass protest on August 27 in New York, according to *Der Tog,* twenty thousand people, including family members of those killed, protested the bloodshed in Palestine. New York City Mayor Jimmy Walker delivered a speech on the steps of City Hall.[57] The *Frayhayt* held a meeting the following day clarifying its position that the Arab riots constituted an uprising. On September 22, the Labor Zionist–allied Jewish National Workers Alliance held a trial against the communists at the Central Opera House, with speeches by the leading Yiddish cultural figures Shmuel Niger-Charney and Alexander Mukdoni. On the same day, the *Frayhayt* held its own show trial at the New Star Casino, where speakers including the journalist and literary critic Kalman Marmor attacked the basic tenets of Zionism.[58] The Soviet Yiddish writers, in solidarity with the communist *Frayhayt,* drafted their own resolution against the "runaways," harshly admonishing Leivick and

Reyzen—poets whom they had recently celebrated in the Soviet Union, in 1925 and early 1929, respectively. The notices section in the Warsaw-based *Literarishe Bleter* states that the union of Jewish pioneers in Moscow had decided to revoke the title of "honorary pioneer" from Reyzen, along with his pioneer kerchief, which they had given him in Moscow.[59] The pioneers also revoked H. Leivick's honorary kerchief. During Leivick's 1925 visit to the Soviet Union, he had been toasted from Moscow to Kiev and had discussed the possibility of emigrating to the Soviet Union in letters with his wife.[60]

That the *Frayhayt*'s most famous poets had turned against the communists was, for the young *Frayhayt* poets, a rift equal to the conflict between the Jews and Arabs in Palestine. As recently as August 25, the *Frayhayt* had run a poem by Reyzen that included the following lines celebrating the Soviet Union:

Un di shtimen fun brider,	And the voices of brothers,
un di trit un di fon	and their footsteps and flag
vekn-oyf in dir lider,	arouse in you songs,
fun a freyd, vos kumt on.[61]	of a joy to come.

In Tanievitsh's indictment of the "runaways," he connects the anti-communist demonstrators, the Zionists, and the poets—including Reyzen—who had left the *Frayhayt*. He describes a clash between political adversaries at one of the many Autumn 1929 protest marches in response to the Palestine events:

> "You are a pogromchik," a Zionist shouts.
> "But I'd like to tell you a few things, Mr. Jew [Reb Yid]," the "pogromchik" says.
> "With pogromchiks there's nothing to talk about!" shouts the Jew louder and sympathizers gather around him. The worker is not afraid, for his comrades in arms are also gathering around him.[62]

Buried in Tanievitsh's description of the rally is a poignant observation of the breakdown of communication in the debate about Palestine. For Tanievitsh and Teyf, the mainstream Jewish press (including the socialist papers) failed to support the communists' anti-Zionist call and therefore also failed the promise of diaspora nationalism, which the communists viewed as necessarily grounded in the Comintern and Moscow. At public rallies, as well as in political writing, the communists insisted on the point that the Zionists, together with the British, were fully responsible for the unrest in Palestine. Although Zionism did play a role in the violence, the Party's tragic simplification was in conflating class revolution with a religious-national revolution.

The *Frayhayt*'s opponents, including Reyzen, Leivick, and Boreysho, could not accept the equation of nation and class, for, they pointed out, doing so came dangerously close to the flawed Russian Revolutionary philosophy of condoning antisemitic violence waged in the name of peasant solidarity. In their letter of resignation from the *Frayhayt,* Leivick and Boreysho recalled the Bundist Vladimir Medem's statement, in the wake of the 1903–1905 pogroms in the tsarist empire, that "the blood of pogroms is the oil that will grease the wheels of the Russian Revolution."[63] Medem's statement, Leivick and Boreysho declare, remained the shame of his life. The *Frayhayt,* they continue, "which in the first moment reacted humanely to the events, is now re-creating the theory of 'Jewish blood on the wheels of an Arab revolution.'"[64]

By September 1929, the source of the disagreement had moved from Palestine to the Yiddish literary community, and writers on both sides saw themselves as victims. With the exception of Reyzen, who was in his fifties, the poets who had left the *Frayhayt* were not much older than the majority of the poets who stayed. Nonetheless, the *Frayhayt* poets, abandoned by their role models, saw a generational divide between the aesthetics of the "runaways" and the politics of the communists. Ayzik Platner's "Tsu di antlofene" (To the runaways) begins with a bitter address: "You writer-aesthetes / you poets of refined taste! / What will become of your sadness?" (Ay shrayber-estetn, / Faynshmeker-poetn! / Vos vet es zayn dort bay aykh mit'n umet?). Platner (1895–1961), like Teyf and Tanievitsh, turns to Reyzen's "Vinter-lid" to describe an older generation that has abandoned a revolutionary fight:

'Hulyet, hulyet beyze vintn,	'Blow, blow angry winds,
haynt iz ayer tsayt'.	now your time has come.'
Far di oygn vakst dos lid,	This song grows before my eyes,

yede shure greser.	each line greater.
s'iz yedes vort—a shnit.	every word—a cut.
Un yeder ferz—a meser . . . [65]	And every verse—a dagger . . .

Like Tanievitsh's article, Platner's accusation against Reyzen is in the spirit of the many protests and trials staged by the *Frayhayt* and its opponents over Palestine. Platner marks his poem, "New York, September 16. In the time of the holy war against the communists." Platner here describes a crusade against the Communist Party for its stance on Palestine. What we see in the poem is a poignant lament of a reader who has been abandoned by his childhood inspirations. Platner, who had once been a member of Poale Zion, would move permanently to the Soviet Union in 1932. He accuses the poets who had left the *Frayhayt* of petit-bourgeois values, indifference to the struggle, and fear. "In Gastonia," Platner continues, "the struggle has already flared up on all the streets, but Leivick got scared."[66] The Loray Mill strike of April–September 1929 in Gastonia, North Carolina, had mobilized the Communist Party USA, particularly following the death of the poet and union organizer Ella May Wiggins, who was killed on September 14, 1929.[67] Platner thus accuses the "runaways" of collectively betraying the workers of the world and choosing nationalism over class consciousness.

Aaron Kurtz also connects Palestine to the strikes in Gastonia in his September 22 poem "Mishpet" (Trial). Kurtz draws a line between those who are with the workers and those who are not. He opens by condemning the aestheticism of the "runaways":

Ver vet mishpetn	Who will judge
un ver vet shtrofn	and who will punish
di shleyfer fun rafinirtn vort	the polishers of the refined word
vos zaynen fun	who ran away
dem shvern kamf antlofn?[68]	from the hard struggle?

The accusation of aestheticism ("polishers of the refined word") is consistent with the demonization, in the 1920s, of right-wing fellow travelers in the Soviet proletarian writers' organizations MAPP (the Moscow Association of Proletarian Writers) and RAPP (the Russian Association of Proletarian Writers).[69] Soviet critics, in effect, attempted to link nationalism and the abandonment of workers to an aesthetic isolationism—a nebulous-enough connection so as to justify rejecting intellectual opponents on the grounds of their obsession with form. Kurtz levels similar charges against the *Frayhayt* "runaways." "Your deed," Kurtz's poem continues, "blesses the medieval fruits upon us, / your deed is a seal upon the actions of the black clan."[70] In keeping with Third Period communism, Kurtz rejects socialists as social fascists. The Klan, the embodiment of racism, was an American analogue to European fascism.[71] By likening the opponents of the *Frayhayt* to the "black clan," Kurtz accuses them of Jewish clannishness and aligns them with both racial bigots and factory bosses. Kurtz negatively compares the *Frayhayt* "runaways" to Ella May Wiggins. "As a danger-flag over the world," Kurtz writes, "Flutters / the thorny life of Ella May Wiggins! / But you sing, together with / the clan, the old song of borders."[72]

Aaron Kurtz (1891–1964), a Party member since 1926, had left his Lubavitcher Hasidic family in Vitebsk as a teenager, joined the circus as a hairdresser, and in 1910 immigrated to the United States, where he published Mayakovskian experiments with revolutionary poetic form in the 1910s and 1920s.[73] One of the most devout communists among the Yiddish poets, Kurtz remained with the Party longer than most of his comrades, publishing a poem for Stalin's birthday as late as December 1949.[74] Kurtz later sought ways of integrating Jewish tradition with a workers' collective during the Popular Front period. However, in the crisis of 1929, he made every effort to equate Jewish clannishness to white American racism in its adherence to a national and religious ethos. He makes this explicit in his poem "Di vant" (The wall), published two days before "Mishpet" in the *Frayhayt*. Identifying the Western Wall as a password connecting Zionism to religious fervor, Kurtz deconstructs the wall as a symbol, presenting it as a dangerous relic that feeds an unjust power structure, a "dead Jesuit-wall that is a knife-like border between human and human."

Di vant, di vant,
tsekrishlt un farshimlt,
di toyte tsien-vant—farheylikt un farhimlt.
Di vant, di vant,

The wall, the wall,
crumbling and moldy,
the dead Zion-wall—made heavenly and holy.
The wall, the wall,

fun vistn, midberdikn gloybn—	of bleak, desert faith—
a nets far shtarbndike gleyber,	a net for dying believers,
a kval—far di, vos roybn.[75]	a wellspring for robbers.

Focusing on the materiality of the "crumbling and moldy" (tsekrishlt un farshimlt) wall, Kurtz shifts the wall's metaphorical purpose from holy relic to dangerous remnant—a divisive border that must be dismantled. Having recoded the meaning of "Vant" (Wall) as an anti-Zionist password, Kurtz then turns to the revolutionary task of his generation:

Mayn zeyde iz shoyn toyt,	My grandfather is dead,
un es shlisn zikh di vegn fun mayn tatn.	and my father's paths are closed.
Der zun muz oyfraysn di vant oyf shtoyb:	The son must rend the wall to dust:
es kon der zun zikh nit farratn.[76]	the son cannot deceive himself.

Like many American poets of his generation, Kurtz favored vers libre, opting for slant rhymes over perfect rhymes. His choice of rhymes and slant rhymes, however—*toyt*/*shtoyb* (dead/dust), *tatn*/*farratn* (father/betray)—furthers the rhetoric of desacralizing a monument of past generations. The lines fall into loose iambs, and the disjointed lengths help to illustrate the deconstruction of a past order. Aaron Kurtz ridicules religion across his oeuvre, regardless of the tone or poetic genre. He frequently juxtaposes his (correct) communist fervor to the (misled) Hasidism of his upbringing. The incidents in Palestine helped Kurtz to explain the deep opposition between revolutionary commitment and Judaism.

In response to being expelled from the Y. L. Peretz Yiddish Writers' Union, between September and December 1929, those writers who remained with the *Morgn Frayhayt* expressed political solidarity with the Comintern by forming the *Frayhayt* Writers' Union—a group that eventually became the Proletarian Writers' Union, Proletpen, with Kurtz at the helm.[77] Kurtz was eager, in 1929, to denounce the "Zionists with holy stars of David" (Tsiunistn mit mogen-Dovid heylikn)—a conflation of religion and politics that would have left many religious Jews and Zionists uncomfortable.[78] But this simplification was intentional: a new generation, he proclaimed, must destroy the archaic religious constructs that have become Zionist symbols.

Dos folk, dos folk	This people, this people
muz nemen in di hent di sharfe zeygn	must pick up the sharp saw
fun dem fayerdikn dor un brengen	of its fiery generation and itself
zikh aleyn dos lang gegarte vor:	bring about this long-craved
tsezegn un	truth: saw up and
tseshpaltn,	split apart,
tsemoln biz tsu shtoyb	grind unto dust
dem viln fun Britanishn pirat, ineynem	the British pirate's will, together
mit	with
dem lign fun	the lie of
dem Tsiunistishn 'moshiekh,' tsemoln	the Zionist 'messiah,' grind it to
biz tsu shtoyb[79]	dust

The felicitous internal rhyme between the phrase "fayerdikn dor" (fiery generation) that must usher in the "lang-gegarte vor" (long-craved truth) suggests a new eschatological system—a revolutionary messianism— to destroy and replace outdated superstition and nationalism in one blow.[80] Kurtz's choice of the Germanic "vor" (truth / reality) not only works to complete the provocative rhyme but also conjures Marx and Engels's "objective truth" (gegenständliche Wahrheit), which is rooted in practical reality as opposed to theory.[81] When Kurtz declares the need to grind the "lie of the Zionist 'messiah' . . . to dust," he is calling attention to religious remnants as objects to be dealt with in a material, practical way, as well as holding one version of utopia against another. He is also combining Zionist, religious, and (British) imperialist hierarchical structures into a single adversary. To align Arab frustrations with the Comintern's proletarian cause, communist venues returned to well-worn passwords that were mobilized for revolutionary struggle before the Revolution. Thus, Kurtz aligns religious symbolism with British imperialism, and the Zionist utopian project with religious Judaism, meanwhile exalting the communist utopian project as a rational alternative to nationalism, religion, and imperialism.

Menke Katz (1906–1991) similarly targets Jewish collective nostalgia in his own rendition of "Tsu di antlofene" (To the runaways), which he dedicates "to the quartet of abandoners." Rather than highlighting the *Frayhayt* departure of the "runaways" from the Party, he accuses

them of indulging themselves in a lachrymose spirit of self-pity and
tribalism:

Hot zikh tsetsundn	You've kindled
klayzl-troyer iber velt—	prayer-house-sadness the world over—
Zayt ir farshvundn,	You've disappeared,
vi eykhe-klangen fun undzer feld.[82]	like lamentation-sounds from our field.

Katz connects the urge to write poems of destruction to clannishness
and to the religious rituals that the Party has abandoned. Like Kurtz in
"Di vant," Katz turns to the materiality of the Western Wall to find a
metaphor for the stagnant religious—and aesthetic—practices that the
Frayhayt rejects: "You've longed, / like dust on the 'ancient wall' / to
shudder in the night."[83] Katz simultaneously rejects religion and national
mourning. His is not only a critique of Judaism but a manifesto for a
new generation of Jewish poets who must resist the trappings of bourgeois nationalism.

Iz aykh atsind farblibn:	Now all you have left is
vi a farloshener himl	to hang like a spent candle
heyngen in beys-medresh-land;	in synagogue-land;
iz aykh atsind farblibn:	now all you have left is
mit a harb fun shiml	to sit with a moldy hump
zitsn bay a fentster	by a window
un zoygn fun der midber	and suckle sandy
zamdike geshpenster.[84]	desert ghosts.

Katz enriches his poem with images of Jewish tradition, even as he sen-
tences the runaway poets, as a result of their tribalism, to "hang . . . in
synagogue-land."[85]

   "As poetry has become more subjective," Harold Bloom reminds
us, "the shadow cast by the precursors has become more dominant."[86]
The 1929 clashes over Palestine represent a particularly politicized
manifestation of Bloom's "anxiety of influence." The Yiddish writers
who left the *Frayhayt* took pains to affirm their commitment to world
revolution, and often to anti-Zionism, even as they rejected the current
Party platform, and the remaining *Frayhayt* poets built their identities in
large part on their rejection of these "runaways." The true conflict be-

tween these groups, it is important to reiterate, lay not in whether to support the Zionists or communists but in how to define the boundaries of their internationalism.[87]

THE "RUNAWAYS" RESPOND

The *Frayhayt* poets' demonization of the "runaways" might have been tolerable on its own, but the accusations in the communist press were painful in another way. The campaign against them included the Soviet Yiddish writers, who had no choice but to align itself with the communist *Frayhayt*. That Dovid Bergelson, the great Yiddish prose writer, who was then still in Berlin, also aligned himself outwardly with the *Frayhayt*, along with the Soviet Yiddish writers Peretz Markish and Der Nister, was almost too much to bear.

The poets who published in the splinter journal *Vokh* took pains to convey their continued support of the Soviet Union's basic revolutionary project while condemning the Comintern's position on Palestine. Avrom Reyzen published a poem titled "Groye teg" (Gray days) in the first issue of *Vokh,* in which he uses basic revolutionary passwords—"kamfn" (struggles), "brider" (brothers), and "makhnes" (squadrons)—to contrast the past spirit of revolution with the current climate:

Groye teg vider . . .   More gray days . . .
nor mir gedenken   but we remember
di kamfn, di lider   the struggles, the songs
di makhnes, di brider,   the columns, the brothers,
un vartn un benken.[88]   and wait and long.

Aaron Glantz-Leyeles declared, "We have absolutely not become Zionists because of the Palestinian tragedy. If possible, we have become even bigger opponents of political Zionism than before."[89] Esther Shumiatcher and Peretz Hirschbein, having just left the Soviet Union, found themselves caught between their desire to support their friends in the Soviet Union and Palestine. The couple welcomed *Vokh* as a golden mien, a venue for expressing their disdain for the recent *Frayhayt* position but continuing to assert their belief in world revolution. Shumiatcher published an excerpt from her Crimea cycle discussed in Chapter 1, "Yung iz erd un royt iz blut" (Young is the earth and red is blood) in the November 29 issue of *Vokh,* a month before her book appeared in print. The excerpt describes enthusiastic Jewish migrants from shtetls to the colonies in Crimea and Kherson. She omits, however, the end of the cycle, where she asserts that brethren from around the world, "by the Vistula and by the shores of the Hudson, / and by the La Plata and by the Jordan's southern path . . . envy you your labor."[90] Shumiatcher still openly admires Soviet Jews, but by leaving this ending out of the 1929 *Vokh* version of the poem, she deemphasizes her recent belief in the Soviet Union as the center of an international community.

In forming *Vokh,* Leivick, Boreysho, and their colleagues embraced the polemic with the *Frayhayt* as part of their responsibility to their readers. In an editorial for the first issue of *Vokh,* "Farvos mir zaynen aroys fun der 'Frayhayt'" (Why we left the *Frayhayt*), Leivick ridicules the communists' performance of revolution:

> It's been four weeks since we left the *Frayhayt* and came to a medieval nightmare. Innocent women and children have shed blood—mocked by people, by communists, who carry ideas about saving the world; the hands of pogromchiks are sanctified, greeted as the hands of revolutionaries. The speeches of Olgin and Melekh [Epstein], insolent and bossy; letters from readers all in the same style, every one of them. And after that—the sham trial. Witnesses, prosecutors, anxious complaints, distorted letters, false intonation, smokescreens, the outcry: guilty. Guilty . . . and after that—telegrams from Shakhne Epshteyn and the Kharkov writers, who now call us "renegades." Excommunication. Excommunication. Kherem. Kherem.[91]

The *Vokh* editors accused the *Frayhayt* writers of misusing the terms "pogrom" and "revolution," concluding that the communists had appropriated passwords from a Jewish international Left for a cause that now supported violence against innocent Jewish lives. For their part, the "runaways" were using Party passwords against the communists, appropriating religious terminology that the Party had explicitly rejected to explain the communist poets' conformist behavior. The biblical word *kherem,* originally signifying condemnation to death or destruction, is used in Jewish law to mean "ban" or "excommunication." Leivick's use of the word is significant: by accusing the communists of overzealous adherence to the Party, Leivick rejects the accusation that he and his fellow "runaways" have succumbed to nostalgia for religious Judaism. The reference to excommunication evokes, moreover, Spinoza, the seventeenth-century philosopher excommunicated from the Jewish community in Amsterdam.[92] The battle between Left and Left occasionally resembled the kind of show trial against religion that had gained popularity in the Soviet Union in the early 1920s, theatrical trials that, as Anna Shternshis has discussed, were waged "against the Sabbath, Passover, and Yom Kippur [and] served both philosophical and practical purposes."[93] Both sides repurposed rhetoric from the Soviet campaign against religion in their competition over who better served Leninist antireligious philosophy.

Leivick, in a poignant soliloquy, "Royte tikhelekh" (Red kerchiefs), wonders if he must return scarves that Soviet Pioneer scouts had given him five years earlier, now that his honorary membership had been revoked.

Ikh nem aroys fun shuflor di dray royte tikhlakh.	I take out of the closet the three kerchiefs.
Ibershikn zey tsurik?—tsu vemen? Vuhin?	Should I send them back?—to whom? Where?
Zey veln forlorn geyn.	They will be lost.
Saydn ibergebn zey tsu eynem, vos iz kosherer fun mir, komunistisher fun mi, un iz mer roe tsu trogn di tikhlekh.	Or should I give them to someone who is kosherer than me, more communist than me, and is worthier of wearing the kerchiefs.
Kinder farlangen—darf men zeyer farlang derfiln.	Children give, so one must honor their gift.
*	*
az ikh bin nit roe mer—dos iz on tsveyfl.	I am no longer worthy—this is beyond doubt.
Ikh bin in kherem.[94]	I am banned.

However, Leivick notes, now that the pioneers had issued a resolution against the deserters, the poet is uncertain what he should do with these red kerchiefs.

H. Leivick's former commitment to the Revolution was beyond dispute. His 1906 arrest and subsequent escape from Siberia was well-known in American and Soviet literary circles. Moreover, by the 1920s, Leivick, who had been a founding member of the New York modernist group, Di Yunge, was among the most celebrated Yiddish poets in the world. Leivick's departure from the *Frayhayt* was, no less than Reyzen's, seen as an act of betrayal: he had published there as recently as August 25. His Sacco-Vanzetti poems, discussed in the introduction to this book, had inspired a younger generation of Yiddish speakers to become politically active.[95] In "Royte tikhelekh," Leivick explicitly compares the Party to Rabbinic Judaism. In the same soliloquy, he names Shakhne Epshteyn—editor of the Moscow daily *Der Emes*—the celebrated former members of the modernist Kiev-grupe Peretz Markish and Leyb Kvitko, and the Soviet proletarian poet Chaim Gildin:

Shakhne Epshteyn hot getsundn shvartse	Shakhne Epshteyn has kindled black
likht un geblozn in shofer: —tekiye!	lights and blown in the shofar: —*tekiya!*
Markish hot untergekhapt mit an asonans:—	Markish took over with an assonance:—
shevarim!	*shevarim!*
Kvitko hot untergetantst:—true!	Kvitko danced further:—*teruah!*
Gildin:—tekiye, shevarim, true!	Gildin:—*tekiya, shevarim, teruah!*
And all together:—tekiye ge-do-la![96]	And all together:—*tekiah ge-do-lah!*

The utterances—*tekiya, teruah, shevarim*—are associated with the blasts of the shofar used in a traditional excommunication (*kherem*) ceremony. Epshteyn, Markish, Kvitko, and Gildin—Yiddish writers at the heart of the Soviet literary project—are thus compared to the gatekeepers of religious Judaism, and the Party rhetoric they intone is compared to the antiquated ritual of formal exclusion. Leivick published this poem on October 18, just after Yom Kippur, which fell on October 14 in 1929. Leivick's sins against the Party (he suggests with a melodramatic flare) are unforgivable.

Leivick delivers his own harsh verdict in return. Not only are the communist writers like religious authorities in their adherence to rituals and rules; they are like bourgeois shopkeepers (*kremer*) in their obsession with exchange value. Leivick mercilessly attacks the Soviet writers for expecting the "runaways" to sacrifice Jews in Palestine as payment for their Soviet colleagues' earlier hospitality:

Zenen zey farblibn di greste kremer.—	They remain the biggest
Tsol zey far di oyfnames, tsol zey!	shopkeepers.—Pay up for the
	reception, pay them!
Far a banket in Kiev tsol zey op mit	For a banquet in Kiev pay up with
Hevron.	Hebron.
Far a lyame in Kharkov—mit Tsfat.	For a party in Kharkov—with Tsfat.
Nit mer un nit veyniker.[97]	No more and no less.

Leivick accuses the communists not only of religion but of capitalism. The American communists have deemed Leivick ungrateful, he continues sardonically, for he now knows that his warm Soviet reception was only "thanks to the intervention of Aaron Kurtz and Ayzik Platner with the Soviet proletariat." In the long prose poem, Leivick reflects on his positive relationship to communism and his disdain for the current rigidity of international Party politics. "I love the pioneer kerchief because it has its roots in the red flag," he continues, and then wonders, "is it really possible that children, themselves rescued from pogroms, should protest someone because they condemn pogromchiks?" In a final, bitter line, Leivick addresses the *Frayhayt* writers: "Dear people of Union Square, send me the names of your cleanest and kosherest.—I have all three kerchiefs ready for him." (Libe layt fun Yunyon Skver, shikt mir tsu dem nomen fun ayer reynstn un kosherstn.—ikh halt greyt far im ale dray tikhlekh).[98]

In a poem published on October 18, 1929, Leivick extends the clash between two groups of poets and their respective futures by comparing both the *Frayhayt* and the "runaway" poets to fathers:

Zey rufn mikh on farreter,	They call me a traitor.
un nemen tsu zeyere zin, un geyen avek	and take their sons, and go away

in park arayn, vu falndike bleter	to the park where the autumn yard worker
der osyendiker shoymer klaybt in fule zek.	gathers falling leaves in full sacks.
Zey lozn zikh tantsn mit di zin tsuzamen,	They dance with their sons,
zey zingen a loyb aza tsu a merders shverd,	they sing a paean to a murderer's sword,
biz der himl brent oys in zayne letste flamen,	until the sky burns up in its last flames,
un es nidert arunter di nakht oyf der erd.[99]	and the night lowers over the earth.

If the communist's poem-sons are learning a murderous dance, Leivick's son has been murdered:

Un mayn zun ligt a derkoyleter oyf breter,	And my son lies shot on boards,
zayn kindisher haldz iz, vi geven, din;	his childish neck is as thin as before;
ikh tayne tsu im: zun mayner, zey rufn mikh farreter—	I complain to him: son, they call me traitor—
di hulyendike tates mit di tantsndike zin.[100]	the reveling dads with their dancing sons.

Leivick here returns to Reyzen's fin-de-siècle revolutionary password, *hulyet* (revel), calling the revolutionary fathers "hulyendike" (reveling). If the communists anticipate a laughing, swirling future, then the future of the left-wing antiassimilationist Leivick is bleak: his revolution will not bear living children.

The spirit of revolution belongs to the young and spirited, and Leivick, having precociously joined an older generation's revolution, now mourns his replacement by the more radical American *Frayhayt* poets. In one blow, Leivick disowns the overly joyful *Frayhayt* poets and predicts a bleak future for his own Yiddish lyric poetry.

Poets on both sides of the divide lamented the culture of trials and accusations. Shifre Vays (1889–1955) published a poem in the *Frayhayt* on November 3 criticizing accusations against the Party. However, Vays's approach to the dispute is tender—almost familial. The accusations (*taynes*) that surround the *Frayhayt* writers are "like mama's talking-to's" (Vi mame's shtrof-reyd), "Like hungry children's-cries" (Vi hungerike kinder-geshrayen), which do no good, for life now is ferocious—"a camp of brown bears" (A makhne broyne bern), "a wood full of wild lions" (A vald mit vilde leybn): "One wrong step / and they'll devour our flesh" (Eyn krumer trot—/ Un s'fartsukn undz di laybn). Vays's assonant rhyme of "leybn" (lions) with "laybn" (lives) is reinforced by the dialectical relationship between the threat and the threatened. In the climate of trials and grievances, too, Vays suggests, it had become tedious to distinguish aggrieved from aggressor. Vays, at forty, was only a year younger than Leivick, and like Leivick, she had become involved in the Bund during her eastern European youth. And yet her choice to uphold the Party position in 1929 aligns her with a younger generation of poets. For Vays, there is tenderness, and even desire, between the two generational camps that touch but cannot speak to one another. She closes her poem,

Taynes,	Accusations,
vi tropns regn	like raindrops
oyf tseshpaltene felder,	on cracked fields,
oder vi kushn, ven doyres farvebn.	or like kisses, when generations overlap.
Nor mir kenen itst andersh nit vern:	But we can't become otherwise now:
A tseflakerter vald unzer lebn.[101]	Our life is a wood on fire.

The *Frayhayt,* as Vays expresses here, had passed a point of no return: clear lines had been drawn between the Yiddish writers who remained with the Party paper and those who left.

By mid-October, the whirlwind of trials had grown unbearable. Nakhman Mayzel, the editor of Warsaw's *Literarishe Bleter,* entreats his colleagues in an October 11 editorial to stop. He describes the series of events in New York, the Soviet Union, Warsaw, and Palestine, including the departure of Reyzen, Leivick, Boreysho, and Raboy from the *Frayhayt;* the resolutions carried out in New York, Moscow, Kharkiv, and Minsk; a Warsaw resolution against the prose writer and playwright Sholem Asch for his condemnation of the Comintern's position; the exclusion of the *Frayhayt* writers from the New York writers' union and the exclusion of the American Yiddish section of the Soviet territorialist organization IKOR from the *Frayhayt;* as well as the departure of twenty writers from the mainstream Warsaw Yiddish daily newspaper, *Haynt*, who had turned against the Warsaw writers' union. "So deeply has our Yiddish life been shaken from within thanks to events from without."[102]

POETRY AND TRUTH

How did a story about Palestine become a story about poets? Perhaps because poets, and the journals that published them, viewed themselves as the guardians of ethical truth. As Hans-Georg Gadamer has formulated, "The truth of poetry consists in creating a 'hold upon nearness.'"[103] In 1929, there was nothing nearer to the revolutionary generation of Jewish poets than the concept of group struggle. Both the Jewish and Arab struggles fit this category, but choosing one struggle over the other, the leftist Yiddish poets split into two camps. By reconstituting key terms from Jewish history, including "pogrom" and "uprising," the *Frayhayt* writers sought to return to language according to their own conscience. All of the poems published in 1929 about the events in Palestine or their aftermath lay claim to an ethical truth through a meditation on the terms that the Jewish revolutionaries of the early twentieth century had held dear. But who got to determine a collective truth? At one anti-*Frayhayt* trial, the literary critic Shmuel Niger-Charney recalled the two Russian terms for truth—ontological truth (*istina*, or in Yiddish *gerekhtigkayts-emes*) and factual truth (*pravda,* or *varhayts-emes*)—and suggested that the *Frayhayt* poets were creating institutions of alternative ethical authority to evade factual truth. This included the invention of new proletarian poets: "Suddenly, overnight, tens of new Yiddish writers grew up! They know most of them aren't writers, . . . but when one has 'to mobilize,' one takes babies from the cradle, workers from the sweatshops, and makes them into writers."[104] Leivick, in his first *Vokh* editorial on October 4, 1929, accused the *Frayhayt* writers of betraying fundamental Marxist-Leninist principles: "they have not shed light on the events in Palestine as true independent-minded communists."[105] For Niger-Charney and Leivick, the *Frayhayt*'s breech of truth through its reinterpretation of sacred passwords along Party lines was a breach of conscience. Each side in the 1929 divide laid claim to its own ontological truth, be it the correctness of the Arab workers whose land had been appropriated by an imperialist project or the correctness of Jews' right to reside in Palestine.

The primacy of Palestine eventually shifted to other events, as the communist press took up other concerns, closer to home. Less than two months after the attack on Hebron, the stock market crashed on Wall Street, ushering in worldwide economic depression. Immigrant workers' newly desperate situation contributed to the already toxic climate of political divisions. As we will see in Chapters 3 and 4, the Scottsboro trials in the US South and the Spanish Civil War would eclipse the immediacy of Palestine, and the poetics of rupture—of pogroms, revolution, and even religion—would shift to other significant concerns. By the mid-1930s, with the ascent of fascism in western Europe, some of the "runaways" made tenuous amends with the Left under the auspices of the Popular Front. Continued altercation in Palestine still prompt returns to the lines that separated the leftist Yiddish writers nearly a century ago.[106] As we shall see in the final chapter of this book, it was not until after the 1939 Hitler-Stalin pact, when a great many more *Frayhayt* writers abandoned the newspaper and bemoaned their ties to the Party, that the poets at the center of the 1929 debates would attempt to make amends with each other.

The most significant breech of truth in the 1929 rift may have been in the forfeiture of ambiguity. In a speech during World War II, H. Leivick, who had again worked with the Party during the Popular Front of the mid-1930s, uttered a chilling statement, suggesting that the rifts—the "penny wars" among Jewish writers—"at a time when the Nazis are annihilating us" may have prevented other groups from jumping to Jews' defense: "And who knows whether many thousands of Jews, who were killed, wouldn't have been saved had our Jewish literature here in our land stood up at the right moment, kindled hearts, driven people to action."[107] Whether or not Leivick was correct, by separating a painful event into competing grievances, the Yiddish poets on each side of the 1929 divide claimed partial truths based on the certainty in their individual positions. By choosing sides in 1929, they failed to evoke widespread empathy for the Palestinian Arabs or empathy within the Party for the Jewish victims of the uprising. In the polarizing environment of 1929, any other response may have been impossible. However, as Jacques Derrida argues in his 1993 *Spectres of Marx,* the language of past politics always haunts the present: "If he loves justice at least, the 'scholar' of the future, the 'intellectual' of tomorrow should learn it and from the ghost."[108] Returning to the poetic debates of 1929 nearly a century later allows us to take a step toward restoring a larger, and more complex, picture. Were the winds of the desert angry or cruel, revolutionary or sinister? If the poetry of 1929 refused to allow for both truths, perhaps our reading of it nearly a century later can.

3

SCOTTSBORO CROSS

Translating Pogroms to Lynchings

In 1931, nine young black men were falsely accused of raping two white women on the roof of an Alabama freight train. The Scottsboro trial, which began in March of that year and lasted over a decade, absorbed the American leftist literary imagination. Many of the Yiddish poems that appeared at the height of the trial present crucifixion or pietà scenes. Malka Lee's 1932 "Gots shvartser lam" (God's black lamb) describes a mother mourning her son. Berish Weinstein similarly ends his 1938 "A Negro Dies" with a weeping mother longing "To die with him on a Negro cross."[1] Menke Katz, in his 1935 "Di lintshndike kro" (The lynching crow), describes the night hanging "on every tree like a crucified Negro."[2] In the earlier decades of the twentieth century, American Yiddish modernists too had described African Americans, often simultaneously exoticizing and identifying with America's perennial Other. Earlier Yiddish poets had also written crucifixion poems: the irony of Jesus's Jewishness and the hypocrisy of a murderous Christian majority had led Jewish modernists to develop the crucifixion motif in pogrom poems. For the Party-aligned Yiddish poets, African Americans had replaced Jews as the martyred minority in their adopted

country, and Scottsboro crosses represented a widespread effort to translate modernist pogrom poems to poems about lynching. The image of
the suffering Jesus became a way of translocating tropes about Jewish
sacrifice to a non-Jewish, African American minority.

Poems describing lynchings filled American Yiddish journals and
newspapers during the early 1930s. Malka Lee (born Malka Leopold,
1904–1976) includes in her 1932 collection the following description of a
landscape perverted by race violence:

Zey hobn im aroysgefirt	They led him outside
mit nakete fis, gebundene hent.	with bare feet, and bound hands.
Fun dorem zamd zayn hoyt farbrent.	His skin burnt by southern sand.
Oylik iz plutsling gevorn zayn layb,	his flesh became suddenly oily,
zayn shvartser guf in trern tseshaynt . . .	his black body sparkled in tears . . .
Der vald hot zikh geboygn vi fun meser shnit	The woods bowed low as if cut by a knife
oyf tsurik, oyf tsurik—	go back, go back—
Gots shvartser lam	God's black lamb
hot zikh gerisn fun shtrik . . . ³	tore himself from the rope . . .

In this lynching scene, Lee identifies the victim with Jesus—the ultimate New Testament "Lamb of God."⁴ The Scottsboro trial mobilized
Yiddish writers across the Left, inviting a degree of rapprochement following the rift over Palestine. Malka Lee was a case in point: she had
shifted from the communist *Frayhayt* to *Vokh,* the Yiddish journal
founded in protest against the Party's stance on the 1929 uprisings in
Palestine. She returned to Party-aligned newspapers during the Scottsboro trial, publishing poems about race violence among other topics
of social concern. Antilynching poems, more than the other themes
described in this book, cut across party lines. Although the Communist Party helped to underwrite the defense and publicized the trial
abroad as evidence of white racism in the United States, communists
were not alone in empathizing with black Americans.⁵ The historian
Hasia Diner has observed, "All of the newspapers, despite their ideological differences and regardless of their definition of Jewish culture
and identity, seized on the image of American blacks and stressed the
close parallels between them and Jews."⁶

The leftist Yiddish poets were not only drawing from their Yiddish modernist role models. English-language writers also used images of the crucifixion to describe Scottsboro. Most famously, Langston Hughes described crucifixions in his 1931 "Scottsboro" and "Christ in Alabama." The English-language Jewish poet Muriel Rukeyser (1913–1980), who reported on the trial, included sections on Scottsboro in her 1935 cycle "The Lynchings of Jesus."[7] The conversation among Yiddish writers and their readers was, however, a closed one. Writing in a language and alphabet foreign to most non-Jews, Yiddish poets could describe African Americans with little chance of engagement with the community they were describing. Most of these poems were not translated into English at the time they were written. Like the Yiddish poems about Sacco and Vanzetti, China, and Palestine, poems about lynchings must be read as works for and about Jews. The Yiddish leftists had, it can be assumed, a concrete objective: to convince a working-class Jewish readership to empathize with African Americans on the basis of their collective memory of European pogrom violence. This meant recognizing Jews' relative privilege as white Americans, despite pervasive antisemitism in the United States. However, by linking themes of anti-Jewish and anti-black violence, Yiddish poets were also working to build support for an internationalist identity in the United States, one with the strength and numbers to overcome both racism and antisemitism.

Scottsboro, the Alabama town where the defendants were incarcerated, became a password for racial inequality in the United States, and poets titled their works "Scottsboro" to signal their support for the nine young black men and the Comintern-sponsored International Labor Defense (ILD), which sponsored their defense and had underwritten Sacco and Vanzetti's defense a few years earlier.[8] The historian Robin Kelley has highlighted positive outcomes of the communists' involvement in the case: "They reversed the poles of criminalization, turning young black men—and young working-class white women—into victims and the state into the criminal. It opened a path for thinking about incarcerated black people as 'class-war prisoners.'"[9] A conversation about class struggle and Scottsboro was taking place among left-wing Yiddish writers internationally. In Romania in 1936, Zishe Bagish published a collection of translations, *Dos gezang fun Neger-folk* (The song of the Negro people), which included a large selection of translations of Langston Hughes's poems, with commentary.[10] Left-wing theater groups around the world staged performances and recitations based on the Scottsboro trial in Yiddish and other languages. The Argentinian Yiddish writer Leyb Malakh's dramatization of the Scottsboro trial, *Mississippi*, was performed around the world, including in interwar Warsaw by the director Mikhl Vaykhert.[11] Alyssa Quint reads Vaykhert's staging of *Mississippi* as part of a larger embrace of deparochialization in interwar Warsaw: "In both substance and form," writes Quint, "Vaykhert sought to cancel borderlines that disrupt the pathways of empathy and identification between those in the audience and those on the stage."[12] If in Europe the Scottsboro boys helped expand the boundaries of leftist Jewish internationalism, for many Jews in the United States, Scottsboro heightened concerns about antisemitism and invited a renewed commitment to combating all forms of American ethnic discrimination.

The passwords generated during the Scottsboro trial opened doors in two directions: terms borrowed from pogrom poems admitted African Americans into a Jewish fold and were aimed at evoking empathy among Jewish readers. Passwords borrowed from African American poets as well as from published letters between the defendants and their mothers brought Jewish writers and readers into an African American conversation about race in the United States. These terms helped to reinscribe writers' and readers' identities from Jews to workers. We must recall that internationalism, in the eyes of the Comintern, was based on ethnicity and not on existing nation-states. The Party-aligned writers who took up the cause of Scottsboro viewed African Americans as a distinct people, with a distinct ethnicity similar to other immigrant cultures. As Nikhil Pal Singh has posited in *Black Is a Country*, African American culture has been "denied ethnic honor (the honor of having 'ethnicity')."[13] The 1930s saw several competing, and in some cases complementary, visions of a distinct black ethnicity, from Marcus Garvey's Pan-Africanism to the Nation of Islam to the Communist Party's vision of an independent black belt state to W. E. B. Du Bois's vision of a "relatively autonomous sphere of black public discussion, interaction, and exchange."[14] Jewish immigrants to the United States, having been excluded from European nation-states, were quick to recognize the actual inequality in the idea of American nationhood, and Party-aligned writers recognized the African American voice as essential to the Communist International, a project centered well outside the US borders, in Moscow. As the Yiddish poet Y. E. Rontsh (1899–1985) articulated in 1940, "The Negro problem isn't unique to America. The question of human equality and race- and national-equality is a world problem."[15] It would be a mistake to read the Yiddish Scottsboro poems purely as manifestations of empathy. That the Scottsboro trial unfolded against the backdrop of the rise of Nazism in Germany lent Jewish poetry more urgency in seeking solidarity across ethnic lines.

To explore how Yiddish internationalists borrowed from pogrom poems to write about American racism, I turn, in the next section, to the emergence of two motifs in Yiddish modernism in the first three decades of the twentieth century: poems about crucifixions and poems about African Americans. I then discuss Malka Lee and other leftist Yiddish writers who combined these two motifs in the 1930s to create a new, antifascist poetics of martyrdom that blurred ethnic, and in some cases ideological, differences. In the third section, I discuss those Party-aligned Yiddish writers who explicitly borrowed passwords like "Scottsboro," "lynch law," and references to the activist Angelo Herndon from the trial and from contemporaneous African American poetry. I focus, in particular, on Y. E. Rontsh's Scottsboro poems. In the fourth section, I offer a close reading of Berish Weinstein, a poet who was not close to the Party but who published pogrom and lynching poems side by side in the 1930s, often reusing images and terms to more tightly combine the two themes. I conclude with a discussion of how the race poems of the 1930s contributed to a complex conversation among Jewish immigrants about their role in a United States that, they had learned, was not always the land of the free. This conversation continues, even after the last of the Scottsboro Boys were posthumously pardoned in 2013.

SACRIFICE IN YIDDISH MODERNISM

In Malka Lee's poem "Gots shvartser lam," a black Jesus is hanged in the US South. By calling her subject "God's black lamb," Lee asks her readers to interpret him as a modern-day Jesus. Although the most prominent depictions of the crucifixion portray Jesus nailed to a cross, Jesus is also sometimes described as having been hanged on a tree. In Acts, in the New Testament, for example, we find, "The God of our fathers raised up Jesus, whom ye slew and hanged on a tree."[16] In Christian tradition, as in Jewish, Jesus is referred to as a hanging man. Moreover, in the Bible, the hanged man is considered a form of blasphemy. "Cursed is everyone who is hung on a pole." Paul makes a bold interpretive move when, in his letter to the Galatians, he infers from this that the hanged man might absolve others of this curse: "Christ redeemed us from the curse of the law by becoming a curse for us."[17] Lee, along with her fellow Jewish poets who described a racialized Christ, was confronting her Jewish readers with an uncomfortable rewriting of religious tradition, one in which the Yiddish-speaking community has been redeemed by the sacrifice of an African American.

Lee closes her poem with the victim's mother, who witnesses the death of her martyred son in a landscape where even nature is marked by violent wounds:

In mitn der nakht a geshtalt	A figure in the middle of the night
iz gelofn iber fintstern vald—	went running across the dark wood—
ir layb vi erd shvarts gekarbt,	her body notched like black earth
der veg royt opgefarbt . . .	the road is painted red . . .
vuhin zaynen zey ale avek?	where have they all gone?
Boymer mit mesers un hek—	Trees full of axes and knives—
nor eyn boym blutikt bizn shtam . . .	But one tree bleeds down to its trunk . . .
Iber im geyt oyf Gots shvartser lam—	Above, God's black lamb succumbs—
Ir zun—ir Tam. . . . [18]	her son—her Tom. . . .

In this black American pietà, Lee broadens her portrait of the victim to emphasize his role as the sacrificed son, albeit a nearly anonymous one. The meter becomes more even in these final lines: I have attempted, in this translation, to approximate Lee's loose trisyllabic verse, which suggest the rhythm of the mother's frantic search. The poem ends with the tragic death of her son, a single irreplaceable individual whose identity is pronounced in four monosyllabic words: "Her son—her Tom" (Ir zun—ir Tam). Casting an African American man in the role of "God's lamb" and, therefore, his mother as the mourning Virgin, Lee draws on two key recurrent motifs in earlier Jewish modernism: the crucifixion as an ironic symbol for the murder of an innocent (usually Jewish) victim, and fascination with the marginalized Other.[19]

Scholars have also long discussed Jewish artists' enigmatic use of Christian images to show the irony of European antisemitism; excellent examples can be found in the work of David Roskies, Efraim Sicher, Matthew Hoffman, Janet Hadda, Neta Stahl, and Avraham Nowersztern.[20] However, the cross occupied a new space in the Jewish social consciousness when Yiddish writers transferred it from a metaphor about Jews to a metaphor about African Americans. The translocation of a Jewish Jesus to a black Jesus during the politically charged 1930s reflected the shift among Yiddish writers, which had become more pronounced since the Sacco-Vanzetti case, from an ethnically to an inter-ethnically oriented poetics.[21]

The Christian cross became a popular symbol for Jewish suffering among Yiddish modernists in the first three decades of the twentieth century. Yiddish poets and prose writers, including Sholem Asch, Lamed Shapiro, Uri Tsvi Grinberg, and Anna Margolin, presented the image of Jesus in pogrom poems to signify Christian hypocrisy.[22] Marc Chagall, who began painting crucifixions in 1908, called Christ a symbol of "the true type of the Jewish martyr."[23] The Yiddish and Hebrew poet Uri Tsvi Grinberg published his provocative 1922 "Uri Tsvi farn tseylem INRI" (Uri Tsvi before the cross INRI) in the shape of a cross in his modernist journal *Albatros*.[24] *Tseylem* (cross) is a powerful password in Yiddish poetry, for its literal meaning is both "icon" and "icon of idolatry." The *tseylem* is thus always already blasphemous within Jewish tradition and forbidden to Jews. Grinberg, standing before the cross, admonishes his "brother" Jesus, who, from his crucifix on high, turns a blind eye to the Jews hanging on similar crosses below:

—Fargliverte oygn zeen nisht: dir tsufisns: a kupe opgeshnitene Yidn-kep. Tsrisene taleysim. Tseshtokhene parmetn. Vayse layvntn mit blut-flekn.[25]

—Frozen eyes can't see: At your feet: a mound of severed Jewish heads. Torn prayer shawls. Stabbed Scrolls. Blood-splattered white linens

Grinberg's blinded, European Jesus justifies the poet's turn toward Zionism. A year after publishing this poem, Grinberg left Europe for Palestine.[26] By contrast, Malka Lee employs a Jesus figure to highlight the martyrdom of the United States' perennial other, the African American, at the height of the Scottsboro trial. Writers sympathetic to the Party were especially apt to extend the role of Christ—the embodiment of both martyrdom and chosenness—to other marginalized groups. Lee, along with a number of fellow poets in the 1930s, evokes the crucifixion in poems about African Americans to suggest that the solution to ethnic violence lay in alliances among workers, rather than in nationalism.

Lee also explored the crucifixion motif in her descriptions of Europe. Unlike Grinberg, who ironically associates the cross with Jewish victimhood, Lee allows the cross to connote a more universal mourning. For Lee, death is associated with the church rituals of her native Monastrishtsh, in Carpathia. "In Yezus' nomen" (In Jesus's name) appears in her 1932 book of poems and describes Christians marking death in an eastern European shtetl:

Ligt shtarbndiker, mit lipn ofene, krume,	The dying lies with lips open, crooked,
oyf vent—bilder heylike, frume.	on the wall are pictures, holy, pious.
Shmeykhlt Yezus tsum goysesdikn a shtumer,	Jesus smiles at the silent dying man,
tselemt shtarbndiker zikh in Yezus' nomen . . . [27]	the dying crosses himself in Jesus's name . . .

This poem does not depict violence. However, it offers a reversal of the human and the sacred, wherein the crucifixion on the wall pales in comparison to the dying human. "Zangen un tslomim" (Corn and crosses), published in her 1940 book *Gezangen* (Songs), presents the transformation of life-giving crops to graveyards:

Amol flegn oyfgeyn di felder mit zoymen,	Once the fields would grow with seeds,
amol flegn zingen di felder mit veyts.	once the fields would sing with wheat.

| Itst ligt farzeyt di erd mit harugim, | Now the earth lies planted with martyrs, |
| vu a goldene zang—a hiltserner krayts. . . . [28] | where a golden ear of corn was, a wooden cross. . . . |

The poem presents a nameless landscape of death at the beginning of World War II: the static crosses of Christian European churchyards have replaced a fertile farmland. Scholars of Jewish modernism have generally focused on expressionist uses of the cross as an ironic symbol of Jewish martyrdom. But the cross is also a password that enables Jewish poets to cross over, quite literally, to the experience of a Christian Other. Lee's cross poems of the 1930s brought her outside the Jewish community to mourn human tragedies across religious lines.

Yiddish poets described African American lynching victims long before the Scottsboro case, and some modernists evoked the crucifixion to do so. The poet Yehoash (Solomon Bloomgarden) addresses God in his 1919 poem "Lintshen" (Lynching), on behalf of a new Christ:

Der vos ruft dikh, reyst dikh, greyst dikh—	He who calls You, tears You, extols You—
iz fleysh gevoren,	has become flesh,
iz a shvartser layb gevoren . . . [29]	has become a black body

Yehoash goes on to admonish God for his own impiety, calling him "desecrator" (farshvekher):

Kuk on dayn verk:	Behold your work:
a shvarts layb mit blut bashtraypt,	a black body striped with blood,
a ponem pekh mit oysgekerte vayslen,	a tar face, the white of its eyes turned inside out,
a royter tsung geshvoln	a red tongue swollen
tsvishn shimerdike tseyn . . . [30]	between shimmering teeth . . .

As Merle Bachman has observed, the poem loses its way in the description of the body: "It fastens the reader's gaze on the black body in a way that suggests fascination with the very spectacle it is attempting to condemn."[31] The poem at once exalts the lynching victim, disconcertingly merging racial features and the wounds inflicted.

The Introspectivist poet Reuben Ludwig (1895–1926), who immigrated from Kiev as a child, offers a similarly grotesque portrayal of an African American victim with his 1923 "Ver hot tseshosn dem krekhtikn niger" (Who shot the leprous nigger). The title itself is a provocation to anger: by using a deeply offensive English-language slur—a password for the lynch mob Ludwig is condemning—the poet forces his Yiddish readers to confront the murderous racism in their adopted country. The unnamed perpetrator is guilty of the most heinous of murders: "Who crumbled / Little bits of bone marrow / Into a river of blood?" (Ver hot tsebreklt / pitslekh tserisenem markh / oyfn blutikn taykhl?).[32] The United States, for the immigrant Yiddish poet, is marked by the blood of its nonwhite martyrs. However, it is difficult to disentangle Ludvig's and Yehoash's outrage at American race violence from their own fascination with the black body. Although racial exoticism is present in the Party-aligned poets too, in the 1930s, we see a transition in Yiddish poetry from portraying the desecrated black body as spectacle toward identifying African Americans more consistently with Jews.

Malka Lee, in a gesture similar to Ludvig's, titled a 1933 poem "Niger in sobvey" (Nigger in the subway) when it first appeared in the communist *Frayhayt,* a choice that highlights the racism projected on the African American protagonist by the people around him and echoes the reclamation of the term in contemporaneous African American poetry. (She changed the title to the neutral "Der Neger in sobvey" [Negro in the subway] when she included the poem in her 1940 collection.) The poem describes an encounter on a New York subway train, with a man speaking to a car full of strangers about his lynched brother in the South. Lee, unlike most of her modernist predecessors, gives the African American protagonist a voice: "Oh Lord, give the killers your retribution. My brother's body's swinging from a pine" (O Lord, di merder gib zey dayn shrof! / Oyf a sosne vigt zikh mayn bruder's guf).[33] The kinship between the protagonist and his murdered "brother" recalls Uri Tsvi Grinberg's use of the term "brother" in "Uri Tsvi farn tseylem": "I have slaughtered brothers. I have brothers in the Red Army gang. And I have brothers younger than them, who plant eucalyptus trees in the swamps of Hadera. Malaria eats them, the wailing of jackals."[34] In Neta Stahl's reading of this poem, a brotherhood with Jesus cannot compare to the more compelling brotherhood with other Jews. Malka Lee, evoking the New York black man's kinship to a lynch victim, highlights the coexistence of multiple group identities in the United States. "Neger in sobvey" is arguably a response to Aaron Glantz-Leyeles's 1926 poem "In sobvey" (In the subway), which describes a black man squeezing against a white woman on a crowded subway. Ever a threat in this close encounter between strangers is the "noose of the gallows" (shleyf fun tliye).[35] Rather than simply describing the African American Other as Glantz-Leyeles does, Lee dramatizes the relationship between black and white New Yorkers in this subway performance: "Back and forth the Negro starts to pace. The other passengers wear their disgrace" (Ahin un tsurik der Neger er shpant / ver es fort mit, trogt di shand). The suffering of their African American neighbors, Lee asserts here, should make white Americans uncomfortable. Lee, despite her status as a Jewish immigrant to New York, recognizes her relative privilege vis-à-vis the African American subject. The poem ends with a challenge to her Yiddish readers: "He sees the murderer's face in every white" (in yedn vaysn zet er dem merders bild).[36] Y. E. Rontsh described Lee's poetry about the United States as written "with love and with pain." In her 1932 volume, "she sees the Chinese laundryman as a foreigner in this country; in his eyes blossom pure fields. She suffers over 'God's Black Lamb'—the lynched Negro. And the unemployed are 'young, healthy as giant oak trees, brooms in hand, lips pursed.'"[37] Lee's New York was a cross-section of workers across ethnicities, and her Yiddish poetry was a forum for making her readers uncomfortable with the realities of US racism.

In "Gots shvartser lam," Lee's landscape of martyrdom extends to the trees themselves. Recall that, as the protagonist, Tom, is being led to the lynch scene, "The woods bowed low as if cut by a knife," and, moreover, the mourning mother finds the one tree that "is bleeding to its roots."[38] The lynch tree that appears throughout Lee's American race poems is a southern crucifix, an unwilling accomplice to tragedy, and a cousin to the cornstalks that are replaced by crosses in her "Zangen un tslomim." Lee's attention to the tree as a living, vulnerable centerpiece in her southern crucifixion poems unites the modernist motifs of the cross and the lynching to adopt the lynch tree as a poetic password that is both closely tied to the crucifixion and unmistakably American.

The poems about lynchings that appeared during the Scottsboro trial present an emotional intimacy between the victim and the reader. In some cases, poets explicitly describe intimacy between blacks and Jews. Menke Katz presents the black-Jewish relationship as a tragic love story in "Di lintshndike kro" (The lynching crow), which Katz published in his 1935 collection on proletarian themes *Der mentsh in togn* (The dawning man). Katz tells the story of a Jewish woman, Tilly, and her African American lover, John. As in Lee's poem, Katz's African American protagonist is akin to the trees surrounding and obscuring him:

Zol gole sheynkayt far undz reydn:	May naked beauty speak for us:
Dayn yikhes zaynen kukuruze-felder un shtoltse kiparisn,	Your pedigree is cornfields and proud cypress trees,
iz vos az du bist tunkl vi uralt fun velder,	so what if you're as dark as primeval forests,
s'hot Got undz fun eyn mentshn-shtam gerisn.[39]	God plucked us from one human trunk.

Katz's poem is redolent of the "Song of Songs." However, the forested metaphors presage the couple's tragic fate. As Tilly's belly swells with their child, the couple foresees the familiar story about to unfold: "John, my John!/Lynchers lurk at your life!" (Dzhon, mayn Dzhon!/Lintshers loyern af dayn lebn!). As a lynch mob, led by Tilly's boss, searches the town for John, "Night hangs on every tree like a crucified Negro" (Oyf yedn boym hengt nakht vi a gekreytster Neger). John is lynched, and Tilly moves to New York, where "A crushed barrel sits *shiva* for him."[40]

The lynch tree here, as in Lee's "Gots shvartser lam," is part of an American wilderness wounded by race violence.[41] These wounds, which mark the United States, are passwords, connecting Jews' past trauma with the African American trauma they were now witnessing. The lynch tree, as an extension of the murdered body, is the centerpiece in a well-known English-language indictment of racism, Abel Meeropol's 1937 "Strange Fruit": "Southern trees bear a strange fruit/Blood on the leaves and blood at the root."[42] Meeropol, a first-generation American and child of eastern European Jewish immigrants, was a member of the Communist Party. In his poem, Meeropol employs passwords familiar from the language of political activism around Scottsboro.[43] Meeropol's words, which are today inextricable from Billie Holiday's 1939 recording, make the wounds of race violence in the United States speak. The Yiddish lynching poems of the 1930s reveal the magnitude of the conversation among Jewish immigrants about ethnic violence in the United States.

CHRIST IN ALABAMA

Black modernists, like their Jewish colleagues, used the cross to describe race violence before Scottsboro. Black crucifixions presented a Christian American mainstream with similar irony to the Christological Yiddish pogrom poems of Uri Tsvi Grinberg or paintings of Marc Chagall. "Look you on yonder crucifix," writes Frank Horne in his 1925 "On Seeing Two Brown Boys in a Catholic Church," "Where He hangs nailed and pierced." Whereas the Yiddish poets who portrayed the cross in pogrom poems were flirting with apostasy, Horne opens his poem by commending his personae: "It is fitting you should be here." And yet, like Grinberg's Jewish Jesus, Horne's brown boys are very much in the wrong place: "Look you well, / You shall know this thing."[44]

During the Scottsboro trial, African American poets were increasingly critical of Christian hypocrisy, particularly those poets closely aligned with the Party. Langston Hughes's Scottsboro crosses bear martyrs who are the illegitimate offspring of a racist society. In his 1931 "Christ in Alabama," Hughes mobilizes racist language to expose the Christian hypocrisy in the US South:

> Most holy bastard
> Of the bleeding mouth:
> *Nigger Christ*
> *On the cross of the South.*[45]

Hughes's "bastard" Christ is the child of a black woman and the "White Master above." The racist epithet that describes him is, as Cary Nelson convincingly argues, evidence of "the spiritual power of black

Fig 3.1   Prentiss Taylor, cover image for Langston Hughes, *Scottsboro Limited: Four poems and a Play in Verse*, 1932. *Credit:* Archives of American Art, Smithsonian Institution

suffering. . . . 'Nigger' is always 'Nigger Christ,' whether or not the sacred name is spoken, or so the poem insists in its fourth and final stanza."[46] Hughes, in this poem, alters a racist dog whistle, reclaiming it as a password that is a call to action against racial inequality.

Hughes republished "Christ in Alabama" together with his play *Scottsboro Limited* and three other poems in a 1932 chapbook, *Scottsboro Limited,* which was sold to benefit the Scottsboro defense (figure 3.1). The cover illustration for *Scottsboro Limited,* by Prentiss Taylor, featured the nine Scottsboro defendants against the backdrop of a cruciform telephone pole. Also included in the chapbook was Hughes's 1931 "Scottsboro," in which Christ leads a march of revolutionaries to the Scottsboro Boys' jail cell.

> Who comes?
> Christ,
> Who fought alone.[47]

Christ is followed by John Brown, Nat Turner, Lenin, Gandhi, and other revolutionary leaders. The procession is an international one. Michael Thurston has observed that "in all five of the pamphlet's texts, but especially in the play, 'Scottsboro Limited,' and in the short poem, 'Scottsboro,' Hughes explicitly makes the defendants representatives of and grounds for an interracial politics."[48] Like his Jewish counterparts, during the Scottsboro trial, Hughes was generating internationalist passwords that could translocate trauma between ethnic communities.

Frank Marshall Davis uses the same marked language Hughes does to reclaim Christ in his 1937 "Christ Is a Dixie Nigger": "My Christ is a black bastard. . . . They all knew Christ's father was Mr. Jim who owns the big plantation."[49] Stacy Morgan reads Davis's personalization of Christ as a leftist password: "Adopting a mode of irreverent direct address that was in keeping with a prevalent leftist antagonism toward organized religion during the 1930s, Davis insists, 'I've got a better Christ and a bigger Christ . . . one you can put your hands on today or tomorrow.'"[50] Because of the Communist Party's role in the defense, the broader public suspected all Scottsboro activists of Party affiliation, further alienating them from mainstream white America. Davis describes this alienation further in the poem:

> They called him a Communist and a menace to the Existing Relationship
>   Between Black and White in the South
> Sheriff and judge debated whether to open the hoosegow and tell
>   reporters the mob stormed the jail or let the state lynch him on the
>   gallows.[51]

The Party's involvement in the trial complicated the widespread association of Jews as well as African Americans with communism in the United States. That a Jewish lawyer, Samuel Leibowitz, defended the Scottsboro boys deepened the relationship. Moreover, as the trial proceeded in the United States, the Nazi Party came to power in 1933, and the Spanish Civil War broke out in 1936, with the Italian and German fascists supporting the Francoist rebels against the democratically elected Spanish Republic. According to Glenda Gilmore, "as non-Communist

African Americans marshaled to fight Fascism, Communists drove home its similarities to the Scottsboro injustice."[52]

Yiddish- and English-language poets alike were increasingly aware of the similarity between Nazi anti-Jewish legislation and the Alabama court system, which could be seen as institutionalizing a culture of pogroms and lynchings, respectively. By the late 1930s, the Scottsboro Boys faced the very real prospect of legal lynchings. Clarence Norris, who was nineteen at his arrest, making him the oldest of the Scottsboro Boys, was convicted and sentenced to death by electric chair on August 19, 1938. The sentence was commuted in July.[53] Langston Hughes, in his "August 19th . . . : A Poem for Clarence Norris," exposes the parity between the lynch mobs that threatened the Scottsboro defendants and the court that would condemn them. "For if you let the 'law' kill me, / Are you free?"[54] Another important figure in the Scottsboro case was Angelo Herndon, who was arrested in 1932 and subsequently imprisoned for organizing a mixed-race rally on behalf of the Scottsboro Boys. Langston Hughes's 1935 play *Angelo Herndon Jones* presents Herndon as a figure who can unite black and white Americans in their struggle against inequality. Hughes's Herndon declares at one point, "I am the working class. Black and white unite to fight!"[55]

The young Yiddish proletarian poet Yuri Suhl (M. A. Suhl, 1908–1986) pays homage to the Scottsboro Boys and Herndon in two poems, published side by side in his 1935 collection, *Dos likht af mayn gas* (The light on my street): "Geblibn volt shoyn haynt fun zey . . ." (What would remain of them today . . .) and "Andzhelo Hoyrndon krigt di post" (Angelo Herndon gets the mail). "What would remain of them today . . ." opens with a description of the lynch trees awaiting the young men:

Geblibn volt shoyn haynt fun zey	What would remain of them today
nayn beymer opgesmalyete,	nine singed trees,
a nit-derbrente petlye oyf a tsvayg.	a partly-burnt noose on a branch.
A shtik farglivert blut in kore-karbn	A bit of dried blood on the notched bark
un ergets vu oyf dr'erd	and somewhere on the ground
a farroykherter beyn,	a smoldering bone,
a farkoylter sharbn.[56]	a charred skull.

The gruesome depiction of the lynch tree that remains an ever-present threat is punctuated by an English-language call to action on their behalf. The poem ends:

Hot gezogt di komunistishe partay,	So says the Communist Party,
hot gezogt di Ay. El. Di.:	so says the ILD:
The Scottsboro Boys Shall Not Die!	*The Scottsboro Boys Shall Not Die!*
Angelo Herndon Must Be Free![57]	*Angelo Herndon Must Be Free!*

By rhyming "ILD" and "free," Suhl bridges the Yiddish and English, modeling the kind of inter-ethnic integration he envisioned in the struggle for the Scottsboro Boys. Suhl creates another cross-linguistic rhyme between "Party," which, pronounced "partay" in his Galician dialect, rhymes with "die." These inter-lingual rhymes reappear in "Andzhelo Hoyrndon krigt di post" (Angelo Herndon gets the mail), which describes, over several pages, the activist waiting anxiously for his daily newspaper delivery. When it arrives, "Angelo swallows every word":

Un ot—	And here—
A ruf af ershter zayt,	A call on the first page,
es ruft di kompartay,	a call from the Communist Party,
es ruft di Ay. El. Di.:	a call from the ILD:
The Scottsboro Boys Shall Not Die!	*The Scottsboro Boys Shall Not Die!*
Angelo Herndon Must Be Free![58]	*Angelo Herndon Must Be Free!*

Suhl, by ending both Scottsboro poems with the rallying cries, in English, that had become unifying passwords throughout the course of the trial, aligns Yiddish- and English-speaking communists in their struggle for justice. Suhl's Herndon is aware of the ever-present threat of a "legal lynching." As he waits, a neighbor cries out from a death cell, where "the priest now gives him / the last spoonful of paradise" (der galekh git im itst / dos letste lefele ganeydn ayn).[59]

Whereas the Yiddish poems about China and Palestine draw almost exclusively from Jewish and other European models, the Scottsboro poems reveal the clear influence of black poets and of journalism surrounding the case. The Party sent several of the Scottsboro defendants' mothers on a speaking tour of the United States in 1931. The following year, Ada Wright (the mother of two of the defendants, Andrew and Roy Wright) made appearances across Europe with the ILD's national secretary, J. Louis Engdahl.[60] Open letters by the Scottsboro mothers were published in left-wing papers in the United States and abroad. As Kwando Kinshasa has observed of these letters, "As they found increased access to the public through media savvy political organizations they also became sophisticated in their attempts to reach the hearts and minds of thousands of curious and outright sympathetic readers and listeners."[61] These letters made their way into poetry across languages. Betsalel Fridman, in his 1931 poem "Skotsboro" (Scottsboro), evokes the defendants' correspondence with their mothers, suggesting that salvation would come in the form of the Party:

Geleyent dayn briv, Mame Powell,	We've read your letter, Mama Powell,
geshribn mit fleyts fun dayn blut.	Written with your gushing blood.
shtark zikh, fartsveyflte mame,	Keep strong, desperate mother,
yeder khaver far Skotsboro tut.[62]	Every comrade works for Scottsboro's good.

Leftist Yiddish writers would have been aware not only of the letters published broadly in the left-wing press but also of the black culture magazine *Opportunity,* the American proletarian journal *New Masses* (edited by Mike Gold), and the literary magazine *Contempo.*[63] Y. E. Rontsh, who wrote extensively on African American culture, appears to borrow directly from Richard Wright in his 1936 poem "Skotsboro" (Scottsboro), which begins,

Ikh hob gezen di shvartse mase kniyen	I've seen black masses on their knees,
in ekstaz far yezusn dem reter;	Ecstatic for Jesus the savior,
un oygn glotsike nit oyfgehert tsu gliyen,	And glowing eyes' eternal gaze,
un hent mazoliste geshtrekt zikh un gebetn.[64]	And calloused hands stretched out in prayer.

The poem traces the development of black workers' political awareness, from exploitation to revolution. Rontsh ends his poem with his black subjects rejecting religion and standing up to fight. What matters is

"Not Jesus-Lord, not spirituals, not genuflection" (Nit Yezus-lord, nit 'spiritshuels', nit koyrim faln) but only Scottsboro and the "fight against the enemies" (kamf mit sonim).[65] Rontsh published his poem two years after Richard Wright's "I Have Seen Black Hands" appeared in the *New Masses* in 1934.[66] Both poems juxtapose black bodies moving from work toward rebellion. Wright, who begins by stating his own racial identity, focuses on material need:

> I am black and I have seen black hands, millions and millions
>   of them—
> Reaching hesitantly out of days of slow death for the goods they
>   had made, but the bosses warned that the goods were private and
>   did not belong to them [. . .][67]

Wright's conclusion evokes the possibility of solidarity across cultures:

> I am black and I have seen black hands
> Raised in fists of revolt side by side
> With the fists of white workers [. . .][68]

Wright recalls writing his poem after his first visit to a John Reed Club, "coining images of black hands playing, working, holding bayonets, stiffening finally in death."[69]

Rontsh's "In Alabama" (first published in the *Frayhayt* under the title "A gut dzhab gemakht" [Done a good job]) casts the church as a civic space where the white lynch mob plans to gather the following day. "In Alabama," like "Skotsboro," presents a church haunted by hypocrisy. This is especially evident in the final stanza of "In Alabama":

S'shpet. Di flamen tsukn shoyn.	It's late. The flames are dying down.
—A gute nakht, mir trefn zikh in kirkh.	"Good night, we'll meet again in church."
—Ikh koyf zikh morgn a por shikh.	"Tomorrow I'm going to buy new shoes."
—Loz grisn ale heymishe.[70]	"My regards to the family."

Rontsh's depiction of a white lynch mob gathering souvenirs takes the commodification of the black body—a historical working body in the United States—to its most horrific conclusion.

Rontsh explicitly connects lynchings to revolution in "Neger-arbeter" (Negro-worker), the opening poem in his 1935 cycle "Shvarts un royt" (Black and red), which also includes "Scottsboro," "In Alabama," and "Bluegrass"—a poem dedicated to Angelo Herndon:

Es groyt nokh fun a lintsheray der roykh,	It's still gray from the lynch smoke,
Es kortshet zikh in angstn guf;—	A body writhes in agony;—
Dokh iz zayn vays gelekhter mutik-hoykh,	Yet his white laughter is bold and loud,
Un hekher nokh—tsum kamf der ruf.[71]	And louder yet—the call to struggle.

In his essay on African Americans in Yiddish poetry, Rontsh suggests, "It was natural that the attention of the socially inclined poets [sotsial-geshtimte dikhter] should have been directed toward the situation of the Negro."[72] This was, according to Rontsh, especially true for the writers belonging to, or under the influence of, the Proletpen group (to which Rontsh belonged)—a group that formed in the wake of the Palestine disturbances.

The Party's sponsorship of the Scottsboro Boys' defense compelled writers and readers to view the case not merely as an example of US racism but in connection to a broader project of an international workers' revolution. The Party's role in the Scottsboro case, it must be acknowledged, complicated the trial for the defendants, opening everyone involved to scrutiny for their (real or perceived) affiliation with communism. The Yiddish Party-aligned poets, however, by writing extensively about race violence during the Scottsboro trial, were normalizing the African American subject as part of an expanded Jewish poetics of collective suffering. This expansion can be seen in poetry by writers who had no Party affiliation whatsoever.

FROM REYSHE TO CAROLINA

Rontsh was no doubt correct when he argued that the Proletpen writers had the firmest grasp on the Scottsboro motif, for the trial was at the center of the Party's activity in the United States. However, noncommunist writers who began describing lynchings in the 1930s reveal the extent to which the translocation of Jewish trauma was becoming mainstream. Berish Weinstein (1905–1967) is best known for his 1947 book *Reyshe: Poema* (Rzeszow: A poem), a eulogy for his home shtetl in Galicia between Lviv and Krakow. The book won the Moyshe Leyb Halpern Prize. Much of his earlier verse, too, focuses on violence wrought on Europe's Jewish communities. A poet whose work could move seamlessly between the romantic pastoral landscape and unbearable violence, Weinstein was politically unaffiliated, but deeply committed to describing the horrors of violence. He had written about pogroms, slaughterhouses, and lynchings since the early 1930s. Weinstein published "A Neger shtarbt" (A Negro dies) in 1938 in the journal *Yidishe Kultur.* The poem begins with linguistic connections between the African American subject of the poem and Jewish cultural signposts:

A Neger in mitn feld blutikt untern heln meser;	A Negro, in the middle of the field, bleeds beneath a bright blade.
shtarbt in a tamuz-tog fun a heysn khalef.	dies, one Tammuz day, of a hot slaughtering knife.
In der sharf shpizn-oyf ale grozn, ale tsvaygn.[73]	Every blade of grass, every branch glints spear-like off the sharp metal.

"Tammuz," a month in the lunar calendar falling between June and July, is a password that admits the African American personae into Jewish time. Tammuz is, moreover, the month leading up to the ninth of Av (Tisha B'Av), a day of mourning commemorating the destruction of the Temple. On Tisha B'Av, lamentations (*kinot,* singular *kina*) are recited that recall significant Jewish tragedies throughout history, from the Crusades to the murder of Jews in the 1648 Cossack uprising. Weinstein's reference to Tammuz suggests that his poem be read as a Jewish lamentation and that the lynching be placed into the history of tragedies mourned within the Jewish community. Marc Caplan has suggested that Yiddish depictions of racism presented unique linguistic challenges because of the specificity of the language to the Jewish context: "Does the perspective of the description assume that [African Americans] are identical to Jews, or inversely Other?"[74] Weinstein's attempt to align the two groups poetically, rather than politically, demonstrates the malleability of Yiddish poetic passwords in the 1930s.

Weinstein's poem may be a *kina*—a Jewish lamentation—but his black protagonist dies on a cross:

Di shkiye fartsert dem tog mit shar-lekhn brand.	The sunset devours the day in scarlet blazes.
Feygl nidern farnakhtik tsum Neger nokh fartsikung arop.	Birds swoop low with the evening for leftover meat.
Di Negerishe mame mit a zhmenye groz redt tsum mes;	The Negro mother, her hand full of grass, is talking to the dead man,
visht dos blut fun zayn moyl, fun zayn haldz.	Wiping the blood from his mouth and from his neck.
Ale ire finger klamern zikh inem toytns hor	All her fingers cling tight to the corpse's hair,
mitsushtarbn afn krayts fun a Neger.[75]	to die along with him on a Negro cross.

Weinstein's christological lamentation is capacious enough to incorporate Jewish and Christian mourning. The tragedy of a senseless killing, moreover, saturates the serene southern setting. As in Malka Lee's poetry, Weinstein's deceptively idyllic landscape is saturated with death, from the blazing sunset to the ravenous birds to the grass, which the victim's mother has rent in her anguish. Weinstein's closing image, as in Lee's "Gots shvartser lam," is a pietà scene: a black mother cradles her son in her arms.

The poem's final, haunting tableaux is preceded by a disturbing series of images that alternate between human emotion and animal sacrifice:

Di tsung tsvishn zayne breyte lipn farhakt,	Tongue, clamped between broad lips,
makht vilder oyszen dos tsegosene shvartse mis.[76]	Makes the drained black corpse look stranger still.

The black body is compared to a calf, and the prominently displayed body parts create a spectacle of a racialized Other. Merle Bachman has quite accurately compared Weinstein's poems to Yehoash's 1919 "Lintshen": "The details are stereotypical: tar face, shiny teeth, thick lips."[77] However, Weinstein's African American poems become more complex when read in the context of his broader oeuvre, in which violence, animal slaughter, and the crucifixion are strategically juxtaposed.

"A Neger shtarbt" appeared two years after the publication of Weinstein's 1936 book *Brukhvarg* (Broken pieces). The book is divided into cycles, which treat immigration, pogroms in Europe, African Americans, and scenes from an animal slaughterhouse. In all of the sections of *Brukhvarg,* the "broken pieces" of community tragedies appear in unsettling detail. "Henkers" (Executioners), dated "Germany, 1933," is part of Weinstein's cycle about pogrom violence titled "Tslomim" (Crosses). The poem commemorates the 1927 massacre of communists—many of them Jews—that took place under the Nazi official Joseph Goebbels in the Wedding district of Berlin.[78] Weinstein describes the branding and unclothing of bodies in prison cells. As at the end of "A Neger shtarbt," the wounded victims' bodies are compared to meat: "Wounds drain and congeal to raw meat" (Vundn klepn un rinen oys in vild fleysh).[79] The slaughtered human, whether a German Jewish communist or an African American, is reduced to flesh, drained of blood as in the process of preparing kosher meat.

Reading the poems together, it would appear that, with "A Neger shtarbt," Weinstein was rewriting his earlier poem, replacing victims in Germany with an African American one. "Henkers," like "A Neger shtarbt," begins with an image of bloody slaughter:

Di hak kilt un blutikt, di hak roysht un trift.
Oyf der sharf shpaltn zikh heldzer un shpringen op.
Fun varemen shnit farloyft der blend mit pare,
s'blut tsit op shnel un heys fun kiln shtol.[80]

The axe cools and bleeds, the axe gushes and drips.
Necks split open and spring from the blade.
The steamy gleam anticipates the warm gash,
The blood drains fast and hot from the cool steel.

The cool, bleeding axe in the pogrom poem becomes, in the later piece, a "bright knife" (heln meser). In both, the blade is a disaggregated agent of death. In "Henkers," necks split on a blade, and in "A Neger shtarbt," the victim dies "of a hot slaughtering knife" (fun a heysn khalef).

Weinstein's blades are simultaneously agents of a gruesome massacre and attractive objects, distracting the reader's attention by reflecting the incongruous beauty of the landscape. Moishe Nadir, who commends Weinstein for his wordplay, criticizes him for beautifying his scenes of violence: "Earth-trembling in ruby flames, a pogrom beneath rosy-blueness, a lynching under amber-and-rose,—what could be more beautiful?" Weinstein's aestheticization of death may be, as Nadir claims, "a colorful film image" (a kolirt film-bild).[81] However, the terrifyingly vivid raw human bodies in Weinstein's pogrom and lynching poems also serve to liken the Jewish and African American figures. As "A Neger shtarbt" portrays the teeth and lips of the murdered man, "Henkers" also reveals the victim's grotesque transformation:

In zamd lesht zikh s'roy-fleysh fun opgehaktn kop.
Tseyn klamern di lipn un lebedik shlogn nokh di shleyfn.
Durkh ibergedektn tukh otemt nokh der guf.[82]

The open wound of a decapitated head is extinguished in the sand;
Teeth clench the lips; the still living temples throb.
Through its covering cloth, the body continues to breathe.

Weinstein objectifies not only the African American body. The murderers, in Weinstein's "Henkers," have separated what was human from the Jewish body, turning fingers, feet, and lips into inanimate objects. Here, as in Weinstein's poems about race violence in the United States, the animal metaphors he applies to the human corpse defamiliarizes the violent act that has taken place. These references to meat conjure the image of a perpetual ritual slaughter.[83]

Weinstein presents both poems against the backdrop of the cross. "Henkers" appears in a cycle titled "Tslomim" (Crosses) between poems titled "Nones" (Nuns) and "Apostoln" (Apostles), suggesting an ironic resemblance between the three professions and linking the murder at the center of the poem to the martyrdom of Christ. Both "Henkers" and "A Neger shtarbt" end, like Malka Lee's "Gots shvartser lam," with crying women. In "Henkers," a Jewish girl cries out:

Henkers shayern op di flekn, farrikhtn zikh
laytish dem kneytsh fun kleyd.

Executioners scrub off the spots and neatly
adjust their clothes.

| Durkh tsugenoglte tirn shrayt di nakht fun | Through the nailed-shut doors the Wedding |
| Veding mit a yidisher tokhter.[84] | night shrieks with a Jewish girl. |

Weinstein's Yiddish-speaking American readers would have been aware of the Nazi-led massacres in Wedding. These readers would also have caught the bilingual double entendre of the "Wedding night" (nakht fun Veding): the girl, who may or may not be the betrothed of one of the victims, is figured as a violated bride. The similarity of the images in "Henkers" and "A Neger shtarbt" suggests that Weinstein translocated a poem centered on anti-Jewish and anticommunist violence to describe his adopted homeland, where African Americans, rather than Jews, were the victims of frequent ethnic violence.

Weinstein, using overlapping passwords to describe Jewish and black martyrs and mourners, was allowing his eastern European past to alter his understanding of the United States. But he also appears to have used his observations of American race violence to make sense of the rising antisemitism in Europe. Weinstein, with his poems "Henkers" and "Haknkreyts" (Swastika), was among the first American Yiddish poets to describe the Nazi atrocities. At that point, Hitler, whose early victims were Communist Party members or supporters, was decried primarily by political poets. Although the literary *Tsukunft* and communist *Frayhayt* published articles and poems about Hitler in the early 1930s, the populist *Der Tog* rejected Weinstein's "Haknkreyts" in 1933, suggesting he approach a literary journal instead. (By the 1940s *Der Tog* readily published Weinstein's poems.)[85]

Throughout Weinstein's 1936 volume *Brukhvarg*, he deploys his frequently-used passwords for slaughter: *shkiye* (sunset), *vundn* (wounds), *halef* (slaughtering knife), *sharf* (sharp), and *shkhite* (ritual slaughter). In his 1933 "Haknkreyts," Weinstein's ubiquitous shining blade transforms humans into meat:

Oyf di finger trogt emitser dem gringn blend fun meser,	Someone carries the lightweight flash of a knife,
un shtilt di sharf on haldz fun mentsh.	sating the blade with a human neck.
Unter zayne negl sheyln zikh vundn	Wounds open under his fingernails
un unter zayn tsung shtarbn heldzer.[86]	and necks die under his tongue.

"Yidn" (Jews), a poem from the same cycle, begins with a description of a Sabbath that will soon be desecrated by a pogrom:

Shtotishe beymer hobn yung getsitert mit frishe bleter	City trees trembled, young with fresh leaves
un vi alemeol shabes, hot oyf der erd getrift s'likht fun der zun,[87]	and as always on the Sabbath, the sunlight drips onto the earth,

The scene jarringly transforms from life to death: "Gentiles have ruined this day with stones and sticks" (Goyim hobn kalye gemakht aza tog mit shteyner un mit shtekns).[88] Weinstein would mirror the pastoral setting with his grassy summer day in "A Neger shtarbt." Moreover, in "Idn," as at the end of "A Neger shtarbt," crosses signify cruelty rather than salvation. A procession of "seven priests in robes with silver crosses" (zibn galokhim in kitlen mit zilberne tslomim) carries a bronze Jesus through the streets. "And in those silver crosses Jews suffer in their last confessions to God" (un in di zilberne tslomim paynikn zikh Yidn mit vide tsu Got).[89] As in Grinberg's 1922 "Uri Tzvi farn tseylem," Jesus is powerless to save the doomed Jews, who are reflected, as they await the procession of Christians, in the priests' crosses.

Weinstein makes explicit his translocation of the Jewish cross to the African American cross in his 1936 "Lintshing" (Lynching). This poem opens with an image now familiar from the English- and Yiddish-language Scottsboro crosses: a lynch mob is enacting a southern crucifixion:

S'fartsikn dikh vayse vilde hent mit a gefunenem shtrik,	White wild hands snare you with a stray rope,
un es kreytsigt a yuli-boym dayn Negerishn haldz;	And a July tree crucifies your Negro neck,
in dayn shverer rayfkayt, in zayn fuler bliung.[90]	In your heavy ripeness, in its full bloom.

Weinstein writes this poem, we must note, in the second person, addressing a victim of lynching. God, the Christian interlocutor is told, will not respond. As in "Yidn," Jesus is a symbol of violence, not of mercy, and has become the mirror image of the lynched man:

Got, far vemen s'hot getrert dayn
  zingendik gebet azoy troyerik,
ken zikh far dir atsind nisht vayzn,
  s'shparn im di fis, di tsugenoglte hent,
er ken afilu nisht zayns an oyg efenen
  mit a trer nokh dir;
onnemen s'letste vort dayns far a
  vide—r'iz aleyn gekreytsikt.[91]

God, before whom your singing
  prayer wept so mournfully,
won't appear before you now, his
  feet split, his hands nailed,
he cannot even open an eye with a
  tear for you
Or accept your last word as a
  confession—He himself is
  crucified.

Weinstein uses the same term for the last Christian confession, *vide* (He-brew: *viduy*), that he uses in "Idn" to describe the final act of the shtetl Jews as they await the terror of the church procession. The *vide*—a con-fessional prayer—is most commonly associated with Yom Kippur. A dif-ferent confession, the deathbed *viduy*, is a final prayer recited at the perceived approach of death and ends with the Shema. However, the *vide* that Weinstein's Jews say appears to be a confession before an execution, which, according to the Mishnah, would ensure "a portion in the world to come," regardless of the person's sins.[92] In both poems, the Hebrew term is used, and Jesus appears as a symbol of the violence wrought by a Christian majority. The lynching victim, whose final *vide* cannot be heard by his crucified God, is directed toward a community that in-cludes Jews, African Americans, and communists. The poem ends with an explicit connection between lynching and the rise of Nazism:

Neger, nit oyf dir bloyz iz gefaln der goyrl
  fun farlendung.
A sakh, a sakh, shtarbn azoy vi du. Aza
  toyt iz itst a mode aza,
azoy nokh shtarbn—shtarbt men haynt
  umetum—
in Veding, in der Leopold-shtot un in
  Karolayna.[93]

Negro, the fate of destruction
  has befallen not only you.
Many, many die like you. Such a
  death is now in fashion,
and so, still dying—they now die
  everywhere—
in Wedding, in Leopoldstadt and
  in Carolina.

Weinstein does not explicitly advocate the kind of world workers' revo-lution that we find in Rontsh's "Skotsboro" or in Langston Hughes's *Scottsboro Limited.* The passwords he uses to conflate lynchings and pogroms are not Party shibboleths per se. Nonetheless, Weinstein's poetry of the 1930s is an indisputable example of the interethnic poetics of the age of internationalism, and as such, it is a poetry of the shared passwords of struggle against inequality.

That Weinstein was part of an internationalist zeitgeist in his 1930s poems is more apparent in his subsequent move away from this kind of direct equation between oppressed groups. Weinstein would continue to write poems about African Americans through the 1940s, comparing, for instance, African Americans to the Jewish diaspora: "In the Harlem ghetto, in such Exile, / Even God becomes a Negro" (In Harlemer geto, in aza goles, / vert afilu fun Got a Neger).[94] However, after World War II, we find fewer explicit comparisons between anti-Jewish pogroms and American lynchings in Weinstein's poetry. In the version of "Lintshing" he included in his 1949 collected poems, Weinstein removed the last line of the poem, "in Wedding, in Leopoldstadt, and in Carolina." The 1949 edition of the poem ends with "Like this they now die everywhere—."[95] The truncated line reflects the changing times: after World War II, the death camps eclipsed the pre-WWII violence in the Wedding district of Berlin and the Leopoldstadt district of Vienna—events that had been anti-Leftist and antisemitic. However, by eliminating the direct analogy between race violence in the US South and antisemitic violence in Germany, Weinstein discarded a key signpost of Leftist internationalism in the 1930s: the simultaneous outcry against Nazi antisemitism and US racism. As I discuss in the final chapter of this book, the Holocaust turned American Jews' focus inward, toward the rebuilding of Jewish culture. The age of internationalism yielded to an age of renewed particularism.[96]

The Yiddish poets who described race in the aftermath of the Scottsboro trial were finding language to forge a uniquely American version of internationalism. As Steven Zipperstein has demonstrated, many American Jews on the Left viewed Russian antisemitic violence as a call to action against US racism. "Conflation of the sins of Kishinev with those of American lynching would surface as an item of paramount concern on the American Left, with pogroms and lynching increasingly viewed as evil twins."[97] Yiddish writers depicted African Americans as a working nation in its own right at the same time they were portraying themselves as Jewish members of an international working community.

BEYOND EITHER / OR

As Ta-Nehisi Coates has recently written, "slavery was but the initial crime in a long tradition of crimes, of plunder even, that could be traced into the present day."[98] The Yiddish poets who wrote about lynchings were drawing their readers' attention to a tradition of institutionalized crime in the United States. Moyshe Leyb Halpern wrote of white culpability in his "Salyut" (Salute), which he published in *Vokh* in January 1930, a year before the framing of the Scottsboro Boys. It is significant that Halpern chose *Vokh*—the venue that his friends and colleagues Leivick and Boreysho had founded after leaving the communist *Frayhayt* over the Palestine crisis—for a poem about culpability with respect to a racial minority. "Salyut" describes a lynch mob that is as patriotic and pious as it is bloodthirsty. All white Americans, including Jews, must take responsibility for the murder of young African Americans. Halpern includes in his indictment the poetic persona, who has done nothing to stop the lynching:

Un der himl iz bloy—im geyt on—	And the sky is blue—all the same to him—
un bam vint iz a simkhe mit der fon,	and the wind celebrates with the flag,
un ikh—a geshlogener hunt—nit a vort.	and I—a beaten dog—not a word.
Nit arayngeleygt gornisht—a shutef tsum mord.[99]	I did nothing—an accomplice to murder.

The guilt of the silent onlooker is magnified by the realization that the Jewish poet, who still suffers from the recent pogroms in eastern Europe ("a beaten dog"), occupies a new position of power. Ruth Wisse views this poem as a statement about the Yiddish poet's inability to intervene: "The loathsome scene of lynching that Halpern fashions is made up entirely of stereotypes, and it is this sense of 'saluting' his subjects that turns the poet against himself." Wisse suggests that "while others in *Voch* wrote as if their opinions mattered and took pride in the pacific nature of Yidishism, Halpern exposed its weakness—and his own."[100] Halpern's defeatism notwithstanding, by placing a poem about white racism in this splinter publication, he is nonetheless asserting his continued commitment to internationalism and his right to criticize his adopted homeland in the wake of his rejection of the Comintern's position on the Arab uprisings against Jews in Palestine.

The Scottsboro trial drew several of the Yiddish poets who had left the Party-aligned venues in 1929 back into the left-wing antifascist fold. As we will see in the next chapter, the Spanish Civil War inspired writers from across the Left to align themselves with the antifascist cause. Michael Denning has suggested that "the most effective part of Popular Front public culture was . . . the mobilization around civil liberties and the struggle against lynching and labor repression."[101] The unrest in Palestine discussed in Chapter 2 divided leftist Yiddish poets into those who viewed Jews in Palestine as the perpetrators of an unjust power structure and those who identified them as victims of continued antisemitism on an international scale. In the United States, unlike in Palestine, identifying with a suffering marginalized people did not necessarily mean identifying Jews as oppressors. The race theme in the United States, and the ILD's role in the Scottsboro defense, helped to bring writers from across the political Left together around a common cause. Many of the 1929 *Frayhayt* "runaways" joined the Popular Front, a left-wing artistic coalition that began to emerge in the United States following the stock-market crash of 1929 and became widespread during the European elections in the mid-1930s. This included H. Leivick, who occasionally published in the *Frayhayt* in the mid-1930s.

The Yiddish poets who described racism in the United States still faced antisemitism and economic depression in their adopted country. Nonetheless, the recent memory of pogroms, the reality of lynchings, and their relative safety as white Americans led Jews to reassess their relationship to the privileged majority. Leivick acknowledged this as early as 1922 in his poem "Negershes." Leivick resists the temptation to assume understanding of the black condition in the United States:

Ikh veys, Negers, kh'vel gornish endern in aykh,	I know, Negroes, I won't change places with you,
nisht fun dernoent un nisht fun dervaytn;	not from close up and not from far away;
Mir veln nisht vern eyns, nisht vern glaykh,	we won't become one, we won't become equal,
Un undzere hoytn veln zikh nisht baytn.[102]	And we won't trade skins.

Leivick goes on to draw the very comparison he has just resisted, turning a statement of cautious political solidarity toward self-reflection about the role of the Jew in white America.

Dukht zikh,—Vos?—ikh bin an ibergepeynikter aleyn,	I suppose—What?—I am a solitary sufferer,
an oyfgehangener, vi ir, oyf shtrik fun rase;	a hung man, like you, on a race-rope;
mayn oyszen iz far aykh nit veyniker gemeyn,	to you my looks are no less vile,
vi dos oyszen fun a yedn fun a lintsher-mase.[103]	than the looks of anyone from the lynch mob.

Leivick included "Negershes" in a cycle of poems on African American themes in his 1932 book *Naye lider*. Publishing his cycle in the racially divided 1930s, Leivick contemplates his own responsibility to an African American community. Whereas Halpern accepts responsibility for his failure to intervene, Leivick insists on an unbridgeable divide. In his 1927 poema "A briv fun Amerike tsu a vaytn fraynt" (A letter from America to a distant friend), the poet admits to the feeling before blacks: "that my every act / stabs them to blood, hurts them" (az mayn yede banemung / shtekht zey durkh biz blut, tut zey vey).[104] Leivick, who asserts that neither he nor his father nor his grandfather has committed a crime before African Americans, rejects personal guilt in US racism, differentiating between the Jewish immigrant and other white Americans. He recognizes his relative privilege, but stops short of assuming responsibility, of identifying as what Bruce Robbins calls a "beneficiary" of an unjust system.[105] Rontsh observes, of Leivick's unsettled relationship to his African American subject, "he feels a kinship to him but at the same time a deep abyss divides them."[106] Nevertheless, by pointedly choosing not to identify with the victims of lynchings, Leivick demands consideration of different peoples with different histories. Leivick registers a subtle critique of the simple equation of Jewish and non-Jewish suffering.

How should a Jewish poet speak out against racist violence in the United States? Michael Rothberg responds, in *The Implicated Subject*, to what Hannah Arendt called the "vicarious responsibility for things we have not done" by proposing a view of memory and trauma that resists "the either / or logic of the zero-sum game."[107] American leftist Yiddish poets in the 1930s found themselves between a privileged majority and threatened minority. In their poems about lynchings, they developed a language to describe this liminal place, to simultaneously address the terrifying, mounting antisemitism in Europe and the horrific American analogue to fascism. If they were not yet able to fully move beyond a zero-sum game, these poets were using the Jewish passwords and modernist imagery that had explained European pogrom culture to enter and navigate US racism. In the process, they demanded that their readers recognize the dangers of violent nationalist movements worldwide.

4

NO PASARÁN

Jewish Collective Memory in the Spanish Civil War

"THE PRECIOUSNESS and cheapness of words," Irving Weissman wrote in his diary in Spain in 1938. "The blood and sweat in them." Weissman, the American child of eastern European Jewish immigrants, was a member of the Young Communist League and in his mid-twenties when he volunteered to fight in the Spanish Civil War. He joined the Abraham Lincoln Brigade and fought to defend the Spanish Republic, with its newly elected Popular Front government, from the right-wing military rebellion. His diary includes fragmented notes about his assignment, the first draft of several chapters of a novel, overheard phrases ("The Jews are running the brigade!"), and scrawled ideas, many of which are meditations on the significance of leftist concepts and passwords: "The nature of political work—internationalism." "Internationalism— love of Spanish people."[1] Weissman never published his novel. But he returned from Spain safely and survived his trials and imprisonment in the 1950s for treason as a Communist Party member. He visited Spain again in the 1970s and later wrote of an encounter there with two young English tourists. "We came from countries as small as postage stamps," Weissman told the young men, "and from countries as large as oceans.

We came to deliver the future as a gift to the world."[2] Spain, for the idealists who volunteered to defend the Republic between 1936 and 1938, was the site of a bright new future. For leftists, and particularly for Jews, the rise of Nazism in Germany, fascism in Italy, and the military coup in Spain made it increasingly apparent that the alternative to this future was a tyranny tantamount to the Inquisition.

Poets describing the Spanish Civil War optimistically saw in Spain a darkness-to-light teleology and created narratives that would deliver the country, and all of Europe, from the horror of fascism and Nazism. W. H. Auden, who visited Spain at the beginning of the war, wrote, in his widely circulating poem-pamphlet *Spain, 1937,* "Yesterday the Sabbath of witches; but to-day the struggle."[3] The rejection of religious tyranny was especially urgent for Jewish writers for whom the Inquisition and Expulsion from Spain—a near-biblical episode in collective memory—echoed everywhere in the emergence of fascism. Yiddish poets around the world hastened to depict Spain as the epicenter of current and past pain. The Soviet Yiddish poet Peretz Markish wrote, in his 1938 book *Lider vegn Shpanye* (Poems about Spain), "I'm yet again your guest! The honor is familiar!"[4] The Mexican Yiddish poet Jacobo Glantz, in his 1936 book *Fonen in blut* (Flags in blood), described the "Hebrews" of Spain's past rising from their graves to fight, "together with the bricklayer, against the Inquisition."[5] The American Yiddish poet Aaron Kurtz, in his 1938 book *No Pasaran,* describes the descendant of Marranos fighting in the trenches with the International Brigades and replacing Hebrew prayers with the communist slogan "¡No Pasarán!," a passphrase that, ironically, means "They shall not pass."[6] Jewish writers who identified ideologically with the Comintern-sponsored International Brigades found in the war not only a theme for their progressive rationalist worldview but a reason to address via communist revolution a history of trauma dating back to the fifteenth century. With this poetic return to Spain came a Comintern-inspired Jewish aesthetics that merged past, present, and future. These three Party-aligned poets, Peretz Markish, Aaron Kurtz, and Jacobo Glantz (1902–1982), each of whom devoted an entire book to Spain during the Spanish Civil War, offer key case studies in how the war affected a Jewish poetics of internationalism.

By the time the Spanish Civil War broke out in 1936, Left-aligned writers around the world had built a pragmatic alliance aimed at quelling the rise in fascism across Europe. After the deep rifts sewn during the hardline Third Period, the Comintern formally adopted the Popular Front in 1935 in hopes of containing the rise of fascism and Nazism.[7] Like the Scottsboro case in the United States, the Spanish Civil War evoked the sympathies of Left-identified Yiddish writers and readers spanning multiple continents, from the Soviet Union to the United States, Latin America, and Europe. This included Jews who had moved away from the Party in 1929 over the Palestine uprisings. The rise of Hitler confirmed, for many Jewish writers, the role of Soviet communism as a viable alternative to a fascist trend that threatened the lives of Jews among other groups. In response to the need for alliances across parties, the International Workers Order (IWO) sponsored a World Yiddish Cultural Congress in Paris in 1937, during which Leivick and other "runaways" from the Party again collaborated with the Comintern.[8] H. Leivick, in a speech at the Yiddish Writer's Congress, declared, "I believe, that one needn't be afraid to speak about our conflicts openly."[9] Jewish writers also participated in the 1937 Second Writers Congress in Defense of Culture in Madrid, Valencia, Barcelona, and Paris. The Yiddish writer Gina Medem describes a young Jewish soldier in a crowd greeting the writers on the street, holding a copy of the Parisian Yiddish newspaper *Naye Presse*. "He waved the newspaper like a flag, waiting for a member of the congress to declare himself a Jew."[10] For Jewish communists and communist sympathizers, the fascist rebels who rose up against the Spanish Republic in 1936 confirmed the inextricability of Jewish survival and the Soviet-led challenge to fascism worldwide. The journalist Melech Epstein later wrote, "no ethnic group in Europe or the United States was so deeply touched by the Spanish civil war as was the Jewish, [who] felt, by and large, that the struggle among the barren hills of north and central Spain was a proving ground for Hitler and Mussolini."[11] Of the thirty-five to forty thousand foreign volunteers for the International Brigades, estimates of Jewish involvement fall between thirty-five hundred and ten thousand total volunteers, and some scholars maintain that Jews made up a third of the American Abraham Lincoln Brigade.[12] The Naftali Botwin Company, a unit of the International

Brigades, used Yiddish as its official language.[13] These volunteers included Zionists, as well as anti-Zionist assimilationists.[14] Others, including Markish, Glantz, and Kurtz, fought on a literary front. As Cary Nelson writes in the introduction to his anthology of American poetry of the Spanish Civil War, "Just how quickly poetry took a significant place in the war remains startling even today."[15] For the purposes of this chapter, I focus on the Yiddish poetic cycles by Markish, Glantz, and Kurtz, three writers sympathetic to the Communist Party writing in distinct cultural contexts and all of whom present the past, present, and future in a way that corresponds both to thematic historical movement and to changes in poetic form. These three books about the rise of fascism in Europe on the eve of World War II—Brecht's "dark times"—represent the beginning of a Jewish genre of literature about the horrors of Nazism. That Hitler would wage a mass genocide against the Jews of Europe was still beyond these writers' worst nightmares.

A triadic past-present-future structure can be traced in all three of the cycles I examine, all of which synthesize the Inquisition and news reports about the Spanish Civil War to yield a collective, utopian future. This triadic structure bears a useful resemblance to Marx and Engels's adaptation of Johann Gottlieb Fichte's thesis-antithesis-synthesis model of social change.[16] The structure that tends to emerge in long Yiddish poems about the Spanish Civil War depends on three symbiotic modes—the lachrymose motif of Jewish liturgical tradition, the documentary spotlighting of a Spanish Other in need, and the glimpse of a rational, communist new order as envisioned through experimental, agitprop-inspired genres, including placard poems and revolutionary prophesy. Yiddish poetic cycles dedicated to Spain, by embedding themselves in a historical process, fulfill a similar function to historical novels, which, according to Georg Lukács, are significant because "their authors have tried to show artistically the concrete *historical genesis* of their time." Furthermore, as with the historical novel, "only a real understanding of these [social historical and human moral] forces in all their complexity and intricacy can show their present disposition and the paths which they can take towards the revolutionary overthrow of Fascism."[17] The cycle of poems that follows this structure thus simultaneously experiments with diverse poetic forms and motifs and strives to be historically self-conscious. The darkness-to-light arc of the past-present-future themes, moreover, lends the cycles the tone of a religious redemption narrative that borrows from Judaism and Christianity, even as the content of the poems remain strictly anticlerical. As Michael Löwy has observed, modern secular messianic movements at the turn of the twentieth century blurred the distinctions between secular, Jewish, and Christian messianic thought: "the messianism of the prophets joined with the Apocalypse of the Gospel, and the two entered into a relationship of elective affinity with modern revolutionary ideas."[18] The arc of the Spanish Civil War narrative in all three of the cycles I discuss, as a redemption narrative, offers a place for a Jewish past and an internationalist future.

For Jews, despite the increasing totalitarianism of the Stalinist administration that supported the International Brigades, Soviet ideology was far superior to fascist Spain and its Nazi allies, and a great many Jewish volunteers cast their lots with the Comintern-sponsored International Brigades.[19] Still, it is impossible to do justice to the political nature of the Yiddish Spanish Civil War poetry without acknowledging the controversies surrounding Party-aligned art, even among the like-minded. Many pro-Republican memoirs of Spain, including George Orwell's 1938 *Homage to Catalonia*, cast doubt on the virtues of the Soviet forces in Spain. Auden, who revised his "Spain" multiple times, ultimately deemed it too ideological in tone, called it "trash," and removed it from his collected works.[20] Hannah Arendt criticized Bertolt Brecht for writing in praise of the Party even "during the Spanish Civil War, when he must have known that the Russians did everything they could to the detriment of the Spanish Republic, using the misfortunes of the Spanish to get even with anti-Stalinists inside and outside the Party."[21] Marc Chagall rejected appeals to portray the Spanish Civil War on canvas and wrote disdainfully that his rival "Picasso may spit on Spain, even on Paris; but my colors come from Pokrova Street in Vitebsk. And are indeed Jewish."[22] The role of the Party in the Spanish Civil War remains a controversial topic in the twenty-first century. However, though the singular influence the Soviet Union exerted on discourse around the Spanish Civil War may have been overly partisan for some people, it challenged others to reconcile group affinity with internationalist politics and to find suitable forms to do so. As Harsha Ram has written, "Soviet literature at once reified the nation and relativized its importance by inserting it into a federal structure that reconfigured relations between local, regional, and central actors."[23] Jewish communists and fellow travelers, regardless of whether they were in the Soviet Union, similarly sought ways of integrating national concerns into an internationalist structure.

Chagall was an exception that proved the rule: his public refusal to depict the Spanish Civil War surprised many fellow Russian-born Jews, especially those on the Spanish front. Many Yiddish writers, even those outside the Soviet sphere, linked fascist Spain to the rise of Nazism in Germany. The decidedly non-Stalinist Yiddish poet Kadye Molodowsky ends her 1937 poem "Tsu di volontyorn in Shpanye" (To the volunteers in Spain) with the cautious fantasy of joining the war effort:

Kh'vel nokh oykh efsher nemen a biks oyf di aksl.	I too will still maybe take a rifle on my shoulder.
Un oyb kh'bin alt shoyn dertsu,	And if I'm too old for that,
vel ikh onton a vaysn khalat	I'll don a white robe
un vern a shvester—	and become a nurse—
un firn baym orem a krankn soldat.	and guide by the arm a sick soldier.
Kh'vel nokh oykh efsher—efsher— efsher[24]	I too will still maybe—maybe—maybe

Civil War Spain was a place for virility, for fantasy. And it was a place that allowed leftist Jews to reimagine what it meant to be a Jew without abandoning a broader struggle.

That Yiddish poetic portrayals of Spain synthesized Jewish, Spanish, and Party interests was possible due in part to changing literary policy within the Communist International. The rise of fascism in the 1930s led the Party to abandon the hardline antisocialist doctrine of the Third Period and seek a more inclusive policy. This decision came about alongside the rise of the Popular Front in western Europe—an alliance that united the communists, socialists, and radical parties.[25] The policy of promoting Popular Front writers, adopted at the 1935 Seventh Party Congress, reflected this desire for political inclusivity.[26] This more liberal literary atmosphere encouraged Party-aligned poets to reconcile internationalism with national interests in their antifascist verse. Not only did the outbreak of the Spanish Civil War lead writers across the Left to equate antifascist ideology with the specific case of Spain, but by 1936, Jews were aware that fascism presented as great a threat to Jewish life in Europe as to Spanish democracy. Communist Yiddish poets of the interwar years like Aaron Kurtz who had previously favored overtly political topics began integrating themes of Jewish memory into their work. This Judaizing of communist themes, which would become essential to Soviet and Soviet-aligned poetry during World War II, for all practical purposes began with Spain.

Although all three poets viewed Moscow as the center of their political aspirations, their lives in Moscow, New York, and Mexico City affected their view of the Party, Spain, and Nazism. For Markish, the Soviet military support of Republican Spain meant that literature about the threat of fascism was highly patriotic. Mexico, where Glantz lived, was the only other foreign government that supported Republican Spain, and scholars have argued that the Spanish Civil War had an important impact on the outcome of the Mexican Revolution.[27] Kurtz's book was well received in his American communist, Yiddish-speaking milieu but was an act of protest against his country's noninterventionist policy. In all three countries, the Yiddish poetry of the Spanish Civil War has been all but completely forgotten, obscured in short order by the poetry of World War II. The Cold War rendered the antifascist cause in the Spanish Civil War dangerously close to Soviet communism. The war in Spain allowed poets to integrate a crucial national concern for many Jews at the time—the threat of Nazism in Europe—into existing concerns of the Comintern.

Since none of the three poets I address here—Peretz Markish, Aaron Kurtz, and Jacobo Glantz—visited Spain, their books attest to the ideology surrounding the Spanish Civil War rather than personal experience. Past, present, and future motifs are marked by Jewish, Spanish, and communist passwords, respectively. In all three poets' Spanish Civil War cycles, the distant past is represented through Jewish collective memory. Nonetheless, references to the Inquisition demonstrate how the Spanish Civil War was crucial to combating both antisemitism and anticommunism. Yiddish poets' insistence on historical atrocities in the Jewish past simultaneously served as a Jewish call to arms to fight the fascist rebels and as one example of the dangers of Christian conservatism. All of the poems' present tense is in Spain, and as we shall see, the poets tend to adopt a documentary tone when describing current events. The Spanish soil, described from a distance in all three volumes, is exoticized and even sexualized. Therefore, if the "past" segments of these books offer a temporal exoticizing and distancing, the "present" segments, which are often framed by letters, news reports, photos, or other documentary genres, represent a geographical distancing. All three Spain cycles culminate in poems that present forward-facing, utopian ideals that drew many of the International Brigaders to Spain. The content of these future-oriented sections is a collectively imagined utopian future. These are often the most formally innovative poems in the volumes. They present new, populist forms replete with Party passwords and inspired by agitational slogans, popular songs, and the placard poems that began emerging shortly after the Bolshevik Revolution. Taken together, these three elements of the Spain poems suggest a compatibility between Jewish tradition and communism.

PAST

Peretz Markish's representations of Jewish suffering made him the Yiddish poet laureate of the Russian Revolution. Born in 1895 in the Ukrainian shtetl of Polonnoye, he completed a traditional Jewish elementary education (heder) and even worked for a cantor before serving in the Russian army during World War I. A member, together with Dovid Hofshteyn and Leyb Kvitko, of the poetic trio in the Revolutionary Kievgrupe, Markish went on to cofound the Warsaw-based *Literarishe Bleter* in 1924 with Israel Joshua Singer, Nakhman Mayzel, and Melekh Ravitch. Those who knew him as a young man often remarked on his striking good looks, his strong voice, and his shocking poetry of revolution.[28] In the years following his 1926 return from Warsaw to the Soviet Union, he wrote increasingly Party-aligned poetry, and the Spanish cycle, referencing the most pressing international topic of the time, bolstered his credentials as a Soviet poet. Nonetheless, he opens his long poem "Spain" by placing the war on a continuum of historical Jewish suffering. "Mounds of ash from my past," he writes, are piled in cemeteries beside the new bodies. For Markish, the war is a modern Inquisition that has targeted communists as well as Jews as its heretics:

Kh'bin nokhamol dayn gast! Der shtolts iz mir fartroyt!	I'm yet again your guest! The honor is familiar!
Ikh hob di shvue nit farhit. Dem neyder nit getsaytikt;	The ancient ban is still in place. I haven't kept the oath;
Af dayn besalmen fun di lesterer, bam ployt,	In your graveyard for transgressors, by the fence,
tliyen nokh berglekh ash fun mayn amol, fartsaytns![29]	still smolder ash heaps from my past, from long ago!

Through this figurative return to Spain, Markish simultaneously upholds the memory of his ancestors and breaks with traditional religious practice.[30] Markish's reference to the desecrated oath recalls an edict allegedly in place since the fifteenth-century Expulsion, forbidding Jews from visiting Spain.

Spain may have been a site of Jewish collective suffering, but it also spawned its own diaspora, and the legacy of Jewish suffering has been viewed, paradoxically, as a source of Jewish strength. Jewish memory writing on the European diasporic experience, as Yosef Hayim Yerushalmi shows in his seminal work *Zakhor,* can be traced to the Expulsion from Spain, which engendered a large body of liturgical and even historical literature in the subsequent century. The expulsion from Spain, which, Yerushalmi reminds us, emptied western Europe of its Jews, "altered the face of Jewry and of history itself."[31] Moreover, even for those Ashkenazi Jews who had no direct tie to Sephardic Jewry, Spain stood as an example of Jewish heroism through suffering. Ismar Schorsch, for example, has written of the "myth of Sephardic Supremacy" in western European Jewish culture.[32] By invoking the Inquisition, Markish also proudly invoked his own possible Sephardic family background. According to family lore, an ancestor, Lorenzo Markish, was an admiral with Portuguese roots.[33]

Markish, opening his poem with past moments of violence, employs an established password to evoke what Maurice Halbwachs has called "external" or "social" memories as well as the "internal" or "personal" memories of his own experience.[34] The "external" memories are of the Inquisition. As for the "internal" memories, readers would immediately recognize in "Spain" the modernist pogrom poems that Markish had published a decade and a half earlier. In particular, the piles of ash ("berglekh ash") recall his 1921 *Di kupe* (The mound), which, as noted in Chapter 1, portrays a mound of bodies after a pogrom during the Ukrainian Civil War. In *Di kupe,* piles of corpses after a pogrom are compared to "filthy wash": "A kupe koytek gret—fun untn biz aroyf iz!" (A mound of dirty laundry—from the bottom up!).[35] In both poems, the dead, piled into mounds, have been humiliated. The "filthy wash" that is discarded in the 1921 poem gives way to "bones of my grandfathers" that are "mocked" in "Spain." Whereas in *Di kupe,* the mound itself speaks, presumably to God, in "Spain," the poet's voice describes the piles:

Es zaynen nokh berglekh ash fun mayn amol tsezayt do	Still here the ash heaps from my past are scattered
mit kvarim fun gefalene in shlakht banand;	alongside the graves of those fallen in battle;
Vel ikh nit ufvekn s'gebeyn fun mayne zeydes,	I will not rouse the bones of my grandfathers,
in shpot getribene fun land tsu land,[36]	goaded in mockery from land to land,

With these mounds of history, Markish views memory in strikingly similar terms to Halbwachs, for whom "history indeed resembles a crowded cemetery, where room must constantly be made for new tombstones."[37] Markish's external and internal cemetery of history is, like Halbwachs's, crowded by the dead.

The humiliated mound was an image that Markish returned to time and again throughout his career, including in his 1929 "Brothers," where he describes the many Soviet citizens who have succumbed to typhus.[38] Markish's perpetual return to these death mounds undermines his simultaneous loyalty to the Party's rhetoric of progress. His many mounds, intriguingly, also recall the romantic Marxism of Walter Benjamin. Benjamin, in his critique of Stalinist dialectical materialism, "Theses on the

Philosophy of History," portrays an angel of history who "would like to stay, awaken the dead, and make whole what has been smashed."[39] Markish, like Benjamin's angel, may have his wings caught in the storm "called progress" but he continues to gaze steadily at the wreckage of the past. That the Spanish Civil War occasioned a return to Markish's mounds of Jewish history attests to the tendency, among Party-aligned writers, to embrace Jewish national solidarity in the face of the fascist threat.[40] Markish viewed the outbreak of the Spanish Civil War as a catastrophe on the level of the Revolutionary pogroms sixteen years earlier—a catastrophe shared by Jews, Spaniards, and leftists across Europe. "Spain" thus offers an internationalist message, while weaving into it two lachrymose Jewish strands—the rise of Nazism and the Inquisition.

Markish would return to his mound again during World War II, when, in a 1941 speech to the Jewish Antifascist Committee shortly after Hitler's invasion of the Soviet Union, he spoke of the Nazi desecration of Jewish villages: "Mountains of corpses and ashes are all that remains of towns in which Jews had lived for almost a thousand years."[41] Writing of this 1941 speech, David Shneer suggests, "By referencing his own famous poem and the long history of Jewish responses to destruction, Markish was placing the current Nazi wave of violence against Jews on the backdrop of this history."[42] The Soviet critic Sergei Narovchatov later called the Spanish poems the beginning of a "new period of Peretz Markish's creativity":[43] the Spain cycle opens a period when Markish increasingly described the rise of European fascism, save for the brief period after the Hitler-Stalin nonaggression treaty. Although Narovchatov downplays the increasing presence of religious themes in Markish's works, he astutely links the Spain cycle to Markish's later World War II poems.[44] Gennady Estraikh has explored how, a few years later, Markish "created in his post-Holocaust writing a space in which to explore a thematics of rebellion in a way that combined his understanding of Communism and Jewishness."[45] Markish is clearly already working to describe a coexistence of Judaism and communism in the Spain cycle.

The cycle has received little attention from Markish scholars, in part, no doubt, because during the brief Hitler-Stalin alliance (1939–1941) that followed the Spanish Civil War, overtly antifascist poems were outlawed in the Soviet Union. Devoted communists after 1939 had to place their trust in Stalin's policy, and as Lisa Kirschenbaum has aptly noted, "The memory of the war in Spain potentially complicated such determination to follow the party line."[46] And yet when Markish first published "Spain" in the *Naye Folkstsaytung* in 1936, it very much reflected the Soviet zeitgeist. Spain filled the pages of Soviet papers for the duration of the conflict, from the summer of 1936 through the spring of 1938.[47] Esther Markish would later recall noticing a newspaper clipping of her husband's "Spain" in the study of the Party chief of Abkhazia, during a writers' convention over New Year's 1937–1938.[48] Markish includes in his poem the ironic suggestion that art itself becomes irrelevant during war: "A shining sword in your hand / should be three times lighter than the castanets' song" (Zol in dayn hant a blitsndike zayn di shverd / Un dray mol laykhter vi di lid fun kastanietn!).[49] Markish's appeal to the struggle against fascism in Spain did not hurt his public recognition. He received the Lenin Prize and became a candidate for Party membership in 1939, which he finally received in 1942.[50]

Markish purportedly said, in the 1930s, "We look to the past . . . not to strengthen our bond to it, but so the future might enter us more quickly."[51] With "Spain," Markish managed to place national collective memory in service to a current struggle against fascism. In the second half of "Spain," Markish writes of the "blood-enraged storm / Of Swastika and Inquisition" (Blut-tsebushevetn tsug / Fun haknkreyts un inkvizitsie).[52] Markish, however, shifts continuously between dangers confronting Jews in particular (the swastika and the Inquisition) and dangers confronting all people, especially Spaniards. The next line begins, "For every murdered child—pay!" (Far yedn umgebrakhtn kind— batsolt!).[53] The international concern about Spanish civilians shifts the conversation from the local to the universal, moving the literary work out of the past into the present and toward the future.

Markish is not alone in merging a poetics of Jewish memory with communist internationalism. The American poet Aaron Kurtz (1891–1964), in his poem "Kol Nidre," depicts a Jew—Dovid Rom of Lemberg, who we learn has Marrano ancestry—in the trenches outside Cordoba with non-Jewish comrades. The poem begins with a Yiddish translation of the Kol Nidre prayer for the Day of Atonement, and the words of the prayer become passwords that bring the International Brigaders—Jewish and non-Jewish—into a historical, Jewish fold:

. . . ale nedorim	. . . All vows
un ale isurim	and all prohibitions
vos mir hobn genumen af zikh—zaynen	that we have taken on ourselves—are
botl.[54]	null.

Dovid goes on to commune with his Spanish ancestor:

Herst di elterzeydes reyd	Hear great-grandfather's speech
fun 1481,	from 1481,
reyd—tsupndike shtiker harts—	speech—tugging pieces of heart—
fun Shpanyes mitlalter-kelers,—[55]	from Spain's medieval cellars,—

By referencing 1481—the beginning of the Inquisition—Kurtz, like Markish, links historical Spanish anti-Jewish violence to contemporary anti-Jewish and anticommunist violence.[56] Moreover, in Kurtz's "Kol Nidre," the tradition of collective Jewish prayer is at the center of the poem, though it yields to the power of collective struggle. Dovid from Lemberg is joined in reciting the Kol Nidre not by a traditional minyan of ten Jewish men but by his Spanish and German comrades in arms, Pedro and Johannes:

Un Pedro fun Madrid,	And Pedro of Madrid,
un Yohanes fun Hamburg,	and Johannes of Hamburg,
helfn zingen di tfile fun Shpanishn Yid,	help sing the Spanish Jew's prayer,
gezungen fun eynikl Dovid	sung by his grandson Dovid
fun Lemberg.[57]	of Lemberg.

The traditional prayer of atonement bonds the three soldiers and admits Dovid's ancestor into the circle of comrades.

Kurtz, like Markish, distanced himself as a teenager from the religious milieu of his childhood. As I have discussed in Chapter Two, Kurtz was raised in a Lubavitcher Hasidic family outside Vitebsk (now Belarus), left home at the age of thirteen, and immigrated to the United States in 1911. He began publishing Yiddish poetry, often experimenting with avant-garde form, in the early 1920s. As we have seen in the case of his Palestine poems, Kurtz frequently attacked religious Judaism as an oppressive system that must yield to a rational, proletarian world order.

Although Kurtz emphasizes the international collective in his poetry—especially after joining the Communist Party USA in 1926—he nonetheless shared with Markish a desire to connect Jewish distant memory, recent experiences of the pogroms, and the antifascist effort in Spain. In another poem, Kurtz's "Yosl," the protagonist has escaped death in Poland, "to come—to death and to mold life" (tsu kumen—af toyt un af lebn zikh meldn).[58] Jewish voices heard throughout Kurtz's book suggest that a long Jewish history of trauma in the diaspora is precisely what has prompted Jews to volunteer to fight in Spain. Kurtz opens his poem "Di letste levaye" (The last funeral), for example, with the command, "Die, feudal Spain / corpse," followed by the promise, "We will blow you up to the highest heaven / in your medieval cathedrals."[59] For Jewish communists, religion was part of the past, but past religious persecution helped to justify a collective future. By linking fascism to the medieval persecution of Jews, Muslims, and Protestants, the Yiddish poet made a strong argument for fighting the political conservatives who touted Spain's Catholic legacy.

The most grotesque combinations of feudal and modern Spain come from Jacobo (Yakov) Glantz (1902–1982), who immigrated to Mexico from Novovitebsk in Soviet Ukraine in 1925. Like Markish and Kurtz, Glantz received enough religious education to integrate Jewish themes into his avowedly secularist verse. He began writing poetry in Russian but shifted to Yiddish in Mexico, where, in addition to writing, editing, and painting, he worked as a dentist and later owned a restaurant.[60] Mexico, impoverished as it was after its own revolution, was the only foreign country to offer the Spanish Republic badly needed financial assistance, sending, according to Adam Hochschild, "a gift of 20,000 rifles, ammunition, and food."[61] Moreover, in the 1930s, Mexico offered asylum for numerous Spanish Civil War veterans, as well as antifascists from Spain and Germany.[62] The coalescence of Mexican interests in the Spanish Republic and Jewish concerns about the rise of fascism coincided with Glantz's long-held agenda—"a Jewish need to enter and be part of Latin American culture," according to Adina Cimet.[63] Glantz's belief in integration may have motived him to write his 1936 *Fonen in blut* (Flags in blood), a book illustrated by the leftist American visual artist William Gropper and that, like the works of Markish and Kurtz,

places Jewish collective memory of the Inquisition in service to proletarian internationalism. In the poem "In vandervaytkayt fun mayn folk"
(In the wide wanderings of my people), resurrected Jewish corpses from
the Inquisition fight alongside the Loyalists. Streams of blood awaken
corpses, and they begin to agitate for the fight for a "new Spain" (far
Shpanye a banayter). Hearing the cry of their ancestors,

Zenen oyfgeshtanen fun di kvorim di Hebreyer	The Hebrews have arisen from their graves
un eyntsikvayz,	and one at a time
beynervayz,	bone at a time,
beyn un beyn,	bone by bone,
gelozt zikh geyn	let themselves out
un rufn:	and they call:
onton zikh in gufn.—	Dress yourselves in bodies.—
Un ineynem mitn moyrer kegn inkvizitsye,	And together with the bricklayer against the Inquisition
zikh ayngeshribn in di reyen fun militsye—[64]	register in the ranks of the militia—

Glantz allows a felicitous rhyme to set the "reyen fun militsye" (ranks
of the militants) directly against the "Inquisition" (inkvizitsye) itself
and visually highlights the couplet by printing it in boldface. The Republican cause is thus presented as a unique opportunity to correct
a past moment of Jewish martyrdom and not only to fight a modern
insurrection.

"Blood is always blood," Glantz writes in his introduction, explaining
the book's political emphasis. "I, hearing the cry of a people in a bloody
tragedy day and night, squeezed 'between the walls' of neutrality and
snobbish diplomacy,—can't dream, but become feverish."[65] Todd Presner
has discussed the paradoxical intellectual origins of twentieth-century
"muscular Judaism": "It epitomized the rebirth of the strong Jew as
drawn from Jewish history and mythology; but, at the same time, many
of the anti-Semitic stereotypes of Jewish degeneracy were internalized
in its conceptualization."[66] The notion that the Jew had to reform
him- or herself depends on a stereotype of past Jewish passivity. So,
too, the leftist Yiddish poets who wrote about Spain had to reconcile
this history of Jewish non-violence and anti-Jewish violence in Europe

with a current willingness to fight, and possibly kill, opponents. Esther Shumiatcher, who, we recall from Chapter 1, moved away from the Party in 1929, returned to internationalist themes during the Popular Front period but called attention to the strain between her Jewish background and her support of the war effort. She begins her poem "Ikh bin a Yid" (I am a Jew) with a rousing call to a Yugoslav, a Russian, a Yankee, and a Jew to "Arise, and come defend Madrid!" and then undercuts this cry: "I can't hold a gun:/my grandfather was a poor Jew./My grandmother read the Tsene Urene/and translated it literally."[67] Shumiatcher, who a decade earlier, in her poems about China and the nascent Soviet Union, had deemphasized her Jewish identity in favor of internationalism, now wrote in support of the International Brigades as a Jew. She goes on to write of the rebel Spanish Catholics, who, in their campaign against the Spanish Loyalists, also constituted a threat to the Jews:

Madrid, Madrid!	Madrid, Madrid!
Tsi iz es vor?	Is it true?
A tliye brent.	A gallows burns.
es tselemt zikh a frumer katolik,	a devout Catholic crosses himself,
un zogt dem yidn tsu	and promises the Jew
dos getlekhe glik.[68]	divine happiness.

The "Jew" in Shumiatcher's poem simultaneously evokes the Jewish allies of the Republic, collective Jewish memory of the Inquisition, and those Jews across Europe who are similarly threatened by the rise of Franco's Nazi allies.

The allegory of medieval Spain, however, appealed to conservatives and Republicans alike. As Paul Preston has shown, in response to the Republic's anticlerical legislation, antisemitic sentiments, present to some degree since the Middle Ages even with Spain's minuscule Jewish population, returned, and "the bilious rhetoric of the Jewish-Masonic-Bolshevik conspiracy was immediately pressed into service."[69] For Jews, however, the Inquisition had been the defining antisemitic episode in European history, and for those who accepted the Comintern's secularist ideology around Spain, anti-Catholic actions were carried out in the interest of eradicating religious bigotry. Moreover, acceptance of violence helped to combat the stereotype of Jewish passivity. Speaking to leftist Jewish volunteer militiamen on the Aragon front, Melech Epstein suggests as much: "Four and a half centuries ago, Jews were driven from Spain to many lands, and the country was boycotted by them. Now young Jews from many lands are hurrying to Spain to rescue her, and perhaps the whole of Europe, from fascist domination."[70] The utopian poets who wrote Spanish Civil War cycles sought a reconciliation of the historical interests of Spain's persecuted Jewish community and contemporary anticlerical communist interests. Past trauma, that is, was only worth evoking if it could serve a progressive future.

This was, let us remember, a moment when Jewish thinkers from across the political spectrum, from Zionism to Bolshevism, sought antecedents for a new vision of Jewish military power. Jacobo Glantz's book, published by the "Gezbir" society, which was formed to support the Soviet autonomous Jewish region of Birobidjan, might be read as offering an alternative, like Birobidjan itself, to Zionism. Glantz reminds his readers that it is "the grandchildren of Jewish martyrs / from Toledo and Madrid" who have joined the struggle.[71] The image of ethnic Jews fighting side by side with non-Jews, like Kurtz's collective Kol Nidre prayer, not only expresses an internationalist hope for the future but compares a touchstone in Jewish collective trauma—the Inquisition—to the Loyalist struggle in contemporary Spain. In this Comintern revision of the lachrymose motif in Jewish memory, the past, rather than serving "competitive victimology" (to use Dominick LaCapra's term), can be redeemed through its comparison to other groups' historical and current tragedies.[72]

Un s'hobn eyniklekh fun Yidishe martirer	And the grandchildren of the Jewish martyrs
fun Toledo un Madrid	of Toledo and Madrid
geshafn batalyonen—	have formed battalions—
(un oysgefarbt di fonen	(and dyed their flags
mit blut fun 'Krist un Yid'—)[73]	with the blood of "Christian and Jew"—)

The relationship between the prodigal Jewish "grandchild" and the ancestral martyrs of the Inquisition is here, as in Kurtz's "Kol Nidre" and Markish's "Spain," a crucial part of the Jewish poetics of Spain. The

Inquisition evoked a tradition of Jewish memory but one that has been revised to suggest a multiethnic collective.

The Jewish historian Salo Wittmayer Baron began criticizing what he called the "lachrymose" tendency in Jewish history in 1928.[74] Like Baron, Glantz, Kurtz, and Markish all reject the notion that suffering should set Jews apart from other nations and embrace the idea of Jews' intimate connection and integration into a multiethnic world. However, all three poets harness a lachrymose tradition to draw attention to a contemporary tragedy of universal concern. Markish challenges a community of Europe's Jews to view the Spanish Civil War as equal to the tragic stories of the past. For Kurtz, the task of collectively remembering transfers from the Jews to the International Brigade. And for Glantz, the war folds history toward the present, reincarnating medieval victims as comrades in arms. For communist Yiddish writers, group memory added Jewish historical meaning to the collective struggle against the fascists. However, this historical meaning only held value if they could demonstrate that Jewish collective concern could be transferred from Jewish memory to the present conditions of Spain.

PRESENT

"I've seen your picture. / Azure eyes—sharp and mild" (Kh'hob gezen dayn bild / Azyere oygn—sharf un mild).[75] Jacobo Glantz opens his poem "Di oygn fun Lina Odena" (Lina Odena's eyes) with a description of a photograph, widely published in Popular Front newspapers in 1936. Lina Odena, a twenty-five-year-old communist, found herself behind Nationalist lines and shot herself to prevent capture. With this reference to a widely known contemporary story, Glantz employs visual documentary evidence—a form of communist factography—to create a present tense in his cycle. Steven Lee has discussed factography, which sought the "precise fixation of fact," as an artistic mode that "cast the non-European Other in a radical, experimental light."[76] The same might be said of Spanish subjects who, in all three Yiddish cycles, serve as a means of overcoming the past. The documentary image of Odena offers a stagnant, fleeting vision of the Spanish present—one that links medieval Spain with a dawning, revolutionary future:

Oygn—vos farmogn	Eyes—that possess
letstn goysesdikn likht	the last dying light
fun kloysterdike mnoyres,	of church candelabras,
un oygn vos balaykhtn veln dos gezikht	and eyes that will light the face
fun tsukunftike doyres.[77]	of future generations.

Odena's immortalized gaze bears witness to an irretrievable past at the dawn of a new era. The present itself is a means to an end.

In popular culture, Odena came to symbolize a young Republican Spain that chooses death over captivity. As Tabea Alexa Linhard has demonstrated, this narrative was both gendered and racialized, for poems and Romanceros of the time often cast Odena's suicide as an act preventing inevitable rape by North African soldiers.[78] Glantz's poem does not mention rape. In fact, he dedicates the poem to the "Revolutionary woman, who fell in battle outside Talavera," suggesting uncertainty about the nature of her demise. However, Glantz does employ the common image of Spain as a counterpart to the male revolutionary, a role often symbolized by the communist activist Dolores Ibárruri (better known as La Pasionaria), who famously stated, "It is better to be the widows of heroes than the wives of cowards."[79] Foreign writers often cast Spanish characters, especially women, as exotic bodies awaiting a hero, pregnant with a new society, mourning a beloved soldier, or defying a master. Even the most progressive poetic tributes to Republican Spain often portray a country in need, reflecting a power dynamic that, as Christina Klein has pointed out, likened the Popular Front to the earlier missionary movement.[80] However, even as they figured Spain itself as a woman in need, Party-aligned poets presented women in Spain overwhelmingly as citizens who, without a history of combat, took weapon in hand to overthrow fascism. They were portrayed simultaneously as comrades in distress and icons of strength.

Male and female figures emblematic of Spanish culture emerge throughout Glantz's book to symbolize a renewal of an ancient landscape. In "Oyf farnakhtikn step fun La Mantsha" (On the evening steppe of La Mancha), Sancho is suddenly loath to follow Quixote's dreams:

S'hot shtolener trot fun geshikhte	The steel tread of history
di alte khaloymes tsetrotn . . .	has trampled old dreams . . .
Es sheylt zikh durkh khmares gedikhte	It peels itself through thick clouds
der tovl fun naye gebotn . . . [81]	the tablet of new commandments . . .

The Marxist-Hegelian march of history replaces the quixotic fictions of old Spain with a new order, and, Glantz suggests, this new order will be more realistic, more rational. This new secularist faith, of course, borrowed liberally from religious form, even as it waged war on religious content. As Igal Halfin has written of Russia, "Imbuing time with a historical teleology that gave meaning to events, Marxist eschatology described history as moral progression from the darkness of class society to the light of Communism."[82] Marxist Yiddish literature, however, offers a unique example for understanding how a community negotiated between a shared religious tradition and a shared commitment to secularism. This communist teleology led all three poets to firmly place their Jewish images and associations in the past; while their depictions of Spain could remain in the fleeting present, and depictions of a Soviet-style utopia were reserved for the future.

The merging of a Marxist eschatology with the reality of widespread Spanish Catholicism is especially apparent in "Royter Kristus" (Red Christ), where Glantz depicts a revolutionary Christ who "shows soldiers the way / through church ruins" (vayzt dem veg soldatn / durkh di kloystershe ruinen).[83] This is the Christ of revolution, akin to the many black Christs discussed in Chapter 3 and to the Christ of Alexander Blok's 1918 "The Twelve," who leads a motley group of Red Army soldiers through a Petersburg snowstorm.[84] A symbol of compassion and justice, Glantz's revolutionary Christ offers an antidote to Franco's Catholic collaborators: "Today Christ is a red leader / at the Somosierra front" (Haynt iz Kristus—royter firer / Oyfn front fun Somesiera).[85] The poem is dated October 11, 1936, several weeks after the Republican fighters surrendered to the fascists at the Somosierra mountain pass, north of Madrid. Glantz, writing in the first months of the war, describes what he assumes will be a transitional, revolutionary moment. His Loyalist heroes are martyrs—saints of a new, revolutionary religion, bound only to the present moment.

Peretz Markish had been using reportage to bridge the past and future since the Russian Revolution.[86] As in his earlier writing on the Russian Revolution, Markish employs the Revolutionary mode of factography to ground utopian ideals and past trauma. As Seth Wolitz has written of Markish's 1922 *Radyo*, "Markish carefully angles his appeal to the Jewish reader by attacking the old ways and insisting that the ruins left by the [Russian] Civil War must be left behind in the past."[87] Markish's Spanish characters are similarly rooted in the kind of fleeting present he described, when he wrote, during the Bolshevik Revolution, "My name is now" (Mayn nomen iz atsind).[88] And indeed, Markish frequently compares the "now" of Spain to the Russian Revolution. In "Spain," Markish compares the Republicans' road to Madrid to decisive battles in recent Russian history:

di trit di shtolene tsum vinter-palats,	the steely footsteps to the Winter Palace,
der laybn-gang tsum zig fun Perekop![89]	the life-giving march to the victory at Perekop!

By evoking the Winter Palace and the battle of Perekop—the Crimean city where the Red Army defeated the White Army—Markish is comparing the Loyalist struggle against the rebels to the two phases of the Bolshevik Revolution, the overthrow of the tsar and the war that followed it. In "Balade vegn delegat" (Ballad of a delegate), the speaker explicitly connects the two countries:

—az vi vayt iz den funanden bizn lebn?	—so how far is it from there to life?
—az vi vayt iz den biz Moskve fun Madrid?[90]	—so how far is it to Moscow from Madrid?

The idea that Moscow represents life as well as the spiritual center of revolution reflects the geographical power balance of Comintern poetics and distinguishes this volume from Markish's poetry of the Bolshevik

Revolution of nearly two decades earlier. By the late 1930s, Markish's allegiances were with the Party, centered in Moscow—his home since 1926.

The quintessential embodiment of traditional Spain appears in Markish's "Toreador," in which the bullfighter has exchanged his bull for the combined specter of fascism and the Inquisition. Like Glantz's Lina Odena, Markish's toreador is both anachronistic and revolutionary:

Nu, fokher oyf dayn roytn tukh, toreador,	Well, fan up your red cloth, toreador,
es vart dos folk, der umgeduld farzidt dort,	your nation waits, anticipation boils there,
nit keyn buhay vet haynt aroys dir tsu der por,	no bull is coming out today to fight with you,
es geyt dos fintstere geshpenst fun inkvizitors![91]	the Inquisitors' dark specter is approaching!

The toreador's red cape becomes a red flag—a visual and tangible fabric connecting a Spanish cultural icon of masculinity to Bolshevik iconography. The poem ends with the line, "And like a flag it should float into the heights!" (Un vi a fon zol er a shveb ton in di haykhn!).[92] The inquisitors of the past have become a specter—a ghost that continues to haunt the present. This poem was probably a response to news coming from Spain's Republican fighters, which included the well-publicized story of a former bullfighter, Melchor Rodríguez, an anarchist who, perhaps paradoxically, became an important voice for pacifism.[93] In Markish's call to action, the bullfighter is summoned to fight the Inquisition—a historic battle against injustice.

Markish's cycle is infused with stories of Spain and with distinctly Spanish passwords and passphrases that evoke these stories. Markish integrates La Pasionaria's well-known slogan into the opening poem, "Shpanye (Spain):

Az—liber zayn iz an almone fun a held,	For—it is better to be a hero's widow,
eyder a vayb fun a farflukhtn pakhdn![94]	than the wife of an accursed coward!

In Markish's Yiddish rendition, the line is seamlessly incorporated into the poem: attribution would have been superfluous. Markish follows this tribute to the heroism of Spanish women with the heroism of Spanish children:

S'baveynen kinder nit in feld zeyere tates,	Children on the field don't mourn their fathers,
di biksn nemen zey mit shtolts fun toyte hent,	they take the rifles proudly from dead hands,
un shvue af di lipn fayerdike flatert,	and a vow on their fiery lips flutters,
un greytkayt shtarbn in di oygn brent![95]	and readiness to die burns in their eyes!

For many people observing Spain from afar, the most moving stories from Spain involved children. Eleanor Roosevelt, despite her husband's nonintervention policy, worked to raise money to feed Spanish children.[96] The Introspectivist poet Aaron Glantz-Leyeles, in his "Shpanishe balade" (Ballad of Spain), conjured "Pepito," a boy of four forced to flee Spain for France:

Pepito falt un heybt zikh, Pepito heybt zikh, falt—	Pepito falls and gets up, gets up and falls again—
Pepito iz shoyn gantse, shoyn gantse fir yor alt.[97]	Pepito is already a four-year-old young man.

Portrayals in the Yiddish press of the youngest and most vulnerable victims of the war were inextricable from Jews' fear for the broader implications of Nazism. Leyeles wrote in an *In Zikh* editorial about the threat of fascism to Spaniards and Jews alike: "Is there no mercy? No, not these days. A small, old culture, maybe the oldest in Europe, is attacked and plundered—there isn't a peep, there isn't a rousing of conscience. . . . So, beloved humankind, look at the Basques. This is your mirror nowadays." Leyeles maintains hope that the Basques, who survived the "cruel pirates" of the past, "will similarly overcome their contemporary enemies": "As we will overcome ours, which are the same."[98] A Trotskyist, Leyeles was openly disdainful of colleagues like Aaron Kurtz who were unabashedly devoted to the Soviet Union, yet news from Spain bridged left-wing political divides.[99]

Both Aaron Kurtz and Jacobo Glantz composed Spanish lullabies for children whose parents had died or were fighting the fascists. Several Spanish characters in Kurtz's *No Pasaran* are parents awaiting their children. The old, blind Karmelita waits for her children "to return her Spain to her" (zoln ir tsurikbrengen ir Shpanye). Karmensita, a woman about to give birth, lies feverish in a hospital. It is unclear whether the future holds life or death:

Arum, oyf tishlekh, blien kveytn,	Around, on little tables, bloom flowers,
Ershtn mame-shmeykhl vekn-oyf di duftn.	Their scent should awaken the first maternal smile.
Neyn. Dos glien vundn oyf halb-toyte,	No. These are wounds blossoming on the half-dead,
Dos flien toyt-buketn funderluftn.[100]	flying death-bouquets dropped from the sky.

These parental figures personify the revolutionary moment of anticipation. Bertolt Brecht and Margarete Steffin use a similar conceit in their 1937 one-act play *Señora Carrar's Rifles*, which centers on a mother who, having lost a son, becomes convinced she must join the Republican forces.[101] The emphasis on parents and children envisions Spain as both effeminate and immature—an old nation rendered inexperienced by revolution.

The Spanish landscape itself became a symbol of the embattled present. Kurtz's "Andaluzyer landshaft" (Andalusian landscape) is labeled parenthetically "from a painter's letter." The artist describes natural beauty ("Spain: splendor / of a thousand Colorados"), which gives way to the pathetic fallacy of war.

A hayntikn moler in Shpanye	A contemporary painter in Spain
geyt nit on dos amolike moln.	doesn't care to depict the past.
Antikn	Antiques
zaynen mer nit keyn teme:	are no longer a theme:
In khoruve templen ligt ashik tseshosn	In ruined temples, obsession with old times
di altertum-manye,	lies shot to ash,
di teme iz—toyt oyf di berg, toyt in di toln,	the theme is death on mountains, death in valleys,

brenendike brikn,	burning bridges
vos himl-fayern tsenemen	that heaven's fires consume
un lebns gerangl in di feld-shpitoln.[102]	and life's struggle in field hospitals.

The painter is only able to depict the present in the midst of its destruction—death on mountains and in valleys, burning bridges. The past, significantly, no longer has a place.

Kurtz's choice of the letter-poem is important to his documentation of contemporary Spain. Kurtz writes, in his introduction to *No Pasaran,* that the book's contents are based largely on documentary material, including "letters from the Spanish front, correspondences, and conversations with returned brigaders. The names of the heroes in this book are not fictitious."[103] Kurtz's letters reflect the fascination with the documentary among poets, across languages, in the Popular Front period. The letter-poem lent English-language writers like Langston Hughes and Muriel Rukeyser a diversity of dialects and perspectives.[104] Leftist Yiddish poets, too, used letters to channel the voices of the politically disenfranchised, from the convicted Italian anarchists Sacco and Vanzetti to the Scottsboro defendants and their mothers to the American men and women fighting in Spain.

To include Spain in a decades-long international struggle for revolution, Yiddish poets who were writing from afar carefully drew their descriptions from current reportage. Crucial to all three cycles, however, is the sense that Spain is prepared to lose its national particularity to a new internationalism. Thus, Glantz's Odena witnesses a change in world order at the moment of her death; Markish mentions Madrid and Moscow in one breath; Kurtz's Andalusian landscape artist must dismantle the old to make way for the new. For the Revolutionary poet, of course, the present moment cannot hold and must usher in a utopian future.

FUTURE

The protagonist in Aaron Kurtz's "A briv fun a kranknshvester" (A letter from a nurse) writes, "it smells / of poplars and death / in my hospital" (es shmekht / mit topol un mit toyt / in mayn shpitol).[105] She describes four men who died that night: an Austrian miner, a Moorish hunter, a Sigeter Hasid, and a German poet. Each dying man glimpses a version of the future, and each makes a statement before death. The Moor, presumably one of the many North Africans forced to fight in Franco's army, cries, "The Moors, *all* the Moors, / Must cross sides" (Di Murn, *ale* murn, muzn desertirn).[106] This sentiment likens Kurtz's poem to Langston Hughes's 1937 "Letter from Spain," a poem written in the voice of an African American volunteer who receives a Moorish prisoner's last breath:

> We captured a wounded Moor today.
> He was just as dark as me.
> I said, Boy, what you been doin' here
> Fightin' against the free?[107]

Hughes's semifictional narrator urges the North African to see the connection between Spanish colonialism and slavery and through this connection to reject the Francoist rebels.[108] Kurtz's North African comes to the conclusion of his own accord, blessing a freer future with words that merge instruction and prophesy.

If Hughes's African American protagonist recognizes himself in the still-enslaved dying Moor ("Then something wonderful'll happen / To them Moors as dark as me."),[109] then Kurtz, who was raised in a Hasidic milieu, presents his own twin in his Hasidic figure, who realizes that fighting the fascists in Spain is an extension of his religious beliefs:

O, ikh bentsh di groyse tsayt	Oh, I bless this great time
vos hot gelernt mir vi zikh tsu shlogn	that has taught me how to fight
far ofene tir un toyer tsum erdishn	for open doors and gates to an earthly
gan-edn.[110]	Garden of Eden

A few years earlier, the fusion of religious prophesy with communism would have bordered on heresy for religious Jews and communists alike, but the overt antisemitism expressed by the fascist rebels and their Nazi allies allowed for a new framing of Jewish tradition that could, at least in the realm of poetry, coexist with revolutionary ideals. This proposed coexistence often took the form of utopian slogans that, repeated, can be likened to internationalist prayers. These prayer-like slogans form the third component of the Comintern-aligned Yiddish Spain cycle. The future-oriented poems in all three volumes discussed in this chapter are the clearest in their communist ideology. They are also the most formally surprising, with internationalist mantras appearing as refrains and with poems written in the form of Republican placards. The future poems, as well, find the poets experimenting with the dissolution of subjectivity to evoke a diversity of voices.

Jacobo Glantz and Peretz Markish, like Kurtz, indulge in visions and dreams through prophetic figures, often at the moment of death. In a poem dedicated to the memory of the poet Federico García Lorca, assassinated early in the war in his hometown of Granada, Glantz writes of future generations:

O, dayn vort,	Oh, your word
dos vort fun vorn,	the word of warning,
vort fun dor	word of a generation
vos vert geborn	being born
in yamen blut fun dayn Granade.[111]	in seas of blood from your Granada.

By depicting the poet as a martyred prophet, Glantz also renders him a warrior.

Markish creates a more explicit prophet-warrior with "Agitprop Pancho Video," a poem about a sniper who arises from the grave to shout Republican agitational propaganda (agitprop) to enemy soldiers. The refrain, "Pancho Video is not just a sniper, / Pancho Video is agitprop!" (Pantsho Video iz nit bloyz a snayper, / Pantsho Video iz oykh agitprop!) envisions Pancho as a poet, prophet, and warrior.[112] Words, Markish implies, are as important to the war as bullets are. During the Spanish Civil War, poems were disseminated in much the same way as pamphlets and placards, which blurred the boundaries between art and agitprop.[113] Loyalist posters presented easily digestible images and caricatures: a businessman with a top hat and swastika represents the fascist-capitalist connection in Europe. A poster for the Syndicalist Party depicts the many arms of the Popular Front threatening a caricatured businessman standing atop a swastika (figure 4.1).

Pro-Republican poems often recapitulated the slogans and visual symbolism found in poster art, binding more tightly the poem's

Fig 4.1 Disciplina. Unified Command. Syndicalist Party. Manuel Monleón. Comité Obrero de Control., UGT-CNT. Lithograph. *Credit:* Southworth Spanish Civil War Collection, Special Collections and Archives, University of California San Diego Library

revolutionary message with the spirit of the people. Many of Kurtz's letter-poems in *No Pasaran* are polyphonic in the Bakhtinian sense, where multiple autonomous voices form a collective dialogue. In a poem titled "Der orkester" (The orchestra), labeled "A letter from Dave," Kurtz describes a musical ensemble, which functions as a harmonious international collective:

Undzer orkester shpilt, in shpiln herstu di harmonye	Our orchestra plays, in it you hear the harmony
fun hundert felker in eyn brigade:	of a hundred nations in one brigade:
der gitarist—a romantisher Venetsyaner,	the guitarist is a romantic Venetian,
der karnetist—a zakhlekher Belgrader,	the cornetist—a matter-of-fact Belgrader,
fidl shpilt a Yid	a Jew plays the violin
un oyf vos du vilst—	you name it—
Daytshn Shvedn Yenkis, Indianer![114]	Germans Swedes Yankees, Indians!

Kurtz's international symphony invokes the spirit of the dream future—a utopia that has not yet been attained but that might be akin to the International Brigades. The orchestra, "in the hinterlands not far from the trenches," plays "The Spanish anthem / and the International," thus producing a collective of nations in content and form.[115]

Kurtz had long sought new forms for poems that could inspire the working Yiddish-speaking masses. His 1927 *Plakatn* (Placards), which he published a year after joining the CPUSA, adapts the genre of Revolutionary street placards. The poems in *Plakatn* are shapely, waving across the page like flags with alternating very short and very long lines of blank verse. They are Mayakovskian, emphatic, occasionally punctuated with English phrases. The short lines, meant to conjure placards at a rally, appreciate mass slogans as an integral part of poetry. The placard poem is made up largely of passwords, from the title to the one-word lines that often close a section. In one poem, "Yunyon Skver" (Union Square), Kurtz writes,

Di fete shtiftates fun shtot, di kalte balebatim dayne,	The city's fat stepfathers, your cold masters,
hobn nit keyn nakhes fun dayn havershaft mit mir,	take no pride in your friendship with me,
dem nar,	the fool,
vos kumt aher fun ale vilde vinklen	who comes here from all the world's
fun der velt un putst dikh oys	wild corners and dresses you up
in bender un	in volumes and
fonen.[116]	flags.

L. Khanukov, writing for the communist *Frayhayt,* praised Kurtz's tireless quest for usable poetic forms and called *Plakatn* "already a book of a ripe poet, who has found his way in life." He remarks further on Kurtz's ability to feel "the power of the awakened masses. He is their tribunal."[117]

With the letter-poems in *No Pasaran,* Kurtz was again experimenting with a formal mode gaining prominence in leftist poetry. The letter form, like the placard poem, allowed Kurtz to loosen his grip on the individual voice, opting instead for the voice of a collective. However, whereas the placard poem suggests voices in unison, verbally capturing the exclamatory atmosphere of a protest, the letters that populate *No Pasaran* salvage the individual experiences that compose that collective. Kurtz's inclusion of Civil War passwords and passphrases, often in Spanish ("¡No Pasarán!," "Salud!," "Viva la Espagna!"), and at the end of a poem merges the individual voice with a collective spirit, binding his diverse cast of characters more tightly together and reinforcing the discourse of collectivity. In a discussion of poetry and discourse, Anthony Easthope observes poetry's potential "to bring the signifier into a reinforcing relation with the signified, so giving the poetic message a quality of 'reification' able to convert it into an 'enduring thing.'"[118] Kurtz's mobilization of Spanish passwords is aimed precisely at converting the political message into such an "enduring thing." Hannah Arendt makes a similar, but more circumspect, observation about the aesthetic and political coalescence of slogans, viewing slogans as signifiers "designed to translate the propaganda lies of the movement, woven around a central fiction . . . into a functioning reality."[119] Although agitation around Spain cannot be completely uncoupled from the strictures of the Soviet 1930s, to dismiss the poetry of Party sympathizers on the grounds of politics would be to miss the aesthetic innovation involved in their particular exaltation of the signifier.[120] Even Arendt's discomfort with slogans demonstrates the power of political literature in Popular Front poetry. As Cary Nelson has noted, "for a moment in the 1930s, verbal creativity and political slogans were considered poetic partners."[121]

The political slogan as password, however, takes on the additional function as a cipher, a key that gives the reader access to the singular historical moment the poem describes.[122] Thus, Paul Celan, in his poem "As One," meditates upon the relationship between passwords and the thing itself that they gesture towards. Celan writes,

Dreizehnter Feber. Im Herzmund	Thirteenth of February. In the heart's mouth
Erwachtes Schibboleth. Mit dir, Peuple	An awakened shibboleth. With you, Peuple
De Paris. *No pasarán.*[123]	De Paris. *No pasarán.*

The slogan here is a password to an otherwise indeterminate moment. It gives access, to the reader who knows the relevant internationalist references, to the untranslatable language of world revolution. Moreover, as

Derrida observes of Celan's poem, "One should specify that untranslatability does not stem only from the difficult passage (*no pasarán*), from the aporia or impasse that isolates one poetic language from another." The uniqueness of the moment is coded by "the multiplicity of languages within the uniqueness of the poetic inscription: several times at once, several languages within a single poetic act."[124] "¡No Pasarán!," as a slogan, came into use among Republicans fighting to defend Madrid from rebel forces. The Spanish Civil War slogan, used in Celan's German poem, or Kurtz's Yiddish book, encodes multiple languages into a poetic utterance, creating a stronger password, as it were, to protect the moment being described.

Glantz's volume, like Kurtz's, emphasizes Revolutionary optimism even as it memorializes the war's early casualties. In a brief preface, the editorial team expresses hope that the poems "should serve the broad Jewish masses in their struggle against bloody fascism."[125] Toward the end of the collection, Glantz shifts from poems about individuals toward collectivist slogans. He employs the same "placard" (plakat) form that Kurtz used in his 1927 book *Plakatn*, a form that became widely popular with the emergence of proletarian poetry of the 1920s, and included short lines, associative metaphors, and identifiable workers' slogans. One poem, titled simply "Plakat" (Placard), responds to the September 1936 battle at Talavera de la Reina by heralding a new era:

A naye era	A new era
heybt zikh on in Eyrope.	is beginning in Europe.
Sopet	The newspaper vendor.
der tsaytungs-farkoyfer.	gasps.
Zayn kol vi a shoyfer	His voice like a shofar
ruft un vornt un gornt	calls and warns and yearns
in luft.	to the sky.
—Di luft iz ful mit dinamit[126]	—The sky is full of dynamite

Although the battle at Talavera devastated the Republican army, the defeat led to an international call to defend Madrid. As the historian Antony Beevor puts it, "The communist slogan that 'Madrid will be the grave of fascism' was powerfully emotive and the battle for the capital was to help the party to power."[127] Glantz's shocked newspaper vendor, a modern town crier, announces the headlines, which would be posted on the streets alongside placards. Like Kurtz's Hasid in "A briv fun a kranknshvester," Glantz's newspaper vendor also reinscribes Jewish tradition onto an internationalist message: the shofar, rather than heralding a new Jewish year, heralds a new era for all workers.

"A lid vegn banker Khid in a shloflozer nakht fun Madrid" (A poem about Gid the banker on a sleepless Madrid night) is parenthetically labeled "in the style of a placard" (plakatish). The eponymous banker, Gilberto Gid, is plagued by visions of Christ and an image of "A bloody banknote." But rather than saving Gid,

Got tut on	God puts on
a shvartsn kapushon	a black cape
un geyt fun shtub aroys . . . [128]	and leaves the house . . .

True to the placard form, the poem is composed of fragmented images: short stanzas recall the visually compelling posters that were ubiquitous at the time—visual works of agitprop flaunting clear, readily digestible messages. The image of Jesus donning a soldier's black cape can be likened to war posters that, despite the Republic's anticlerical actions, accuse the nationalists of Christian hypocrisy.[129] In one Popular Front poster, an International Brigader stands before a female symbol of international peace, whose cruciform posture and dove suggests a truer understanding of Christianity than that put forth by the church (figure 4.2).

Glantz's meandering poem ends with a reminder that the Loyalist forces are watching (and punishing) the actions of the fascists and their allies:

Bavakht iz yeder trot	Guarded is every step
un shpan!—	and stride!—
NO PASARAN![130]	¡NO PASARÁN!

The "guarded step" simultaneously evokes war propaganda and the biblical lines from Isaiah 21:6, "Go set up a sentry." The poem describes the necessity of barring passage, and the use of an internationalist slogan in a Yiddish poem itself creates an aporia—an impassable barrier. The slogan bars passage to those who should not have access to the original context. After all, as Derrida reminds us, "the barred passage, *no pas-*

Fig 4.2 "El Frente Popular de Madrid Al Frente Popular del Mundo," Poster advertising the International Brigades. *Credit:* Library of Congress / Corbis / VCG via Getty Images

arán: this is what aporia means."[131] Like the biblical watchman, Glantz's implied Loyalist guards are prophet-soldiers, watching for the enemy and for the dawn of a new era.

Peretz Markish, the only poet of the three to have made his home in Soviet Russia, uses more Soviet reference points in his Spain cycle than Kurtz or Glantz do. In the poem "Commander Diestro," which closes Markish's volume, the eponymous character, a philosophy student who takes up arms after a bishop shoots his father, is a Spanish Vasily Chapaev, the decorated Red Army commander from the Russian Civil War who had died in battle. Chapaev's name was, by then, a password for wartime heroism: "Just like that Chapaev once fought!" (Ot azoy s'amol geshlogn zikh Tshapaiev!).[132] Whereas "Spain" begins with a tragic return to the Inquisition, Diestro leads a group to successfully occupy a church. Again evoking Chapaev, Markish contributes to the view of Spain as a new theater for world revolution. The poem ends with a vision of victory. Diestro, his arms wounded, is taken to the hospital, where the battle continues to play out in the commander's mind:

On bavustzayn z'er gelegn a mesles dort,	He lay there unrecognized for twenty-four hours,
vi a kholem iz adurkhgegan di shlakht,	like a dream he went back through the battle,
un gekumen, vi a vunder, iz der zig,—	and it came, like a wonder, victory,—
s'hot farlangt azoy dos folk, di republik![133]	this nation has so longed for the Republic!

Like the dying Robert Jordan in Ernest Hemingway's *For Whom the Bell Tolls*, Diestro does not see victory but dreams victory. His anonymity, by the end of the poem, emphasizes the unimportance of the individual in the face of a collective future, but his role within that collective is that of the dying prophet.

Comintern-aligned Jews, faced with the foreboding rise of fascism across Europe, placed their hope in the Spanish Republic. The American volunteer Hyman Katz wrote in a letter in 1938, "Don't you realize that we Jews will be the first to suffer if fascism comes?"[134] Ilya Ehrenburg, who traveled to Spain as a Soviet newspaper correspondent, felt optimistic in 1936 when France voted in the Popular Front candidate, Leon Blum. "I rejoiced with the others: after Spain—France! It was clear now that Hitler would not succeed in beating Europe to her knees. . . . I think back to the spring of 1936 as to the last happy spring of my life."[135] The desire to see an end to the fascist threat helps to explain the tenacity with which supporters of the Republic clung to the hope of victory. The future-oriented poems in Markish's, Glantz's, and Kurtz's Spain cycles express the same collective will.

CODA: SPAIN TO WORLD WAR II

From the moment Stalin and Hitler signed a nonaggression treaty in 1939, the prospect of World War II overshadowed the defeat in Spain for Jewish leftists in and outside the Soviet Union. Problematically for Yiddish writers, the Soviet-German alliance in 1939 meant that Soviet writers were, for a period of several months, prohibited from denigrating fascism.[136] When, following the Nazi invasion of the Soviet Union, anti-German literature was again published, Markish wrote several World War II works that used passwords to place Nazism in the context of Jewish history, much in the same way he had used historical Jewish passwords to place the rise of fascism in the context of Spanish Jewish history in 1936.

The Spanish Civil War returned to Yiddish literature as a password for martyrdom during World War II.[137] Markish's *Trot fun doyres* (Footsteps of a generation) finds a young widower, Metek, searching for the words to discuss his wife's death in the Spanish Civil War with his father-in-law. Metek thinks of the biblical Joseph's brothers as he prepares to show his father-in-law "the bloody party card of his daughter, who gave her life for freedom in Spain." The return to the motif of Spain in this story of a Jewish family during World War II universalizes the fight against Hitler from a Jewish concern to a long war against fascism. It also shows the role of the Spanish Civil War, and the Comintern, in the development of Jewish literature. Metek hopes to convince his father-in-law "that with his daughter's blood too would be written the history of the freedom-movement not only in Spain but . . . in the whole world."[138] Spain, even during World War II and despite the defeat of the International Brigades and Republic, remained a heroic moment, a moment when Jews stood up to fight the injuries and injustices of history.

"Everybody knows how the war ended," Muriel Rukeyser wrote, in the opening to her posthumously published Spanish Civil War novel *Savage Coast*.[139] In hindsight, the Spanish Civil War devastated the liberal ideals of freedom and justice that inspired not only the leftists who joined forces with the Loyalists but also moderate democracies that stood by. However, Jewish ideological investment in the International Brigades offers a crucial context for the literature of trauma associated with the Holocaust. So, too, the Yiddish poetry of the Spanish Civil War introduced a modern poetics of antifascism in Europe, one that aped the fascist uses of history and met violence with violence. The cycles considered here, each in its own way, integrate a traumatic past, contemporaneous documentary accounts of Spain, and collective slogans that prophesied a progressive future. That all three poets merge national memory, their current antifascist commitment, and Marxist eschatology demonstrates the ubiquitous artistic devices that Yiddish internationalist poets deployed in Spain.

5

MY SONGS, MY *DUMAS*

Rewriting Ukraine

THE YIDDISH POET Avrom Sutzkever (1913–2010) wrote on multiple occasions of a meeting he had in Moscow, in the winter of 1944, with the Russian Jewish poet Boris Pasternak (1890–1960). Sutzkever, who had fled the Vilna Ghetto to fight with Soviet partisans a few months earlier, claims to have read one of his ghetto poems to the Russian poet and, describing the encounter in a poem decades later, recalls a password that was lost in translation:[1]

Ikh hob geleyent mayn geratevetn zhar fun gehenem:	I read my salvaged char from hell:
"A rege is gefaln vi a shtern"—ale verter	"A moment—a *rege*—fell like a star"—all the words
farshtanen, khuts 'a rege.' Nit gekent tsu ir derlangen.	were clear, except "a *rege*." He couldn't reach it.
Der shney iz nit tsegangen.[2]	The snow didn't melt.

In Sutzkever's account, Pasternak's fluent German gave him access to all but the key to the poem, which lay in the Hebrew word for "moment"— *rege*. The poem Sutzkever references opens with the following lines:

A rege iz gefaln vi a shtern,	A moment fell like a star,
hob ikh zi ongekhapt in mayne tseyn,	I caught it between my teeth.
un ven zey hobn oyfgehakt ir kern,	And when they cut open its core,
hot oyf mir a shprits geton a kini-	It sprayed me with a kingdom of
graykh geveyn.[3]	crying.

Sutzkever's Yiddish "rege" (moment) is at once a wound and a time stamp, an irreplaceable password for those who can decipher it. It is, as Derrida has observed of Paul Celan's shibboleths, a cipher for an otherwise inaccessible experience, "the word that opens the possibility of mourning what has been lost without remainder."[4] Regardless of whether the conversation took place as Sutzkever remembered it (Pasternak denied it did), Sutzkever's poetic account of the lost *rege* suggests that on both sides of the Nazi-Soviet border, Jewish culture was disappearing.[5] If in the Vilna Ghetto Yiddish was being systematically murdered, east of the Nazi occupied territory it was giving way to the very internationalism many Yiddish poets had helped to build. In Sutzkever's account, however, he teaches his password to the Russian Jewish poet:

In zayne faykht-geshlifene shvarts-	In his damp-polished black-marble
mirmlne shvartsaplen	pupils,
hot opgeshternt yene rege. Un zi hot a	that *rege* hit him. And for a moment,
rege	forced
dem Rusishn poet mit geler late oykh	the Russian poet to wear a yellow
bahangen.[6]	star.

Sutzkever's "rege," a password to the "kingdom of crying" (kenigraykh geveyn), transforms into the other, fatal, password—the yellow patch. The word's untranslatability at once defines the limits of translation and becomes a vehicle for smuggling experiences across a deadly border. Real or imagined, the encounter offers a redemption narrative for the endangered Yiddish word, which miraculously reaches Pasternak, the Russian poet and master translator.

Pasternak was a generation removed from Yiddish, but his contemporary Soviet Yiddish poets were keenly aware of the loss of a textual tradition. The poet Dovid Hofshteyn had complained to his colleague, the Russian-born Argentinian Yiddish poet Hirsh Bloshteyn, in 1932, that young Soviet Jewish writers had read only a few modern

Yiddish writers, at best: "Our national Jewish culture here lacks cultural tradition [kultur-traditsie]. . . . In our schools you don't study the leaders of our Jewish literature in other languages. . . . If you rip out the foundation, the structure will not hold for long!"[7] At a time when Jewish culture appeared to be falling out of the international celebration of Soviet nations, carefully placed passwords were a mechanism for encoding, and facilitating, forbidden conversations. Although Jewish cultural tradition was thinning in the internationalist Soviet cultural sphere, the avowedly internationalist institution of translation provided a refuge for discussing Jewish tradition, albeit in a coded way. The untranslatable password, embedded in a non-Jewish text, could carry its meaning to a new readership.

By the late 1930s, when Stalin's government increasingly suppressed political self-expression, poets turned to translation as a safe means of supporting themselves and sometimes of conveying political and cultural messages in borrowed texts.[8] Boris Pasternak had shifted from publishing original work to translation in the 1930s, famously rendering Shakespeare and Goethe, as well as several Georgian modernists and the Ukrainian poet Taras Shevchenko into Russian.[9] Soviet Yiddish poets, like their Russian colleagues, found in translation an outlet that lent meaning to the Jewish experience through engagement with canonical works of a neighboring culture.[10] A paradigmatic case of this double role of translation into Yiddish was Dovid Hofshteyn, who in the 1930s translated a selection of world literature that overlapped strikingly with the writers Pasternak translated into Russian—Shakespeare, Goethe, the Georgian poet Simon Chikovani, and Shevchenko. Hofshteyn's translations of Shevchenko, in particular, provided a space for Hofshteyn to hone his poetic form, to write verse about his native Ukraine, and to embed distinctly Jewish passwords in his translations from one of his childhood languages.

In the previous chapters I have examined cases where Yiddish poets shared Jewish passwords with other ethnic groups in an act of internationalist solidarity, from Chinese workers to Spanish Republicans. In the Soviet late 1930s, however, preserving traces of Jewish cultural signs was paramount. This was, after all, a time when Soviet internationalism was changing, and minority cultures not directly tied to geographically defined Soviet republics had fewer opportunities for cultural expression.[11] This became more urgent in the wake of the Spanish Civil War, when Jews in and outside the Soviet Union saw the dangerous strength of Hitler and his allies. Although during World War II Jewish writers did write about Jewish victims of the war, embedding these stories into a larger, antifascist narrative, the late 1930s, which saw the waning of the Popular Front in 1938 and eventually the Hitler-Stalin nonaggression treaty in 1939–1940, were years of repressed Jewish cultural self-expression.[12] During this period, Soviet Yiddish writers expressed their concern about Jewish culture either by writing for the drawer, as Peretz Markish did with his 1940 *Tsu a yidishe tentserin* (To a Jewish dancer), or found coded ways of discussing Jewishness. The historical coexistence of Ukrainian and Yiddish made translations, and discussions, of Ukrainian literature into a coded conversation about the place of Jews in the Soviet Union. Here I examine the covert use of passwords from a non-Jewish literary tradition to converse about Jewish experiences.

TARAS SHEVCHENKO'S IDEAL TRANSLATOR

In 1939, Dovid Hofshteyn published a translation of Taras Shevchenko's 1840 antitsarist poem "Son" (A dream). Shevchenko's original, written in St. Petersburg, is a harsh indictment of the tsar's limitations on Ukrainian rights. Images of the Russian winter reflect the alienation of the marginalized Ukrainian subject:

Upyvaites', benketuite—	Drink, feast—
Ia vzhe ne pochuiu,	I no longer hear,
Odyn sobi navik-viky	Alone for all eternity
V snihu zanochuiu.[13]	I'll sleep in the snow.

Hofshteyn's Yiddish translation echoes, whenever possible, Shevchenko's trochaic meter, as well as his alliterative lines and feminine rhyme scheme. He also finds Yiddish equivalents to match the stark contrast, in the Ukrainian, between those who rejoice and those who disappear, in isolation, in the snow:

Freyt zikh! Hulyet! Shikert! Hulyet!	Rejoice! Carouse! Get drunk! Carouse!
Ikh vel shoyn nit hern—	I'll no longer hear—
aleyn, aleyn ikh vel oyf eybik	alone, alone forever
in shney farglivert vern.[14]	I'll grow rigid in the snow.

The violent rejoicing in the first line, contrasted with the deaf and frozen loneliness that follows, could easily evoke the mass violence spreading across Europe in the 1930s. Hofshteyn's choice of the word "hulyet" (carouse) in place of Shevchenko's "benketuite" (feast) adds an element of rabble-rousing, reminiscent of Avrom Reyzen's well-known Bundist song "Revel, revel, angry winds!" (Hulyet, hulyet, beyze vintn!). The word, which has Ukrainian roots and is connected to the concept of "hooliganism," had come to signify the dangerous merriment associated with riots, boycotts, and unjust violence. Party members used it to describe fascist demonstrations and, as we have seen in Chapter Two, used the word to describe the Jewish outrage against the Party following the violence in Palestine in 1929. Hofshteyn's shift from trochees to iambs in the lines cited above, from "*Freyt* zikh! *Hul*yet!" (Rejoice! Carouse!) to "a*leyn*, a*leyn*" (alone, alone), combined with his repetition of the word "aleyn" (alone) and his alliteration on the consonant *v* and diphthong *ey*, suggest a whispered "vey" (pain), lending the poem a mournful tone. Hofshteyn's "A kholem" is, then, simultaneously a close approximation of Shevchenko's 1840 poem and a new Yiddish work, relevant to Hofshteyn's own time.

Taras Shevchenko (1814–1861) was born a serf. He traveled to the imperial capital in 1831 with his master, Paul Engelhardt. Recognizing Shevchenko's artistic talent, a group of artists and writers collaborated to buy Shevchenko's freedom in 1838. Once free to pursue his career as a painter, Shevchenko enrolled in the Imperial Academy of Arts and gradually became active in the Ukrainian national movement, writing about Ukraine's historical nation-building efforts and speaking out against serfdom from St. Petersburg. (He was later arrested in 1847 as a member of the Brotherhood of Saints Cyril and Methodius, a Ukrainian national movement consisting of writers and intellectuals, and sent into exile.) The imagery in Shevchenko's poem echoes in Hofshteyn's early poems about the Ukrainian landscape, which focus on the isolation of Jews in the Slavic lands. Arguably Hofshteyn's most famous lines are from 1912, and they too compare bitter isolation to the Russian winter:

| In vinter-farnakhtn oyf Rusishe felder! | On winter evenings in Russian fields! |
| Vu ken men zayn elnter, vu ken men zayn elnter?[15] | Where can one be lonelier, where can one be lonelier? |

Translation allowed Hofshteyn to express modern Jewish themes of alienation in terms acceptable to the increasingly Russocentric world of Soviet internationalism. Hofshteyn's poetics of wandering, laced with an understated pride in his Jewish heritage, made him an ideal translator of Shevchenko. In addition to Yiddish and Hebrew, Hofshteyn wrote in Ukrainian and Russian. He translated Shevchenko's writings from both languages, as well as works by Ukrainian modernists including Pavlo Tychyna, Mykola Bazhan, Volodymyr Sosiura, and Pavlo Usen'ko and anonymous folk poets.[16] Shevchenko's condition of alienation and exile as a former Ukrainian serf in the tsarist empire must have resonated with Hoyfshteyn, a Jewish poet who grew up in Ukraine at the end of the tsarist period. It probably also resonated with the more mature Hofshteyn who in the early 1930s witnessed the thinning of Soviet Jewish culture.

Shevchenko was canonized as the official representative of Ukrainian literature in the 1930s, and Soviet translations of his work appeared in multiple languages. Hofshteyn's Yiddish translations of Shevchenko help to reveal the nuances and loopholes in a state-sponsored world-literary project. The ambitious, top-down Soviet literary project strove for pluralism but did so by exalting Moscow as the center of the world's workers and of communist internationalism.[17] State publishing organs promoted translation and published in the multiple languages of the Soviet peoples. This project involved what Katerina Clark has termed the "Great Appropriation," which repackaged local and foreign writers of the past and present to evoke and reflect current Marxist values.[18] Translator-practitioners of this Great Appropriation used a variety of passwords to simultaneously reinforce a Soviet-aligned internationalist project and undermine what increasingly appeared to be Russian neoimperialism.

The Revolutionary Jewish culture that had taken root in the nascent Soviet Union by the early 1920s centered on Yiddish, rather than Hebrew, as its official language. Following the Revolution, Hebrew publication was banned, and most Hebrew writers left soon after.[19] Yiddish publications, to the contrary, had been restricted under the tsar and even banned during World War I, but after 1917 the government encouraged the spread of Yiddish culture.[20] As a result, writers like Hofshteyn continued to write in Yiddish but gradually saw an increased imperative of replacing Jewish reference points with Marxist-Leninist messages. As Soviet Jewish cultural institutions were losing support, Yiddish writers often turned to translation as a means of building a Soviet Yiddish poetry and as a way of discussing the role of minorities in the increasingly Russocentric Soviet cultural sphere. Harriet Murav has demonstrated Jews' key role, as Russian translators, "in the implementation of the policy known as the 'friendship of nations.' Jews transmitted Soviet cultural values to the so-called national minorities and translated their works into Russian."[21] Soviet Jewish translators were representatives of what Naomi Seidman has called, in the context of German Jewry, a "translator culture"—"consummate cultural translators, whether this was highest praise or nastiest insult, wild exaggeration or powerful insight."[22] In the Soviet 1930s, Jews helped to build what was, de facto, becoming an imperial literary project in Russian with their linguistic expertise, while simultaneously spreading canonical Soviet texts through their translations into Yiddish.

If translators into Russian helped to build Russian as the ideal universal language, translators into Yiddish were strengthening a Yiddish language of poetry that acknowledged the complicated coexistence of Soviet national minorities. Hofshteyn had deep roots in the Ukrainian territories, which linked him geographically to Shevchenko. He was born in the small town of Korostyshev in the Kyiv region in 1889, not far from the village of Moryntsi, where Shevchenko was born in 1814. His poetic career began in earnest in interwar Kyiv, in a time of alternating Ukrainian and Bolshevik governments. Ukraine, which had been marginal to Jewish culture compared to centers like Vilnius or Warsaw, moved to the center of Yiddish literature in the years immediately following the Revolution.[23] Hofshteyn was hailed in the interwar years as an innovator of a new, modern Yiddish poetry, and he and a handful of fellow Ukrainian Jewish writers including Peretz Markish, Leyb Kvitko, Dovid Bergelson, and Der Nister (Pinkhes Kahanovitsh) became known as the Kiev-grupe—a group praised for writing Yiddish literature that was universal rather than folkloristic.[24] Hofshteyn was also a member of the Yiddish organization Kultur-Lige, which had its start in Ukraine and sponsored schools, theaters, libraries, and publications. Eventually, this organization was subsumed into the Soviet literary project—a project that Hofshteyn and his Kiev-grupe colleagues joined but only after leaving and then returning to the Soviet Union in the 1920s.

Scholars of postcolonial translation practices and non-European languages have observed the inextricability of what has traditionally been considered distinct realms of form and content. Anthony Appiah has advocated sacrificing smooth translations that favor the target audience for "thick translation," which "challenges us to . . . undertake the harder project of a genuinely informed respect for others."[25] The emphasis on the idiosyncrasies of lesser-spoken languages acknowledges that a worldview, in addition to culturally specific passwords, is embedded within language itself. After all, languages are not perfectly equivalent, and linguistic form, particularly of a dominated language, always already contains cultural content. As Jeffrey Veidlinger has observed in his study of the Moscow Yiddish Theater, minority artists, expected to turn their languages into "thin veils" for Soviet messages, instead "took advantage of the opportunity to utilize their national myths and languages to reenact ancient battles for national independence, to revive long-forgotten heroes, and to recreate the halcyon days of the people's glory in order to ignite their audience's nationalist yearnings."[26] Well before the Revolution, Jewish cultural figures discussed methods of translating world literature into Yiddish and Hebrew. Their goal, according to Kenneth Moss, was to strengthen modern Jewish culture by making it possible to read the classics of world literature in Jewish languages. Approaches to world literature ranged from internationalists like Peretz Markish, the revolutionary poet who eschewed traditional Jewish referents in his writing, to Zionists like Chaim Nachman Bialik, who believed that translations of modern European literature should encourage readers to approach world literature in Jewish languages.[27] Hofshteyn was much closer to

Markish than he was to Bialik in his sensibility, but even his Soviet-commissioned translations reveal a continued investment in Jewish folk themes and styles.

Translation, as a key component of the nascent Soviet world-literary project, was a means of building a network of national literatures in the multiple languages of the Soviet peoples, all of whom were expected to uphold Marxist-Leninist ideals. Yet translation of past texts also allowed for the expression of national concerns that would not have been permitted in new works of Soviet literature. Themes of one group's past national struggle metaphorically recall another nation's similar struggles. Dialect in the original encourages translators to showcase dialect in the target language. Thus, Hofshteyn transforms Shevchenko's ironic, vernacular line "There you have it, Pole, friend, brother" (Otak-to, Liashe, druzhe, brate!) into the equally folksy and ironic "There you have it! Poles, brother-love!" (Ot azoy, Poliakn, brider-libe!). In the process, he preserves the Yiddish speech idioms, "ot azoy" (there you have it) and "brider-libe" (brother-love).[28] By finding a place for Yiddish idiom, Hofshteyn playfully evokes Jewish national solidarity even in a Ukrainian poem.

Lawrence Venuti has coined the term "specular process" to describe how a translation of another national literature can encourage national solidarity and "enable a self-recognition in a national collective."[29] Translators representing empires, nation-states, and national minorities have stimulated national solidarity, Venuti demonstrates, whether by presenting a perceived challenge to a particular national myth, by translating multiple texts for a target readership to demonstrate the "capacity to mediate all other national cultures," or by altering signifiers in a way that fits the current political aspirations or cultural identity of the target language. Venuti offers examples that demonstrate metaphorical political messages that translation offers an imperial project and a national minority. On the one hand, "German culture, created through translation, achieves global domination . . . by forcing the 'foreigner' to appreciate the canon of world literature in German."[30] On the other hand, the Catalan translator Josep Carner rendered the Cheshire Cat of Lewis Carroll's *Alice in Wonderland* in 1927 as the "Castillian Cat" (el gat castellà), a decision, among others, that allowed Carner's readers "to recognize themselves as Catalans."[31] Whereas the Russian-language Soviet school of translation shared much in common with the nineteenth-century German approach to envisioning itself a center of world culture (and therefore of world domination), translation between Soviet national minorities was a means of inserting national identity into the language of the translation. Just as Carner's "Castillian Cat" was a password for Catalan identity in a "Madrid-imposed dictatorship,"[32] passwords that reflected Jewish identity made Hofshteyn's translations of Shevchenko into Jewish literary texts in the Russocentric 1930s.

Hofshteyn's translations of Shevchenko, moreover, reveal how a specular translation process is meaningfully amplified in the exchange between groups that have historically cohabitated, if often uncomfortably. Ukrainians' historical involvement in violent anti-Jewish pogroms left lasting scars on the Jewish collective memory. Ukrainians, for their part, viewed Jews, who had historically worked as tax collectors for Polish magnates or wine and vodka merchants, as contributing to a broad power structure that had oppressed Ukrainian peasants.[33] Whereas Venuti identifies examples of translations that supply political metaphors across languages, we find an even more potent, metonymic, means of national self-expression through translation that occur in relationships of close spatial and temporal proximity. Like many Ukrainian Romantics, Shevchenko occasionally portrayed Jews negatively, as Ukrainians' caricatured antagonists. Despite historical tensions between Ukrainians and Jews, translations between Ukrainian and Yiddish reveal unexpected similarities. Although in the 1930s Soviet Ukrainians and Jews alike saw a censoring of their cultural traditions by the Soviet government, it must be acknowledged that the internationalist efforts to foster a friendship among nations created an institution of minority translation where the Soviet Ukrainian and the Soviet Jewish cultures both preserved elements of group solidarity by closely inspecting each other. Yiddish writers could foster Jewish group solidarity through the unlikely vehicle of Ukrainian literature.

For Hoyfshteyn, translating Shevchenko—a writer who described the same geography Hofshteyn treated in his early poems and whose Ukrainian idioms demanded Yiddish equivalents—perpetuated a sense of national identity formation, albeit through the looking glass of translation. Hofshteyn's translations from the 1930s—a period when Soviet literature was to be national in form only—gave Yiddish readers layered texts that resonated strongly with a Jewish textual tradition.

Hofshteyn's translations of Shevchenko allowed the Yiddish poet to address themes of home, God, and the Ukrainian landscape where Hofshteyn and many of his readers had come of age. The fact that Ukrainians and Jews were often antagonists presented a challenge to the Yiddish translator, who, in keeping with Socialist internationalism, was expected to emphasize friendship between the Soviet peoples. Hofshteyn nevertheless included some of Shevchenko's negative images of Jews, subtly recalling the fraught cohabitation between Jews and Slavs in the region.

The Stalinist 1930s saw both the exaltation and the exploitation of culture in general and of literature above all, as a way of validating and solidifying the Soviet state. As Katerina Clark has articulated, "Writing is a way to give governance to speech."[34] In addition to publishing in Russian (the dominant language), Soviet cultural leaders took pains to publish approved texts in, and to translate from, Soviet minority languages. Maxim Gorky initiated the publishing house Vsemirnaia Literatura (World literature), which published about two hundred books between 1918 and 1924. In 1929, Gorky claimed that thanks to Soviet translation practices, "the literate Russian knows incomparably more about the life of European peoples than these peoples know and have known about Russia and the tribes who have lived amidst the Russian people since ancient times."[35] Translation, Gorky suggests here, whether of Soviet or non-Soviet languages, is proof of the international thrust of the Soviet project. The initial centralization of world literature in the late 1920s was both noticeably bureaucratic and a material windfall for the Yiddish poet. In 1927, Hofshteyn, writing to his friend Daniel Charney about the centralization of literary groups under the umbrella of the All-Russian Association of Proletarian Writers (VAPP) and the Moscow Association of Proletarian Writers (MAPP), sardonically quipped, "They have VAPPed and MAPPed themselves."[36] Nevertheless, the increased bureaucratization of the publishing industry created stable work for Party-aligned writers. By 1928, Hofshteyn wrote to Charney, "I have now situated myself a bit differently. I have a secretary, an office, a telephone, and so forth."[37]

And yet, by the 1930s, Russia was emerging as the dominant center of communist internationalism. The "Velikii perelom" (Great break;

1928–1932), as Yuri Slezkine has shown, hailed a return to increasingly Russocentric content, despite a superficial "extravagant celebration of ethnic diversity."[38] Clark has argued that although internationalism remained a goal of the Soviet literary enterprise, by the late 1930s, "things Russian—Russia's culture, its language, and even its people—were increasingly depicted as a primus inter pares, the pares being the other ethnic groups within the Soviet Union and their cultures."[39] What is clear is that even during this decade of increasingly centralized state power and Russocentric patriotism, translation was a lucrative Soviet enterprise. The newly consolidated state publishing apparatus sought to allow national groups to remain literate in their traditional languages while becoming indoctrinated into Marxist-Leninist ideals. The publishers of Hofshteyn's translations were state-funded institutions that actively promoted the publication of Marxist-Leninist texts in minority languages. These non-Russian-language Soviet publishing houses trod carefully in their treatment of the content they published, focusing on Marxist-Leninist educational and theoretical texts.[40] The State Publishing House for National Minorities, which printed three of Hofshteyn's book-length translations of Shevchenko, was born as a branch of the central State Publishing House, Gosizdat.[41] The Soviet branches of the Yiddishist Kultur-Lige were, during this period, absorbed into the centralized state publishing houses.[42] Harriet Murav points to the 1939 preface to the first issue of the literary journal *Druzhba Narodov* (Friendship of nations) as evidence of the definitive Russocentric turn: "Only a victorious nation can create and nurture all the conditions for the flowering of culture. . . . It discovers them, forces them to sound in a new way and to give birth to new feelings."[43] This centralization of internationalism meant that by the late 1930s, Soviet Yiddish writers, who had used Jewish passwords to emphasize other struggling groups as they had done in the case of China, Palestinian Arabs, and Spanish Republicans, were increasingly drawing literary passwords from other national minorities to highlight the Jewish experience.

Even as Stalin consolidated his dictatorship, the translations published in the late 1930s often tell a story of individual writers experimenting with cultural expression and even inserting national shibboleths between the lines. The institution of translation was important for displaying Moscow's hegemony within a vision of world literature put forth by the Communist International, but as Brian Baer notes, in the Soviet Union, "literary translators came to embody resistance, especially during the worst periods of repression."[44] Even the ever-cautious Pasternak, in his translation of Shakespeare's sixty-sixth sonnet, gestured toward the encroaching dangers of authority, by substituting "thoughts" for "authority," rendering Shakespeare's line "And art made tongue-tied by authority" as "And remember that thoughts will lock the mouth" (I vspominat', chto mysli zatknut rot).[45] Translation could smuggle meaning, whether by alteration or omission. This kind of subtle resistance perpetuated the "universal values" that Baer identifies as "in opposition to what [readers and translators] saw as the tendentious, politicized, and class-based official culture of the Soviet Union."[46] Importantly, translation also offered writers a subtle means of national self-expression.

BETWEEN NATION AND THE INTERNATIONAL

Although Jews are generally assumed to have identified with the culture of the empire that hosted them, instructive exceptions to this rule demonstrate, to the contrary, the admiration that often flowed between Jews and coexisting minority nationalities.[47] A striking example of this is Vladimir (Ze'ev) Jabotinsky, who would eventually lead the Revisionist Zionist movement. Jabotinsky found in Shevchenko a model for the kind of tribalism that he supported in his own nationalist project. In an article in Russian commemorating Shevchenko's centennial, Jabotinsky acknowledges Shevchenko's occasional antisemitism but nonetheless writes admiringly that "he . . . gave his people, and the whole wide world, inviolable proof that the Ukrainian soul is capable of the highest levels of original cultural expression."[48] Hofshteyn did not share Jabotinsky's radical Zionism, but he too undoubtedly found in Shevchenko a poet who stirred his people's linguistic and cultural sensibilities. Hofshteyn, who was censured in 1924 for supporting the teaching of Hebrew in the Soviet Union, left the nascent Soviet state for Berlin and then Palestine, where he published Hebrew-language poems and articles.[49] Only upon returning to the Soviet Union in 1926 to reunite with his young sons did Hofshteyn publicly repent of his support for Hebrew in an open letter to *Der emes:* "I want to again take my place among those who are building a new life for the Jewish working masses in the Soviet Union."[50] Through his translations of Shevchenko, he demonstrated the possibility of minority-group solidarity within a Russian-dominated cultural sphere.

In the aftermath of 1917, some Revolutionary Jewish readers had viewed Hofshteyn as the kind of internationalist poet that the Soviet literary project demanded, whereas others saw him as a nationalist poet who slipped Jewish themes into his work. He fell somewhere in between. The Soviet critic and playwright Yehezkel Dobrushin called Hofshteyn "our first 'not national' poet"—the highest praise a Revolutionary critic could give. Hofshteyn, even in his early verse, employed little overtly Jewish content. His early poetic personae are Whitmanesque wanderers—unfettered by the shtetl or tradition. His 1919 book of poems *Bay vegn* (On roads) includes lines like,

A dank aykh, vander-vegn breyte!   Thank you, wide wanderways!
Far mide glider, vander-shtoyb,[. . .][51]   For tired limbs, wanderdust, . . .

Others, including the fiction writer Dovid Bergelson praised Hofshteyn for integrating Jewish themes with universal themes.[52] Those who were close to Hofshteyn claimed that the poet nurtured an affection for Hebrew that remained hidden from the Soviet public sphere. According to the Soviet literary critic Eliezer Podriatshik, Hofshteyn told him in 1940, "I have woven into [my poems] a language of the holy-tongue spirit and image."[53]

Some readers identified, even in Hofshteyn's seemingly innocuous poetry of wandering, Jewish nationalist passwords. The American Yiddish poet and Party adherent Alexander Pomerantz criticized Hofshteyn in 1943 for describing in his poetry figures still attached to an older generation's bourgeois values. In *Bay vegn,* Hofshteyn writes in the voice of a young man setting out on his own path through the Ukrainian landscape: "with my inheritance from grandfather, with the old stick" (Mit zeydns yerushe, mit shtekn mit altn).[54] Pomerantz faults Hofshteyn for his use of the term "yerushe" (inheritance), evidence, according to Pomerantz, of bourgeois individualism and an attachment to a Jewish cultural inheritance, though he praises Hofshteyn for eventually breaking with the past in Revolutionary poems like "October" and "Protsesye."[55] Alexander Pomerantz, a founder of a series of American proletarian writers' groups and journals, lived in Soviet Kyiv for two years in 1933–1935, where he wrote his dissertation on the American Proletpen writers' union, which he had helped to found in 1929.[56] Like many American Party members, Pomerantz was quick to point out the ideological inconsistencies of his Soviet colleagues. If in hindsight it is difficult to overlook the hypocrisy in such criticism, it is worth acknowledging that Pomerantz's ear was closely attuned to nationalist and internationalist passwords. As Chana Kronfeld has recognized, "Even though Hofshteyn often tried to follow the party line, he never quite managed to rid his poetry of the forbidden cultural and biblical associations."[57] When in 1952 Hofshteyn was sentenced to death alongside twelve fellow Soviet Jewish writers, intellectuals, and cultural figures (including Markish, Bergelson, Kvitko, and Itsik Fefer), the trumped-up charges included his being "a convinced Zionist [who] participated actively in the anti-Soviet activity of Jewish nationalistic organizations during the Civil War and slandered Soviet power in his literary work."[58] The vague charges of anti-Soviet activity bore no connection to Hofshteyn's actual poetry or activities. The charges of Zionism, although fatally exaggerated, were not entirely wrong. Hofshteyn, who had written poetry in Hebrew and had a family in Palestine, must have identified on occasion with Shevchenko's longing to be elsewhere.

Hofshteyn, like many of his colleagues, embraced the project of creating a Jewish colony in Crimea. When the Jewish territorial project failed in Crimea, rather than shifting his gaze as others did toward Birobidjan, Hofshteyn turned to a more organic native space, Kyiv.[59] His cycle, *Kiev*, published in 1936, includes numerous Ukrainian words sprinkled into his Yiddish poems. "Dnieper" opens with a reference to Ukrainian time and space: "It's New Year's again. It's Sitchen, it's January" (Nokh nay-yor shoyn. S'iz Sitshen, s'iz Yanvar). By inserting the Ukrainian name for the first month of the year, Hofshteyn places his book into Ukrainian time and Soviet Kyiv into a Ukrainian space. Further in the collection, the poem "Kiev-hoyptshtot" (Kyiv—capital city) celebrates the 1934 transfer of the Ukrainian Soviet Socialist Republic's capital from Kharkiv to Kyiv. Hofshteyn's *Kiev* includes poems dedicated to the Palace of the Pioneers, the soccer team Dynamo (founded in the 1920s), the historically Jewish Podol region of the city, and "Tsen-Tsien," a Chinese hero who purportedly died defending Kyiv from the White Army.[60] "Mikhaylover monastir" (Mikhailov monastery) welcomes the demolition of the famous monastery in the 1930s and the creation of a government building in its place. Hofshteyn describes the large monastery as a place where Jews were at risk of being attacked. For the thugs who once lurked in the monastery courtyard,

Dos ergste zidlvort iz "zhid,"	The worst invective is "Jew,"
der ergster shpot iz—"komunist."[61]	the worst shame is—"Communist."

The publishers produced fifteen hundred copies of the book and clearly did so hastily, for it is full of errors in typography and pagination. However, these ideological verses remind us that as Hofshteyn was translating Shevchenko, he was attempting to describe a transformation in Soviet Ukraine. Hofshteyn presents a Soviet promised land that has eradicated antisemitism and the ghetto. Kyiv, he suggests, could be both a Soviet Jewish homeland and an internationalist Zion.

That Hofshteyn wrote poetry on both a universal and a national register made him an ideal translator for bringing Shevchenko to Soviet Jewish readers. Hofshteyn's remarkable commitment to bringing Shevchenko and Shevchenko scholarship into Yiddish suggests that Hofshteyn was not merely doing the Party's bidding by helping to translate the newly canonized nineteenth-century Ukrainian poet but that he identified with Shevchenko. His first translations of Shevchenko's poems appeared in a 1927 Yiddish edition of Vladimir Drunin's Russian-language biography of Shevchenko published by the formerly avant-garde Kultur-Lige press.[62] In 1935 Hofshteyn published a translation of Andrii Khvylia's Ukrainian-language biography of Shevchenko.[63] In 1937, he published a collection of Shevchenko's verse for children;[64] and in 1939, Hofshteyn published three book-length translations of Shevchenko's poems and prose: the collection *Lider* (Poems), *Geklibene verk* (Collected works), and the Russian-language novel *A shpatsir mit fargenign un nit on moral* (A walk with pleasure and not without a moral).[65] The following year, he became a member of the Communist Party, a status that rewarded him for his commitment to Revolutionary values and afforded him new professional privileges. Hofshteyn's colleagues Kvitko and Markish also became Party members in this period—Markish in 1939 and Kvitko in 1941. Their engagement with other national minorities undoubtedly played a role in these writers' inclusion as contributing members to the Communist Party of the Soviet Union.

The state publishing apparatus was gradually canonizing representative writers in Russian and national minority languages. The official Russian writers included Pushkin and Dobroliubov. Sholem Aleichem eventually became the representative Yiddish writer,[66] and Ukrainians were given Shevchenko, who was widely celebrated in the spring of 1939, on the occasion of the 125th anniversary of his birth.[67] In April 1939, a monument to Shevchenko was erected in Kyiv, and Nikita Krushchev, who then headed the Communist Party of Ukraine, delivered a speech at its unveiling: "All the peoples of the Soviet Union lovingly translate the poetry of Shevchenko, a Ukrainian poet, into their own languages."[68] That year, St. Vladimir University was renamed Taras Shevchenko University.[69] Soviet publishers were tasked with rapidly producing editions that emphasized protosocialist content and bore introductions highlighting Shevchenko's struggle for a friendship of nations. Newspapers across the Soviet Union ran articles about Shevchenko and examples of his poetry.[70] The Soviet critic and poet Kornei Chukovsky later recalled that in 1939 "poets of all republics and regions of the Soviet Union began an enormous and collaborative collective to prepare a multilingual translation of *Kobzar*."[71] *Kobzar* was the title of Shevchenko's first widely distributed collection of poetry, which appeared in 1840. The title, literally meaning "bard" or "minstrel," referred to the player of a Ukrainian folk instrument, the *kobza,* which traditionally accompanied epic songs—*dumas*—that retold Ukrainian history and folklore. Hofshteyn's Yiddish translations were part of the broad effort to adapt Shevchenko to the Socialist Realist context of high Stalinism.

Curiously, the Yiddish-language monographs about Shevchenko that accompanied the 1939 celebration offered a space for contemporary Jewish academics to discuss how a nation could assert its cultural heritage in the Soviet Union. In a 1939 Yiddish-language biography, Petro

(Peisia) Al'tman writes, "Nowhere ... have the masses valued their kobzar as highly as here in our Soviet Union. ... Under the flag of Lenin-Stalin all peoples live free in our land, they build and create their cultures to be national in form, and socialist in content."[72] Hofshteyn, in a translator's introduction, remarks that "only the proletariat, under the leadership of the Bolshevik party of Lenin-Stalin, led the peasant to battle."[73] The anachronism is not unique to Hofshteyn; the idea that Stalin might have retroactively freed nineteenth-century serfs fit the logic of Socialist Realism. This kind of Marxist seal of approval was expected. As Gennady Estraikh has discussed, "A critical introduction, known among Russian editors as a *konvoi*, or 'safeguard,' was widely used in Soviet publishing as a way of making permissible books by classic writers."[74] However, the discussion of the Ukrainians as a people should not be overlooked as mere Stalinist rhetoric. Rather, it is thinly coded language for discussing the role of national minorities in the Soviet Union. There is, Al'tman and Hofshteyn indicate, a place for closely examining a nation within the socialist state—but it is best if it is someone else's nation.

That Hofshteyn wrote programmatically about the Ukrainian Romantic poet attests to an important aspect of his project: his translations were simultaneously ideological renderings of Shevchenko for a Soviet Jewish audience and linguistic renderings into Yiddish. Indeed, we cannot separate Hofshteyn's translations from the Moscow-centered world-literary project that commissioned them. Discussions of Ukrainian literature, as well as translations, constituted a specular process, by which Jewish writers simultaneously bolstered the Soviet internationalist friendship of nations and engaged in a conversation about the limitations of national self-expression. The Soviet Ukrainian Yiddish literary journals, *Royte Velt* (Red world) and *Prolit* featured regular translations as well as discussions of Ukrainian literature. The proletarian-focused *Prolit* published excerpts translated from Volodymyr Koriak's address to the second VUSPP (All-Ukrainian Union of Soviet Writers) congress, where Koriak clarifies the need to shift the literary focus from peasants to proletarians. "In Ukrainian literature one has always felt the strength in the peasant poetics [poyersher stikhie]. The peasant theme is now being reworked."[75] The satirist Kofsi, who published a humor column in *Prolit* that regularly caricatured Yiddish writers, poked fun at Hofshteyn's poetics of wandering, his allegiance to Ukraine, and his desire to adapt to Soviet literature. A caricature in May 1929 places Hofshteyn on Kyiv's central boulevard, Kreschatik, which is rhymed with "tematik" (thematic):

Kh'gey arum afn Kreshtshatik,	I wander around on Kreschatyk,
ikh bin itst in enderung, in veg.	I am now in a change, on a path.
Vu-zhe nemt men hayntike tematik?	But where does one find a current thematic?
Kh'freg.[76]	I ask.

Kofsi appears to poke fun at Hofshteyn's eagerness to please the Soviet press after his return from Palestine. Hofshteyn, who indeed sought somewhat clumsily to prove his ideological commitment to the Soviet project, found that translation allowed him to simultaneously express his firm belief in Soviet internationalism and create new Yiddish verse. The ideological aspect of the Soviet friendship-of-nations project hardly warrants dismissing Soviet Yiddish translations from Ukrainian as Stalinist court poetry. To the contrary, the poetic license Hofshteyn took attests both to the maturity of Yiddish translation by the 1930s and to Hofshteyn's eagerness to find a means of Yiddish poetic expression, even through the looking glass of Ukrainian subject matter.

HOFSHTEYN'S UKRAINE

As a Jew living in the Soviet Union—a Jew who had chosen the Soviet project over political Zionism but who privately acknowledged his affection for Hebrew and Palestine—Hofshteyn identified with Shevchenko's longing for his native land. Hofshteyn's pogrom poem "Ukrayne" (Ukraine), which appeared in his 1922 book *Troyer* (Sorrow), expresses the ambivalence of one who has never fully belonged. Hofshteyn writes of the

trit banditishe	bandits' footsteps
un lider shikere	and drunken songs
oyf dayne vimlendike markn . . . [77]	at your swarming markets . . .

Despite a generally negative view of Ukraine, the persona admits,

Ikh fil mit libe nokh:	I still feel lovingly:
es hot keyn shoyb do nit geplatst	not a windowpane here has broken
in bergturems in dayne,	on your mountaintops,
vos kukn, loyter nokh,	which look, still clear,
oyf di gevisern fun Dnieper,	over the floods of the Dnieper,
oyf stepes dayne . . . [78]	over your steppes . . .

These sentiments were not far from Shevchenko's 1838 observation, while in the imperial capital, that

Na chuzhyni ne ti liude—	People are different abroad—
Tiazhko z nymy zhyty!	It's hard to live with them!
Ni z kym bude poplakaty,	You'll have no one with whom to cry
Ni pohovoryty.[79]	Or talk.

This poetics of alienation, whether of Jews in Ukraine or of Ukrainians in Russia, connects the two poets despite their different relationships to Ukraine.

After returning to the Soviet Union in 1926, Hofshteyn began writing unambiguously patriotic poems about Soviet Ukraine. Hofshteyn's 1944 poem "Ukrayne" casts Ukraine as a child who has emerged from the violence of the Civil War (1918–1920), a newly grown woman with "motherly pain":

Fun roykh, un fun brokh, un fun ash, un fun shand	From smoke, and from woe, and from ash, and from shame
ikh derze, du derheybst dayn tseshedikte hant,	I see you lift your wounded hand,
ot derheybt zikh dayn kop, vos mit blut iz baklept,	your head rises, pasted in blood,
ikh derze dayn gezikht! O, er lebt, o, er lebt,	I see your face! Oh, it lives, oh, it lives,
dayn nokh kindersher blik mit shoyn mutershn tsar,	your still childish glance now with motherly pain,
un es loykht shoyn di freyd, vos kumt on nokh gefar,	and the joy that follows danger lights up,
der farshtand, vos kumt on nokh fartumlung un grayz,	the knowledge that follows confusion and error,
vi vaser in friling fun unter dem ayz—[80]	like water in the spring from under the ice—

Shevchenko, who frequently wrote in a female first-person voice, also frequently imagined Ukraine as a woman, ravaged, as Susan Layton puts it, "by masculinized Russia, Poland, or her own politically dislocated native sons."[81] In a bizarre sexual unveiling, Hofshteyn depicts a feminized Ukraine, who, violated and battered, is now undressed, admired, and deemed ready for marriage:

Ikh derze: ot derheybt zikh dayn guf, dayn geshtalt,
vos di reshtlekh fun kleyder af im koym zikh halt,
un es faln di shmutsike shmates fun layb—
s'iz tsu zen shoyn, s'a kind a der-vaksns, a vayb,
s'iz a likhtiker kerper mit sheynkayt, vos shaynt
i durkh shand, i durkh shpot, i durkh gvaldtat fun faynt.[82]

I see: now your body, your image is rising,
how your clothing's remains can barely hang on,
and the dirty rags fall from your body—
you can see a child grown into a wife,
it's a stunning body with beauty that shines
through shame, and through mockery, and through the enemy's violence.

Precisely who will betroth the new Ukraine, whether the people, Stalin, or Russia, is vague. By the end of the poem, however, Hofshteyn suggests that the husband is none other than the Yiddish poet himself: "It's Ukraine my home, / Ukraine my land" (Si'z Ukrayne mayn heym, Ukrayne mayn land).[83] The poem is both a reconciliation and a sexual conquest—and indeed, we must assume, a nonconsensual one. The "shame" and "mockery" ("shand" and "shpot") mentioned in the opening and closing of the poem allow for an interpretation that the Soviet people—Jews included—have thrived at Ukraine's expense. Whereas before the Revolution, modernizing Jews viewed Ukraine—the largest territory in the Pale of Settlement—as a marginal site of diaspora, the newly established Ukrainian Soviet Socialist Republic promised many Jews new status and opportunities.[84] This multiethnic space now provided the opportunity to celebrate the "Friendship of Nations" hailed as one of the key values in the Soviet Union.[85]

It is likely that Hofshteyn drew his specular approach to national solidarity in part from Shevchenko himself. The two poets' experiences in the Caucasus, as non-Russian subjects of an empire, contributed to Hofshteyn's connection to Shevchenko, helped to further both poets' credentials as internationalists, and offered both poets a mirror for their own cultural alienation in a distant Other. Shevchenko's 1845 poem "Kavkaz" (The Caucasus) dealt with the Circassian struggle for independence from Russia. The Ukrainian poet made clear his identification with the Circassians in lines addressing them in their struggle with the imperialist Russians: "And you, knights of freedom / God has not forgotten" (I vam, lytsari velyki / Bohom ne zabuti).[86] Like Shevchenko, Hofshteyn, who served in the Russian military in the Caucasus in 1912, included poems about the Caucasus in *Bay vegn*. These poems, as Mikhail Krutikov has observed, placed Hofshteyn "within the established Russian literary discourse of Caucasian 'Orientalism,' which had its roots in the romantic poetry of the 1820s."[87] However, Hofshteyn's poems of the Caucasus reflect a form of self-exoticism that demonstrates the poet's sympathy for the marginalized Other over the Orientalist empire. In the poem "In Armenie" (In Armenia), Hofshteyn writes, "I am brown and stiff, black-eyed just like you" (Kh'bin broyn un shtayf, shvarts-oygik ir tsuglaykh).[88] In Hofshteyn's early poetry of the Caucasus, we find a self-Orientalism similar to that found in Esther Shumiatcher's East Asian cycles. "Black-eyed" (shvarts-oygik) here, as for Shumiatcher, is a password for the marginalized non-Russian, whether Jewish, Armenian, or Chinese.

Hofshteyn's interest in the Caucasus continued into the Soviet period. His 1939 volume *Felker zingen* (Peoples sing), coedited with Itsik Fefer, is a collection featuring a wide variety of Soviet national minority poets, as well as folksongs, translated into Yiddish. Hofshteyn translated several of the Ukrainian poems, as well as poems from Russian, Georgian, Turkmen, and Armenian. The contents are a combination of folksongs emphasizing labor and patriotic songs to Stalin's Soviet Union (Hofshteyn wrote two original Yiddish odes to Stalin in the volume). Hofshteyn's productivity as a translator from national minorities, including his attention to the Caucasus in this volume, undoubtedly contributed to his acceptance by the Party. Notably, Shevchenko's attention to national minorities similarly bolstered arguments for his canonization in the Soviet Union as the poet of Ukrainian anti-imperialism. The Ukrainian writer Hryhorii Epik, in an essay translated into Yiddish and published in *Royte Velt* in 1925, argued that Shevchenko should be viewed as an internationalist: "Shevchenko was no nationalist, as the Ukrainian bourgeoisie [pritsim] maintain. His strongest protest was against the oppression of the Caucasus."[89] The term used here for the Ukrainian bourgeoisie, *pritsim*, literally means "noblemen" or "magnates." For Jews, *pritsim* historically referred, often derogatorily, to Polish nobility. Here, however, *pritsim,* like "foreign fascists," is a password that derogatorily connotes those diaspora Ukrainian nationalists who had fled eastern Europe for the West for their anti-Soviet Ukrainian nationalism. Rebuking those in the Ukrainian diaspora who advocated for an independent Ukrainian nation-state was an important theme among Soviet critics following the Ukrainian Civil War. The debate over the soul of past Ukrainian literature was comparable to debates over the internationalist or Zionist sympathies of earlier Yiddish writers, including Sholem Aleichem.[90] In conversations among Yiddish writers, *pritsim,* an allusion to Ukrainian nationalists, particularly in the Ukrainian diaspora, becomes a password for the dangers of Zionism.

Hofshteyn and Shevchenko also shared strictly formal sensitivities. Hofshteyn's wordplay, alliteration, and internal rhymes complement Shevchenko's alliterative Ukrainian. Take the last line of Shevchenko's most famous poem, "Zapovit" (Testament), where Shevchenko's speaker prepares to leave the hills and valleys of Ukraine to meet his maker:

Vse pokynu i polynu	I will leave it all and I will float
Do samoho boha[91]	To God himself

Hofshteyn finds a similarly alliterative voice for his Yiddish-speaking Shevchenko, who declares that he will:

alts farlozn un zikh lozn	leave it all and let myself go
biz di himlen trogn[92]	to take myself up to the heavens

Not only does Hofshteyn create a new internal rhyme (farlozn / zikh lozn), but he preserves Shevchenko's vowel sounds: "boha" (God) yields phonetically to "trogn" (carry), creating an intertextual rhyme. A more virtuosic example of the preservation of sound appears earlier in "Zapovit," where Hofshteyn renders Shevchenko's "lany shyroko-poli" (wide fields) as "breytpoledike lonkes" (broad-rimmed fields).

The felicitous reappearance of "pole" allows Shevchenko's own surprising long word to shine through in the Yiddish, despite the linguistic distance between the Germanic Yiddish and Slavic Ukrainian. Internal rhymes and alliteration are often the first things Shevchenko's other translators dismiss.[93]

The terms Hofshteyn selects to describe Shevchenko's Ukraine occasionally echo the language he used to describe the Jewish home and shtetl in his own early poems. For instance, in Shevchenko's 1839 "Dumy moi" (My songs), a poem that compares a poet's verse to a mother's children, we find,

Chom vas viter ne rozviiav	Why has the wind not blown you
V stepu, iak pylynu?[94]	on the steppes, as dust?

Hofshteyn translates these lines as follows:

Vos hot vint aykh nit tseveyet	Why has the wind not blown you
in step, vi shtoyb fun vegn?[95]	on the steppes, like the dust from roads?

The translation adheres tightly to the original, the notable exception being that Hofshteyn's dust comes "from roads" (fun vegn), possibly an allusion to his own first collection of poems, *Bay vegn* (On roads). If we take Hofshteyn's translation to be a poetic utterance in its own right, the "vegn" here suggests that the Ukrainian-Yiddish translator views his translations as dust from his first volume, that is, as part of his own larger poetic oeuvre.

In addition to these formal allusions to the Ukrainian original, Hofshteyn preserves Ukrainian passwords in his translations. There is no perfect translation for the Ukrainian-specific "duma" in the opening line—a genre of lyric-epic poem or song traditionally recited to the accompaniment of a musical instrument, usually a stringed *kobza, bandura,* or *lira*—a Ukrainian hurdy-gurdy. The untranslatable "duma" constituted a genre of poem for Shevchenko. Deriving from the verb *dumaty* (to think), it can be translated into "song," "poem," "thought," or "idea." Shevchenko compares these deeply personal *dumas* to children, whom he then compares to flowers: "My songs, my songs" (Dumy moi, dumy moi), "My flowers, children!" (Kvity moi, dity!). Hofshteyn, understanding *duma* to be an untranslatable password, renders the line, "My songs, my dumas"

(Lider mayne, *dumes* mayne). This preserves the original Ukrainian *dumy*, while conveying at least one sense of the meaning into Yiddish. Hofshteyn thus also makes clear that he expects and trusts his readers to understand this Ukrainian reference.[96] Elsewhere Hofshteyn chooses Yiddish variants that phonetically approximate the Ukrainian: Shevchenko's Ukrainian "kvity" (flowers) become "kvaytn," a choice that preserves the sound of the original Ukrainian, unlike another choice for "flowers"— *blumen.* In "dumes" and, more subtly, with "kvaytn," Hofshteyn preserves something of what Jacques Derrida has called a "trace"—the remains of a former signifier.[97] "Duma," a trace of Shevchenko's original, is also a cipher that, like the Spanish Civil War slogans, encodes the poetic act, allowing the poem to guard and grant access to the thing itself, in this case to the existence of the word that Shevchenko gave to his songs. Like Celan's multilingual poems, where, according to Derrida, "what seems to bar the passage of translation is the multiplicity of languages in the same poem, at once," Hofshteyn, by preserving Ukrainian passwords in his Yiddish translations of Shevchenko, acknowledges that Yiddish itself is a language of passwords and a language where others' passwords can resound.[98] At the moment when Soviet literature was increasingly limited by the dictates of the Stalinist state, Hofshteyn's insistence on preserving traces in his translation was also an insistence on preserving the password as a continuation of a cultural tradition. Allowing a glimpse of the original Ukrainian through his Yiddish, Hofshteyn protects the difference between the translation and the original, an act that forces the reader to engage with Shevchenko using at least the occasional Ukrainian word. This act bridges the Yiddish of his translation and the Ukrainian that Hofshteyn's readers are presumed to understand, given their history of cohabitation and conflict with Ukrainians.

Shevchenko wrote this poem in 1839, while a student at the St. Petersburg Academy of Fine Arts. A woman's voice narrates this early poem. Comparing her songs to children, she asks them to return to their native Ukraine "to sing." The following excerpt depicts the poems/children as emissaries back to Ukraine:

V Ukraiinu idit', dity!	Go, children, to Ukraine!
V nashu Ukraiinu,	To our Ukraine,

Popidtynniu, syrotamy,
A ia—tut zahynu.[99]

Wandering aimlessly as orphans,
And I—I'll perish here.

Hofshteyn adds three syllables to the final line of this passage, allowing a long pause to emphasize the distinction between the song-children, who will travel to Ukraine as orphans, and the mother-poet, who expects to remain in exile:

Oyf Ukrayne geyt itst kinder
oyf Ukrayne geyt itst zingen
unter ployt dort vi yesoymim
un ikh—ikh vel shoyn do farz-
  inken . . .[100]

Go now children to Ukraine
go now to Ukraine to sing
behind a fence as orphans there
and I—I'll pass away right here . . .

Hofshteyn adds "itst" (now) to his first two lines, a choice that adds urgency to the mother's request as well as extending the meter to match Shevchenko's multisyllabic Ukrainian. Moreover, in the second line, Hofshteyn forgoes the possessive "our Ukraine," choosing instead to make the children/poems "sing." The solution creates several formal innovations: Hofshteyn replaces Shevchenko's trochaic trimeter with a repeated trochaic tetrameter; he also adds a near rhyme between "kinder" and "zingen" to replace the lost alliteration in "idyt dyty" (go children), in the process reinforcing the metaphor of poems as children. Hofshteyn also subtly shifts to political identity of the poem: his sacrifice of Shevchenko's collective possessive "our Ukraine" (v nashu Ukrainu) softens the notion of Ukrainian nationalism as part and parcel of geographic territoriality. Instead, Hofshteyn's poem-children are told simply to go "to Ukraine" (oyf Ukrayne), an instruction that, in theory, need not be unique to a child of a Ukrainian national. It is worth noting, as well, Hofshteyn's choice of preposition to situate Ukraine: whereas Shevchenko's mother sends her poem-children "to Ukraine," Hofshteyn's "oyf Ukrayne" could be translated into English as "to *the* Ukraine" or into Russian as "*na* Ukrainu." Hofshteyn's choice of "oyf" as opposed to the alternative "in" adopts the Russian grammatical construction of the time, which figured Ukraine as a territory, rather than an independent country.[101] For Hofshteyn and his Yiddish readers, Ukraine would have evoked spatial memory, and even nostalgia, conjuring for some a sense of national ethos, as many Soviet Jews hailed from the region. However, following the establishment of Soviet Ukraine in 1922, Ukraine as a territory could not be formally linked to the hope for an autonomous nation-state still present for Shevchenko and his nineteenth-century Ukrainian readers. Hofshteyn's choice of "unter ployt" (behind/under a fence) renders literally Shevchenko's "popidtynniu"—an idiomatic term for "wandering aimlessly" that literally means "under/beneath fences." The possibility that Shevchenko's orphaned *dumy* are confined to wander "beneath fences" was too tempting an image to resist for a Yiddish poet concerned with the poetics of alienation, for "unter a ployt" (under a fence) is itself a passphrase in Yiddish for the ultimate spatial alienation. A Jewish apostate, when deceased, was buried "behind the fence," separated from the Jewish community. Separation from one's poems, Hofshteyn implies, and by extension from one's national traditions (as he had complained to Bloshteyn back in 1932) is tantamount to a separation from one's community for all eternity.

MARIA

Hofshteyn included his translation of Shevchenko's 1857 narrative poem "Maria" in his 1939 anthology of the Ukrainian poet's collected works. Boris Pasternak translated the same poem into Russian, publishing it in 1938, and the difference between the two poets' approaches illuminates Hofshteyn's use of passwords as cultural signposts in both Yiddish and Ukrainian. The Ukrainian literary critic Dmytro Chyzhevsky has called the poem "the most outstanding example of Shevchenko's 'secularization' of sacred history."[102] Most significantly in Hofshteyn's Yiddish, the character becomes "Miriam," which is understood to have been the original Hebrew name of Jesus's mother and functions as a password that brings the figure closer to Hofshteyn's Jewish readers. Notably, Pasternak, who rendered "Maria" into classical Russian lyric verse in 1938, did not attempt to Judaize Shevchenko's biblical figures, nor does he carry traces of Shevchenko's Ukrainian folk motifs into his translation.

In this poem, Shevchenko, who, as Myroslav Shkandrij has written, "was steeped in the Bible, the Old Testament, and especially the psalms," creates a version of the Christ story that emphasizes Mary over Jesus.[103] It is a classic poem of alienation that, as George Grabowicz puts it, offers a "sublime case" of the illegitimate child.[104] Jesus's mother is not merely human and therefore flawed; Shevchenko emphasizes her child's illegitimacy, includes a sexualized encounter with the holy emissary who impregnates her, and ends the poem with the Virgin Mother dying alone of hunger "under a fence" (pid tynom), thereby including Mary, like the orphaned poems in "Dumy moi," among those who are eternally alienated from their community. Whereas Pasternak's version has Mary dying "u tyna" (by a fence), Hofshteyn, as in "Dumy moi," renders this "hinter a ployt" (under / behind a fence), which likens Mary in death to those who are buried outside the confines of a Jewish cemetery and therefore eternally alienated from their community. Hofshteyn's Judaized Maria—Miriam—thus becomes an individual, alienated from her family and perhaps from her people.

Even as Hofshteyn subtly Judaizes his Mary in his translation, he also preserves Shevchenko's Ukrainianizing of the Virgin. In the passage just before the holy emissary visits Maria, Shevchenko's Mary, "bedecked in flowers" (zakvitchana), resembles a Ukrainian girl at a festival:

Uvecheri, mov zoria taia,	In the evening, like that star
Mariia z haiu vykhozhae	Maria leaves the grove
Zakvitchana. Favor-hora	Bedecked in flowers. Mount Tabor
Nenache z zlata-serebra	As though golden-silver,
Daleko, vysoko siiae,	In the distance, is tall and shining,
Azh slipyt' ochi. [105]	As if to blind the eye.

Hofshteyn preserves Shevchenko's meter. As is often the case in translating the multisyllabic Ukrainian language into Yiddish, Hofshteyn finds himself with syllables to spare in his Yiddish, which he uses to add alliteration:

Farnakht, vi yener heler shtern,	Evening, like that sparkling star,
tut Miriam fun dem vald zikh kern,	Miriam from the woods emerges,
baputst mit blumen. Der barg Tavor,	ornamented with flowers. Mount Tabor,
vi helish-gold, vi zilber-klor,	so sparkly-gold, so silver-clear,
di vayt, di brayt arum bashaynt,	the distant, broad encirclement shines,
bashaynt un mentshn-blikn blendt.[106]	shines and blinds the human eye.

We see here Hofshteyn's selective preservation of Shevchenko's metaphors. The additions of his own alliteration and imagery to Shevchenko's lines suggest coauthorship with the Ukrainian bard. He has added adjectives to both "gold" and "silver": Shevchenko's simple "golden-silver" (zlata-serebra) becomes "bright gold" (helish-gold) and "silver-clear" (zilber-klor). Whereas Shevchenko's Mount Tabor "in the distance, shines on high" (daleko, vysoko siaie), Hofshteyn's mountain is wide, rather than tall—"the distant, broad surrounding shines" (di vayt, di brayt arum bashaynt). Like Shevchenko's, his Yiddish lines are highly alliterative. Here, Hofshteyn flaunts the versatility of Yiddish through his ability to approximate Shevchenko's alliterative patterns. His repeated consonants *v* and *z* echo Shevchenko's sound play on the same consonants. Hofshteyn's rich use of alliteration in his own poetry follows a variety of organizational patterns that complement his subjects and rhymes. As the Soviet critic Fume (Fayvl) Shames observed, Hofshteyn had "an organic musical intuition" and, as a result, "almost always instrumentalized his lines not with one, but with various consonants."[107]

Hofshteyn also takes pains to preserve Shevchenko's Ukrainian imagery. His Miriam remains bedecked with flowers. The Ukrainian "zakvitchana" (beflowered) is a password for a specifically Ukrainian form of femininity, evoking the floral wreathes of Ukrainian folk festivals. As the Soviet critic Leonid Khinkulov observed of this passage, Shevchenko's Maria "is not the mythical 'mother of God,' but a simple peasant girl."[108] The Yiddish "baputst mit blumen" (ornamented with flowers) evokes this Ukrainian festive tradition. The Yiddish "baputst" might describe the way a girl gets dressed up for the Sabbath or a wedding, though there is no one word in Yiddish, as there is in Ukrainian, for the very marked Ukrainian folk practice of covering one's hair and clothing in flowers. Hofshteyn, that is, takes ample license in expanding Shevchenko's eastern-European-scented biblical landscape but leaves intact Shevchenko's sense of place and traditions.

By contrast, Pasternak, who takes license in order to make his Russian 1938 version distinct from the original, leaves out the flowers entirely—a decision that removes the Ukrainian folk motif from the image. Pasternak's tendency to drop Ukrainian specificity, privileging the target readership, is in keeping with the larger Soviet translation project, which privileged loose translations that could reflect, as Harriet Murav has put it, "a unified Russocentric and socialist realist literature."[109]

Iz roshchi, krashe zvezd nochnykh,	From the grove, prettier than night stars,
Vykhodit vvecheru Mariia.	Maria goes out to the evening.
Vdali pred nei Favor-gora,	In the distance before her Mount Tabor,
Litaia, kak iz serebra,	Is cast, as though from silver,
Vzdymaet vvys' boka krutye	The steep slopes billowing up
I oslepliaet. [110]	And blinding.

Pasternak collapses the image of a woman in flowers with Shevchenko's reference to the night and to Mary's resemblance to a star. Pasternak's Mary is "prettier than night stars" (krashe zvezd nochnykh). The Russian poet casts Shevchenko's Mount Tabor entirely in silver, removing the gold, and making it billow. The flowers and woods—natural elements that almost place the biblical scene on the Ukrainian steppe—are reduced to a grove in Pasternak's Russian interpretation. Hofshteyn, for all his added alliteration, does not lose an opportunity to preserve the Ukrainianized landscape. Hofshteyn's close engagement with the original anticipates the kind of hybrid text Anthony Appiah advocates for with his "thick translation." As Murav has observed, "Hybrid utterances decentralize language by pulling against its unifying force."[111] This act itself decentralized the Soviet literary canon.

Following Maria's flower-bedecked entrance, she summons the Holy Spirit with an incantation:

Raiu! Raiu!	Heaven! Heaven!
Temnyi haiu!	Dark woods!
Chy ia, molodaia,	Will I, young as I am,
Mylyi Bozhe, v tvoim raii	Dear God, in your heaven
Chy ia pohuliaiu,	Will I take a stroll,
Nahuliaius?[112]	And have my fill of walking?

Shevchenko evokes the felicitous rhyme between heaven ("Raiu! Raiu!") and earthly forest ("Temnyi haiu!"). The consistent end rhymes of "raiu" (heaven), "haiu" (forest), "molodaia" (young), "pohuliaiu" (wander), and "nahuliaius" (walk my fill), add a sexual euphemism to the layering of heaven and earth. Maria is strolling through God's world, and the experience is pleasurable.

Russian lacks a rhyme between "heaven" (also *rai* in Russian) and "forest" (les). Pasternak solves the problem by changing the rhyme scheme and adding an additional word, "krai" (edge / confine) to rhyme with "rai" (heaven), as well as "chudes" (wonder) to rhyme with "les" (forest). Pasternak finds language to preserve the sublime connection between earth and paradise, though this requires considerable changes, despite the linguistic similarity between Russian and Ukrainian:

Rai bez kraiu, --	Heaven without confines, --
Temnyi les!	Dark forest!
Ia ne znaiu,	I don't know,
Molodaia,	Young as I am,
Dol'go l', Bozhe,	Will it be a long time, God,
Poguliaiu	That I will walk
Sred' tvoikh chudes?[113]	Among your wonders?

Pasternak captures Shevchenko's rhythm and rhyme wonderfully. But his subject has less agency than Shevchenko's Maria. Rather than wondering whether she will tire of her walk, she wonders how long her walk will last. Hofshteyn remains truer to Shevchenko's sentiment of pleasure: Miriam wonders whether she might take another walk. Moreover, Hofshteyn transforms the felicitous Ukrainian rhyme between "heaven" and "woods" into a similarly fortuitous overlap, in Yiddish, between "paradise" and the "Garden of Eden":

O, ganeydn,	O, Garden of Eden,
vald du triber!	you muddy forest!
Vel ikh, meydl,	Will I, a girl,
Got mayn liber,	God my lover,
In ganeydn	into the Garden of Eden
Zikh nokh firn,	come again
onshpatsirn?[114]	to take a stroll?

Hofshteyn's "ganeydn" (Garden of Eden), which appears twice in these lines, is the clearest translation for "paradise," even without Shevchenko's "forest." By evoking the Garden of Eden rather than using a word like *himlen* (heavens), Hofshteyn brings together Shevchenko's woods and paradise, while slipping in a Biblical Hebrew term. "Ganeydn" (Garden of Eden) is a password that allows Hofshteyn to claim the poem as his own: after all, the biblical Ganeydn is not a translation of Shevchenko's New Testament source but the original! Hofshteyn's Eden, like Shevchenko's heaven, is earthly and sexual; Hofshteyn drives the point further by making the forest muddy (triber). By emphasizing the carnal aspect of the poem, Hofshteyn ensures that the translation is appropriate to his own militantly secularist Soviet context. The Garden of Eden may come from Genesis, but it is still a muddy wood. Just as he adds earth to paradise, Hofshteyn further sexualizes God. Shevchenko's ambiguous "mylii bozhe" (dear God) becomes "Got mayn liber" (my beloved God), which connects Mary's song explicitly to her impending conception. Hofshteyn renders Shevchenko's poem more indecent, and therefore more appropriate for an atheist public. Hofshteyn was, after all, translating Shevchenko for a Soviet readership and not only for a Yiddish one.

A MARRANO

In presenting Shevchenko as a national poet whose message could represent the internationalist Soviet collective, Hofshteyn and his fellow Soviet Shevchenko scholars had to decide what to do with Shevchenko's unsympathetic treatment of Jews. Shevchenko, like other Ukrainian writers of the tsarist period, often depicted Jewish characters in stereotypical roles, either as leaseholders in service to the Polish overlords or as tavern keeps who preyed on the vices of poor, overworked peasants.[115] Some critics dealt with this by going to the opposite extreme and praising Shevchenko for his occasional affection toward Jews in an otherwise antisemitic era. Al'tman dismisses "evil claims against the great poet" (beyze rekhiles afn groysn dikhter) concerning his alleged antisemitism and notes that Shevchenko expressed friendship for all peoples (Czech, Caucasian, etc.), including Jews. He offers a bit of biographical apocrypha, in which the great poet was sojourning in a shtetl and helped to put out a fire, saving several Jewish lives.[116] Other Soviet critics focus on the oppression of peasants like Shevchenko by the Polish overlords. Ukraine's Jews, who were often employed in service to the Poles, were believed to be complicit in the process for reasons beyond their control. Khvylia, whose Ukrainian-language monograph on Shevchenko Hofshteyn translated into Yiddish, proposes that Ukrainian nationalists had intentionally misconstrued Shevchenko's hatred of Jewish "exploiters" and collaborators with the Poles as more general hatred of all Jews.[117]

Hofshteyn treads lightly on the subject of Shevchenko's Jewish characters. He did not include a translation of "Haidamaki," a work that describes a Haidamak massacre of Jews and Poles, in his collections of Shevchenko's poetry, although he did translate excerpts included in Khvylia's monograph. His translations include few references to Jews. The few exceptions would have reminded his Yiddish readers that Jews had a place in Ukraine and, therefore, that Ukrainian literature is relevant to Jewish readers. One of these is the novella *Progulka s udovolstviem no ne bez morali* (A walk with pleasure and not without a moral). In one chapter, a family of Jewish tavern keepers appears ridiculous—they never bring their guests tea, and they bargain with the protagonist before allowing him to borrow a book. In the Russian, these are "zhydy," a term that was, by the nineteenth century, increasingly viewed as an antisemitic epithet. In Yiddish, they are simply Jews—"Yidn." Hofshteyn marks their foreignness by making them speak Russian, the language of empire, which grates on the Yiddish narrative as accented and inauthentic. In one passage, Shevchenko describes a Jewish innkeeper who makes an empty promise to bring tea to his lodger:

Zhid skazal: "Zaraz"—i skrylsia za dver'iu.[118]	The Jew said: "Right away [zaraz]," and hid behind the door.
Zaraz,—hot geentfert der yid un zikh bahaltn hinter der tir.[119]	"Right away [zaraz]," answered the Jew and hid behind the door.

That Shevchenko's Ukrainian landscape included Jews, out of place as they were among their Slavic neighbors, was arguably part of what drew Hofshteyn to translate the Ukrainian poet. Subtle allusions to the history of a difficult relationship between Jews and their Slavic neighbors stood in for the Jewish cultural tradition that disappeared with the imperative that art could be national in form only.

In a 1959 article, the Soviet poet and translator Semyon Lipkin suggested that translation is a form of rapprochement. He imagined a future history of Soviet artistic translation, "a book about how the most talented, inspired artistic tranŝlations became a key contributing factor in the formation of a future unified culture of all peoples."[120] Translations, that is, ought to be taken seriously as examples of cultural interaction. "Translated poetry is first and foremost poetry," Lipkin concludes.[121] If we take Lipkin's approach to translation to heart, we begin to see Hofshteyn's Shevchenko as a genre of Yiddish poetry that sheds light on all that occurred between the time the Ukrainian Romantic and the Yiddish modernist took pen in hand. After all, Hofshteyn, like Lipkin, saw translations as original poems. In a 1926 letter to Daniel Charney, he wrote of poems awaiting publication in the New York-based *Tsukunft*, "You have one more poem of mine, a translation."[122]

Avrom Sutzkever, writing from Israel in 1962, describes meeting Soviet writers, following his dramatic escape from the Vilna Ghetto, through the Lithuanian forest, to Moscow in 1944. These included not only Pasternak but also a number of Yiddish poets. Peretz Markish hosted an evening at the writers' union in honor of Sutzkever's rescue. Hofshteyn arrived late and insisted on reading a poem in Sutzkever's honor, which described an unnamed "ergets" (somewhere). Sutzkever reproduced the poem in full nearly two decades later, along with a description of his meeting with the Soviet Yiddish poets. Hofshteyn's poem ends,

Azoy fil ergetsn hob ikh gezen biz her.	I've seen so many somewheres before here.
Un yenem ergets oykh,	And that somewhere too,
ot dem,	the one
vos glantst in yeder trer.[123]	that sparkles in every tear.

Sutzkever describes loud applause that follows. "We understood well which symbolic somewhere the poet meant. The allusion, that he, Dovid Hofshteyn, had already seen the *somewhere* unveiled the poem's deception [hot anthilt di farshleyertkayt funem lid]. The writer, and the majority of those in the audience knew that Hofshteyn had spent beautiful months in 1925 in the land of Israel."[124] We must take Sutzkever's narration with some degree of circumspection. He was, after all, retelling the episode eighteen years later, long after his own immigration to Palestine and after the founding of the State of Israel. If Hofshteyn did read the poem as Sutzkever recalls, the password could have been understood by many to reference the Soviet Union—the safe "somewhere" to which Sutzkever had just escaped. If it is unlikely that all of Sutzkever's Soviet Jewish acquaintances in the 1940s secretly expressed covert Zionism, it is nonetheless likely that at least some of the writers who met the young poet of Vilnius did use Yiddish—the language of passwords—to express their concern for a loss of Jewish culture.

Sutzkever recalls leaving the event with Hofshteyn to walk through Moscow and describes the Soviet poet confiding to him that, even as Jews returned to Ukraine from evacuation, "no one in Kiev needed his Yiddish poems."[125] Hofshteyn attempted to publish in Russian and Ukrainian, but submissions were returned. Sutzkever, for his part, questioned Hofshteyn's allegiance to Ukrainian culture and asked his colleague about a poem he had published about the seventeenth-century Cossack hetman Bohdan Khmelnytsky, the leader of an uprising that led to the death of thousands of Jews in Ukraine.[126] "Why did you need to write a poem about Bohdan Khmelnytsky . . . I saw it in 1940. There was already a ghetto in Warsaw at that time."[127]

The poem in question was probably Hofshteyn's "Denkmol Khmelnytskin" (Monument to Khmelnytsky), which appears midway through the book *Kiev*. If so, Sutzkever's memory is faulty, for the poem includes no reference to the East but, rather, to the North. The poem begins,

Oyb Khmelnitski gevinkt hot keyn tsofn, ahin,
un gemeynt hot de[m] tsar un di pritsishe makht,
hot dem meyn'shoyn tsetrogn der frostiker vint
in di heldishe yorn fun blutikn shlakht.[128]

If Khmelnitsky beckoned up there, to the North,
meaning the tsar and the powerful lords
the frosty wind this meaning then scattered
in heroic years of bloody battle.

Needless to say, the poem is ambiguous. Hofshteyn's allusion to a "frosty wind" (frostike vint) that confused the proper order of things hints at the tsarist cruelty toward Ukrainians that followed Khmelnytsky's yielding of the Ukrainian territories to Muscovy in 1654. The poem continues, "And through toil the correct direction's now found" (Un in mi itst di rikhtike rikhtung gefint).[129] That the new Soviet citizens have resolved this Russian-Ukrainian brotherhood appears, at first glance, to be a renewed celebration of the brotherhood that Khmelnytsky had established (whether reluctantly or willingly) between the Ukrainian and Russian lands.

Sutzkever writes that Hofshteyn later brought him the poem in question and asked, "Well, how do you understand the line 'Your sword is outstretched to the east'?" Hofshteyn's explanation to the bewildered Sutzkever is telling: "'Do you know what I meant by that line,' Hofshteyn said, looking around suspiciously, and leading me by the arm into the nearby wash-room where there was no danger that the telephone receiver should overhear. 'I meant in that line that Khmelnytsky had *once again* stretched forth his sword to the East, to us, Jews.'" This conversation makes more sense if we apply it not to Sutzkever's misremembered line about a sword raised to the East but rather to the line we have above, in which Khmelnytsky "beckoned" (gevinkt) to the North. Thus, buried in Hofshteyn's portrayal of Russian-Ukrainian brotherhood is an anxiety about a renewed antisemitic sentiment infiltrating the northern cities of Russia from the west, perhaps via Ukraine. Sutzkever recalls, following Hofshteyn's explanation, "I was silent. What could I have replied? Only my lips quietly whispered: 'A Marrano—Hofshteyn is a Marrano [a Maran].'"[130]

Sutzkever's story of Hofshteyn, like his story of Pasternak, no doubt contains some mythologizing. But the suggestion that the word "Marrano"—the quintessential password for Spanish Jews who hid their Jewish identity—might have been exchanged between the two poets at the end of the war offers an astute interpretation of Hofshteyn's Ukrainian Yiddish poetry in the years of high Stalinism. As Jewish culture became increasingly thin, Ukraine and Ukrainian history provided a way of discussing Jewish identity. This was not in spite of the tumultuous relationship with Ukrainians but because of it. For all of the stereotypes, Ukrainian cultural memory included Jews, and in an environment where the idea of ethnic solidarity could only safely be conveyed through the looking glass of multinationalism, this would have to stand in for Jewish cultural tradition. This interpretation of Hofshteyn's poem becomes more accessible if we return to Shevchenko, who in 1859 admonished the Cossack hetman, "If only you, drunken Bohdan, / could look at Pereyaslav now!" (Yakby-to ty, Bohdane p'ianyj, / Teper na Pereiaslav hlianuv!).[131] For Shevchenko, whose oeuvre Hofshteyn knew as well as anyone, Khmelnytsky was not a nation builder but a compromiser, whose 1654 treaty with Muscovy led to centuries of Ukrainian subjugation. Hofshteyn's Khmelnytsky was Shevchenko's Khmelnytsky—a fateful unifier, compromiser, and traitor. Placed in the middle of Hofshteyn's 1936 *Kiev* volume, this enigmatic two-stanza poem about confusion was a poem about dangerous unions, about being in the wrong place at the wrong time.

By translating Shevchenko, Hofshteyn was not only conveying Shevchenko's flower-filled Ukrainian landscape, negative Jewish stereotypes included, to a Yiddish-speaking readership; his translations offer a covert narrative about Jewish history, coauthored with the bard of his neighboring Ukrainians. Hofshteyn resolves his own dilemma, expressed to Bloshteyn in 1932 about lost Jewish cultural traditions, by broadening his vision of national literature to include a transnational literary system. The Soviet Great Appropriation of the 1930s may have been imposed from above, but this world-cultural project nonetheless encouraged writers to seek new literary connections. Through Hofshteyn's appropriation of Shevchenko for his Soviet Yiddish readers, he also made Shevchenko relevant to his own lifelong creative project. For a Jewish writer like Hofshteyn, who recognized the political danger of describing deep Jewish cultural traditions, Ukraine's literary history provided new ways of recalling the Jewish past for his readers, through negative and positive images associated with Ukrainian Jews' long history of cohabitation with their neighbors.

6

TESHUVAH

Moishe Nadir's Relocated Passwords

Ikh gedenk keyn nemen nit, gornisht-nisht.	I don't remember any names, not a thing.
S'iz alts in mir shoyn oysgemisht.	Everything is mixed in me.
Aleyn mikh misht der shternshtoyb	I'm mixed, myself, by the stardust
fun Gots fargiltn hengl-troyb.[1]	of God's gilded grape cluster.

The American Yiddish writer Moishe Nadir signed and dated his poem "Neenter" (Closer), "Miami Beach, Florida, May 1943." The poem was probably the last one he wrote: Nadir died the following month in Woodstock, New York, of a heart attack at the age of fifty-eight. With the poem's references to God and its existential uncertainty, it scarcely resembles the exclamatory revolutionary poems he published in Communist Party–aligned newspapers and journals in the 1920s and '30s or the satirical verse that endeared him to readers in the 1910s. It is, like many of Nadir's late writings, a poem of *teshuvah*—a public acknowledgment of return to the Jewish community following a period of apostasy.

Despite the ideological departure of "Neenter" from Nadir's communist poems, it still bears the familiar "Nadirish" virtuosic wordplay, with sounds leading seamlessly to new words and ideas: the "gornisht-nisht" (nothing at all) of the first line blends into the rhymed "oysgemisht" (mixed up) of the second line, which leads to the internal rhyme, "aleyn mikh misht" (I'm mixed, myself) in the third line. In all of his writing, Nadir uses rhyme and alliteration to defamiliarize the sounds of words, vesting them with more power. The repeated "misht" (mixes/mixed) and the rhyming "nisht" (not) create a sense of uncertainty and even self-negation, as though the individual is being mixed into nothingness. Nadir's confessional terms and tone also recall his communist-period confessions, which professed departure from what he came to consider his bourgeois modernist phase to perform *teshuvah*— repentance—to the Party. For communists, *teshuvah* figured into the Soviet genre of self-criticism (*samokritika*), which J. Arch Getty has usefully called an "apology ritual."[2] Moishe Nadir provides a poignant case study in the shift that many Yiddish internationalist poets made away from the Party with World War II. In the late 1930s, it was becoming increasingly apparent that not only Yiddishism but Jewish survival was in grave peril. Elias Tcherikover and Yisroel Efroikin, the editors of a Paris-based journal, *Oyfn sheydveg* (At the crossroads), wrote in April 1939 that in such an environment, "we must honestly and seriously begin to revise our old ideological baggage and leave intact whatever can help keep up the depressed Jewish spirit and revive the frozen national energy."[3] A similar conclusion led Moishe Nadir to relocate religious passwords back to their original Jewish context, the same passwords that he had translocated to exalt communist internationalism over a decade earlier. Nadir's trajectory maps the shifting age of internationalism, from his 1926 travel to Moscow, to his welcoming of the uprising in Palestine, to his eventual disillusionment with Party politics.

"Neenter" was included in Nadir's posthumous book *Moyde ani* (published as *Confession* in English), which appeared in 1944 and was edited by the poet Leon Faynberg and Ghenia Nadir, Nadir's wife of fifteen years.[4] The title of the book references the daily morning *Modeh ani* confessional prayer: "I offer thanks before you, living and eternal King, for You have mercifully restored my soul within me; great is your faithfulness."[5] The term *modeh* (*moyde* in Yiddish), as it is used in the daily supplication, connotes both thanks and repentance. As such, Nadir's title connotes both praise of God and self-criticism in the spirit of his earlier, communist, apologies. Moreover, in typical Nadirish wordplay, his title, with its Ashkenazi pronunciation, approximates the sound of the author's name—"Moy[de] ani" is assonant with "Moy[she] [N]adi[r]." The collection announces itself as a reflection of the author's identity and a departure from the work that came before it.

Traditionally, *teshuvah*—a biblical Hebrew word meaning "turn back"—refers to repentance, either in the context of atonement before and on Yom Kippur or a return to the Jewish covenant with God after a period of nonobservance.[6] Nadir's *teshuvah* for his years of Party alignment is, in many ways, in keeping with the instruction of the medieval Jewish commentator Moses Maimonides, who outlined the need to verbally confess one's transgressions, even at the end of life: "Were a person to have been a sinner all her life and yet repent on the day of her death, and to have died while still repenting, all her sins would be forgiven."[7] However, as the critic Alexander Mukdoni observed in his review of Nadir's last poems, Nadir performed *teshuvah* twice: "Actually Moishe Nadir was already a *ba'al teshuvah:* when he became a communist, he did *teshuvah* for his bourgeois past."[8] Like many religious signposts and experiences, *teshuvah* had been explicitly translocated to a political context in the 1920s and '30s, and the word was often used, among Yiddish speakers, to refer to the confessional mode employed within the Communist Party. Communist confessions, of course, transcended Judaism: Oleg Kharkhordin has identified them with medieval Christian exomologesis (a process of seeking absolution for apostasy; Michel Foucault calls this "knowing oneself"), by which a new Party applicant publicly confessed and atoned for past sins.[9] For Nadir, as for other American Jewish fellow travelers, even informal alignment with Soviet communism required publicly disavowing affiliations that the Party condemned, including religion, Zionism, and what Communist literary critics called "bourgeois modernism," especially during the hardline "Third Period" of the late 1920s and early '30s.[10] The poem "Neenter" is a product of the final transformation that Nadir underwent in the last years of his life, this time from communist atheist to anticommunist Jew.

Nadir's poetic and ideological career, in its many extremes, offers an allegory for the transformations of his leftist Jewish community in the age of internationalism. His hyperbolic self-fashioning and refashioning were

part of his trademark as a poet-provocateur, but they illustrate, in exaggerated form, the changes that many of his fellow leftist poets underwent in the tumultuous age of internationalism, Nadir moved
from empathy to unquestioning support of a Party vision to the liberal Popular Front and finally to disillusionment following the Hitler-
Stalin pact. Nadir's performative conversions dramatize the struggle
of many Jewish writers to align themselves with justice in a decade of
extremism, populism, and nationalism. In the dark times that bridged
the two world wars, group identity—whether political or religious—
often had the dire effect of silencing an individual's humanity. Nadir's
pivot from exclamatory political assertions to self-negating uncertainty in his final poems exposes the inadequacy of public displays of
group allegiance, whether in favor of a nationalist or revolutionary
movement. But it also highlights a tragedy that is not often discussed
in collective memories of World War II: with the unbearable loss of
Jewish lives and subsequent widespread turn inward from internationalism toward the Jewish community came a loss of faith in inter-
ethnic collaboration that has been difficult to regain. Moishe Nadir's
trajectory toward and away from communist internationalism and his
shifting object of *teshuvah* exemplify the relocation of Jewish passwords,
beginning with the 1939 Molotov-Ribbentrop pact. This relocation of
language, from the centrifugal force of communist internationalism to
the centripetal force of Jewish particularism during World War II,
is no less tragic for its inevitability.

Nadir moved between extremes and used exaggerated rhetoric during
all stages of his political and creative life.[11] Born in Narayev, Galicia, in
1885, Isaac Reiss, who took on a variety of pseudonyms, eventually came
to identify exclusively as Moishe Nadir, a pen name redolent of crude
marketplace exchange, literally "Moishe Take-it."[12] Nadir is most often
associated with his humorous sketches, his foppishness, his aphorisms,
and his folk-inspired songs. His 1927 "Der Rebbe Elimelekh," based
loosely on the English "Old King Cole," quickly entered the Jewish folk
canon. Having received a Jewish elementary education in Narayev, he
immigrated to the United States at age thirteen and lived with his parents on Manhattan's Lower East Side. He began publishing articles in

Yiddish in 1902, translated to and from Yiddish, and by his midtwenties had garnered a following for the lampoons he published in Yiddish humor journals.[13] An outspoken sympathizer with the Soviet Union from the mid-1920s until the 1939 Molotov-Ribbentrop pact, he regularly contributed to the communist daily *Frayhayt* (later *Morgn Frayhayt*) and spoke on behalf of Yiddish writers at the Party-affiliated 1935 American Writers' Congress.[14] However, the period between 1939 and his fatal heart attack in 1943, years that witnessed World War II and the demise of the Communist International, found Nadir reassessing his relationship to party politics. As with his other phases, Nadir adopted an exaggerated tone in his break with communism, questioning his faith in world revolution and entering a period of public *teshuvah* as he attempted a return to Judaism.

Nadir's literary life can be divided into three chapters, with two conversions separating them: an early phase, during which he developed his iconoclastic style as a modernist and humorist; his communist period, when he applied his tongue-in-cheek turns of phrase specifically to the Revolutionary cause (albeit with his own nuances); and his dramatic departure from communism. The case of Nadir's double *exomologesis* or *teshuvah* exemplifies the writer's flair for the melodramatic. Nadir's demonstrative conversions also exemplify how fellow travelers often mapped their movement to and from communism onto a religious framework. Allusions to his communist *teshuvah* lent Nadir's writings a tongue-in-cheek religious structure and tone, even as he declared faith in a communist creed. Nadir again applies the format of *teshuvah* to his last poems, which read as far more serious and less ironic than anything he had written previously, bearing as they do the weight of traditional atonement to a Jewish community. Even these late poems reveal traces of the lightly ironic Soviet rhetoric of communist self-criticism (*samokritika*), which he had mastered as a fellow traveler in the 1920s and '30s. Ultimately, Nadir's multiple conversions, his willingness to drastically resituate his identity and allegiances, and his translocation and relocation of Jewish and Party passwords reveal the existential uncertainty that permeated his generation of Yiddish poets in the age of internationalism.

NADIR THE MODERNIST:
BETWEEN LYRICISM AND BLASPHEMY

Moishe Nadir, despite his popularity as a humor columnist, joined the modernist Yunge, a New York–based group of poets, including H. Leivick, Moyshe Leyb Halpern, and Manachem Boreysho, devoted to lyricism and influenced by Expressionism and Symbolism, in the 1910s. In hindsight, the affiliation seems odd, for Nadir's work was far from the earnest lyric verse of neo-Romantics like Leivick and Halpern. Communist sympathizers, Nadir among them, would later view Di Yunge as anathema to Revolutionary poetry and workers' issues, writing "under the flag of aestheticism."[15] Nor did Nadir's writing fit with the mission of the Introspectivist group In Zikh, who criticized the Symbolist impulse of the Di Yunge, devoting their poetry and criticism to exploring form and psychology.[16] Even the inward-focused In Zikh, whose leaders, Aaron Glantz-Leyeles and Yankev Glatshteyn, were Trotksyists, entered the political conversation, occasionally condemning the Soviet sympathizers who published in the *Frayhayt*.[17] Nevertheless, Nadir's association with the modernists calls attention to his development of a lyric voice; his embrace of audacity and clever wordplay fed the linguistic innovations that took place in the 1910s across languages. Nadir's first volume of poems, *Vilde royzn* (Wild roses), scandalized and tantalized readers with its innovative language and erotic imagery. The erotic "miniatures" in this volume were wildly popular, and a few thousand copies of the book were printed—an unprecedented number for a book of Yiddish poetry.[18] In "Amol gevolt zikh shmadn" (I once wanted to be baptized), the persona, attracted to nuns, enters an abbey but decides not to convert, because "the air wasn't filled with anything except 'nun-farts'" (mer vi mit 'nonen-fertskhen iz di luft nit ongefilt geven).[19] In *Vilde royzn*, which was shocking for its vulgarity, Nadir hints, albeit mockingly, at his revolutionary inclinations: "Ikh bet dikh" (I beg you), the poetic persona entreats a woman, "let me be drunk." When sober, he admits, "[I am] so cruel, bitter, revolutionary."[20] In a mock apology at the beginning of the book, Nadir lists those who should not read the book: "very young inexperienced girls, cruel critics, deeply earnest cultural critics, my good wife and a couple of tens of thousands of Jewish people, who dislike my wild roses. A goyish thing. Be warned!"[21] Nadir's love of shock for shock's sake was in place in his Yunge period.

The fun Nadir poked at sentimental poetry, even within his poetry, pushed the boundaries of form and content. Beginning in the 1910s, Nadir was close to a few English-language modernists, including Joseph Kling, who edited the *Pagan* and published English translations of Nadir's poetic improvisations.[22] Nadir's 1919 volume *Fun mentsh tsu mentsh* (From man to man) consists of poetic soliloquies printed in the form of blocks, with each caesura punctuated by a bullet point or colon (figure 6.1). The visual effect recalls a Torah passage, suggesting a translocation of the religious book—the *sefer*—to the secular book. The associative lines read as parodies of Symbolist verse, simultaneously building on and undermining one another. Although the poems resist formal structure, Nadir frequently highlights a word or phrase, as if to poke fun at the very modern lyric genre that includes his own poetry: "Night burned: her green-gray ash fell upon my dream: the burnt out

III די נאכט האט אויסגעברענט ♦ איהר גרין־
גראה אש איז געפאלען אויף מיין חלום ♦
די אויסגעברענטע לבנה ז ו י א ש ט י ק
פּאפּיר פון א קינדער־קרוין האט
איהרע שפּורען איבערגעלאזט אין א וועלט פון
עלפאנטביין ♦ גאלד און לאנגווייליע ♦ איך דארף
נאר א ווייה טון דארויף מיט מיין אטעם און עס
וועט פארלוירען־געהן ♦ פארלוירען־געהן ♦ קיין
סימן וועט נישט בלייבען פון דער נעכטיגער לבנה
וואס האט אזוי הויך און שטאלץ און הערלאאיש
געברענט אויף מיין נעכטיגען הימעל ♦ די שטע־
רען זענען צעריבען אויף ווייסמען מעהל און די
געטער געהען ארום באַרפּיס און עסען דאס ביטער־
געשמאקע שטערענברויט אין וועזען דערפון גע־
זונט און פעט ♦ און איינער אן אלטער גאט
וואס האט זיך איבערגעפרעסען מיט דעם ברויט
וואס איז געמאכט פון צעמאלענע אוניוווערזומס
געהט ארום מיט דריי גוידערם ♦ און יעדער
גוידער איז א וועלט פאר זיך ♦ און אויף יעדען
גוידער וואוינען טויזענד מיליאן מענשען־קינדער
און שאקלען זיך צום מאקס פון א יעדען געוויין
פון דער איבערזאטער גאטהיים ♦ די נאכט האט
9

Fig 6.1 An untitled prose poem from *From Man to Man* (New York: Verbe, 1919). *Credit:* The Yiddish Book Center's Steven Spielberg Yiddish Library

moon *like a piece of paper from a child's crown* left her footprints on an ivory world."[23]

In a 1920 review of *Fun mentsh tsu mentsh,* the critic Shmuel Niger-Charney surmises that Nadir's exaggeration was precisely what affirmed his lyrical tendencies. Nadir, despite elements of satire, cannot be considered a satirist, "for his sensibilities led him, a born lyric poet, to subvert his own lyricism."[24] Niger-Charney's reading of Nadir as a poet so steeped in lyricism that he is bound to discredit it helps to explain the mixture of seriousness with which Nadir took language and the spirit of rebellion that was a part of his gestalt as a dandyish enfant terrible.

With the 1919 formation of the semilegal Communist Party USA, the Jewish Communist Party (Poale Tzion), and Communist International (Comintern), communist-identified Yiddish writers began to create forums for Party-aligned articles and artistic texts.[25] Young Yiddish poets like Alexander Pomerantz and Aaron Kurtz, who embraced communism in the 1920s, found in the movement an opportunity to place Yiddish literature into the context of an international working class. As Gennady Estraikh has observed, the United States had the "strongest and largest phalanx of pro-Soviet Yiddish writers."[26] Nadir and his Yunge colleagues seldom published in the short-lived experimental journals like *Yung Kuznye,* though they occasionally did publish in the more successful communist monthly *Der Hamer* (The hammer, 1926). But it was the communist daily newspaper—the *Frayhayt*—that gave Nadir his enormous readership throughout the 1920s and '30s.

NADIR'S ROMANCE WITH MOSCOW

Moishe Nadir, who was sympathetic to the underground Communist Party of America even before it formally merged with the Workers Party in 1929, joined the *Frayhayt* along with fellow Yunge modernists, including Halpern, Leivick, and Boreysho, at its inception in 1922. By the mid-1920s, Nadir was writing a regular column in the *Frayhayt* in addition to plays, aphorisms, and poems. The Yiddish marionette "Modjacut" theater artists Zuni Maud, Yosl Cutler, and Jack Tworkov included a Moishe Nadir puppet in their entourage in 1926.[27] Also in 1926, the poet

Noakh Shteynberg wrote *A bukh Moyshe Nadir* (A Moishe Nadir book), in which he calls Nadir a "creator of a new style in Yiddish."[28] By 1926—a time when many left-leaning Yiddish writers around the world were declaring their allegiance to the Communist Party—Nadir's star was rising.

Nadir's commitment to the Party was solidified during his 1926–1927 trip to Europe, with stops in Paris, Vilnius, Warsaw, and the Soviet Union.[29] He received a hero's welcome. A Minsk Russian-language paper announced the arrival of the "famous Jewish writer M. Nadir," who hoped to familiarize himself with the building of the Soviet Union.[30] In Warsaw, Peretz Markish (who would, himself, return permanently to the Soviet Union a few months later) called Nadir a Pierrot figure who conjures an elegant carnivalesque: "The carousel is spinning."[31] Melech Ravitch wrote in the Warsaw-based *Literarishe Bleter,* which he coedited with, along with Markish, "It is difficult not to fall in love with Moishe Nadir."[32] The Soviet Yiddish daily *Der Emes* hailed Nadir's visit to Moscow by publishing Nadir's poetic tribute to the city:

O, mume Moskve,	Oh, Auntie Moscow,
ikh fil dem tam-un-reyekh	I sense the taste-fragrance
fun epes, vos iz honik far dem oyg	of something that is honey for my eyes
un dorshtung far di lipn.[33]	and quenching for my lips.

Moscow, the epicenter of the Communist International, appears here to be both desirable and impenetrable. The sweetness in these lines betrays an unwillingness, or inability, to describe the smell, sight, and taste of the city in anything more than vague gestures. Like an infatuated lover, Nadir saved among his papers an unsigned, folded piece of paper bearing a sketch of the Moscow skyline, the Kremlin's Spaskaia tower and the domes of St. Basil's Cathedral looking every bit the center of culture, a city as password for world revolution and the end point of a fellow traveler's pilgrimage.[34]

In a 1927 article in *Der Hamer* in which Nadir describes his trip to Moscow, he defends the city, poking fun at friends who had warned him about shortages: Leivick advised him to bring soap, a Warsaw colleague urged him to get his hair cut before traveling to Russia, and American newspapers suggested that Bolsheviks eat children.[35] Nadir describes his adventures with all the giddiness of a young tourist, noting with satisfaction that when he entered a restaurant expecting nothing, he was served a piece of meat fit for "half the Polish Army."[36] Nadir later characterized the visit as a "pilgrimage" to the "holy land of the Soviets."[37] Nadir spent several months traveling around the Soviet Union and giving readings. In photographs from his trip, Nadir poses with various groups of Soviet writers. He poses in hiking clothes with a group of peasants before the former tsar's winter palace in Crimea; he appears in photos with well-known eastern European writers, including Dovid Hofshteyn, Leyb Kvitko, Peretz Markish, and Israel Joshua Singer.[38] The Soviet actress Klara Jung signed a photograph in English, "To my dear friend M. Nadir as a rememberance [sic] from Moskou from Klara Jung, 10/4/27."[39] The following year, Nadir's book *Fun mir tsu dir* (From me to you) appeared in Soviet Kiev, published by the newly Soviet Kultur-Lige press.[40]

In the mid-1920s, Nadir's love for the Soviet Union resembled romantic infatuation more than religious devotion. Indeed, Nadir flouted Jewish and Christian tradition to display his ardent passion for all things Soviet. In a 1926 letter to Melech Ravitch Nadir described, with characteristic exaggeration, his love for the Soviet Union: "My heart belongs to her, my sisterly bride. And may my right hand forget, etc. (See the Zionist pledge!)." By citing the Zionist pledge, Nadir uses a religious passphrase to satirize his own infatuation. Of this letter, Ruth Wisse writes, "In applying the Zionist pledge—the passage from Psalm 137 that sacrifices the loyalist's right hand should he ever forget Jerusalem—to the Soviet Union, Nadir is burlesquing its religious and national meaning."[41] There is sometimes a fine line between burlesque and religious fervor, and as Nadir would later admit, in pledging his faith in the Soviet Union, he was beginning to accept a religion in its own right, with its own set of practices.[42]

Nadir had been attacking organized religion, often strongly offending his audience, since his first book, *Vilde royzn*.[43] Joel Schechter summarizes Nadir's 1929 play *Messiah in America* as one that "displays no sympathy for fools. The misled public that worships false messiahs in the play exhibits a naïve, all-accepting attitude toward impostor saviors."[44] The Yiddish writer Lamed Shapiro recalls that during an early performance of the play, the hall was in convulsive laughter. "I too laughed, and was ashamed, as though I were laughing at one who had fallen."[45] Had Nadir forgotten, Shapiro wondered, what it meant to long for the Messiah back in his shtetl, Narayev?[46] Nadir's communist faith allowed him to have it both ways: he could freely access Jewish tradition and Jewish passwords in order to ridicule religion in the name of Marxism. And he had an eager audience, plenty of whom understood and supported his translocation of Jewish passwords to support a communist-led workers' movement.

MESSIAH IN UNION SQUARE:
NADIR'S PARTY *TESHUVAH*

Moishe Nadir may have been flirting with communism throughout the 1920s, but his declarations of *teshuvah* to the Party did not come until 1929, when he chose to remain with the *Frayhayt* following the disturbances in Mandatory Palestine discussed in Chapter Two, when the wider Jewish community condemned, and the *Frayhayt* expressed solidarity with, the Arab uprising. In an act of public penance, Nadir dissociated himself from the bourgeois values of the modernist Yunge poets who had left the paper and asserted his decision to identify with the Party in his "Driter period" (Third period):

Kh'hob opgeshnitn mit der nudner birger-velt:	I've split with the dull bourgeois-world:
mit hartn hemd un veykhn kresl,	with the pressed shirt and the soft armchair,
a hoykhe barikade oyfgeshtelt	put up a high barricade
tsvishn mir un dikhter-balebesl.[47]	between me and the petit-bourgeois poets.

The poem is typical of Nadir's procommunist assertions of the time: he acknowledges his earlier ties to the "petit-bourgeois poets" (dikhter-balebesl) and asserts his break with his own past ways. The title, "Driter period," is a password aligning the piece with the official change in Comintern policy following the hardline position Stalin had introduced at the Sixth World Congress of the Comintern, which demanded that communists worldwide fight their opponents, including democratic socialists—now deemed "social fascists."[48] The Third Period, as we have seen, was not only a period when the Party was critical of multinationalism in general, including Jewish fellow travelers; it was a period when the colonial struggle, including the struggle of Arabs in Mandatory Palestine, was considered part of the proletarian struggle for world revolution. Nadir's poetic "Third Period" comes close to the kind of declaration of unquestioning faith the Party expected of Communist Party aspirants. Nadir did not need to do *teshuvah* in order to join the *Frayhayt* in 1922. But in the contentious climate of the Third Period, particularly following the cataclysmic rupture over Palestine, he needed to perform *teshuvah* to assert his intentions to stay.

Nadir constantly used the language of confession in his poems, articles, and feuilletons. In an article published in the *Frayhayt* on September 14, 1929, which he titled "Di tsar-vakkhanalie" (The sorrow-orgy), he attacked the prominent writers, among them Leivick, Roboy, and Boreysho, who left the *Frayhayt* in protest over its support of the Arab rioters and clarified, "I am *not* resigning from the Frayhayt! On the contrary. I am with the Communist Party—more than ever."[49] He ends the article with a call to the "deserters" to realign themselves with the Party: "Look around you, colleagues! Reyzen, Leivick, Raboy! The hysteria will calm, the orgy will spit you out, and where will you be, my former comrades [mayne gevezene khaveyrim]? On what deserted island?—On what desolate stone? Come back!"[50] The command "Come back!" (Kumt tsurik!) is closer to an admonishment than an entreaty.[51] Nadir here makes clear that in order for his former colleagues to rejoin their comrades, they will have to perform *teshuvah* to the community. This is, then, also a decisive assertion that, faced with the same "hysteria," Nadir has proven his allegiance to his people—the workers of the world.

Nadir follows this challenge to his former colleagues with a multipart manifesto: Yiddish-speaking fellow travelers must support the Party in its struggle against Zionist politics, as well as against imperialism and race hatred, must believe that no one people is better or worse than others, and must reject "a culture of Yiddishkayt," not to be confused with a "culture in Yiddish, with the charm, nectar, beauty and richness of our cultural treasures."[52] In this meandering article, Nadir distinguishes between dangerous nationalism and the beauty of Yiddish itself. The paper readily published it, albeit with a disclaimer separating the editors' views from Nadir's manifesto. Alexander Pomerantz later observed the ideological problems with Nadir's article, including "nationalist, humanist and idealistic positions about 'Culture in Yiddish.'"[53] If Nadir's Party ideology was less than perfect, his solidarity with the paper was important, as he was the only "crossover" (aribergekumener) modernist to remain with the paper after August 1929. Nadir expressed similar ideas in a poem of the same period, "Tsu a teyl Yidishe shrayber" (To some Yiddish writers), in which he berates those who left the paper, identifying them as "class traitors" (farreter fun a klas), an epithet that had become a password for those who had quit the *Frayhayt*:

Ikh ken aykh lang, ikh vil aykh mer nisht kenen	I've long known you, I no longer want to know you
ir fintstere farreter fun a klas	you dark traitors of your class
bay dem fayer fun tsvey veltn velkhe brenen	beside the fire of two worlds burning
fareykhert ir zikh shtil a paperos.[54]	you're quietly smoking a cigarette.

Group allegiance, Nadir makes clear in this 1929 poem, should be to class, not nation, and *teshuvah* should be performed before the proletariat.

Nadir, having affirmed his commitment to the Party, was committing to publish articles, stories, and verse that hailed the anti-imperialist struggle and the mobilization of workers. In the introduction to his 1930 book *Derlang aher di velt, burzhoy!* (We want the world; literally "Hand over the world, bourgeois!") Nadir included the following catchy rhyme in boldface:

Ey, burzhoy,	Hey, bourgeois,
gib op di velt un tayne nisht.	give up the world and don't complain.
zi iz dayne nisht.	She isn't yours to claim.
Gib op di velt! Ot-di minut!	This very minute! Give up the world!
Gib op—du hintish blut![55]	Give it up—you doggish blood!

Even in Nadir's children's stories and poems, we find verse celebrating the Soviet Union and American union activism. An "Arbeter vig-lid" (Workers' lullaby) begins, "Hushaby, my little soul, / Daddy's at the strike" (Liulinke, neshome mayne, / Tate iz in strayk).[56] In the months that followed the Palestine uprisings, Nadir contributed a series of feuilletons to the *Frayhayt* under the title "Pen un biks" (Pen and rifle), in which he discussed the rise of proletarian art and literature. Alexander Pomerantz, writing of Nadir's contribution in his 1933 Kiev dissertation *Proletpen,* qualifies his praise: "He expresses a lot of very interesting opinions about the rise of art in general, about bourgeois literature, and proletarian literature, many correct and many unfounded."[57] Despite Nadir's ideological inconsistencies, the *Frayhayt* eagerly published his poems, stories, and articles.

By the 1920s, it was becoming a ritual in and out of the Soviet Union for Party aspirants to express their allegiance through statements of repentance. These statements took various forms, including letters (private and public), poems, and articles. The Soviet official autobiographical genre, broadly defined, included oral and written statements of self-criticism (*samokritika*), as well as the more formulaic questionnaires (*ankety*) that Party members filled out, and curriculum vitae or party autobiographies (*avtobiografii*) that they wrote.[58] Igal Halfin has observed the structural similarity between the communist autobiography and Christian confession: "The achievement of Communist perfection also required an imperfect starting point: an unconscious, ideologically naïve state. At the decisive moment, when the communist autobiographer claimed to have seen the light of Communism, an individual's consciousness and the Party line (which embodied the supra-personal proletarian consciousness) were supposed to be merged."[59] This process of conversion—of formally articulating one's allegiance to the proletarian state—was what enabled writers wishing to make their home in the Soviet Union to transform into "engineers of human souls."[60] Although Christian conversion, which Halfin emphasizes in his study, remains an uncannily accurate model for communist confessionals, *teshuvah,* the ritualized process of returning to religious Judaism was an apter reference point for Yiddish writers.[61] In an open letter to *Der Emes* in May 1926, Dovid Hofshteyn, having spent a year in Palestine, expressed his desire "to again take [his] place among those who are building a new life for the Jewish working masses in the Soviet Union."[62] Here, the act of *teshuvah,* if humiliating, was a serious requirement for reentering the Soviet literary sphere. The verb "moyde zayn" (to admit or confess) and the noun *teshuvah* are ubiquitous passwords in this genre of communist confession. Hofshteyn, in a letter to his friend Daniel Charney from Moscow in 1926, writes of having been "deeply absorbed in doing *teshuvah*" (shtark farton in tshuve ton).[63] Despite its religious overtones, *teshuvah* so perfectly encompasses the self-criticism required to realign oneself with the Party that it is used almost unironically. (Mordechai Altshuler, in his 1979 compilation of letters of Soviet Yiddish writers, refers to Hofshteyn's letter to *Der Emes* as his "*Teshuvah* briv.")[64]

Writers, of course, also engaged half-heartedly or ironically in Party *teshuvah*. Dovid Bergelson, by then a giant in Yiddish prose, shifted his allegiance from the socialist to the communist press in the mid-1920s and wrote an open letter to the editors of the Moscow-based *Der Emes* in March 1926 to apologize for his earlier opposition to the Jewish Section of the Party. Bergelson, who then lived in Berlin, explained— possibly facetiously—that he must remain in the diaspora (*Goles*) a bit longer to atone for his misunderstandings of the Jewish Section's decisions. Bergelson opens his letter, "I confess my mistake" (Ikh bin moyde in dem feler). Bergelson's use of "moyde" as an apologetic password was probably aimed at ridiculing his Evsektsiie (Jewish Section) colleagues. As Harriet Murav observes, Bergelson's letter does more to undermine the form of self-criticism than adhere to it: "The letter is hardly a ringing endorsement of the Soviet Union or Jewish literary life in Moscow; the apology for past errors is lukewarm, and the reason for postponing his return (he would be depressed) is pathetic."[65] However, the editors responded seriously, publishing the letter and noting that "the Jewish Section in no way requires Bergelson to remain in exile."[66] In the 1920s, when the peripatetic Yiddish literary path often led to the nascent Soviet Union, emigration was always a possibility, and Comintern-aligned writers the world over either flirted with the idea of resettling or did resettle in the Soviet Union.[67] Others, like Alexander Pomerantz, lived in the Soviet Union for a few years and returned. Nadir flirted with this possibility during his 1926–1927 visit to the Soviet Union. A declaration of *teshuvah,* like a passport, could ensure a smooth entry when and if the time came to emigrate to the Soviet Union.

Self-criticism and affirmation of Party ties had the corresponding practice of denouncing Party enemies. As Sheila Fitzpatrick has demonstrated, this practice was common in Soviet newspapers, and the genre boundaries between citizen's complaint, letter to the editor, and artistic literary work were always blurry. Fitzpatrick suggests that readers of Soviet papers were writing as much for the experience of seeing their work published as out of moral obligation. "The readers who deluged *Krest'ianskaia gazeta* with so many letters of complaint, denunciation, and enquiry were also spontaneously sending the newspaper 'artistic' production—drawings, poems, and short stories—that they hoped would be published."[68] The *Frayhayt,* like its Soviet counterparts, ran letters from readers who spontaneously adopted the practices of self-criticism and denunciation. One reader wrote in overwrought metaphors, shortly after the Hebron riots, "I feel guilty, that as a worker I was also trapped by the patriotic-chauvinistic fumes. But I quickly came to myself thanks to the clarifications of the *Morgn Frayhayt.*"[69]

Those who criticized the Party used the same terms to ridicule communists' solemn use of the confessional mode. In an essay published in *Vokh,* the splinter journal that emerged from the 1929 rift over Palestine, the poet Aaron Glantz-Leyeles responded with a mock confession: "So let us confess [Lomir deriber moyde zayn]: we write individualistic poems. Whatever shall we do?"[70] In the opening editorial to the first issue of *Vokh,* Leivick compares the communists who faithfully follow the *Frayhayt* editor Moyshe Olgin to children repeating a prayer. "Even in these cynical and soiled days we believe in the human soul, and every human who was at the trial and repeated after Olgin, the way a child says the *Moyde ani,* left the hall guilty and ashamed before themselves [iz aroysgegangen a shuldiker un a farshemter far zikh aleyn]."[71] Here, Leivick is ridiculing the communists' near-religious use of accusation and self-criticism. *Moyde ani,* which explicitly references the daily prayer of thanksgiving, mocks the Party's adherence to a translocated form of Jewish ritual. Leivick follows the mocking comparison to prayer, however, by evoking the more serious issue of the individual's "guilty and ashamed" conscience.

Nadir, by remaining with the *Frayhayt* as his former colleagues departed to form *Vokh,* had to prove his earnest embrace of the Party, and he did so in florid language to match Leyeles's and Leivick's sarcasm. In his speech to the 1935 communist-led American Writers' Congress, Nadir declared, "We love America as one of the most beautiful flowers in the bouquet of the world Soviets of tomorrow." As Eitan Kensky has written of this speech, the message may be earnest, but "there is a little too much embellishment." According to Kensky, "Nadir was prone to take strong positions only to reveal them as the set-up for a joke, and his unabashed declaration of love for the future Soviet America reads like an introduction that will soon be negated."[72] Indeed, Nadir would later negate these statements. Nadir was an iconoclastic cult figure in American Yiddish letters long before the 1930s, and as his colleagues would later admit, it was difficult to reconcile Nadir's famous irreverence with the reverence he claimed to have for the Party.

Nadir's faith in the Party did not hurt him financially. The *Frayhayt* provided a regular paycheck, and Nadir managed to support himself on a combination of this and income from his business ventures, which included a New York café called Nakinka (Nadirs kinstler kafe) and "Nadir Farm," his guest house in Loch Sheldrake, New York.[73] The writers who left the paper in 1929 struggled to subsist in Depression-era America. Nadir's friend Moyshe Leyb Halpern died in August 1932 with insufficient funds to feed and house his family and unable to afford care for a series of ailments.[74] H. Leivick wrote to the playwright Peretz Hirschbein and the poet Esther Shumiatcher of his financial difficulties after leaving the *Frayhayt*. He was prepared, he told his friends, to return to manual labor but could not afford the $200 for a union card.[75] Nadir, in his most zealous phase, attacked his former friends as class enemies time and again in print, despite their material struggles and his relative financial success. Nadir's poem "A velt mit arbet" (A world with work), in which he calls his former comrades "*Frayhayt* tourists," is a particularly dark example of Nadir's "Third Period" poetics:

Der shturem ariber,	The storm is over,
di shoybn tsebrokhn,	the windowpanes broken,
un Reyzen un Leyvik	and Reyzen and Leivick
tsum soyne farkrokhn.[76]	crawl off to the enemy.

If the "Frayhayt tourists" struggled to support themselves after leaving the newspaper, Leivick claimed to be, nonetheless, "in general very happy to have distanced himself a bit from Nadir."[77]

Nadir spent a lifetime alienating former friends, but he remained popular with readers in the 1930s and enjoyed a place among the leftist literati. A photo from 1930 finds Nadir with Mike Gold at the communist Jewish summer camp Nitgedayget, the camp the Russian futurist poet Vladimir Mayakovsky had made famous in the Soviet Union when, after visiting in 1925, he wrote a poem about it:

Tol'ko son li eto?	Is this really just a dream?
Slishkom gromok son.	This dream is too loud.
Eto	These
Komsomol'tsy	Communist youth
Kempa "Nit gedaige"	from Camp "Nitgedayge" [*sic*]
Pesnei	with a song
Zastavliaiut	make the Hudson
Plyt' v Moskvu Gudzon.[78]	flow into Moscow."

Back in Moscow, Mayakovsky was falling out of step with the government-sponsored organization for proletarian literature, and in 1930, the Russian poet took his own life. Mayakovsky's Soviet Jewish colleagues gave up much of their autonomy in 1930 when the Jewish Section (Evsektsiia) of the Communist Party in the Soviet Union was eliminated. Eventually, only the minuscule population of Jews based in the national territory of Birobidjan would be identified as a national community in the Soviet Union, although foreign Yiddish-language groups continued to work within the Comintern until its 1943 dissolution.[79] In 1934, Communist Party Secretary Andrei Zhdanov declared Socialist Realism the only official genre, formally eliminating all experimental groups. Nadir remained, of course, on the Hudson side of Mayakovsky's communist dream, and the distance between New York and Moscow was widening. Whereas Soviet writers, who were supported entirely by the state, had to answer to a single, centralized organization, American poets had the freedom to write what they wanted, as long as they could afford it. After the 1939 Molotov-Ribbentrop non-aggression treaty Nadir retreated from Party politics. Having escaped both the hunger of the Great Depression and the authoritarianism of high Stalinism, he spent the remainder of his short life in a new period of *teshuvah*—this one involving a more traditional penance and return to Judaism.

NADIR'S POST-PARTY *TESHUVA*

Many Jewish leftists who, like Nadir, remained committed to the Soviet project through the rifts over Hebron, finally broke with the Party after the 1939 Molotov-Ribbentrop pact.[80] Some left quietly; others called attention to their change of heart; still others, like Alexander Pomerantz, spoke out against Stalin only after learning of the 1952 execution of the most prominent Soviet Yiddish writers, Markish, Bergelson, Kvitko, and Hofshteyn among them.[81] The unraveling of Nadir's devotion to the Party took place against the backdrop of Hitler's rise to power. As early as the mid-1930s, when the Popular Front movement had softened tensions on the literary left and the Spanish Civil War made the dangers of fascism clear, Nadir's tone was changing. The November 1936 issue of the American proletarian journal *Signal* ran a poem by Nadir, in which the poet despairs of the state of the world:

Mayn gedank iz haynt oysgeven a halbe velt	Today my thought traveled half a world
oyf shtrasn Viner	along Viennese straßes
in vayter Khine,	to far-off China,
bay der komunarn vant,	by the walls of the Paris Commune,
oyf Poylns kresn,	in Poland's borderland *kresy*,
oyf Lites rand	on Lithuania's border
in royter zone fun Pariz	in Paris's Zone Rouge
in overalte gasn fun Madrid	on Madrid's ancient streets
un umetum gezen, gehert, dos faln un dos shtaygn	and everywhere, it saw, heard, the fall and the rise
fun dem tsu-nitsokhn-shpanendikn riz.[82]	of the giant striding toward victory.

With the war in Spain, Nadir's approach to internationalism was shifting from unqualified optimism to uncertainty. Nadir's "thought" returns bearing the dust and smoke of the world's battles. Three years later Nadir broke with the Party. That Stalin, the purported promoter of a friendship of nations, could align himself even temporarily with Hitler was enough to turn Nadir from the Communist International toward anti-communist Jewishness.

Nadir's dramatic ideological about-face meant that he again had a use for the confessional form and the associated passwords he had adopted a decade earlier with his attempts to prove his faith in the Party. This time, however, he used confession to distance himself from Party politics. Nadir's last writings, gathered in the posthumous 1944 volume, *Moyde ani*, include a poem and an essay by the same title. Given Nadir's many personal quarrels, it is no surprise that his efforts at a confession received mixed responses from his colleagues and readers. These responses to Nadir's second act of *teshuvah* illustrate the turmoil in which the American Left found itself during and immediately following World War II.

The publishers preface Nadir's posthumous book with a perplexing apology for its lack of political content: "Due to the war against the 'brown snake,' we have chosen to eliminate all of the political-polemical positions from the material included in the book *Moyde ani*."[83] Unlike Nadir's work in the 1920s and '30s, beloved for its sharp satire and brimming with social commentary, this last volume is deeply contemplative and frequently references Judaism. The editors' choice to omit any poems explicitly related to the Party is indicative of the broader censorship of Party affinities following World War II. Indeed, this may be the first Cold War book of Yiddish poetry. Of course, the volume does not entirely escape politics, for Nadir's many confessional poems read as a disavowal of his earlier communist period. They also serve as a reminder of the cataclysmic change that took place with World War II. The war led many Soviet Yiddish writers to cautiously return to Jewish themes. In the United States, where censorship was not a concern, many Yiddish writers who had remained with the Party were compelled to atone for their neglect of a Jewish community.[84]

Moyde ani opens with Nadir's 1940 prose piece "Moyde-ani: Oytobiografish" (Confession: Autobiographical), in which Nadir revisits his movement toward communism. In it, Nadir breezes through his childhood, his entrance into literature, and his fruitless attempts at faith ("I sought a god and found life").[85] Nadir claims to hail "not from the 'aristocratic class' but from 'pure-proletarian' stock," a statement that recalls the kind of editing individuals did when presenting their life narratives to the Soviet authorities.[86] In actuality, Nadir went to a religious school (heder) as a child, and his father was a salesman and a German teacher.[87] But, as Sheila Fitzpatrick has articulated, "The Life, an all-purpose Soviet identity card, was a work of art, polished to a high gloss."[88] Nadir's identification with the proletariat here is a bit too perfectly in keeping with the communist autobiographical form to take at face value. The strange autobiography becomes more clearly parodic when he describes his dramatic introduction to communism. Around 1922, a former colleague, "X," invited Nadir and Moyshe Leyb Halpern to have a drink and discuss the formation of a new, communist newspaper.[89] Here, Nadir's narrative becomes outlandish, an exaggerated version of what Halfin calls the "moment of conversion," after which "the Communist's consciousness became permanent and perfect, and s/he was now expected to devote him- or herself to the conversion of others."[90] Nadir describes this as hypnosis: "Hypnotized by the enchanting speech of Colleague X, I nodded off, the way a sick child nods off to the tender tones of a Bach concerto."[91] When he came to, Halpern purportedly said, "You're better now, Moishe Nadir. You've found a god now. . . . Mazel tov to you!"[92] The ironic "Mazel tov," placed in the mouth of Nadir's late friend Halpern, is parodic: that the two poets should use the celebratory Jewish term to mark Nadir's conversion to communism calls the entire conversion into question. Indeed, Nadir's self-parody is part of his relocation of Jewish signposts to Jewish meaning. He describes his gradual embrace of communism, first as a sympathizer (*mit-shteyer*) then as a companion (*mit-geyer*), and finally as a fellow traveler (*mit-loyfer*). Nadir writes of developing an iron faith and a steel discipline but abruptly undercuts this faith: "But doubts have feasted on my heart and give me no rest."[93]

"Autobiographical," written in the wake of Hitler and Stalin's non-aggression pact, outlines Nadir's double-conversion narrative, offering the story of a conversion to Party politics in ironic-enough tones to justify Nadir's final *teshuvah*—the return to Jewish cultural particularism that patterned his poetry between, roughly, 1939 and his death. Viewing his 1926–1927 trip a decade and a half later, Nadir highlights key Soviet paradoxes. Despite the ostensible Soviet rational secularism, he observed a people who remained highly literalist in their religion: "They need a god that they can see with their eyes, touch with their fingers." Such a god, Nadir concludes, was by then lying in a marble mausoleum in Red Square.[94] Another paradox involved the fundamentals of Marxist-Leninism—the notion that "material life is everything,

232 SONGS IN DARK TIMES

and ideals, nothing. And therefore everyone must be prepared to give up his life for an ideal."[95] In hindsight, Nadir justified his communist turn as a gradual transition from intellectual skepticism to utilitarian optimism. In the Soviet Union, he saw futile bureaucracy and rampant poverty, but he also saw a new multilingual milieu and industrial development: "I thought that with time it would all stabilize, according to Lenin's prophecy."[96]

Nadir was not the only fellow traveler to become disillusioned as Stalin's plan for "socialism in one country" undermined the vision of world revolution that had united leftists in 1919 with Lenin's Third International. Nor was Nadir the only recent convert from the Party to cynically view his romance with Moscow on religious terms. Arthur Koestler, who had been a Comintern intelligence agent in the early 1930s, later commented, "From the psychologist's point of view, there is little difference between a revolutionary and a traditionalist faith. All true faith is uncompromising, radical, purist; hence the true traditionalist is always a revolutionary zealot in conflict with Pharissean society, with the lukewarm corruptors of the creed."[97] Richard Wright, who left the Party in 1942, later wrote with awe of his own communist writings: "I was glad that they were down in black and white, were finished. For I knew in my heart that I should never be able to write that way again, should never be able to feel with that simple sharpness about life, should never again express such passionate hope, should never again make so total a commitment of faith."[98] Nadir, burdened with similar doubts, attempted to translate his Communist Party faith into a more traditional Jewish faith.

Nadir probably began questioning his poetic trajectory even before 1939, with news of the growing popularity of the Nazi Party. "Far vemen" (For whom) is dated July 1938 and suggests doubts about the efficacy of poetry:

Far vemen zol ikh zingen mayne lider	For whom should I sing my songs,
Ven tife erd-tsiters kumen for in mir?	When deep temblors are emerging inside me?
. . . .	. . . .
Itst veys ikh shoyn, az foyst un pen ineynem,	Now I know that fist and pen together,

Zey zaynen es der tsviling, vos regirt,	Are the twins that govern,
Un az iber ale fidlen, iber ale feders	And that over all the violins, over all the pens
Es hengt di lange shverd un zi diktirt.[99]	Hangs the long sword, who dictates.

Noakh Shteynberg later observed that around this time, Nadir must have been entering "the gray abyss of faithlessness."[100] However, although Nadir claimed to be losing faith in poetry, he did not cease to write and even continued to play with words, now often at his own expense. The repetition of "over all" (iber ale) with reference to the dictatorial sword suggests the *über alles* of the *Deutschlandlied,* an unmistakable password for Hitler's reign. The closing line likens literary dictation to political dictatorship. Nadir, the former author of the *Frayhayt* column "Pen and Rifle" (Pen un biks), was losing faith in left-wing writers' efficacy against the growing threat of Nazism.

Nadir did not clearly express his doubts about the Party until 1939. At this point, Lamed Shapiro would later observe, "when there were no enemies left before his eyes, he turned his rifle on himself."[101] Faynberg, in his foreword to *Moyde ani,* observes the gap between the "Moishe Nadir legend" and "Moishe Nadir—the changing polemicist, whose lashes hurt him far more than those whom he often cruelly and pitilessly hit with his 'pen-and-rifle.'"[102] Nadir later wrote that he threw himself into communism, "not like the generals, who die in bed, or under their beds, but like the suicide brigades, who wrap their hearts in dynamite with the intention of going just one way and not coming back."[103] His *teshuvah,* then, was an attempt at making an unlikely return trip. Although many of his colleagues refused to accept this return, Nadir expresses remorse for the personal attacks he made in the years of his devout adherence to the party. "In the 'holy war,' which I waged for a 'better humanity,'" writes Nadir, "I often bitterly sinned against the individual man."[104]

Nadir's change of heart, which alternately angered and endeared him to his fellow American poets, did not escape the Soviet writers of his generation. The theater director David Lederman describes a 1940 visit in Białystok with Peretz Markish, during which Markish, in secret, shared an article in which Nadir had written, "I nurtured a snake around my neck" (ikh hob oysgehodevet a shlang arum mayn haldz). According to Lederman, a distraught Markish asked, "Just he alone nursed a snake around his neck? Just he alone? And maybe we all nursed the snake? And the time may come when the nursed snake will choke us all."[105] As we have seen, World War II led Soviet, as well as fellow-traveler, Jewish writers to cautiously embrace Jewish religious themes. As Harriet Murav has shown, even in the Soviet Union, where the term "Holocaust" was never used in discussions of the "Great Patriotic War," Yiddish writers eventually turned to liturgical motifs to articulate the Jewish loss amid their continued support of the Soviet narrative of heroism.[106] Whereas Soviet writers struggled to balance nation and multinational communism, Nadir turned toward religion, a move that Nadir's posthumous editors helped to highlight. His *teshuvah* was also a process of relocating passwords to their original context. To do this, Nadir evoked prayer.

Moses Maimonides, writing of *teshuvah* in the twelfth century, maintained, "Only through repentance will Israel be redeemed."[107] For Maimonides, the steps required to achieve forgiveness include stopping the transgression, resolving not to repeat the transgression, feeling regret over the transgression, and confessing verbally to God.[108] If Nadir in his 1940 autobiography maps his movement away from communism, making clear that he will not return to Party politics and demonstrating regret over his earlier transgressions, his 1941 prose poem "A Tfilah" (A prayer) constitutes a verbal confession to God. He begins the piece, "This is a conversation between me and God."[109] After many years of a childish quarrel (*broygez*), the narrator states, "Today I am coming back—for the last time."[110] The short essay, with its emphasis on return before death, evokes Psalm 71: "Cast me not off in the time of old age; when my strength faileth, forsake me not." Nadir repeats the supplication, "Do not abandon me, oh God, do not abandon me! [Farloz mikh nit, o Got, farloz mikh nit!] In my last few steps, last few steps—do not abandon me, Oh God!"[111] The repeated appeals to God are in keeping with Maimonides's final requirement for repentance. But Nadir is praying specifically for his writing: "Make it not mundane, make it not indifferent [Makh nit vokhedik, makh nit glaykhgiltik]—the pen, with which I have really tried—apart from earning my bread—to also serve the people in a pure and decent way."[112] The desire to be "not indifferent" is telling. Nadir, who had so long undermined his own messages with exaggeration, here longs to write poetry that is unambiguously meaningful. Eitan Kensky reads this desire for earnestness in Nadir's final book as a failure: "The exuberance is gone, the comic voice absent, and the serious one that replaced it thoroughly uncompelling."[113] Nadir's willingness to use his own irreverence against himself is what makes his final attempt at poetic truth so poignant. Despite the attempt at penance, Nadir's tone remains exaggerated. The insistence on exclamation points to punctuate each line produces an effect of shouting. The message itself is a desperate longing to write poetry in service to the Jewish people, a people for whom he feels a new sense of responsibility.

Nadir's "Tfilah" resonated with some his fellow poets. The poet Ada Glazer wrote to Nadir, on September 21, 1941, to thank him for "Tfilah": "The prayer moved me to tears." She goes on to lament her inability to write something similar.[114] In a letter dated the eve of Rosh Hashanah, 1941, Aaron Glantz-Leyeles wrote, "Your 'Prayer' really moved me. You are properly praying for all of us who have had the luck to live to this Rosh Hashanah."[115] In the same letter, Glantz-Leyeles responds to a note he had received from Nadir by declaring, "It is time that all of the quarrels, which have come over and under the waves from this dear time of ours should be released—especially between people who get around on word-shmord, art-shmart and other such mild things—that oh and woe to us all."[116] For sympathetic readers like Glantz-Leyeles and Glazer, "Tfilah" was a gesture toward mending the rifts that had fractured New York's Yiddish literary community a decade earlier.

Nadir was attempting to resolve his quarrel not only with God but with fellow writers and even his readers, although Shmuel Leshtsinski later wrote, "Of course the accounts with the personal Moishe Nadir, even now, after his death, are far from over and the totals haven't been completely summed up."[117] In an article that appeared in the May 4, 1940, issue of *Der Tog,* Nadir appealed to his readers, asking, "What should I write to you?" One reader, Hirsh Fugl, cheered Nadir's departure from the communist press in a personal letter: "When you wrote for the *Frayhayt,* I felt sorry for you . . . but now that you're the good old Moishe

Nadir again, write as you know how, and let's all enjoy it and give you back the respect that you earned in the old days."[118]

Nadir's letters to fellow poets suggest a growing admiration for the very colleagues he had condemned a decade earlier. In November 1941, Nadir wrote to Yankev Glatshteyn that he understood why "in those young foolish years" Glatshteyn became "a little angry" at him. He expresses admiration specifically for Glatshteyn's ability to think carefully: "Among Yiddish writers we have more than a few thinking people [denkendike mentshn], but rethinking, contemplative people [nokhdenkendike, komtemplative mentshn], cut from your cloth are few in our writing family.[119] Nadir, who had long written poems about his hometown, Narayev, compliments Glatshteyn on his semiautobiographical *Yash* cycle, which was based on his 1934 trip to his hometown of Lublin.[120] Nadir's reference to "rethinking" suggests that he was also carefully reading Glatshteyn's poems, including his 1938 "A gute nakht, velt" (Good night, world), in which the speaker famously slams the door on the non-Jewish world:

A gute nakht, velt, breyte velt,	Good night, world, wide world,
groyse, shtinkendike velt.	big, stinking world.
Nisht du, nor ikh farhak dem toyer.[121]	Not you, but I am slamming the gate.

Nadir, assuring Glatshteyn that he remained Glatshteyn's "'faithless,' but for all that 'passionate' reader," appears to be modeling his own *teshuvah* on Glatshteyn's poetics of return.[122]

Also in November 1941, Nadir wrote to H. Leivick in a clumsy attempt to mend their rift. "Like the ragged fool [opgerisener nar] that I am, I never reasoned that a poet could and would always remember that someone once refused to kneel before the same icons as he!"[123] Nadir uses the familiar "du" in his letter, whereas Leivick, in his response, uses the formal "ir"; Leivick nevertheless assures Nadir, "I carry no anger toward you" (Ikh trog nit keyn kas oyf aykh).[124] Leivick—the Leivick who had spent time in a tsarist prison and Siberia, who had with Nadir been a member of Di Yunge, and whom Nadir had accused of treachery on the pages of the *Frayhayt* after the 1929 Hebron riot, had no interest in reopening old wounds.

Nadir, however, sought not respite but reconciliation with both man and God. Leivick and Nadir both wrote poems titled "Memameykim"

(Out of the depths), in 1940 and 1942, respectively, which interpret Psalm 130, one of seven penitential psalms:[125]

> Out of the depths have I called Thee, O Lord
> Lord, hearken unto my voice;
> Let Thine ears be attentive to the voice of my supplications.[126]

"Memameykim" (*Mima'amakim*, as transliterated from biblical Hebrew; *De Profondis*, as it is well known in Latin) is important both to the tradition of lament and to prayers of deliverance or thanksgiving.[127] Whereas the psalm begins with a clear first-person narrator, Nadir begins his lament with a rhetorical question:

Ver zingt in fintsternish—fun likht,	Who is singing of light in the dark,
zitsndik in faykhtn tom?	sitting in a damp abyss?
Es iz der dikhter, es iz ikh—	It's the poet, it is I,
der letster aynvoyner fun Sdom.[128]	Sodom's last dweller.

Nadir's poem, beginning with this riddle, is self-critical. The abyss (*tom*) from which the poet hopes to ascend is partly self-inflicted. In the tradition of other poems of lament, Nadir alludes to past sins: if Sodom is a password for the Party, Nadir was indeed one of the last dwellers from among his American Yiddish modernist milieu.

It is likely that Nadir wrote this poem in response to H. Leivick's 1940 "Memameykim," in which the poet meditates on the slurred utterance "memameykim"—translating it into the unusual contraction, "fundertifenish" (fromthedepths), in Yiddish: "Whose cry is this? / Who is falling? / Whose song is this / fromthedepths" (vemens geshray iz dos? / ver fargeyt zikh azoy? / vemens gezang iz dos / fundertifenish). Leivick, locating a single word in its most literal meaning, strips away the many ciphers, as though attempting to reach language itself. For Leivick, who wrote several poems about forgiveness and healing in this period, the utterance "fromthedepths" takes the place of a divine addressee.[129] Leivick relocates the word "Memameykim"—a password, a scar, and a marker of Jewishness—into its original context, suggesting that the word itself is what must be reached. Psalm 130, traditionally recited during the ten days of penitence between Rosh Hashanah and Yom Kippur, had recently been the center of liturgical debates in American

Judaism. Mordecai Kaplan, founder of Reconstructionist Judaism, advocated in 1930 for substituting Psalm 130 for the Kol Nidre prayer on Yom Kippur, arguing that a psalm is more meaningful than "an outworn formula."[130] Nadir and Leivick, in their indirect conversation about poetry and redemption, turned to the Jewish poetic tradition of the psalms as a means of return and an object of return.

Nadir appears to have modeled his final poem, "Neenter," too, on the penitential psalms. In the fourth stanza, we find, "God, where are you? Say yes or no:/Will you come to meet me?" (Got, vu bistu? Zog yo, tsi neyn:/tsi vestu mir antkegn geyn?).[131] In Psalm 102, "A Prayer of the Afflicted," the speaker cries, "Hide not Thy face from me in the day of my distress." Nadir further reiterates this desperate desire for the divine:

Ikh vart un vart, aleyn, aleyn,	I wait and wait, alone, alone,
tsi vet mir Got antkegn geyn?	will God come toward me?
A tsvey-dray trit khotsh biz tsum shvel—	There are only two or three steps to the threshold—
ikh trog im shney-blimlekh in zel.	I carry him snow-blossoms in my soul.
Shema Yisroel—der sof fun lid,	Shema Yisroel—the end of the song,
azoy muz shtarbn yeder yid.[132]	this is how every Jew should die.

Appeals to God appear throughout this poem, as they do in "Tefilah." These appeals recall the "do not abandon me" of Psalm 71, as well as Psalm 70's "Oh Lord, tarry not" (Adonay, al-takhar). Nadir, with his frequent references to the psalms, and his inclusion of "Shema Yisroel," appears to be ritualizing the transition from life to death by infusing his poetry with prayer. The Shema—the prayer that Jews are meant to say while dying—is a password for the ultimate wound and time stamp, death. As Hans-Georg Gadamer helps to illuminate, death is both "the hour of one's utmost forsakenness" and the event that "unites everyone with each other."[133] If the form, which includes clever wordplay, inventive rhymes, and dramatic performance (in this case, of the act of prayer), resembles Nadir's earlier manifesto-like verse, the content differs in important ways. Through his embrace of religion, Nadir, once an ardent secularist, was attempting to turn from irony to sincerity, to restore his passwords to a meaning that holds value for him as he retreats from internationalism.

Some of Nadir's readers welcomed his turn toward Judaism. Leon Faynberg maintained that "with Moishe Nadir there died a great Jew, whose name will remain a legend."[134] The critic Avrom Tabachnik wrote in his 1943 review of *Moyde ani*, "If Moishe Nadir hadn't written another poem besides his last poem 'Neenter,' we could still consider him not only the master of a new, sparkling and shining word-magic, but also one of our most original Yiddish poets."[135] Similarly, the fiction writer Shea Tenenboym remembered Nadir favorably for his "word-art": "The word was his crown and his sword, his scepter and his spear."[136] A reviewer of *Moyde ani* for the *Keneder Odler* dismisses Nadir's politics altogether: "I loved him when he was 'left' and I 'right' and vice versa."[137] Not everyone shared this appreciation of Nadir's final poems. Following the posthumous publication of *Moyde ani*, Nadir's legacy became the subject of debate in the Yiddish press, where reviewers weighed Nadir's formal contributions to Yiddish literature against what many saw as a life of insincere oaths.

Other critics were skeptical of Nadir's sudden change of heart. Lamed Shapiro, while praising Nadir's "word art" (vort-kunst), did not accept Nadir's penance. "They tell me that in recent years Moishe Nadir did *teshuvah*. Hmm . . . *teshuvah*. One of our ancients once grumbled: 'He who says "I sin and I repent I sin and I repent," doesn't have enough left in his hands to make *teshuvah*.'"[138] Shapiro reminds readers of the 1929 rift over Hebron when he recalls Nadir's "blind, maniacal run [that] tramples all borders," even going so far as "welcoming the Palestinian pogroms."[139] Alexander Mukdoni, with a heavy dose of sarcasm, writes of *Moyde ani*, "Here we have before us Moishe Nadir the *ba'al teshuvah*, he does *teshuvah*, he feels remorse for his decade and a half as a communist."[140] Mukdoni views Nadir's *teshuvah* as an indictment of his community: "He didn't beat his own chest with 'I have sinned,' he beat other people's chests with 'I have sinned'; he didn't torment himself, he tormented his former friends, his former colleagues."[141] Shteynberg, despite his glowing 1926 *Moishe Nadir Book*, in his review of *Moyde ani* accuses Nadir of intellectual narcissism and hypocrisy: "From narcissism to cynicism is a short step."[142] Shteynberg further damns Nadir by claiming the latter was never a true communist. "Basically Nadir was asocial—communism was an empty word for him. . . . He didn't put anything into it, other than his own invectives, which come from his hatred for others."[143] Even Faynberg, who coedited Nadir's last book, suggested on the pages of *Der Tog* that Nadir's self-fashioning was a show: "They often cried from all sides that Moishe Nadir fancied himself exclusively a revolutionary, but in truth he is a petit bourgeois poet, who 'dreams of Narayev and knots his pretty neckties.'"[144] Friends and foes alike summed up Nadir's literary life as a series of exaggerated performances.

Elias Tcherikower, one of the editors of the Paris-based *Oyfn Sheydveg* who encouraged a return to Judaism, nonetheless wrote skeptically in 1939 of the Yiddish and Hebrew writers who were urging a return to the metaphorical ghetto: "And in the current dark times, we shift our gaze back, longing for such completeness of soul, for fortification in our afflictions, and we are chasing after the blue bird of the old ghetto. A fantasy."[145] Nadir, ever the performer, was enacting this fantasy. Arguably, the most accurate reading of Nadir's legacy was as a Shakespearian tragedy. Tabachnick, despite his praise of "Neenter," called the book *Moyde ani*, "one big Hamletesque to-be-or-not-to-be monologue."[146] If we read Nadir's oeuvre as a struggle between two confessions, Soviet-aligned communism and Judaism, his life's work appears less to be broken into disjointed segments (precommunism, communism, and postcommunism) than to reflect a tragic dialogue between revolution and Jewish tradition. By World War II, Jewish identity began replacing leftist politics, even for those who had remained with the Party into the 1930s.[147] "We are sinking [Mir geyen unter]," Nadir wrote shortly before his death. "The Nazi is slaughtering us like calves. And before he slaughters us, he unmans us such that not even one in a thousand jumps up in the last death throes onto the Nazi-executioner and bites him in the neck."[148] The "us" had clearly shifted from the workers of the world back to the Jews. For Nadir, as for many Americans on the left, the horrors of World War II signaled the end of a utopian dream. Had he lived beyond 1943, Nadir might have become what Hannah Arendt has termed an "ex-Communist," publicly urging his former friends to "make a confession, own up to a conversion, and form a solid political group."[149] Or he might have found new ways of balancing his exclamatory and lyrical tendencies. His fatal heart attack, however, caught him midconfession, and his last, self-negating works call attention to his inability to reconcile his competing allegiances. As we shall see in the Afterword to this book, some writers did find a way of merging their internationalist faith with a return to a Jewish community.

Exaggerated utterances are often what best embody the spirit of a historical moment. Nadir's communist poems, replete with revolutionary passwords, helped to define the spirit of internationalism in the 1920s and '30s; and his tortured attempt at penance captures the feeling of betrayal that led many Jewish internationalists to retreat into religious group identity by the 1940s. Nadir's second *teshuvah* dramatically altered his legacy. After his death, he was viewed as a writer who moved between political and aesthetic poles. As Faynberg put it, Nadir's poetics consisted of two key elements: "1. tender, dreamy lyricism, and 2. cruel, bilious pathos in protest against the injustice of the world order."[150] Faynberg admits that these two tendencies did not always live in harmony, although when they did work together, the synthesis produced remarkable lyrics.[151] Nadir's two periods of *teshuvah* evince the malleability of a password, which can code a writer's allegiance to an identity, be it proletarian or Jewish. Nadir's dramatic shifts—between lyricism and political protest, between Party and Jewish allegiances, culminating in his attempts at earnest self-negation—expose the apparent irreconcilability of Jewishness and internationalism on the eve of World War II. To draw from collective, national memory while forging international solidarity would require a new, more ambiguous relationship to identity categories. It may also require new passwords.

AFTERWORD

Kaddish

After World War II, leftist internationalism changed. Yiddish poets in the Soviet Union, the United States, and elsewhere turned inward, mourning the genocide that had taken place in Europe. This included the most fervent proponents of proletarian internationalism on both sides of the Iron Curtain. Aaron Kurtz, who wrote passionately against Zionism in 1929 and for the Spanish Republic in 1938, was one of the few American Yiddish poets who did not leave the Party. However, he changed as a poet in the years after the Holocaust, more frequently writing about specifically Jewish loss. In 1944, Kurtz wrote "A milion por shikh," which his wife, the poet Olga Cabral, translated into English as "A Million Pairs of Shoes":

A milyon por shikh	A million pairs of shoes
lign un trakhtn.	Lie thinking.
A milyon por	A million pairs of shoes, all that
lebn-geblibene shikh	survived,
bargn zikh,	Clambering,
rirn zikh,	Creeping,
kletern zikh tsum himl.	Climbing to the sky.
A milyon Yidn hobn zeyere vundn	A million Jews bore their wounds in
getrogn in di shikh.[1]	these shoes.[2]

The empty shoes are traces of their murdered wearers and silent replacements for a community that had perished, together with its wounds. Kurtz, who had presided over the American Proletpen writers' union in the 1930s, remained with the Party far longer than most of his fellow internationalists. At the end of World War II, many of the most doctrinaire poets of the internationalist generation refocused their attention to Jewish wounds.

Moyshe Teyf, we recall, translocated Bialik's 1903 "B'ir haHaregah" in 1929 into a condemnation of Zionism. After the war, Teyf, like Kurtz, turned his attention to Jewish trauma. "Vilne, Zumer 1944" (Vilnius, Summer 1944) begins by evoking the first word of the mourner's Kaddish, *yisgadal* (May it be great):

O yisgadal mayn mames shtot,	O *yisgadal* my mama's town,
O yisgadal tsu dayne vent,	O *yisgadal* to your walls,
O, alte Vilne—golesdiker got,	O, old Vilna—diasporic god,
tsebrokhn bist, farbrent. . . . [3]	you are broken, burnt. . . .

The mourner's Kaddish is an eighth-century Aramaic prayer recited in the company of a minyan (ten Jews, traditionally men). It opens with an exaltation of God's name: "Yisgadal ve'yiskadash shmey rabo" (May it be great and may it be holy the name of the Lord). Teyf's repetition of the opening word, *yisgadal,* has the effect of aporia—an impassable barrier, in this case to prayer. Teyf's salvaged Aramaic word exalts not God but the city, home to a thriving prewar Jewish community. The Nazis liquidated the Vilna Ghetto in 1943, sending its inhabitants to death in the nearby woods of Ponar. The Red Army retook the city in the summer of 1944. Teyf was imprisoned at the height of Stalin's purges, between 1937 and 1941, then volunteered for the front. The poem's narrator is a Jewish Red Army soldier who, entering Vilnius in 1944, protests its silence: "Arise, my mama's city! Don't be silent!" (Shtey uf, mayn mames shtot! Nit shtum!).[4] If Jewish culture was once Teyf's source of internationalist passwords, it has now become the cause for which he is willing to risk everything. Teyf was rearrested in 1948, a year after the release of his *Milkhome lider* (War poems).[5]

Soviet and American Jewish writers mourned in different ways, and the afterlife of internationalism manifested itself differently in each con-

text. By the 1960s, with the Eichmann and Auschwitz trials, the Holocaust was publicly recognized outside the Soviet sphere as a tragic, Jewish
event within World War II. In communist Europe, however, the war was
collectively remembered as a Soviet struggle against fascism. Katie
Trumpener has poignantly summed up the Cold War divide in World
War II memory in East and West Germany: "The West focused almost
exclusively on the Holocaust as deterritorialized genocide; the East, primarily on fascism as imperialist expansionism, on slave labour as cultural subordination and obliteration."[6] Although Stalin formally dissolved the Communist International in 1943, throughout the Cold War,
the rhetoric of internationalism remained official doctrine in the Soviet
Union: Soviet commemoration of war victims emphasized a collective,
Soviet loss rather than a specifically Jewish loss. In the Soviet Union,
Jewish passwords became a means of referencing Jewish collective loss,
particularly in the antisemitic atmosphere of postwar Stalinism. Jewish
culture became part of dissident culture.[7]

If one blind spot in Soviet multiethnicity was the struggle of Russia's
Jews, a corresponding blind spot in the United States was Jim Crow.
Steven Lee has discussed the rivalry that emerged during the Cold War
between an American rhetoric of multiculturalism and a Soviet rhetoric of multiethnicity. "Through much of the twentieth century," Lee
writes, "the United States and the USSR laid competing claims to global
preeminence by touting domestic inclusion, both assailing one another's failures to live up to stated ideals. Segregation in the American South
was a favorite topic for Soviet propaganda, to which U.S. lawmakers
could respond by highlighting antisemitism in the USSR."[8] A by-
product of the treatment of minority rights in the Cold War was that
Soviet and American Jewish activists had different causes for speaking
truth to power: Soviet dissidents and their Western allies emphasized
Jewish loss, whereas American activists fought for racial equality, and
some viewed the Soviet Union as a safe haven for African Americans.
Lee has observed that, despite this apparent "Cold War binarism," the
Soviet Union and the United States shared an "experience of illusion,
disillusion, and compromise that traversed but also reinforced descent-
based divides."[9] In the postwar period, Jewish artists in the Soviet
Union and the United States shared a legacy of internationalism, one

that colored ethnic commemoration and activism in the 1950s, '60s, and '70s.

Despite the increase in antisemitism under Stalin, Teyf and other Soviet Yiddish poets relocated Jewish texts after World War II to a Jewish community, mourning the dead alongside the language they had used to fight for a workers' international. "Postwar work written in the Soviet Union," Harriet Murav has observed, "powerfully engages the central question of twentieth-century literature: living in the aftermath of disaster."[10] After the Hitler-Stalin pact, Peretz Markish wrote a poem that would remain unpublished in the Soviet Union—"Tsu a Yidishe tentserin" (To a Jewish dancer), addressing the alienation of Jewish refugees in the Soviet Union following the Nazi invasion of the Soviet Union. He would go on to commemorate Jewish loss in the war publicly in his two-volume *Milkhome* (War, 1948).[11] Moreover, some of the modernist Yiddish pogrom poems that the internationalist poets had translocated to address other groups' suffering in the 1930s gained new meaning after World War II. Avrom Sutzkever admitted that before the war he did not understand Markish's 1921–1922 pogrom poem *Di kupe* (The mound). He had failed to decode the first-person-singular cry, "Lick not, heavenly tallow, my matted beards!" (Lek nit heylevne himlisher mayne farpapte berd!), or the plural "beards," until he found himself in the Vilna Ghetto, where "the collective mound [kupe] of the years 1941–1943 did have this kind of intertwined plural [tsunoyfgetulyetn mertsol]."[12] The passwords that Yiddish poets had eagerly translocated from pogrom poems to poems about other groups' suffering were redeployed to describe the unimaginable Jewish loss in the war.

Later generations of Soviet Jews would return to Jewish passwords to mourn a lost community and lost words. After the war, the eastern European Jewish lingua franca ceased to be Yiddish, and Jewish passwords became ways of marking a Russian-language poem. The poet and performer Alexander Galich (born Ginzburg, 1919–1977) dedicated his 1970 Russian-language ballad "Kadish" (Kaddish) to Janusz Korczak, the teacher, pediatrician, and orphanage director who accompanied his pupils to Treblinka when the Warsaw Ghetto was liquidated in 1942.[13] Galich describes a verbal aporia reminiscent of Teyf's aborted 1944 Kaddish: "I don't know how to pray, forgive me, Lord God" (Ia ne

umeiu molit-sia, prosti menia, Gospodi Bozhe).[14] Galich's inability to
conjure Jewish words renders the title of his song all the more forceful.
Galich, who did not speak Yiddish, was fascinated by his parents' generation of Soviet Yiddish cultural figures. In his 1973 memoir, he describes visiting a Jewish Section Party meeting in 1948. Peretz Markish,
who was presiding over the meeting and had been friendly to Galich,
threw him out of the auditorium: "You're a stranger here, leave at once!"
Galich recalled that two weeks later, the entire Jewish Section was arrested, and many of them, including Markish, were later executed.
"Now I know that Markish in that very moment when he had publicly
called me a stranger and threw me out of the meeting, was just saving
my young life."[15] The American writer Grace Paley, who met Galich in
Moscow before his 1974 emigration, speculated that Galich viewed the
1960s and '70s as a "new exodus," a time that demanded he write about
the Jews of Russia as a Russian poet and as a Jew.[16] Galich addresses
Stalin's antisemitism in his 1972 "Poema o Staline" (Poem about Stalin).
The leader cannot abide "Sweaty, big-mouthed Jews" (Potnye, mor-
dastye evrei).[17] For Galich, the bard of a generation of Soviet dissidents,
Jewishness was in opposition to the regime.

On both sides of the Iron Curtain, the Kaddish became a metonym
for postwar Jewish mourning, across languages. In Allen Ginsberg's
1957–1959 *Kaddish,* commemoration doubles as a curse of God, of the
self, and of the prayer's subject, Ginsberg's mother, Naomi Levy (1894–
1956), a Party member who had been to the same Yiddish-speaking
communist summer camp, Nitgedayget, that both Moishe Nadir and
Vladimir Mayakovsky had visited. "Blest be your failure! Blest be your
stroke! Blest be the close of your eye!"[18] In 1963, Leonard Bernstein
completed his "Kaddish" Symphony (Number 3), an avant-garde work
that includes a narrator who alternately praises and curses God: "Angry,
wrinkled Old Majesty: / I want to pray" turns to "You let this happen,
Lord of Hosts!"[19] The Kaddish, as the historian David Shyovitz has
shown, was conceived not merely to commemorate the dead but to in-
tercede on behalf of a soul that may still be wandering.[20] The prayer is,
in this sense, a protest to God against a potential injustice. Both Ginsberg and Bernstein present the Kaddish as a password for the lost
Jewish signifier, but both also present their works as protests against

injustice. If their Jewishness did not place them into particular peril in postwar America, both were outsiders as gay men. But both of these Left-identified American Jewish artists also invite, with their Jewish mourning, a universalizing interpretation. Allen Grossman has written of Ginsberg's *Kaddish* that Naomi's death "represents the death of parochial culture."[21] Bernstein, translocating the mourner's Kaddish from a traditional Jewish minyan onto a secular symphony space, reinvents the tradition of Jewish community mourning for a largely non-Jewish community. A distinctly Jewish password was passing, in a non-Jewish language, to a secular, multicultural audience.

Non-Jewish writers, too, entered the genre of Jewish mourning. The English-language poet Olga Cabral (1909–1997), who married Aaron Kurtz in 1951, based her poem "At the Jewish Museum" on an installation piece by Harold Persico Paris. Paris's *Kaddish for the Little Children* was a large, empty black room, displayed in the Jewish Museum of New York in 1975. Cabral describes the entrance to the room, which contains "the alphabet of mysterious / tablets. / May words guide me through this place." The walls of the room "are receding rapidly to the edge / of the visible universe where objects / tend to disappear—"

> where all the names have gone
> the diminutives
> the sweet
> nicknames
> beyond reach of our most cunning
> telescopes[22]

Cabral's poem marks the loss of the most personal of passwords—the names that reference unique individuals. Cabral was born in Trinidad to Spanish and Portuguese parents and raised in Canada. She and Aaron Kurtz lived on Long Island, remained close to the Party, and translated each other until Kurtz's death in 1964. In an intermarriage that was rare in their generation, far enough from the Soviet Union that they could disregard many of the realities of Soviet autarky, they both wrote poems commemorating the victims of the Spanish Civil War, the Holocaust, and US race violence.

Most of the American Yiddish poets I have discussed in this book turned away from Party politics after the war, if they had not already. The revelations of Stalin's atrocities, the encroachment of the Cold War into American and Soviet lives, and the tragic death of most of the world's Yiddish speakers rendered the messianic excitement of the 1930s unsustainable. In postwar Yiddish poetry, Jewish suffering featured far more prominently than it had in the age of internationalism, although some poets did continue to write about other marginalized groups, particularly those who lived to see the civil rights era. According to Olga Cabral, one of Aaron Kurtz's last works was his "Kaddish," which he dedicated to the four African American schoolgirls killed in the 1963 Alabama church bombing.[23] Rather than supplanting Jewish pain with the pain of others, Kurtz mourns multiple tragedies. It is worth citing the poem at length:

Yisgadal veyiskadash . . .	*Yisgadal veyiskadash . . .*
Ponem al ponem mit Eyb Linkoln,	Face to face with Abe Lincoln, face to
ponem al ponem mit	face with
dem Negershn martirerfolk	the Negro martyrs
zogt a rov kadesh. Ikh bin nit	a rabbi says Kaddish. I am not
Keyn kadesh-zoger. Nor di mames	a Kaddish-sayer. But today mamas
iber der velt hobn haynt biter	the world over bitterly wept
Geveynt un baveynt di fir kleyne	and mourned the four small black
shvartse meydelekh—	girls—
Hob ikh af dem rovs kadesh geen-	I responded to the rabbi's Kaddish:
tfert: *omeyn!* Un gehert hob ikh	*omeyn!* And
nit dem rov aleyn, nit dem rov aleyn:	I heard not the rabbi himself, not the
gehert hob ikh	rabbi: I heard
iber der velt	across the world
a milyon mayne yesomim zogn kadesh:	A million of my orphans saying
unter veynendike volkns—[24]	Kaddish: beneath weeping clouds—

Aaron Kurtz, at the end of his life, drew passwords from the Jewish mourner's prayer, along with the image of a "million" orphans from his own Holocaust poem, extending Jewish pain to a wider community. Kurtz, three decades after Scottsboro and the rise of fascism in Europe, imagines a single community united by a Jewish password. This Kaddish, Kurtz asserts, is the same as the one spoken in Babylon and during the Spanish inquisition, "the same / As in Bialik's *City of Slaughter,* the same / as I hear in Auschwitz, in Ponar, in the Warsaw Ghetto and Babi Yar."[25] In this long poem, Kurtz references individuals who have fought for injustice across national boundaries, from the African American singer and writer Paul Robeson to Hirsh Glik, the poet whose Vilna ghetto song "Zog nit keymmol" (Never say) Robeson had famously sung on numerous occasions, in Yiddish. Kurtz continues:

Un do zog ikh	And here I am saying
dem zelbikn kadesh mit mayn folk . . .	the same Kaddish with my people . . .
vos hilkht	that echoes
mit Hirsh Gliks kol un mit zayn	in Hirsh Glik's voice and with his
parol.[26]	password.

Aaron Kurtz, the poet who had titled his Spanish Civil War book *No Pasaran* and who had described the Western Wall as "crumbling and moldy" in 1929, recognized the importance of the password (*parol*) to community. Glik's lyric "Never say (that you are traveling the last road)" becomes a formula for uniting a postwar Jewish community on behalf of the African American victims of racism. Kurtz, one of the last believers in the age of internationalism, maintained his faith that suffering was not to be guarded within an isolated national community; it was to be translated.

APPENDIX

Poems from the Age of Internationalism

H. LEIVICK, "A SACCO-VANZETTI YEAR"
(A YOR SAKO VANZETI)

Ir hot zikh ayngeshnitn in unzer zikorn,
vi an ongegliter meser in a vund;
o, vemen nokh azoy hot der toyt gekent portn
in aza farzigltn bund?

Haynt, azoy vi farayorn,
Tsharlstonen iber der erd dem talyens fis;
s'iz nokh afile nit fartsoygn gevorn
mit keyn haytl der Fulerisher bis.

Dos zelbe shlekhts fun kateyger tsu kateyger,
der zelber foyst, di zelbe makht;
o, mir fargesn nit di vayzers fun zeyger
vi zey hobn getrift mit blut in oygust-nakht.

In yener nakht, oyf ongeglite shteyner,

You've cut into our memory
like a hot knife in a wound;
oh, whom else could Death have taken
in such a sealed bond?

Today, like last year,
the hangman's feet dance the
    Charleston across the earth;
Fuller's bite hasn't even been covered
with a scab.

The same evil from accuser to
    accuser,
the same fist, the same power;
oh, we won't forget how the clock
    hands
dripped with blood that August night.

That night, on the glowing stones,

hobn mir ale gevoyet vi mide velf,
ven es zaynen gefaln oyf undz, vi
s'faln beyner,
di letste reges fun der shtunde tsvelf.

we all howled like tired wolves,
when they fell on us, like falling
bones,
those last moments of the twelfth
hour.

Ober in yener nakht hobn mir oykh
zalbenung gegosn
oyf tfise-shlos, oyf rigl un kayt,
un farpeynikter korbn iz gevorn
khosn,
un vi a shtul fun bazetsns—der shtul
fun toyt.

But that night we poured ointment
too
on prison locks, on bolts and chains,
and the tortured victim became a
bridegroom,
and the bridal chair was the electric
chair.

Fun gerekhter monung, fun optsol atake
hern zikh shoyn, hern zikh shoyn trit;
vi a glok klingt der klang Sako,

From a just petition, from retribution
footsteps still echo, echo;
how the sound Sacco rings out like a
bell,

Un vi zikh Vanzeti zidt.

And how Vanzetti sizzles.

ESTHER SHUMIATCHER, "AT THE BORDER OF CHINA" (BAYM RAND FUN KHINE)

Froy un muter
baym rand fun Khine un Ind!
Es hengen di korbn fun ayere akslen
gelodn mit umet un mi.
Es hengen di trukene brustn, vi
fartruknte loglen
in blend funem dorshtikn vist.
Un s'viklen trantes farfoylte ayer
faroremtn guf—
af ayere lipn glit a fariglter flukh.

Wife and mother
at the border of China and India!
Baskets hang from your shoulders,
laden with sadness and toil.
Your breasts hang barren as empty
leather flasks
in the dazzle of parched waste.
And the rotten wreckage wraps your
meager body—
on your lips glows a sealed curse.

Froy un muter
baym rand fun Khine un Ind!
Es shviblen di borvese trit fardungen
tsu eybiker protses
af gliendn zamd.
Ir lodt ayere teg in grunt funem shif
ineynem mit koyl-

Wife and mother
at the border of China and India!
Your barefoot steps swarm, bound to
their eternal trial on
burning sand.
You load your days on the bottom of
the ship along with

shvartsn shtoyb.

Un s'vert ayer yugnt farbrent in flam
    funem fintstern royb,
es rizlt farkhalesht gezang fun oygn
    bazoymte mit krenklekhn royt:
Mir garn un vartn af ru funem toyt.

Froy un muter—
ariber mayn kop hengen himlen in
    gelaytertn bloy,
vigt zikh di zatkayt af zangen in feld
    farn shnit.
Un umetik nidert af lebn, harts
    mayns, der toy
baym rand fun Khine un Ind . . .
Royen zikh lebns af bergele mist.
Fayf, fayfl, a lid mir, in vind un in vist.

Rinshtok iz heym far heymloze hent.

Brekele guf hot hunger farlendt.

Hot zikh der vey afn mistbarg gemert—

emitsns lebn iz oysgeyn bashert.
Ver s'hot gezindikt antkegn di hent,

der hot dos lebn geflikt un geshendt.

the coal-black dust.

And your youth is consumed by the
    flame of this dark pillage,
a faint song trickles from eyes lined
    with a sickly red:
We crave and await death's rest.

Wife and mother—
over my head hang clear blue
    heavens,
the fullness swings on ears of corn
    before the harvest.
The dew hovers sadly over life, my
    heart,
at the border of China and India . . .
Lives swarm on a mound of trash.
Whistle me a song in the wind, in the
    void.

Homeless hands find a home in the
    gutter.

Hunger has ruined a crumb of a body.

Here on the trash heap, sorrow
    has grown—
somebody's life is bound to expire.
Whoever has sinned against these
    hands,
he has plucked and dishonored this life.

MOYSHE TEYF, "SING, DESERT WIND" (ZING, VINT FUN MIDBER)

Kum gey in shkhite-shtot
zolst zen mit dayne oygn . . .
"Shkhite-shtot," Kh. N. Bialik

Arise and go to the city of slaughter
you must see with your eyes . . .
"City of Slaughter," Ch. N. Bialik

Dayne groyzame verter, a "dikhter fun
    Levonen,"
kuk oyf zey,
dermon zikh un dertseyl:
In shoen peynlekhe, bay vey-geshray
    fun kinder,

Your cruel words, a "poet of Lebanon,"

look upon them,
remember and recount:
In painful hours, in children's
    moaning,

vos hostu gezukht,
un vu hostu gefunen retung?
Vey tsu der heyliker heym
—a shkhite-shtot!
Vey tsu dem heylikn nakhtleger
—a blutiger mizbeyakh!—
ir—fun keynem gezalbte,
ir—gest nit gebetene,
vos hot ir gegazlt di bloy-vayse farbn

fun undzere erlekhe himlen?
Neyn!
Biz tsentn dor
zey veln shoyn nit opvashn
dos blut umshuldike, vos ir hot do
    fargosn!
Mit bayzer nikhterkayt
fun ayer tatn Shaylok
hot ir oyf falshe vogsholn
gevoygn erd baroybte,
—shtiker fleysh fun kinder—
to trinkt fun fule krugn
nit keyn vayn fun Karmel-vayntroybn,
nor a getrank fun kraytekher!
Vayl azoy hot bafoyln der vint der
    gerekhter

Fun midber,
fayer fun oyfshtand,
vos geyt oyf tsu himlen tsu heyse
tsu himlen fun mizrekh!

O, ir oreme Shimshons,
shvindzikhtike zin fun Makabi,
vos knien far shveln fun henker

un lekn a beyn fun groyzamen,
    blutikn moltsayt.
Vey tsu der heliker heym
—a shkhite-shtot!—
vey tsu dem heylikn nakhtlenger

what have you sought,
and where have you found salvation?
Woe to the holy home
—a city of slaughter!
Woe to the holy resting places
—a bloody sacrificial altar!—
no one has anointed you,
you are uninvited guests,
why have you stolen the blue and
    white colors

from our honest sky?
No!
Even the tenth generation
will not wash away
the innocent blood you've spilled
    here!
With the evil sobriety
of your father Shylock
on false scales you have
weighed stolen land,
—bits of children's flesh—
so drink from full tankards
not the wine from Carmel-grapes,
but an herbal potion!
For this is how the wind of justice has
    sent its message

From the desert,
fire of rebellion
that reaches the hot heavens
the heavens of the East!

O, you poor Samsons,
consumptive sons of Maccabee,
who kneel at the executioners'
    thresholds
licking a bone from an atrocious,
    bloody meal.
Woe to the holy home
—a city of slaughter!—
woe to the holy resting places

—a blutiker mizbeyekh!—
tsu aykh, farfirte brider,
zol dergeyn mayn kol,
tsu di erlekhste fun ayere kolonen:
Gleker fun derleyzung shvaygn oyf
   Levnen!
Nu, zayn genug tsu trogn aykh

di shvere last fun falsher libshaft
tsu a fremder heym
un tsu a fremder shprakh!
Eyn shprakh hobn doyres in ondenk
   gelozn:

Tfises—ir vig,
pulver un fayer—ir muter getraye.
Brider farfirte fun 'heylikn goles,'

Shtrekt oys di hent
tsu di rayter, vos kumen fun midber
   oyf kemlen!

Zol lebn di sho,
ven oykh unter ayere himlen
vet oyfgeyn un vimlen
di fon fun Moskver Kreml! . . .

—a bloody sacrificial altar!—
To you, wayward brothers,
my voice should reach,
to the most honorable of your columns:
Bells of redemption are silent in
   Lebanon!
Well, it should be enough for you to
   carry
the heavy burden of false love
for a foreign home
and a foreign language!
One language generations have left as
   a memento:

Prisons are her cradle,
dust and fire are her true mother.
Brothers led astray out of our "holy
   diaspora,"
Stretch out your hands
to the riders who come from the
   desert on camels!

May the hour arrive,
when beneath your skies
there too will rise and fill the air
the flag of Moscow's Kremlin! . . .

SHIFRE VAYS, "ACCUSATIONS" (TAYNES)

Taynes,
vi mames shtrof-reyd,
shnaydn in undz,
vi in alte boymer
tempe zegn,
nor mir
kenen andersh itst nit vern.
Dos lebn arum undz:
A makhne broyne bern.
Ayn krumer trot—
mir shteyen in gefar
ayngeshlungen vern.

Accusations,
like mama's talking-tos,
cut into us,
like dull saws
in old trees,
but we
can't be any other way.
This life around us:
A band of brown bears.
One crooked step—
we stand in peril
of being devoured.

Taynes,
vi hungerike kinder-geshrayen,
shpizn undz in hartsn.
Mir hern,
nor mir kenen itst andersh nit vern,
dos lebn arum undz:
A vald mit vilde leybn.
eyn krumer trot—
un s'fartsukn undz di leybn.

Accusations,
like hungry children's-cries,
poke us in the heart.
We hear,
but we can't become otherwise now,
this life around us:
A wood with wild lions.
one crooked step—
and they'll devour our lives.

Taynes,
vi tropns regn
oyf tseshpaltene felder,
oder vi kushn, ven doyres farvebn.
Nor mir kenen itst andersh nit vern:
A tseflakerter vald undzer lebn.

Accusations,
like raindrops
on cracked fields,
or like kisses, when generations weave.
But we can't become otherwise now:
Our life is a wood on fire.

MALKA LEE, "GOD'S BLACK LAMB" (GOTS SHVARTSER LAM)

Zey hobn im aroysgefirt
mit nakete fis, gebundene hent.
Fun dorem zamd zayn hoyt farbrent.
Oylik iz plutsling gevorn zayn layb,
zayn shvartser guf in trern
    tseshaynt . . .
Der vald hot zikh geboygn vi fun
    meser shnit
oyf tsurik, oyf tsurik—
Gots shvartser lam
hot zikh gerisn fun shtrik . . .

They led him outside
with bare feet, and bound hands.
His skin burnt by southern sand.
His flesh became suddenly oily,
his black body sparkled in tears . . .

The woods bent as if from a knife
    wound
go backward, go back—
God's black lamb
tore himself from the rope . . .

Azoy hot men zayn zeydn gebundn
    tsum boym.
Oyf lipn—galiker shoym . . .
Foystn vi hek tseshvungen in roym.
Shpilt tam oyf tseyn oys dem vint,
arum im tantsn mentshlekhe hint.
Far yedn hunt a beyn . . .
Zayn guf iz mer nit vi laym . . .

This is how they bound his grand-
    father to a tree.
Bilious foam on his lips . . .
Fists like axes swinging in space.
Tom plays the wind on his teeth,
around him dance human dogs.
For every dog a bone . . .
His body is nothing more than
    clay . . .

Fun eygenem guf shoyn farfremdt,	Already estranged from his own body,
Git er zikh iber in hintishe hent . . .	He gives himself over to dog-like hands . . .

In mitn der nakht a geshtalt	A figure in the middle of the night
iz gelofn iber fintstern vald—	went running across the dark wood—
ir layb vi erd shvarts gekarbt,	her body notched like black earth
der veg royt opgefarbt . . .	the road is painted red . . .
Vuhin zaynen zey ale avek?	Where have they all gone?
Boymer mit mesers un hek—	Trees with axes and knives—
Nor eyn boym blutikt bizn shtam . . .	But one tree bleeds down to its trunk . . .

Iber im geyt uf Gots shvartser lam—	Above, God's black lamb succumbs—
Ir zun—ir Tam. . . .	Her son—her Tom. . . .

PERETZ MARKISH, "SPAIN" (SHPANYE)

Kh'bin nokhamol dayn gast! Der shtolts iz mir fartroyt!	I'm yet again your guest! The honor is familiar!
Ikh hob di shvue nit farhit. Dem neyder nit getsaytikt;	The ancient ban is still in place. I haven't kept the oath;
af dayn besalmen fun di lesterer, baym ployt,	in your graveyards for transgressors, by the fence,
tlien nokh berglekh ash fun mayn amol, fartsaytns!	still smolder ash heaps from my past, from long ago!

Es zaynen nokh berglekh ash fun mayn amol tsezayt do	Still here the ash heaps from my past are scattered
mit kvorim fun gefalene in shlakht banand;	alongside the graves of those fallen in battle;
vel ikh nit ufvekn s'gebeyn fun mayne zeydes,	I will not rouse the bones of my grandfathers,
in shpot getribene fun land tsu land,	goaded in mockery from land to land,

vos zaynen, vi di shof, farurteylte un shtile,	Which are, like sheep, condemned and silent,
hakhnoedik-gebundene un ayngehilt in shrek,	humbly-bound and draped in terror,
gegan af shayters fun Kordove un Kastilye	gone to the bonfires of Cordova and Castile
unter dem kirkhnklang fun Got- gezalbte hek.	beneath the church-bell pealing of God-anointed hatchets.

Di zelbe henker-hek, vos hobn zikh
    atsind farmostn
Iber dayn kop dem shtaygndikn-
    ufgevigt un grod;
Kh'bin nokhamol dayn gast! Dayn
    layb-bruder fun Moskve!
Kh'bin nit aleyn. Un nit in vogldikn
    navenad!

Mayn goyrl itst funsnay mit dir
    farbind ikh,
ven payn un shverd af teg af dayne
    blankt;
ikh trog dir far dem bund di khokhme
    un dem vunder
fun mayn bafrayt un durkhgelaytert
    land!

Tsu pruv iz ufgevekt dayn laydndike
    erd
dos harts fun folk nit gebn af tsu tretn.—

Zol in dayn hant a blitsndike zayn di
    shverd
un dray mol laykhter vi di lid fun
    kastanyetn!

Fun lender khoreve, fun blutikn
    farfleyts,
bazoyfene mit shand fun shayterdike
    roykhn,
hot iber dir a hoykh geton der
    blutdorshitker krayts,
hot zikh di hak tsebushevet in dayne
    hoykhn.

Zey brekhn oys di letste tropns pest

un giftn oysgezoygene ba keyverdike
    verem;
zey loyern af ash fun dayne shtet, vi a
    geshpenst,

The same hangman's-hatchets now
    vying for your head
rising-swinging, and straight;

I'm yet again your guest! Your
    blood-brother from Moscow!
I'm not alone. And not a roaming
    wanderer!

Once again I bind your fate with mine,

when sword and anguish gleam upon
    your days;
I bring you for this union the wisdom
    and the wonder
of my country—freed and purified!

Your suffering earth has woken to the
    challenge
a people's heart that won't be
    trampled over.—
May the sword flash in your hand,

three times lighter than the song of
    castanets!

From devastated lands, from bloody
    flood,
Drenched in the shame of bonfire
    smoke,
the bloodthirsty cross rose above
    your head,
the hatchet ran rampant in your
    highlands.

They break out the final drops of
    plague
and poisons drained from grave
    worms;
specter-like, they lay in wait on the
    ash of your cities,

un trogn um in virblvintiker
    farshverung—

Farat, un royb, un mord, un shrek,

un ongeroybte rekht, un broyt, un
    knekhtshaft;
a yeder trot mit beyner bet dem veg,

un yeder tsvayg mit sharbns iber-
    flekht zikh!

Nor dayn gevag un mut un gayst
    tseblit,
tsu shlakht iz munter-ufgeloykhtn
    yeder,
s'bavofenen zikh denkmols alte fun
    Madrid,
un s'vartn af der rey yesoymim fun
    Toledo!

Un klor iz dir der veg ba yedn knal
    itst,
mit rufn likhtike in dr'heykh itst
    klingen op
di trit di shtolene tsum Vinter-Palats,

der laybn-gang tsum zig fun Perekop!

Dayn goyrl vi a barg—in dr'haykh zikh
    shpreyt,
un fun dayn ufshtayg—hert zikh iber
    yam dos shpanen,
aroysgeshikt host af gerangl
    kind-un-kayt
tsu heylikn mit blut di felder dayne,
    Shpanye!

Dayn gayst hot keynmol nit gebrent
    nokh azoy hel,
dayn harts hot keynmol nit gekvelt
    mit aza frakht dort;

swirling in a conspiracy-whirlwind—

Treachery, and robbery, and murder,
    and terror,
and slavery, and stolen bread and
    rights;
at every step the road is embedded
    with bones,
and every branch with skulls is
    intertwined!

And yet your grit and might and spirit
    blossoms,
everyone is cheerfully lit for battle,

armed and ready are Madrid's old
    monuments,
and the orphans of Toledo wait in
    rows!

The road is clear to you now, bullets
    crackling,
you now can hear, in bright calls from
    above,
the steely footsteps to the Winter
    Palace,
the life-giving-march to the victory at
    Perekop!

Your fate is like a mountain,
    spreading upward,
and far across the sea—they heard
    your ascent,
you've sent your kith and kin to join
    the struggle
to sanctify your battlefields with
    blood, Spain!

Your spirit has never burned so bright
    as it does now,
your heart has never overflowed with
    such a load;

az—liber zayn iz an almone fun a
  held,
eyder a vayb fun a farflukhtn pakhdn!

for—it is better to be a hero's widow,

than the wife of an accursed coward!

S'baveynen kinder nit in feld zeyere
  tates,
di biksn nemen zey mit shtolts fun
  toyte hent,
un shvue af di lipn fayerdike flatert,
un greytkayt shtarbn in di oygn brent!

Children on the field don't mourn
  their fathers,
they take the rifles proudly from dead
  hands,
and a vow on their fiery lips flutters,
and readiness to die burns in their
  eyes!

Ven s'lign derfer, vi di shof fartsukt,
iz vet keyn shteyn keyn eyntsiker zikh
  nit farzitsn,
nor durkhbrekhn dem blut-
  tsebushevetn tsug
fun haknkreyts un inkvizitsiye!

When villages lie, like ravaged sheep,
then not a single stone will lie
  unturned,
but will break through the blood-
  raging procession
of swastika and Inquisition!

Far yedn umgebrakhtn kind batsolt!
Far yedn boym, in blut farflektn,
vet zey der groyser tsorn funem
  folk
mit berg mit mekhtike tsebreklen!

For every murdered child pay!
For every tree, stained with blood,
the great fury of the people will
  make
them crumble with mighty mountains!

S'zaynen nokh berglekh ash fun
  mayn amol tsezayt do
mit kvorim fun gefalene in shlakht
  banand;
vel ikh nit ufvekn s'gebeyn fun mayne
  zeydes,
in shpot getribene fun land tsu
  land,

Still the ash heaps from my past are
  scattered
alongside the graves of those fallen
  in battle;
I will not rouse the bones of my
  grandfathers,
goaded in mockery from land to
  land,

Vos zaynen, vi di shof, farurteylte un
  shtile,
hokhnoedik-gebundene un ayngehilt
  in shrek,
gegan af shayters fun Kordove un
  Kastilye
unter dem kirkhnklang fun Got-
  gezalbte hek.

Which are, like sheep, condemned
  and silent,
humbly-bound and draped in terror,
gone to the bonfires of Cordova and
  Castile
beneath the churchbell-pealing of
  God-anointed hatchets.

Mayn goyrl fundosnay mit dir farbind
  ikh,
ven payn un shverd af teg af dayne
  blankt;
ikh trog dir far der shlakht di
  khokhme un dem vunder
fun mayn bafrayt un durkhgelaytert
  land!

Vi shneyen af di Pireneyen-berg,
hot zikh tseshpreyt der rum fun dayne
  zin un tekhter,—
s'iz nit faran keyn mer bafligldik
  gever,
vi dos gever fun mut un folkstsorn
  gerekhter!

Once again I bind your fate with mine,

when sword and anguish gleam upon
  your days;
I bring you for this battle the wisdom
  and the wonder
of my country—purified and freed!

Like snows upon the Pyrenees,
your sons and daughters spread their
  glory,—
there are no swifter arms than these,

than the weapons of courage and the
  people's just fury!

AARON KURTZ, "KOL NIDRE"

. . . ale nedorim
un ale isurim
vos mir hobn genumen af zikh—
  zaynen botl.

Herst di elterzeydes reyd
fun 1481,
reyd—tsupndike shtiker harts—
fun Shpanyes mitlalter-kelers,—.

Un Pedro fun Madrid,
un Yohanes fun Hamburg,
helfn zingen di tfile fun Shpanishn Yid,
gezungen fun eynikl Dovid
fun Lemberg.

Un s'hobn eyniklekh fun Yidishe
  martirer
fun Toledo un Madrid
geshafn batalyonen—
(un oysgefarbt di fonen
mit blut fun 'Krist un Yid'—)

. . . All vows
and all prohibitions
that we have taken on ourselves—are
  null.

Hear great-grandfather's speech
from 1481,
speech—tugging pieces of heart—
from Spain's medieval cellars,—.

And Pedro of Madrid,
and Johannes of Hamburg,
help sing the Spanish Jew's prayer,
sung by his grandson Dovid
of Lemberg.

And the grandchildren of the Jewish
  martyrs
of Toledo and Madrid
formed battalions—
(and dyed their flags
with the blood of "Christian and Jew"—)

DOVID HOFSHTEYN, "UKRAINE" (UKRAYNE, 1944)

Fun roykh, un fun brokh, un fun ash,
    un fun shand
ikh derze, du derheybst dayn
    tseshedikte hant,
ot derheybt zikh dayn kop, vos mit
    blut iz baklept,
ikh derze dayn gezikht! O, er lebt, o,
    er lebt,
dayn nokh kindersher blik mit shoyn
    mutershn tsar,
un es loykht shoyn di frayd, vos kumt
    on nokh gefar,
der farshtand, vos kumt on nokh
    fartumlung un grayz,
vi vaser in friling fun unter dem ayz—

Ikh derze: ot derheybt zikh dayn guf,
    dayn geshtalt,
vos di reshtlekh fun kleyder af im
    koym zikh halt,
un es faln di shmutsike shmates
    fun layb—
s'iz tsu zen shoyn, s'a kind a der-
    vaksns, a vayb,
s'iz a likhtiker kerper mit sheynkayt,
    vos shaynt
i durkh shand, i durkh shpot, i durkh
    gvaldtat fun faynt.

S'iz a yunge, a zoybere, zikhere kraft,
    Vos zikh vert, vos zikh laytert on
    ufher un lakht,
vos vet gikh zey farheyln, di
    veyen, di shand—
S'iz Ukrayne mayn heym,
Ukrayne mayn land.

From smoke, and from woe, and from
    ash, and from shame
I see you lift your wounded hand,

your head rises, pasted in blood,

I see your face! Oh, it lives, oh, it
    lives,
your still childish glance now with
    motherly pain,
and the joy that follows danger lights
    up,
the knowledge that follows confusion
    and error,
like water in the spring from under
    the ice—

I see: now your body, your image is
    rising,
how your clothing's remains can
    barely hang on,
and the dirty rags fall from your body—

you can see a child grown into a wife,

it's a stunning body with beauty that
    shines
through shame, and through
    mockery, through the violence
    of the enemy.

It's a young, a pure, sure strength,
That becomes, that continues to
    cleanse itself and laughs,
That will soon heal the pain, the
    shame.
It's Ukraine my home,
Ukraine my country.

MOISHE NADIR, "CLOSER" (NEENTER)

Ikh gedenk keyn nemen nit,
  gornisht-nisht.
S'iz alts in mir shoyn oysgemisht.
Aleyn mikh misht der shternshtoyb
fun Gots fargiltn hengl-troyb

Meraglim tsvey—di nakht, der tog—
zey gibn mikh a gringen trog
fun her tsu hin, dernokh tsurik,
tsum vinkl fun mayn krotkevik.

Dort blayb ikh lign—volf antvolft,
a bintl beyn, nit nokhgefolgt,
nor fil farfolgt un fil farshimft

far mayne un far dayne zind.

(O, tararames un hu-has
fun dikhterishn shtern Mars!)
Got, vu bistu? Zog yo, tsi neyn:
Tsi vestu mir antkegn geyn?

O eylt zikh tsu, fraynt Adashem!
Es zinkt mayn oyg, es falt mayn pen.
ver shtarbt in mir? A fremder man—
bakentlekh iz mir bloyz zayn hant.

Mit finger on a shum control
Un mit an ekholozn kol,
a moyl vos past mir shoyn nit mer
un oygn—yeder oyg a trer.

A mider-mider man, antnutst,
oysgevashn, oysgeshtutst,
an foyst farkvetsht a kvaynrit
fun Narayevs karshntsvit.

Un vu tsu trogn iz nito
dem kop, dem-o fun zilber-blo,
dos harts dos-o, der nes-lamter
fun shlofmitlen, mit shlof bashvert.

I don't remember any names, not a
  thing.
Everything's mixed up in me.
I'm mixed, myself, by the stardust
of God's gilded grape cluster.

A pair of spies—the night, the day—
they hoist me gently
from here to there, and back again,
to the corner of my cave.

There I lie—a wolf unwolfed,
a pile of bones, unfollowed here,
but plenty tortured and plenty
  offended
for my, and also for your, sins.

(O, crashing cymbals and hoo-has
from the poet-planet Mars!)
God, where are you? Say yes or no:
Wilt Thou come to meet me now?

O hasten here, Comrade Hashem!
My eyesight sinks, it falls, my pen
who dies in me? Some unknown man—
I vaguely recognize his hand.

With fingers that have lost control
and with an unresounding voice,
a mouth that doesn't suit me now
and eyes that are each eye a tear.

A tired-tired man, used up,
washed out, gussied up,
a flower branch clutched in his fist
from Naraiev's cherry tree.

And there's no place to take it to
this head, this one of silvery-blue,
this heart, this one, this magic lamp
of sedatives, with sleep encumbered.

Mit glaykhgilt, oysgegilt, gekilt
dem fayermarsh, vos kh'hob geshpilt.
Di lave rint fun kroyn fun barg—
un ikh in tol zits shtil un vart.
***

Indifferent, ungolded, cold
the fire-march that I have played.
The lava runs from mountaintop—
and I in the valley sit still and wait.
***

Ikh vart un vart, aleyn, aleyn,
tsi vet mir Got antkegn geyn?

I wait and wait, alone, alone,
will God come to meet me now?

A tsvey-dray trit khotsh biz tsum
    shvel—
Ikh trog im shney-blimlekh in zel.

Only two or three steps to the
    threshold—
I carry him snow-blossoms in my
    soul.

Shma Yisroel—der sof fun lid,
azoy muz shtarbn yeder Yid.
*

Shema Yisroel—the end of the song,
this is how every Jew must die.
*

Ikh shrayb dos alts mit tempn shtift
in mayn heroglifn-shrift.
Mayn froy aleyn nor ken dem sod
fun yedn kotsherdikn os.

I write all this with blunted lead
in my hieroglyphic-hand.
My wife alone knows the cipher
to my every twisted letter.

Zi vet, ven der tog vet glien,
Es opshraybn oyf dem mashin.
Nor shtarb ikh on mayn froy derbay,

She will, with the glow of day,
type it up on her typewriter.
But I'll die without my wife
    beside me,

Shtarbt oykh mayn letster
    oysgeshray.

and my last outcry will die inside me.

AARON KURTZ, "KADDISH"

Yisgadal veyiskadash . . .
Ponem al ponem mit Eyb Linkoln,
    ponem al ponem mit
dem Negershn martirerfolk
zogt a rov kadesh. Ikh bin nit
keyn kadesh-zoger. Nor di mames
    iber der velt hobn haynt biter
geveynt un baveynt di fir kleyne
    shvartse meydelekh—
Hob ikh af dem rovs kadesh geentfert:
    omeyn! Un gehert hob ikh

Yisgadal veyiskodash . . .
Face to face with Abe Lincoln, face to
    face with
the Negro martyred people
a rabbi says Kaddish. I am not
a Kaddish-sayer. But today mamas
    the world over bitterly
wept and mourned the four little
    black girls—
I responded to the rabbi's Kaddish:
    amen! And I heard

nit dem rov aleyn, nit dem rov aleyn:
gehert hob ikh
iber der velt
a milyon mayne yeseymim zogn
kadesh: unter veynendike volkns—
vi alte, oysgeveynte taleysim—a
milyon mayne yesoymim zogn
kadesh.
Der rov hot ongeton a shvartsn kitl in
dem shvartsn tog un geyt
in shvartsn marsh durkh shvartser
eybikayt
mitn Negershn folk: dem rovs kehile
haynt
iz ingantsn shvarts. Shvarts zaynen
di zingendike tfiles vos dos folk do
zingt.
Un di tfiles hilkhn haynt
vi di shvartse lider, un di lider hilkhen
haynt
vi mayn gants folk mitn Barditshever,
mit Robsonen, gebirtikn,
zol zogn kadesh nokh di fir Neger
meydelekh
vos zuntikdike vayse mentshn hobn
in shvartsn zuntik oyfgerisn
in a shvartser kirkh fun a vayser,
vayser shtot.
Yisgadal veyiskadash . . .
A folk—a farshvartst folk in a
takhrikhim-vayser shtot.
Ver es geyt mit mir un ver es geyt mit
Got. Nor ale
geyen zey eyn veg un ale hobn zey
eyn plan: der veg, der veg—der
derleyzndiker veg
tsum kapitan
vos zitst un vart zey zoln kumen un
nokhzogn un nokhzingen

not the rabbi himself, not the rabbi: I
heard
across the world
a million of my orphans saying
Kaddish: beneath weeping clouds—
like old, cried-out tallises—a million
of my orphans saying
Kaddish.
the rabbi donned a black robe on this
black day and walks
in the black march through black
eternity
with the Negro people: the rabbi's
congregation today
is entirely black. Black are
the prayers that this people is
singing.
And the prayers echo today
like black songs, and the songs echo
today
like my whole people, the ones from
Berdichev, with Robeson, natives,
who must say Kaddish today for the
four Negro girls
whom white folk in their Sunday best
tore apart on a black Sunday
In a black church in a white, white
city.
Yisgadal veyiskodash . . .
A people—a blackened people in a
shroud-white city.
Whoever walks with me and whoever
walks with God. But all
walk one path and they all have
one plan: the path, the path—the
path of redemption
to the captain
who sits and waits for them to come
and repeat after and sing after

zayn ruf un zayn monen vos es zogn
    tsu vi baners un
di fonen fun
drayhundert oder hundertoyznt yor.

Ikh zog *omeyn*—iz der kadesh dokh
    derzelbiker
vos in goles bovl, derzelbiker vos ba
    di shayters
in Shpanye un Portugal, derzelbiker
fun geyresh Daytshland, geyrush
    England, derzelbiker
vos in Bialiks Shkhite-Shtot,
    derzelbiker
vos ikh her in Oyshvits, af Ponar, in
    Varshever
geto un Babi Yar Derzelbiker kadesh

vos ikh hob nokh mayn mamen,
    yinglvayz gezogt.
Derzelbiker kadesh vos shvartse
    shturems durkh shvartse
velder trogn iber shvartsn gehenem
    fun der velt.

Robson zogt dem Barditshever
    kadesh breygezlekh-monendik
mitn Barditshevers kol. Un ikh zog
Leyvi Yitskhoks kadesh onklogndik
    Eyrope un mayn land, onklogndik
    Got aleyn
mitn kol fun mayne zeks million far
    mayne gazoyvns
vi far di lintshvelder fun dorem—alts
    eyn kadesh,
alts eyn klog, derzelbiker
vos Perets un Reyzen un Markish
    hobn gezogt. Zog ikh *omeyn!*
Un do zog ikh

his call and his command that they
    pledge like banners
and flags that have flown
for three hundred or a hundred
    thousand years.

I say *omeyn*—the Kaddish is the same

As in the Babylonian exile, the same
    as in the pyres
In Spain and Portugal, the same
As in the expulsion from Germany,
    expulsion from England, the same
As in Bialik's City of Slaughter, the
    same
As I hear in Auschwitz, in Ponar, in
    the Warsaw
Ghetto and Babi Yar. The same
    Kaddish
That I said for my mother, as a child.

The same Kaddish that black storms
    through black
woods carry over the world's black
    hell.

Robeson says the Berdichev Kaddish,
    angrily demanding
with a Berdichever's voice. And I say
Leyvi-Yitskhok's Kaddish, accusing
    Europe and my country, accusing
    God himself
with the voice of my six million before
    my gas chambers
as before the southern lynch-
    forests—the same Kaddish.
The same lament, the very same
that Peretz and Reyzen and Markish
    said. I say *amen!*
And here I am saying

dem zelbikn kadesh mit mayn folk
un mit di felker fun der gorer velt.
   Yisgadal
Veyiskadash—alts der zelbiker
   hartsraysndiker, himlshrayendiker
Kadesh, vos hilkht durkh di
   kvure-koymens
fun Hitlers krematories, vi der kadesh
   vos hilkht
mit Hirsh Gliks kol un mit zayn parol.

Yisgadal
Veyiskadash: gegroyst un geheylikt
   zol dayn nomen zayn
af eybik, "o kapitan, mayn kapitan".
Yisgadal
Veyiskadash: gegroyst un geheylikt
   zol ayer nomen zayn
af eybik, Buker T. Vashington, Fred
   Dogles un
Dzhak Braun.

Zay visn, velt, vayse velt: ven ikh
veyn—veyn ikh nit
aleyn, vi in *mayn* geveyn klogt
dem Negershn folks geveyn!—Omeyn.

Omeyn.

---

the same Kaddish with my people
and with the people of the whole world.
   Yisgadal
Veyiskodash—the same heart-
   wrenching, heavenward-crying
Kaddish, that echoes through the
   funeral-chimneys
of Hitler's crematoria, as the Kaddish
   that echoes
in Hirsh Glik's voice and with his
   password.
Yisgadal
Veyiskodash: may your name be great
   and holy
forever, "O Captain, my captain."
Yisgadal
Veyiskodash:great and holy may your

name be forever, Booker T. Washington, Fred Douglass, and
Jack Brown.

Be advised, world, white world: when I
cry—I am not crying
alone, for in *my* weeping resounds
the weeping of the Negro people!
   —Amen.

Amen.

NOTES

PREFACE: THE OPTIMISTS

1. "Aaron Kurtz, Poet and Yiddish Writer" (obituary), *New York Times,* May 31, 1964, 76.

2. For an excellent study of the American Yiddish Introspectivist (In Zikh) movement, see Sarah Ponichtera, "The Fragmented Self: Individualism in Yiddish Introspectivism," *Jewish Studies Quarterly* 18, no. 3 (2011): 290–317.

3. Nariman Skakov, "Reorientalism: From Avant-Garde to National Form," unpublished ms., quoted with permission from the author.

INTRODUCTION: YIDDISH PASSWORDS IN
THE AGE OF INTERNATIONALISM

1. Bertolt Brecht, *Svendborg poems*, in *The Collected Poems of Bertolt Brecht,* trans. and ed. Tom Kuhn and David Constantine (New York: Liveright Publishing Corporation, 2019), 660.

2. H. Leivick, "A yor Sako Vanzeti," in *Lider* (New York: Fraynt, 1932), 114. All translations are my own, unless otherwise specified.

3. Marc Caplan includes the *kateyger* in the trope of "the demonic voice speaking ultimate truths" in his reading of Max Horkheimer and Theodor Adorno's *Dialektik* and Mendele's *Di klyatshe.* See Caplan, "The Smoke of Civilization: The Dialectic of Enlightenment in Sh. Y. Abramovitsh's *Di Klyatshe,*" in *Arguing the Jewish Canon: Essays on Literature and Culture in Honor of Ruth R. Wisse,* ed. Justin Cammy, Dara

Horn, Alyssa Quint, and Rachel Rubinstein (Cambridge, MA: Harvard University Press, 2008), 464.

4. The *kategor* had, by the early Midrashic period, become associated with ministering angels, and by the medieval period, the kategor is associated with Satan. My thanks to Mira Balberg for her help with this etymological history.

5. Y. L. Peretz, *Di verk fun Yitzkhok Leybush Peretz,* 12 vols. (New York: Jewish Book Agency, 1920), 4:17.

6. The proverb is attributed to Rabbi Levi and can be found, among other places, in Yerushalmi Rosh Hashanah 3:2. See *The Talmud of the Land of Israel,* vol. 16, *Rosh Hashanah,* ed. Jacob Neusner (Chicago: University of Chicago Press, 1988), 85.

7. Anita Norich, *Writing in Tongues: Translating Yiddish in the Twentieth Century* (Seattle: University of Washington Press, 2016), 100. Ruth Wisse has discussed the importance of this story to Jewish socialist leaders "who in fact complained of the chronic passivity of the workers." Wisse, *I. L. Peretz and the Making of Modern Jewish Culture* (Seattle: University of Washington Press, 1991), 50.

8. Brecht, *Svendborg poems,* 660.

9. For an overview of Sacco-Vanzetti poems in Yiddish, see Jordan Finkin, "In the Pot, Half-Melted: Sacco-Vanzetti Poems and Yiddish American Identity," in *Choosing Yiddish: New Frontiers of Language and Culture,* ed. Lara Rabinovitch, Shiri Goren, and Hannah S. Pressman (Detroit: Wayne State University Press, 2013), 47–64. On Stalin's left turn in 1927–1928, see Jacob A. Zumoff, *Communist International and US Communism, 1919–1929* (Leiden: Brill, 2014).

10. Gershon Shafir has compared early Zionism to "a variety of Eastern European nationalism, that is, an ethnic movement in search of a state." Gershon Shafir, *Land, Labor and the Origins of the Israeli-Palestinian Conflict, 1882–1914* (Berkeley: University of California Press, 1996), 8.

11. Yuri Slezkine, *The Jewish Century* (Princeton, NJ: Princeton University Press, 2004), 35–36.

12. The distinction between "nation" and "ethnicity" was at the heart of Soviet Nationalities Policy, and non-Soviet communist writers often used "nation" to refer to a distinct ethnic group, regardless of whether this group had been given a territory. I discuss the Soviet nationalities question more extensively later in this Introduction, as well as in Chapters 1 and 5. The transnational network of Yiddish writers on the left can be compared to what Kris Manjapra in his study of Southeast Asian political activists has called a "global ecumene"—a broad network of anticolonial leftists. Kris Manjapra, "Communist Internationalism and Transcolonial Recognition," in *Cosmopolitan Thought Zones: South Asia and the Global Circulation of Ideas,* ed. Kris Manjapra and Sugata Bose (New York: Palgrave Macmillan, 2010), 159–177. Katerina Clark has applied Manjapra's concept of the ecumene in her treatment of leftist writers in the 1930s. See Clark, "Indian Leftist Writers of the 1930s Maneuver among India, London, and Moscow: The Case of Mulk Raj Anand and His Patron Ralph

Fox," *Kritika: Explorations in Russian and Eurasian History* 18, no. 1 (Winter 2017): 63–87.

13. For a good discussion of the Soviet Jewish agricultural project, see Jonathan Dekel-Chen, *Farming the Red Land: Jewish Agricultural Colonization and Local Soviet Power, 1924–1941* (New Haven, CT: Yale University Press, 2005).

14. Robin D. G. Kelley, *Hammer and Hoe: Alabama Communists during the Great Depression* (Chapel Hill: University of North Carolina Press, 1991), xx–xxi.

15. Helen Graham and Paul Preston, *The Popular Front in Europe* (Basingstoke, UK: Macmillan, 1987), 4.

16. Michael Denning, *The Cultural Front: The Laboring of American Culture in the Twentieth Century* (London: Verso, 1997), 21.

17. Jean Baudrillard, *Passwords* (London: Verso, 2003), xiii.

18. Jacques Derrida, *Sovereignties in Question: The Poetics of Paul Celan,* ed. Thomas Dutoit and Outi Pasanen (New York: Fordham University Press, 2005), 22.

19. On the origins of Yiddish, see Dovid Katz, *Words on Fire: The Unfinished Story of Yiddish* (New York: Basic Books, 2004).

20. Avrom-Yitskhok Trivaks, "Di Yidishe zhargonen," in *Bay unz Yuden,* ed. M. Vanvild (Warsaw: Farlag Pinchas Graubard, 1923), 159. See also Robert A. Rothstein, "Argots," in *The YIVO Encyclopedia of Jews in Eastern Europe,* accessed June 18, 2018, http://www.yivoencyclopedia.org/article.aspx/Talk/Argots.

21. Raymond Williams, *Keywords: A Vocabulary of Culture and Society* (New York: Oxford University Press, 1976), 20–21.

22. Adam B. Seligman and Robert P. Weller, *Rethinking Pluralism: Ritual, Experience, and Ambiguity* (Oxford: Oxford University Press, 2012), 68.

23. H. Leivick, quoted in Benjamin Harshav and Barbara Harshav, *American Yiddish Poetry: A Bilingual Anthology* (Berkeley: University of California Press, 1986), 675.

24. Emma Goldman and Alexander Berkman, "Sacco and Vanzetti," originally published in the New York anarchist journal *Road to Freedom* in August 1929, reprinted in *Sacco & Vanzetti,* ed. John Davis (Melbourne, Australia: Ocean, 2004), 107.

25. Finkin, "In the Pot," 50.

26. Finkin, 61–62n24.

27. Homi Bhabha, discussing the condition of late twentieth-century migrants, presents culture in the postcolonial era as "both transnational and translational." Homi Bhabha, *The Location of Culture* (New York: Routledge, 1994), 247.

28. John Dryden, "From the Preface to *Ovid's Epistles,*" in *Translation Studies Reader,* 2nd ed., ed. Lawrence Venuti (New York: Routledge, 2012), 38.

29. Walter Benjamin, "The Task of the Translator," in *Selected Writings, Volume I: 1913–1926,* ed. Marcus Bullock and Michael W. Jennings (Cambridge, MA: Harvard University Press, 1996), 256.

30. Marc Caplan has highlighted this shift in his analysis of Peretz's address at the 1908 Czernowitz conference. Marc Caplan, "Y. L. Peretz and the Politics of Yiddish,"

in *Czernowitz at 100,* ed. Kalman Weiser and Joshua A. Fogel (Lanham, MD: Rowman and Littlefield, 2010), 91.

31. Jacques Rancière, *Politics of Literature* (Malden, MA: Polity, 2011), 19. Originally published in French in 2006.

32. Moishe Nadir, "Fun fremde kvaln" (Arabish), in *Morgn Frayhayt,* October 20, 1929, 7.

33. Jonathan Culler, *Literary Theory: A Very Short Introduction* (Oxford: Oxford University Press, 2011), 95–96.

34. Nadir, "Fun fremde kvaln," 7.

35. Jacques Derrida, "Différance," in *The Critical Tradition: Classic Texts and Contemporary Trends,* 3rd ed., ed. David H. Richter (New York: Bedford / St. Martin's, 2007), 932–949.

36. Bhabha, *The Location of Culture,* 234.

37. Naomi Seidman, *Faithful Renderings: Jewish-Christian Difference and the Politics of Translation* (Chicago: University of Chicago Press, 2006), 153. Seidman here focuses on the case of writers in German.

38. As discussed in the Afterword, an exception was Aaron Kurtz, who was married to the English-language poet Olga Cabral, who translated a few of Kurtz's postwar poems close to the time they were written. See Gayatri Chakravorty Spivak, *Can the Subaltern Speak?* (Basignstoke: Macmillan, 1988).

39. Marina Tsvetaeva, "Poema kontsa" (1924), in *O liubvi* (St. Petersburg: Azbuka-klassika, 2009), 292.

40. Tsvetaeva, 292.

41. Citing Tsvetaeva, Derrida posits, "If all poets are Jews, they are all, the poets, circumcised or circumcisers." *Sovereignties in Question,* 55.

42. Leivick, "A yor Sako Vanzeti," 114.

43. As Moshik Temkin has noted, Stalin worked to adopt Sacco and Vanzetti's popularity as a Party cause, despite the fact that anarchism had been banned in the Soviet Union. See Temkin, *The Sacco Vanzetti Affair: America on Trial* (New Haven, CT: Yale University Press, 2009), 35–36.

44. Jonathan Frankel, *Prophesy and Politics: Socialism, Nationalism, and the Russian Jews, 1862–1917* (Cambridge: Cambridge University Press, 1981), 134.

45. As Kenneth B. Moss has observed, "The turn of the century brought the first Hebrew and Yiddish journals devoted explicitly to 'Jewish culture,' and the relaxation of government restrictions on Jewish cultural life after the 1905 Revolution allowed more formal institutions to develop." Moss, *Jewish Renaissance in the Russian Revolution* (Cambridge, MA: Harvard University Press, 2009), 9.

46. On Lenin's early rejection of the Bund as an example of bourgeois nationalism, see his writings on the Jewish proletariat: Vladimir Ilyich Lenin, *Collected Works,* vol. 6 (Moscow: Progress, 1964), 330–336.

47. David Fishman, citing Vladimir Medem's 1904 essay "Social Democracy and the National Question," describes national-cultural autonomy as the equality of languages and the ability of groups to use these languages in education and cultural institutions without interference from the state. Fishman, *The Rise of Modern Yiddish Culture* (Pittsburgh: University of Pittsburgh Press, 2005), 73–74.

48. See Esther Schor, *Bridge of Words: Esperanto and the Dream of a Universal Language* (New York: Metropolitan Books, 2016).

49. Rosenfeld's sweatshop ballads began appearing in the early 1890s, and they were popular enough with American Jewish readers that by the end of the decade they appeared in English translation. Morris Rosenfeld, *Songs from the Ghetto,* trans. Leo Wiener (Boston: Copeland and Day, 1898).

50. Fishman, *Rise of Modern Yiddish Culture,* 52.

51. Fishman, 61.

52. Lenin and his party viewed the Bundists as too closely aligned with bourgeois nationalism.

53. David Roskies notes that in these folk songs, "Even when the singer invoked historical facts, the relics of the violence were organized into public symbols and thematic formulas, so that the details were applicable anywhere and only the place-name would have to be changed." Roskies, *Against the Apocalypse: Responses to Catastrophe in Modern Jewish Culture* (Syracuse, NY: Syracuse University Press, 1984), 81.

54. Roskies, 80.

55. Steven J. Zipperstein, *Pogrom: Kishinev and the Tilt of History* (New York: Norton, 2018), 103.

56. See Chaim Nachman Bialik, "B'ir ha Haregah," originally published as "Masa' Nemirov" (Hazeman: Measef Iesifrut ulemad'a), no. 3 (July–September 1904): 3–15. David Aberbach has discussed the similarity between Bialik and Yeats as modern, national, poets. Aberbach, *National Poetry, Empires and War* (New York: Taylor and Francis, 2015).

57. Quoted in Zipperstein, *Pogrom,* 115n23.

58. Quoted in Zipperstein, 108.

59. Maurice Halbwachs, *On Collective Memory,* edited, translated, and with an introduction by Lewis A. Coser (Chicago: University of Chicago Press, 1992) 53.

60. Filippo Tommaso Marinetti, "Manifeste du Futurismo," *Le Figaro,* February 20, 1909.

61. As Stephen C. Hutchings has proposed, modernists' response "was to set out along the path of resemiosis—the discovery of new nets of signs and new objective / subjective realities to which they might refer." Hutchings, *Russian Modernism: The Transfiguration of the Everyday* (Cambridge: Cambridge University Press, 1997), 228.

62. Benjamin Harshav, *Language in the Time of Revolution* (Stanford, CA: Stanford University Press, 1993), 150.

63. Moss, *Jewish Renaissance*, 9.

64. Uri Tsvi Grinberg later shifted to Hebrew and moved permanently to Palestine.

65. Peretz Markish, *Di kupe* (Poeme) (Kiev: Kultur-Lige, 1922), 16.

66. Seth Wolitz, "A Yiddish Modernist Dirge: *Di kupe* of Perets Markish," *Yiddish: A Quarterly Journal Devoted to Yiddish and Yiddish Literature,* ed. Joseph C. Landis, 6, no. 4 (1987): 56–67.

67. Aaron Glantz-Leyeles, "Chronicle of a Movement: Excerpts from Introspectivist Criticism," no. 11, translated in Benjamin and Barbara Harshav, *American Yiddish Poetry: A Bilingual Anthology* (Berkeley: University of California Press, 1986), 785–804.

68. Pericles Lewis, for example, has discussed the nationalist impulse in European modernist prose, observing that "the old God was dead, but in the nation many intellectuals and popular movements found a new God." However, cultural-centered discussions of Jewishness took a very different, more dispersed, form. Lewis, *Modernism, Nationalism, and the Novel* (Cambridge: Cambridge University Press, 2000), 5.

69. Chana Kronfeld, *On the Margins of Modernism: Decentering Literary Dynamics* (Berkeley: University of California Press, 1993), 195. As Allison Schachter has argued more recently, both Yiddish and Hebrew modernism offer counternarrative to the place-based nationalism of most European modernisms and even of Zionism. See Schachter, *Diasporic Modernisms: Hebrew and Yiddish Literature in the Twentieth Century* (Oxford: Oxford University Press, 2012), 3–28.

70. Ernst Gellner, *Nations and Nationalism,* 2nd ed. (Ithaca, NY: Cornell University Press, 2006), 6.

71. Ezra Mendelsohn has argued that the decline of the Bund marked the "decline of the Jewish left in general." Mendelsohn, *On Modern Jewish Politics* (Oxford: Oxford University Press, 1993), 141.

72. Cecile Kuznitz, *YIVO and the Making of Modern Jewish Culture: Scholarship for the Yiddish Nation* (Cambridge: Cambridge University Press, 2014), 4.

73. Moss, *Jewish Renaissance*, 113.

74. Moss, 169. Moss notes that the Kultur-Lige rejected affiliation with the Proletkult groups in Ukraine, 234.

75. The government dissolved the organization in 1921, and by the early 1930s, Soviet literature became highly centralized, with the only publication venues being state run and with the 1932 dismantling of all literary groups outside the Soviet Writer's Union.

76. As David Brandenberger, Yuri Slezkine, and others have shown, "proletarian internationalism" eventually gave way to a turn toward a form of nationalism in the de facto Russocentric Soviet state. See Brandenberger, "Proletarian Internationalism, 'Soviet Patriotism' and the Rise of Russocentric Etatism during the Stalinist 1930s," *Left History: An Interdisciplinary Journal of Historical Inquiry and Debate* 6, no. 2 (1999): 83–103; and Slezkine "The USSR as a Communal Apartment, or How a

Socialist State Promoted Ethnic Particularism," *Slavic Review* 53, no. 2 (Summer 1994): 414–452.

77. Gennady Estraikh, "The Kharkiv Yiddish Literary World, 1920s–Mid-1930s," *East European Jewish Affairs* 32, no. 2 (2002): 80.

78. The journal was printed in Vilna. For a brief discussion of *In Shpan*, see Gennady Estraikh, *In Harness: Yiddish Writers' Romance with Communism* (Syracuse, NY: Syracuse University Press, 2005), ix.

79. *Spartak,* October 1925, 2.
Note: I have translated the term *"byt"* as "daily life." Roman Jakobson has, however, argued that the word is untranslatable, so closely is it tied to a particular kind of day to day existence that is unique to Russia. See Roman Jakobson, "On a Generation that Squandered its Poets," in *Language in Literature* (Cambridge: Harvard University Press, 1990).

80. Kimberlé Williams Crenshaw, "Demarginalizing the Intersection of Race and Sex: A Black Feminist Critique of Antidiscrimination Doctrine, Feminist Theory and Antiracist Politics," *University of Chicago Legal Forum* 1989, no. 1 (1989): 138–167.

81. Michael Rothberg, *Multidirectional Memory: Remembering the Holocaust in the Age of Decolonization* (Stanford, CA: Stanford University Press, 2009), 102–103.

82. Harriet Murav, *Music from a Speeding Train: Jewish Literature in Post-Revolutionary Russia* (Stanford, CA: Stanford University Press, 2011), 172.

83. Vladimir I. Lenin, *Sochineniia,* vol. 25, 229, quoted in George S. N. Luckyj, *Literary Politics in the Soviet Ukraine, 1917–1934,* rev. ed. (Durham, NC: Duke University Press, 1990), 177.

84. See Richard Breitman, *FDR and the Jews* (Cambridge, MA: Harvard University Press, 2013).

85. Leivick, "A yor Sako Vanzeti," 114.

86. Derrida has observed, "Whoever inscribes the year, the day, the place, in short, the present of a 'here and now' attests thereby his or her own presence at the act of inscription." Derrida, *Sovereignties in Question,* 16. Leivick had written a longer poem the year of Sacco and Vanzetti's death. "Sacco and Vanzetti's Wednesday" (Sacco un Vanzettis Mitvokh) opens with the place and date of the planned execution, August 10. In a last-minute stay of execution, following protests, the date was moved back to August 23. H. Leivick, "Sako un Vanzetti's Mitvokh," in *Ale Verk* (New York: Posy-Shoulson, 1940), 280.

87. Vladimir I. Lenin, speech at the Sixth All-Russian Congress of Soviets, session of November 8, 1918, in *Sobranie sochinenii,* vol. 15 (Moscow, 1922), 550, 555, quoted in Milorad M. Drachkovitch and Branko Lazitch, "The Communist International," in *The Revolutionary Internationals, 1864–1943,* ed. Milorad M. Drachkovitch (Stanford, CA: Stanford University Press, 1966), 165.

88. In a discussion of literary modernism in the post–World War I period, Pericles Lewis notes that "the Paris Peace Treaties of 1919 and the founding of the League of Nations appeared to contemporary liberals to ratify the victory of the liberal principle

of national self-determination championed by the Allies over the imperialism of the Central Powers. Under the Treaties, the Allies attempted to 'redraw the political map [of Europe] on national lines' and thus to establish an international system of liberal nation-states." Lewis, *Modernism, Nationalism, and the Novel,* 51n1.

89. Kevin McDermott and Jeremy Agnew note that "the idea of a Third Period made its debut at the Seventh ECCI [Executive Committee of the Communist International] Plenum in November–December 1926 and it was not Stalin who first introduced the notion, but Bukharin." McDermott and Agnew, *The Comintern: A History of International Communism from Lenin to Stalin* (New York: St. Martin's, 1997), 68.

90. Anouar Abdel-Malek, *Social Dialectics: Nation and Revolution,* vol. 2, trans. Mike Gonzalez (Albany: State University of New York Press, 1981), 86–87.

91. Steven S. Lee, *The Ethnic Avant-Garde: Minority Cultures and World Revolution* (New York: Columbia University Press, 2015), 33.

92. Katerina Clark, *Moscow, the Fourth Rome: Stalinism, Cosmopolitanism and the Evolution of Soviet Culture, 1931–1941* (Cambridge, MA: Harvard University Press, 2011), 104.

93. Gennady Estraikh, *Evreiskaia literaturnaia zhizn' Moskvy, 1917–1991* (St. Petersburg: Evropeiskii universitet v Sankt-Peterburge, 2015), 73–74. Estraikh cites "Tsu ale yidishe shrayber in Eyrope un in Amerike," *Der Emes,* April 15, 1926. Estraikh notes that the signatories included Teyf, Halkin, Gildin, Kipnis, Fefer, Kvitko, and Leyb Gol'dberg—the brother of the American Yunge poet Menakhem Boreisho.

94. Nadir and Markish quoted in Nora Levin, *The Jews in the Soviet Union since 1917* (New York: NYU Press, 1988), 214. Gennady Estraikh notes that Markish came into the Soviet circle especially fast. He was considered a "Soviet poet who just wanted to see the world." Estraikh, *Evreiskaia literaturnaia zhizn' Moskvy,* 87. See also Joshua Rubenstein and Vladimir P. Naumov, eds., *Stalin's Secret Pogrom: The Postwar Inquisition of the Jewish Anti-Fascist Committee* (New Haven: Yale University Press, 2001), 145.

95. Shmuel Charney wrote under the name S. Niger, a pseudonym with clear American racial connotations, which has sparked debate in the Yiddish scholarly community over how best to identify this important historical literary critic. I have chosen throughout this book to use a hyphenated form of his family name and pseudonym, which I believe clearly identifies him without erasing Niger-Charney's choice to call himself by a loaded racial epithet. For a good discussion of the historical racial implications of this pseudonym, see Eli Bromberg, "We Need to Talk about Shmuel Charney," *In geveb: A Journal of Yiddish Studies* (October 2019), accessed May 18, 2020, https://ingeveb.org/articles/we-need-to-talk-about-shmuel-charney.

96. Estraikh, *Evreiskaia literaturnaia zhizn' Moskvy,* 104. Estraikh cites Y. Lifshitz, "Opklayb fun der Leyvik-Niger korespondents," in *Pinkes far der forshung fun der yiddisher literature un prese* (New York, 1972), 446–448.

97. As Terry Dean Martin writes, "While Lenin and Stalin opposed the creation of a Russian nation-state, they accepted the principle of the nation-state and sought to

create the basic essentials of the nation-state—a national territory, elite, language, and culture—for each Soviet ethnic minority." Martin, *The Affirmative Action Empire: Nations and Nationalism in the Soviet Union* (Ithaca, NY: Cornell University Press, 2001), 341.

98. Martin translates Stalin's natsional'naia kultura as "symbolic ethnicity." Martin, 13. Martin cites Herbert Gans, "Symbolic Ethnicity: The Future of Ethnic Grups and Cutures in America," *Ethnic and Racial Studies* 2 (1979): 9–17. Martin, 5.

99. Terry Martin cites Stalin's declaration, at the June 1930 party congress: "The period of the construction of socialism in the period of the flowering of national culture, socialist in content and national in form[.]" Martin, 155. Martin cites *XVI s"ezd VKP/b/. Stenograficheskii otchet* (Moscow, 1930), 55–56.

100. Joseph Stalin, *Sochineniia*, vol. 7, 137–38, quoted in Luckyj, *Literary Politics*, 177. Stalin later would widely use the phrase "national in form and socialist in content."

101. Alexander Pomerantz notes that one of the events that changed the course of the Yiddish Proletpen group was the development by the leadership of the Comintern of the Communist Party USA. See Pomerantz, *Proletpen: Etyudn un materyaln tsu der geshikhte fun dem kamf far proletarisher literature in Amerike* (Kiev: All-Ukrainian Academy of Science, 1935), 21–22.

102. Kelley, *Hammer and Hoe*, xviii.

103. The approach to the Party outside the Soviet Union often fell on racial and national lines. Rossen Djagalov has noted, for example, that "African (-American) activists found the sectarian Third Period [. . .] more congenial to their demands than the broad anti-fascist Popular Front phase declared by the Comintern in 1934, which enlivened communist parties in Western Europe and North America." See Djagalov, *From Internationalism to Postcolonialism: Literature and Cinema between the Second and the Third Worlds* (Montreal: McGill University Press, 2020), 15.

104. Baudrillard, *Passwords*, 3.

105. Denning, *The Cultural Front*, 121.

106. Both Olgin and Epshteyn were former Bundists; but as Eli Lederhendler comments, Epshteyn was a full-fledged Party member, and Olgin, at that time, was a centrist. See Lederhendler, *Ethnicity and Beyond: Theories and Dilemmas of Jewish Group Demarcation* (Oxford: Oxford University Press, 2011), 35.

107. Although the *Morgn-Frayhayt* continued publishing until 1988, its popularity waned after World War II.

108. Tony Michels, *A Fire in Their Hearts: Yiddish Socialists in New York* (Cambridge, MA: Harvard University Press, 2005), 238.

109. Estraikh notes that Litvakov, when he took up the editorship of *Der Emes,* noticed a dearth of Yiddish writers. Estraikh, *Evreiskaia literaturnaia zhizn' Moskvy*, 59.

110. See D. Charney, "Vi Dovid Berelson iz farnart gevorn keyn Rusland," *Der Tog-Morgn-Zhurnal*, August 5, 1956; Estraikh, *In Harness;* and Mikhail Krutikov, "Narrating the Revolution: From 'Tsugvintn' (1922) to *Mides-hadin* (1929)," in *David Bergelson:*

From Modernism to Socialist Realism, ed. Joseph Sherman (Abingdon, UK: Legenda, 2007), 167–182; and Sasha Senderovich and Harriet Murav, "David Bergelson's *Judgment*: A Critical Introduction," in Dovid Bergelson, *Judgment,* trans. Harriet Murav and Sasha Senderovich (Evanston: Northwestern University Press, 2017) .

111. Estraikh, *Evreiskaia literaturnaia zhizn' Moskvy,* 87. Estraikh cites Rubenstein and Naumov, *Stalin's Secret Pogrom,* 145.

112. On the Yiddish communist press, see Gennady Estraikh, "The Yiddish-Language Communist Press," in *Dark Times, Dire Decisions: Jews and Communism,* ed. Jonathan Frankel (Oxford: Oxford University Press, 2005). For an in-depth discussion of Comintern Yiddish writers, see Estraikh, *In Harness,* 65–101.

113. The second conference of the union, in 1930, formally acknowledged Proletpen. Gennady Estraikh, "The Stalinist 'Great Break' in Yiddishland," in *1929: Mapping the Jewish World,* ed. Hasia R. Diner and Gennady Estraikh (New York: NYU Press, 2013). Dovid Katz, writing specifically of the American Yiddish Left, has noted, "Whoever left after the Ribbentrop-Molotov pact of 1939 was sufficiently kosher. But those who waited until confirmation of the Moscow murders of the writers in 1952 were banished from the canon." Katz, "The Days of Proletpen," in *Proletpen: America's Rebel Yiddish Poets,* ed. Amelia Glaser and David Weintraub (Madison: University of Wisconsin Press, 2005), 13.

114. Joshua M. Karlip, *The Tragedy of a Generation: The Rise and Fall of Jewish Nationalism in Eastern Europe* (Cambridge, MA: Harvard University Press, 2013), 312.

115. Alan M. Wald, *Trinity of Passion: The Literary Left and the Antifascist Crusade* (Chapel Hill: University of North Carolina Press, 2007), 14.

116. Hannah Arendt, *Men in Dark Times* (San Diego: Harvest Harcourt, 1955), 239.

117. Ronald Grigor Suny, *The Revenge of the Past: Nationalism, Revolution, and the Collapse of the Soviet Union* (Stanford, CA: Stanford University Press, 1993), 87.

118. Djagalov, *From Internationalism to Postcolonialism,* 25.

119. H. Leivick, "Vider geshtorbn a shokhen," in Harshav and Harshav, *American Yiddish Poetry,* 738. English translation ("Again a Neighbor Died") by Harshav and Harshav, 739.

120. See Mikhail Bakhtin, "Author and Hero in Aesthetic Activity," in *Art and Answerability: Early Philosophical Essays,* trans. Vadim Lapunov (Austin: University of Texas Press, 1990), 25–36.

121. Rothberg, *Multidirectional Memory,* 12.

1. FROM THE YANGTZE TO THE BLACK SEA: ESTHER SHUMIATCHER'S TRAVELS

1. The poems include "May lid" (May song), "Tsu Kadye Molodovski" (To Kadye Molodovsky), "Baym rand fun Khine" (By the border of China), "Glustike" (Desired), and "Dershtoynene mi" (Amazing toil). *Royte Velt,* nos. 7–8 (July–August 1928): 62–64.

She opens the last stanza to Molodovsky with the lines, "Here, Kadye, you are greeted from Russia's little Mother, the Volga, / A red joy is growing in the fields here."

2. Shumiatcher, "May lid," 62. (The poem would later appear in Shumiatcher's collected works.)

3. Shmuel Niger-Charney would later call Hirschbein "a representative of his generation . . . who not only dreamed the dream of Zion, as well as the socialist dream of the new youth, but, like other Yiddish writers at the beginning of the 20th century, devoted himself to Reb Israel and, of course, to himself." Quoted in Joseph and Chana Mlotek, *Pearls of Yiddish Poetry,* ed. Mark Mlotek, trans. Barnett Zumoff (Jersey City, NJ: KTAV, 2010), 282.

4. Shumiatcher met Hirschbein when she was chosen to give him flowers on a visit he made to the Calgary Jewish community. Hirschbein subsequently became ill with the Spanish flu and returned to the Shumiatcher house to convalesce. Shumiatcher had written poems in English as a child and devoted herself to Yiddish poetry in her decade of travel following her marriage. Jessica Hirshbein, private correspondence. See also Faith Jones, "'Wandering Is Your Fate': Esther Shumiatcher-Hirschbein Writing across Boundaries," *Canadian Jewish Studies/ Études juives canadiennes* 11 (2003): 20.

5. David Shneer, *Yiddish and the Creation of Soviet Jewish Culture: 1918-1939* (162)

6. Esther Shumiatcher, "Albatros," in *In shoen fun libshaft,* 30.

7. Jones, "Wandering Is Your Fate," 16.

8. Osip Mandelstam, "Amerikanka," in *Sobranie sochinenii v 4 tomakh,* vol. 1 (Moscow: Art-Biznes-Tsentr, 1993), 92.

9. H. Leivick, "A Briv fun Amerike tsu mayn vaytn fraynt (poeme)," *Royte Velt,* no. 7 (July 1929: 1-7).

10. Gennady Estraikh discusses the visits of the *Frayhayt* editor Moyshe Olgin, as well as Winchevsky, Leivick, Reyzen, and Nadir extensively in *Evreiskaia literaturnaia zhizn' Moskvy, 1917-1991* (St. Petersburg: Evropeiskii universitet v Sankt-Peterburge, 2015), 102-108.

11. On Dreiser's visit, see Estraikh, 95; and Theodore Dreiser, *Dreiser Looks at Russia* (New York: Horace Liveright, 1928), 163-164.

12. Walter Benjamin, *Moscow Diary,* ed. Gary Smith, trans. Richard Sieburth (Cambridge, MA: Harvard University Press, 1986) 127. As Gennady Estraikh has noted, "Truth to tell, in the mid-1920s the Soviet Union could indeed look like an exciting place." Estraikh, *In Harness: Yiddish Writers' Romance with Communism* (Syracuse, NY: Syracuse University Press, 2005), 83-84.

13. Estraikh, 66. Estraikh cites the following sources on these visits: F. Hofshteyn, *Mit libe un veytik: vegn Dovid Hofshteyn* (Tel Aviv, 1985), 9-17; Dror Abend-David, "Gender Benders and Unrequited Offerings: Two Hebrew Poems by Rachel Bluwstein-Sela and Dovid Hofshteyn," *Prooftexts* 31, no. 3 (2001): 210-228; A. G. Senchenko, "Poezia sovetskoi Ukrainy," *Literaturnaia gazeta* 5 (February 24, 1936).

14. For a discussion of US passports and the changes they underwent, see Craig Robertson, *The Passport in America: The History of a Document* (Oxford: Oxford University Press, 2010). Hirschbein wrote extensively of his travels. See, for example, his book of essays about his travels in the early 1920s, *Arum der velt (rayze ayndrukn)* (New York: Literatur, 1927).

15. Shachar Pinsker has called Hebrew fiction a "literary passport." See Pinsker, *Literary Passports: The Making of Modernist Hebrew Fiction in Europe* (Stanford, CA: Stanford University Press, 2010).

16. Shumiatcher, "May lid," 62.

17. Edward Said observes that in Western Orientalism, "Something patently foreign and distant acquires, for one reason or another, a status more rather than less familiar." Said, *Orientalism* (New York: Vintage Books, 1979) 58.

18. Jones, "Wandering Is Your Fate," 23.

19. Faith Jones cites this review, which Ravitch himself cites in a 1958 article. Neither Jones nor I have found the original article. See Jones, 34; Melech Ravitch, "Ester Shumyatsher-Hirshbayn," *Keneder Odler,* December 19, 1958, 3-4.

20. Jones, "Wandering Is Your Fate," 22. Jones observes that Melech Ravitch, for example, "apparently abhorred" the book. Jones cites Ravitch, "Ester Shumyatsher-Hirshbayn," 3-4.

21. According to Samuels, Foa "exploit[ed] her difference to a public fascinated by the Romantic, oriental other." Maurice Samuels, *Inventing the Israelite: Jewish Fiction in Nineteenth-Century France* (Stanford, CA: Stanford University Press, 2010), 24.

22. An analysis of Shumiatcher's travel poetry also reveals the shortcomings of applying a postcolonial analysis of Western Orientalist thought to Soviet- and Soviet-aligned literature. As Nathanial Knight has noted, "the stark dichotomy between Orient and Occident around which Said's analysis hinges transforms in the Russian context into an awkward triptych: the west, Russia, the east." Knight, "Grigoriev in Orenburg, 1851-1862: Russian Orientalism in the Service of Empire?," *Slavic Review* 59, no. 1 (2000): 77, quoted in Susanna Soojung Lim, *China and Japan in the Russian Imagination, 1685-1922: To the Ends of the Orient* (New York: Routledge, 2013), 13, 181n34.

23. Boris Pilniak records the couple's planned itinerary in his *Rasskazy s Vostoka* (Moscow: Ogonek, 1927), 13.

24. As Joshua A. Fogel has shown, the Chinese military guards insisted on the use of Russian, which many of them knew, rather than Yiddish. Fogel, "The Japanese and the Jews: A Comparative Analysis of Their Communities in Harbin, 1898-1930," in *New Frontiers: Imperialism's New Communities in East Asia, 1842-1953*, ed. Robert Bickers and Christian Henriot (Manchester, UK: Manchester University Press, 2000), 98-99.

25. Chinese writers were, themselves, in dialogue with communists and anarchists as they developed revolutionary genres. See, for example, Arif Dirlik's *Anarchism in the Chinese Revolution* (Berkeley: University of California Press, 1991).

26. Alexander Blok, "The Scythians," in *The Russia Reader,* ed. Adele Marie Barker and Bruce Grant (Durham, NC: Duke University Press, 2010), 13–15.

27. See, for example, Velimir Khlebnikov's 1918 manifestos, "An Indo-Russian Union" and "Asiaunion," in *Collected Works of Velimir Khlebnikov,* vol. 1, *Letters and Theoretical Writings,* trans. Paul Schmidt, ed. Charlotte Douglas (Cambridge, MA: Harvard University Press, 1987), 341–343.

28. Sergei Eisenstein, "The Cinematographic Principle and the Ideogram," in *Film Form: Essays in Film Theory,* ed. and trans. Jay Leyda (New York: Harcourt, 1949), 28–44.

29. As Lee puts it, "Tret'iakov offered an alternative model for the Soviet-centered ethnic avant-garde, one that broke from fanciful, mythological notions of revolutionary history and non-Western cultures." Steven Lee, *The Ethnic Avant-Garde: Minority Cultures and World Revolution* (New York: Columbia University Press, 2017), 86.

30. Pilniak had a cameo in a film, *Go to the People,* by the well-known Chinese filmmaker Tian Han. See Elizabeth McGuire, *Red at Heart: How Chinese Communists Fell in Love with the Russian Revolution* (Oxford: Oxford University Press, 2017), 105. Alexander Bukh has suggested that Pilniak was probably the first Soviet writer to visit Japan or China. See Bukh, "National Identity and Race in Post Revolutionary Russia: Pil'niak's Travelogues from Japan and China," in *Race and Racism in Modern East Asia: Western and Eastern Constructions,* ed. Rotem Kowner and Walter Demel (Leiden: Brill, 2013), 183.

31. Katerina Clark, "Boris Pilniak and Sergei Tretiakov as Soviet Envoys to China and Japan and Forgers of New, Post-Imperial Narratives (1924–1926)," *Crosscurrents: East Asian History and Culture Review* 28 (September 2018): 34, https://cross-currents.berkeley.edu/e-journal/issue-28/clark.

32. Quoted in Bukh, "National Identity and Race," 188. Bukh cites Boris Pilniak, *Kitaiskii Dnevnik, Sobranie sochinenii: Povesti s Vostoka* (Moscow: Gosudarstvennoe izdatel'stvo, 1930), 183–188.

33. Bukh, 185.

34. According to Valijko Vujacic, Pilniak believed the Russian people would ultimately "take a form of flight from the Westernized elite culture of imperial *Rossiia,* or, better still, its conquest and assimilation by a pre-Petrine *Rus'* reincarnated by the Bolsheviks and pitted against the 'mechanized West.'" Vujacic, *Nationalism, Myth, and the State in Russia and Serbia* (Cambridge: Cambridge University Press, 2015) 164. Peter Alberg Jensen has called Pilniak "the first celebrity of early Soviet literature." See Jensen, *Nature as Code: The Achievement of Boris Pilnjak* (Copenhagen: Rosenkilde and Bagger, 1979), 65.

35. See Dany Savelli, "Shest' neizdannykh pisem Borisa Pil'niaka o ego pervom prebyvanii na Dal'nem Vostoke (v Kitae i v Iaponii) v 1926 g," *Cahiers du Monde Russe* 42, no. 1 (January–March 2011): 142.

36. Pilniak, *Rasskazy s Vostoka,* 12.

37. Pilniak, 17.

38. Pilniak, 13.

39. Boris Pilniak, "Chinese Story," in *Chinese Story and Other Tales,* trans. Vera T. Reck and Michael Green (Norman: University of Oklahoma Press, 1988), 17.

40. Pilniak, 17–18.

41. Pilniak, 25.

42. Esther Shumiatcher, "Saygon," in "Baym rand fun khine," *Hamer,* April 1927, 10.

43. Vladimir V. Mayakovskii, "Ia," *Russkaia poeziia serebrianogo veka. 1890–1917 Antologiia,* ed. Mikhail Gasparov (Moscow: Nauka, 1993), 561.

44. Peretz Markish, *Di kupe* (Kiev: Kultur-Lige, 1922), 5; first published in 1921. Translation consults David Roskies, *Against the Apocalypse: Responses to Catastrophe in Modern Jewish Culture* (Syracuse, NY: Syracuse University Press, 1984), 100.

45. Shumiatcher, "Saigon," 10.

46. Pilniak, "Chinese Story," 18. Bukh writes of this passage, "Depictions of cultural differences or curiosities are rare and appear only when the author experiences a physical reaction, such as when he sees the dead bodies floating in the Yangtze river or when he devotes a paragraph to the rotten smell that permeates everything in China." Bukh, "National Identity and Race," 186n52.

47. Pilniak, "Chinese Story," 18.

48. Shumiatcher, "A betler," in "Baym rand fun khine," 10.

49. As Katerina Clark has observed, despite the fact that Pilniak was, like Sergei Tretiakov, expected to provide a reappraisal of the East that avoided the nineteenth-century trappings of exoticism, he nonetheless portrays China as sleepy and in decline. Clark compares Pilniak's images of Asia to those of Pierre Loti, whose *Last Days of Peking* was a negative example for the positivist Soviets. See Clark, "Boris Pilniak and Sergei Tretiakov," 17.

50. This comparison is similar to Pilniak's Chinese writings, in which, Bukh has observed, "Again and again Pil'niak sees scenes from the Russian Revolution in China, including pillage, rape and the burning down of whole villages." Bukh, "National Identity and Race," 187; Bukh cites Pilniak, *Sobranie sochinenii,* 184–186.

51. Peretz Hirschbein, "Nit Rusland nor Ratenfarband," *Der Tog,* January 20, 1929, 3. Hirschbein includes, in this group, the Japanese revolutionary poet Akito.

52. Hirschbein, 3.

53. "Letter from Hirschbein to Leivick" (undated), Hirschbein files, RG 315, Folder 23, p. 1, YIVO, New York.

54. Cathy Caruth, *Unclaimed Experience: Trauma, Narrative, and History,* 20th anniversary ed. (Ithaca, NY: Cornell University Press, 2016), 8.

55. Shumiatcher, "Baym rand fun Khine," *Royte Velt,* 63–64. (The poem had already been published in *Hamer,* July 1927, 5. It would later appear in Shumiatcher's collected works.)

56. Shumiatcher, "Baym rand fun Khine," *Royte Velt,* July–August, 1928, 63–64.

57. See, for example, Robert A. Rosenstone, "Reds as History," *Reviews in American History* 10, no. 3 (September, 1982): 297–310.

58. This premise for a united front would prove simplistic. As Arif Dirlik has articulated, "From 1926 onward, with signs of serious tension in the United Front, this facile description of the goals of the Chinese Revolution was challenged first in Moscow and then in China. It is not clear how the various factions in the Comintern reacted to the first coup d'état by Jiang Jieshi (Chiang K'ai-shek) after the Zhongshan incident in March 1926, but it seems likely that some disagreement was responsible for the restatement of the Comintern position on China in the Seventh Plenum of the Executive Committee of the Comintern in December 1926, a few months before Trotsky's open opposition to the Stalinist line in China." Dirlik, *Marxism in the Chinese Revolution* (Lanham, MD: Rowman and Littlefield, 2005), 48.

59. Clark, "Boris Pilniak and Sergei Tretiakov," 16.

60. Chaim Nachman Bialik, "B'ir haHarega," in *Mishirei hazoam* (Odessa: Halperin and Schweizer, 1906), 6. The passage can also be found in *Kol shirei Khaim Nakhman Bialik* (Tel Aviv: Dvir, 1962), 357. I thank Prof. Dovid Katz for his help with the Ashkenazi transliteration of Bialik's Hebrew. "In the City of Slaughter," trans. A. M. Klein, in *The Literature of Destruction: Jewish Responses to Catastrophe,* ed. David G. Roskies (Toronto: University of Toronto Press, 1990), 160–168. I have chosen to provide the Ashkenazi transliteration of the poem, as this would have been used by most Yiddish readers in pre-Revolutionary Eastern Europe.

61. Roskies writes of World War I, "The kind of face-to-face violence, blind hatred, and persecution that Jews were subjected to during World War I was such native ground that the selective recording of history came into play once more and the Jewish tragedy was kept separate from world events." Roskies, *Against the Apocalypse,* 92.

62. See Eric J. Hobsbawm on the rise of the modern nation in *Nations and Nationalism since 1780: Programme, Myth, Reality,* Second Edition (Cambridge: Cambridge University Press, 2012), 102.

63. Alan Mintz discusses the modernist focus on a particular experience in his study of Agnon's Buczacz stories, *Ancestral Tales: Reading the Buczacz Stories of S. Y. Agnon* (Stanford, CA: Stanford University Press, 2017), 16. On the rise of nationalism in the western European novel, see Pericles Lewis, *Modernism, Nationalism, and the Novel* (Cambridge: Cambridge University Press, 2000).

64. Markish, *Di kupe,* 5. My translation consults Roskies, *Against the Apocalypse,* 100.

65. Esther Shumiatcher, "Nisht shend!," *In shoen fun libshaft: Lider un poemes* (Vilna: Vilner farlag fun B. Kletskin, 1930), 194.

66. Boris Pilniak, "Olenii gorod Nara," in *Povesti i rasskazy* (Moscow: Sovremennik, 1991), 462.

67. Shumiatcher, "Baym rand fun Khine," 63–64.

68. Lamed Shapiro, "The Cross," in *The Cross and Other Jewish Stories,* trans. Leah Garrett (New Haven, CT: Yale University Press, 2007), 8.

69. This is section IX of Markish's first edition of *Di kupe.* Peretz Markish, *Di kupe* (Warsaw: Kultur-Lige, 1921), 11.

70. Esther Shumiatcher, "Homel, 1905–1928," *In Shoen fun Libshaft,* 213; trans. Jones, "Wandering Is Your Fate," 24.

71. Shlomo Lambroza, "The Pogroms of 1903–1906," in *Pogroms: Anti-Jewish Violence in Modern Russian History,* ed. John D. Klier and Shlomo Lambroza (Cambridge: Cambridge University Press, 1992), 207–210.

72. Hans Rogger, "Conclusion and Overview," in Klier and Lambroza, *Pogroms,* 342.

73. Shumiatcher, "Nito a freyd aza," *Royte Velt* 1 (1921): 30.

74. Shumiatcher, 30.

75. Shumiatcher, 30.

76. Slavoj Žižek discusses this emergence of subjecthood, proposing that "it is this very transubstantiation which distinguishes Subject from Substance. 'Subject' designates that X which is able to survive the loss of its very substantial identity and to continue to live as the 'empty shell of its former self.'" Žižek, *Interrogating the Real* (London: Bloomsbury, 2005), 187.

77. Esther Shumiatcher, untitled poem marked "Homel, 1928," in *In shoen fun libshaft,* 65.

78. Esther Shumiatcher, untitled poem marked "Kyoto, 1926," in *In shoen fun libshaft,* 100.

79. Pilniak, *Rasskazy s Vostoka,* 18. Pilniak was also associated with the moon. His 1926 *Tale of the Unextinguished Moon (Povest' nepogashennoi luny)* was the story of the death of a Soviet commander and had made Pilniak a politically suspect writer. See Clark, "Boris Pilniak and Sergei Tretiakov," 10.

80. Ravitch, "Ester Shumyatsher-Hirshbayn," 3, cited in Jones, "Wandering Is Your Fate," 20.

81. Esther Shumiatcher, untitled, in *In shoen fun libshaft,* 214.

82. "Tsigeyner," dated "Crimea, 1928," in *In shoen fun libshaft,* 66.

83. According to Jonathan Dekel-Chen, in 1921 the population of Crimea was 720,000, which was 51 percent Ukrainian and Russian, 25 percent Tatar, and 6 percent German, with a small Jewish community of "mostly urban merchants and shopkeepers" that had been present for centuries. Dekel-Chen, *Farming the Red Land: Jewish Agricultural Colonization and Local Soviet Power, 1924–1941* (New Haven, CT: Yale University Press, 2005), 16.

84. Dekel-Chen, 21.

85. Dekel-Chen, 22.

86. Esther Shumiatcher, "Oyf felder Krimmer un Kherson," part 1 of "Yung iz erd un royt iz blut," in *In shoen fun libshaft*, 233.

87. Esther Shumiatcher, "Nisht andersh," in *In shoen fun libshaft*, 169.

88. As Harriet Murav has articulated, "The Soviet Union offered Jews the twin opportunities to remake themselves and relocate themselves in a body politic that gave them a home and a national home in Jewish settlements in Southern Ukraine, Crimea, and later the Jewish Autonomous Region of Birobidzhan." Harriet Murav, *Music from a Speeding Train* (Stanford, CA: Stanford University Press, 2011), 67.

89. Gennady Estraikh writes, "These days were auspicious: 17 November 1926 Kalinin, Chairman of the Central Executive Committee of the USSR, gave a speech at the meeting of the society for land development of Jewish workers (OZET) and designated the northern steppe of Crimea as the region of the Jewish farming colony. . . . Tens of foreign Jewish writers and public figures visited the new colonies, describing them in their reportage, poems, stories and novels." Estraikh, *Evreiskaia literaturnaia zhizn' Moskvy*, 82. As Estraikh notes, in 1928, Birobidjan became the major source of interest. Mikhail Kalinin was the formal head of the Soviet Russian state.

90. Dovid Hofshteyn, "Fun Krimmer tsikl," *Royte Velt* 1 (January 1927), 28.

91. The name Anakim derives from *anaq*, meaning "long neck." See Rodney Steven Sandler and Rodney S. Sadler Jr., *Can a Cushite Change His Skin? An Examination of Race, Ethnicity, and Othering in the Hebrew Bible* (New York: Bloomsbury, 2005), 44. The term *Anakim* means "Canaanite" and references the Judao-Slavic peoples who are part of the historical imagination. Paul Wexler has noted that Yiddish has retained traces of the "now obsolescent Kipchak Turkic language spoken by Karaites in the Crimea and in the Belarusian and Ukrainian lands." Wexler, *Two-Tiered Relexification in Yiddish: Jews, Sorbs, Khazars, and the Kiev-Polessian Dialect* (Berlin: Mouton de Gruyter, 2002), 515.

92. Khane Levin, "Krime motivn," *Royte Velt*, August 1929, 37–39.

93. According to Jonathan Dekel-Chen, Soviet authors "argued that religious conservatism enslaved Palestine's Jewish inhabitants, whereas life on the Crimean steppe liberated colonists." Dekel-Chen, *Farming the Red Land*, 102. Zvi Gitelman has also written about the competition between Soviet Jewish settlements and Zionism: "Jewish agricultural colonies would steal the thunder from the Zionists, who boasted about their communal settlements in Palestine, and they would populate and secure border regions in the Crimea, Ukraine, Belorussia—and later the Far East." Gitelman, *A Century of Ambivalence: The Jews of Russia and the Soviet Union, 1881 to the Present*, 2nd ed. (New York: YIVO, 2001), 94.

94. Esther Shumiatcher, "Der mistbarg iz groys," in *In shoen fun libshaft*, 272.

95. Shumiatcher, "Baym rand fun Khine," *Royte Velt*, July–August 1928, 64.

96. Murav, *Music from a Speeding Train*, 28. Murav cites Yurii Slezkine, *The Jewish Century* (Princeton, NJ: Princeton University Press, 2004), 191.

97. Markish, "Shloyme Ber in Krim," *Royte Velt,* February 1927, 5.

98. Walter Benjamin, "Theses on the Philosophy of History," in *Illuminations,* trans. Harry Zohn (New York: Schocken, 1968), 253–264.

99. Shumiatcher, "Yung iz erd un royt iz blut," in *In Shoen fun Libshaft,* 276.

100. Naomi Seidman, *A Marriage Made in Heaven: The Sexual Politics of Hebrew and Yiddish* (Berkeley: University of California Press, 1997), 124.

101. Aron Horowitz, in "An Encounter with Peretz Hirschbein," quotes a conversation he had much later with the Yiddish playwright in Calgary: "Somebody mentioned 'Palestine.' It seemed to me that Hirschbein was glad of the opportunity to tackle this subject. To quote him, 'I asked Bialik: How is Palestine going to solve the Jewish problem? At the most, there could be there about a million Jews in about twenty years. If and when this maximum number is reached, there will probably be by then about twenty million Jews in the rest of the world (this was said while Hitler was in the midst of *his* 'final solution' of the Jewish problem). How could one million Jews influence twenty million?!" Horowitz, *Striking Roots: Reflections on Five Decades of Jewish Life* (Oakville, ON: Mosaic, 1979), 88.

102. Nachman Mayzil, "Mit der heyser brokhe oyf di lipn: Tsum opforn fun Perets Hirshbeyn un Esther Shumiatcher fun Poyln," *Literarishe Bleter* 45 (November 8, 1929): 877.

103. Esther Shumiatcher, "Honik fun Birebidzhan," in *Ale Tog* (New York: Erd un heym, 1939), 114.

104. Esther Shumiatcher, "Dos Khinezerl Van-pu," in *Ale Tog,* 118.

105. For a discussion of Shumiatcher's critics, see Jones, "Wandering Is Your Fate."

2. ANGRY WINDS: JEWISH LEFTISTS AND THE CHALLENGE OF PALESTINE

1. Chaim Nachman Bialik, "B'ir haHarega," in *Mishirei hazoam* (Odessa: Halperin and Schweizer, 1906), 5. The passage can also be found in *Kol shirei Khaim Nakhman Bialik* (Tel Aviv: Dvir, 1962), 356. I thank Prof. Dovid Katz for his help with the Ashkenazi transliteration of Bialik's Hebrew. "In the City of Slaughter," trans. A. M. Klein, in *The Literature of Destruction: Jewish Responses to Catastrophe,* ed. David G. Roskies (Toronto: University of Toronto Press, 1990), 160–168. I have chosen to use the Ashkenazi transliteration of Bialik's poem, as this is the pronunciation used in pre-revolutionary Eastern Europe.

2. Moyshe Teyf, "Zing, vint fun midber! . . . ," *Frayhayt,* October 13, 1929, 7. Further quotations from the poem refer to this source and are cited parenthetically in the text.

3. The American socialist *Forverts,* for example, ran a headline on August 24, 1929, labeling the events in Palestine a "pogrom" and ran a series of photos the following day, titled "Pogrom pictures."

4. Statistics cited in Hillel Cohen, *Year Zero of the Arab-Israeli Conflict: 1929* (Waltham, MA: Brandeis University Press, 2015), xxi.

5. Nevertheless, several Arabs risked their lives to save Jewish neighbors.

6. "29 Dead, 150 Wounded in Battles between Jews and Arabs in Jerusalem: England Sends Warships and New Troops to Palestine," *Morgn Frayhayt,* August 25, 1929, 1.

7. "Over 100 Dead," *Frayhayt,* August 26, 1929, 1.

8. "Ver iz shuldik in Palestine," *Morgn Frayhayt,* August 27, 1929, 1. This notice announces an assembly the following day, August 28, in Irving Plaza.

9. Olgin's article of August 29 is cited by Menachem Boreysho. Boreysho also notes that the Soviet *Der Emes* on August 28 printed an article about "the imperialist provocation in Palestine." Boreysho, "Der Moskver 'Emes,' di Nyu Yorker 'Frayhayt' un di Palestiner pogromen," *Vokh* 1, no. 1 (October 4, 1929): 7.

10. See, for example, "Di pogromen in Palestine," *Forverts,* August 27, 1929, 4. An English translation of this article is available: "The Pogroms in Palestine," trans. Tony Michels, in *Jewish Radicals: A Documentary History,* ed. Tony Michels (New York: NYU Press, 2012), 298–300.

11. See Michel Foucault, *Fearless Speech* (Cambridge, MA: MIT Press, 2001).

12. Gerard Genette, *Paratexts: Thresholds of Interpretation* (Cambridge: Cambridge University Press, 1997), 2. Originally published in French in 1987. According to Genette, "Any text is a hypertext, grafting itself onto a hypotext, an earlier text that it imitates or transforms" (ix).

13. Hillel Cohen, *Year Zero of the Arab-Israeli Conflict 1929,* trans. Haim Watzman (Waltham, MA: Brandeis University Press, 2015); Matthew Hoffman, "The Red Divide: The Conflict between Communists and Their Opponents in the American Yiddish Press," *American Jewish History* 96, no. 1 (March 2010): 1–31. Numerous examples point to the connection communists made between Palestine and imperialism around the world. See, for example, an article from the *Morgn Frayhayt* on December 24, 1929, "Nokh Palestine—dorem Afrike" (After Palestine—South Africa), signed "An Ortign" (A local). The subtitle reads, "Vuks fun der revolutsionerer bavegung in di Englishe kolonyes."

14. Sheila Fitzpatrick, *On Stalin's Team: The Years of Living Dangerously in Soviet Politics* (Princeton, NJ: Princeton University Press, 2015). See, in particular, chapter 2, "The Great Break," 43–63.

15. Gennady Estraikh, "God velikogo pereloma," in *Evreiskaia literaturnaia zhizn' Moskvy: 1917–1991* (St. Petersburg: Evropeiskii Universitet, 2015), 136–157.

16. Ruth Wisse, "Jewish American Renaissance," in *The Cambridge Companion to Jewish American Literature,* ed. Hana Wirth-Nesher and Michael P. Kramer (Cambridge: Cambridge University Press, 2003), 190.

17. Scholars have long discussed the political relationship between Palestine (and later, Israel), and international stakeholders, from both a Jewish and an Arab perspective.

As Edward Said has written, "If . . . Palestine was the site of a contest between a native presence and an incoming, basically European / Western form of advanced culture, then it has followed that a considerable part of the contest was conducted outside Palestine itself." Edward W. Said, *The Question of Palestine,* 2nd ed. (New York: Vintage Books, 1992), 19. The 1929 Yiddish debates over the Party's role in Palestine complicates the discussion of Western interests.

18. Moishe Nadir, "Tsion vakkhanalia," *Morgn Frayhayt,* September 29, 1929. The text also appears in Nadir, *Nayste verk,* vol. 6 (New York: Frayhayt, 1931), 49. In it, Nadir harshly condemns those colleagues who left the paper.

19. Nadir, "Tsion vakkhanalia."

20. Edna Nahshon, "Art and Politics: The Case of the New York Arteff Theatre (1925–1940)," in *Politics of Yiddish: Studies in Language, Literature and Society,* ed. Dov-Ber Kerler (Walnut Creek, CA: AltaMira, 1998), 136.

21. Hoffman, "Red Divide," 5.

22. In one jointly authored editorial, the editors make clear that they are unaffiliated with any political party, connecting the leftist turn in the United States to the natural American tendency to assimilate. "Vokh," *Vokh* 1, no. 1 (October 4, 1929): 3. Trotsky himself, who was, like many of the *Vokh* contributors, an avowed anti-Zionist, when asked about the Palestine events, responded, "Unfortunately, I am not thoroughly familiar with the facts to venture a definite opinion. I am now studying the question." He noted that the uprisings appeared to involve a combination of national liberationists, "reactionary Mohammedans and anti-Semitic pogromists." See "On the 'Jewish Problem,'" an interview that first appeared in *Class Struggle,* February 1934, reprinted in Leon Trotsky, *On the Jewish Question* (New York: Pathfinder, 1970), 24. My thanks to Tony Michels for helping to explicate this point.

23. Cohen, *Year Zero,* 42. "Di maske hinter velkhe er shist," *Frayhayt,* September 2, 1929.

24. William Gropper cartoon, "Er shtelt ayn ru un ordnung in Palestine," *Frayhayt,* September 1, 1929, 10.

25. Joseph Foshko cartoon, "Er derkent zikh nit in shpigel," *Der Tog,* August 23, 1929.

26. William Gropper cartoon, "Di maske hinter velkhe er shist," *Frayhayt,* September 2, 1929.

27. Joseph Foshko cartoon, "Ikh halt di 'situatsie' in di hent!," *Der Tog,* September 4, 1929.

28. Aaron Glantz-Leyeles, "Dem Muftis arbl," in *Vokh* 1, no. 1 (October 4, 1929): 13.

29. Israel Bartal has suggested that early Zionists intentionally affected Cossack images in order to project strength in Palestine. See Bartal, "Hanukkah Cossack Style: Zaporozhian Warriors and Zionist Popular Culture (1904–1918)," in *Stories of Khmelnytsky: Competing Literary Legacies of the 1648 Ukrainian Cossack Uprising,* ed. Amelia Glaser (Stanford, CA: Stanford University Press, 2015), 139–152.

30. On the suppression of Hebrew in the Soviet Union, see Kenneth Moss, *Jewish Renaissance in the Russian Revolution* (Cambridge, MA: Harvard University Press, 2009), 225.

31. David Shneer, *Yiddish and the Creation of Soviet Jewish Culture: 1918–1930* (Cambridge: Cambridge University Press, 2004), 47.

32. These included the People's Publishing House (Folksfarlag) in Kiev as well as the stock company and Hebrew-language writers' collective Devir in Odessa, both in then-independent Ukraine. Shneer, 123; Moss, *Jewish Renaissance*, 168.

33. Moyshe Teyf, *Oysderveylts: Lider, balades, poems,* ed. Tsevi Hirsh Smoliakov (Jerusalem, 1966), 204. The editors include a note at the beginning of the autobiographical essay, indicating that the essay was written in Russian at the request of the editors and translated into Yiddish by Y. Rabin.

34. Y. L. Peretz translated Bialik's original Hebrew poem "B'ir haHaregah" (originally published as "Ma'asa Nemirov") into Yiddish in 1906. Vladimir Jabotinsky translated it into Russian in 1904. Bialik's poem was reissued in Warsaw in 1922 in Bialik's own Yiddish translation, and a 1922 edition of Jabotinsky's Russian translations was issued in Berlin.

35. Adrienne Rich, "When We Dead Awaken: Writing as Re-vision" (1971), in *On Lies, Secrets, and Silence, Selected Prose* (New York: Norton, 1979), 35.

36. Yehezkel Dobrushin, "Teyfs zhanr (Vegn zayn band lider un poemes)," in *Sovetishe dikhtung* (Moscow: Emes, 1935), 146. See also Khayem Beyder, Boris Sandler, and Gennady Estraikh, *Leksikon fun Yidishe shrayber in ratn-farband* (New York: Congress for Jewish Culture, 2011).

37. Dobrushin, "Teyfs Zhanr," 158.

38. Aaron Vergelis, introduction to Moyshe Teyf, *Izbrannoe* (authorized translations from the Yiddish) (Moscow: Sovetskii pisatel', 1958). As Vergelis notes, "Teyf byl i ostaetsia lirikom" (Teyf was and remains a lyric poet). Vergelis cites Bergelson's comments in *Literaturnaia gazeta,* 1935: "Teyf poistine zamechatel'nyj poet, original'neishee darovanie" (Teyf is truly an exceptional poet, with a most original gift; 3). Teyf shifted from writing in Yiddish to writing in Russian in 1958, near the end of his life.

39. Bialik, "In the City of Slaughter," in Roskies, *The Literature of* Destruction, 163.

40. The leaders of the Communist Party in Palestine were, at that point, largely still eastern European Jews, who represented a vanguard that the Comintern hoped to replace with Arabs being educated in Moscow's University of Toilers of the East. Avner Ben-Zaken, "From Universal Values to Cultural Representations," in *1929: Mapping the Jewish World,* ed. Gennady Estraikh and Hasia Diner (New York: NYU Press, 2013), 136–137.

41. H. N. Bialik, "In shkhite shtot," in *Fun tsar un tsorn* (Berlin: Klal-Farlag, 1922), 22.

42. Katerina Clark, *Moscow, the Fourth Rome* (Cambridge, MA: Harvard University Press, 2011), 20.

43. Bialik, in *The Literature of Destruction*, 167–168. The Yiddish reads as follows: "Run to the dismal desert—go insane! / Rip your soul into a thousand pieces [. . .] and hurl your cry up to the storm" (In visten midber loyf—un ver meshuge! / Tserays oyf toyzent shtiker dayn neshome . . . Un dayn geshrey zol aynshlingen der shturem). Bialik, "In Shkhite Shtot," 23.

44. Betsalel Fridman, "Palestine," *Morgn Frayhayt*, September 27, 1929, 5.

45. Quoted in "Saul Tchernichovsky," in *The Modern Hebrew Poem Itself*, new and updated ed., ed. Stanley Burnshaw, T. Carmi, Susan Glassman, Ariel Hirschfeld, and Ezra Spicehandler (Detroit: Wayne State University Press, 2003), 43.

46. Fridman, "Palestine," 5.

47. Ben-Zaken, "From Universal Values to Cultural Representations," 129. Ben-Zaken cites "A Resolution of Admission of the PCP as Section of the Comintern," in *Lehud o byahad: Yehudim ve Aravim' al pi mismachi ha-Comintern* (In separation or together: Jews and Arabs according to the documents of the Comintern), ed. Leon Zehavi (Tel Aviv, 2005), 21–22.

48. Ben-Zaken, "From Universal Values to Cultural Representations," in *Mapping the Jewish* World, ed. Hasia R. Diner and Gennady Estraikh (New York: New York University Press, 2013), 131. On the Third Period embrace of anticolonialism at the Sixth World Comintern Congress, see Anouar Abdel-Malek, *Nation and Revolution*, vol. 1 of *Social Dialectics*, trans. Mike Gonzalez (Albany, NY: SUNY Press, 1981), 86–87. This policy had an important effect on the relationship between the Comintern and colonial struggles around the world, including in China, following the 1927 massacre of the Chinese communists by the Kuomindang, former Soviet allies.

49. In the memory book for the shtetl of Luboml, the authors note that the youth movement in the shtetl was spurred on by young intellectuals from the nearby city of Cheml, "mostly members of Poale Tsion or the Bund": "[They] awakened our youth to political activities and lively debates on relevant topics. . . . Under the influence of these fellows we began reading socialist literature; we lustily sang the songs 'Hulyet, Hulyet Beyze Vinten' ('Whirl, Whirl You Angry Winds') by Avrom Reyzen, 'Hemerl, Hemerl Klap' ('Pound Away, Little Hammer') by Y. L. Peretz, etc." Berl Kagan and Nathan Sobel, *Luboml: The Memorial Book of a Vanished Shtetl* (Jersey City, NJ: KTAV, 1997), 84.

50. Avrom Reyzen, "A vinter-lid," in *Di lider in tsvelf teyln*, 4.

51. Jonathan Frankel has written of the constant threat of arrests facing the Bund's core membership beginning in the 1890s. See Frankel, *Crisis, Revolution, and Russian Jews* (Cambridge: Cambridge University Press, 2009), 61.

52. See Avrom Reyzen, *Epizodn fun mayn lebn*, vol. 1 (Vilna: B. Kletskin, 1929), 151–153.

53. Reyzen, *Epizodn*, vol. 2 (Vilna: B. Kletskin, 1929), 211. He describes the Zionist café in Dzielne in Warsaw, which was located off a little yard, where loud, argumentative voices could be heard. "If the café opened right onto the street," Reyzen later wrote,

"there is no way they would have been able to so freely do battle in it." Reyzen, 212. Socialists would come to the Zionist café, Reyzen recalls, and he and his friend Nomberg, as well as other socialist intellectuals like Lipa Novogrudsky, would argue with the Zionists. By contrast, Reyzen recalls, Kotik's Café, on 31 Nalevkes Street, was where Bundists and frustrated writers would gather along with Zionists and young people of other political stripes. This was a quieter café, Reyzen notes, in part because Kotik kept a variety of newspapers that people would try to read and in part because the socialists feared that spies may be lurking about. Reyzen, 214–216.

54. Reyzen, "A vinter-lid," 4.

55. Dovid Tanievitsh, "Huliet, huliet, beyze vintn!," *Morgn Frayhayt,* September 4, 1929, 5.

56. Tanievitsh, 5.

57. "20 Thousand People Take Part in a Protest against the Bloodshed," *Der Tog,* August 27, 1929, 1.

58. Edna Nahshon references these splits in "Art and Politics: The Case of the New York Artef Theatre (1925–1940)," in *Politics of Yiddish: Studies in Language, Literature and Society,* ed. Dov-Ber Kerler (Walnut Creek, CA: AltaMira Press, 1998), 136.

59. Nakhman Mayzil, "Fun vokh tsu vokh," *Literarishe Bleter,* October 25, 1929, 852. H. Leivick, "Royte tikhelekh," *Vokh,* October 18, 1929, 14.

60. On September 18, 1925, the Moscow Jewish theater hosted a banquet in honor of Leivick, who came from America "with the purpose of creating contacts among Soviet-Jewish literature and translation of Jewish literature abroad." Estraikh, *Evreiskaia literaturnaia zhizn' Moskvy,* 103. Estraikh cites "A banket dem kh'Leyvik," *Der Emes,* September 27, 1925, and B. Kats, "Nyu-york-Varshe-Moskve: der disput fun dikhter Leyvik mit di Yidishe komunistn in Moskve," in *Haynt,* October 30, 1925. Estraikh notes, further, that Leivick wrote to his wife, "I feel much, much better here than in Poland and in other countries," and she indicated her readiness to join him. Estraikh, *Evreiskaia literaturnaia zhizn' Moskvy,* 104. Estraikh cites a letter from Leivick to his wife published in *Di Goldene Keyt* (1988), 44–48.

61. Reyzen, "Ferzn," *Frayhayt,* August 25, 1929, 7.

62. Tanievitsh, "Huliet, Huliet, beyze vintn!," 5.

63. Vladimir Medem, cited in Oleg Budnitsky, *Jews between the Reds and the Whites, 1917–1920,* trans. Timothy J. Portice (Philadelphia: University of Pennsylvania Press, 2012), 467.

64. "Der aroystrit fun Yidishe shriftshteler fun *Frayhayt*" (Declaration of Leivick and Boreysho), *Literarishe Bleter,* September 27, 1929, 770.

65. Ayzik Platner, "Tsu di antlofene," *Morgn Frayhayt,* September 28, 1929.

66. Platner, "Tsu di antlofene."

67. See John A. Salmond, *Gastonia 1929: The Story of the Loray Mill Strike* (Chapel Hill: University of North Carolina Press, 1995).

68. Aaron Kurtz, "Mishpet," *Morgn Frayhayt,* September 22, 1929, 7.

69. See Katerina Clark and Evgenny Dobrenko, "The Organization of Proletarian Art: The Cultural Revolution," in *Soviet Culture and Power: A History in Documents, 1917–1953* (New Haven, CT: Yale University Press, 2007), 50–75.

70. Kurtz, "Mishpet," 7.

71. Matthew Hoffman has discussed the effect of "Third Period Communism," which was initiated in the summer of 1928, on the "Great Break" in American Yiddish politics that followed the uprisings in Palestine. Hoffman, "Red Divide."

72. Kurtz, "Mishpet," 7.

73. Alexander Pomerantz accused Kurtz of being too formalist in his writing. Pomerantz, *Proletpen: Etyudn un materyaln tsu der geshikhte fun dem kamf far proletarisher literature in Amerike* (Kiev: All-Ukrainian Academy of Science, 1935), 237.

74. Aaron Kurtz, "Dem bafrayers geburtstog" (The liberator's birthday), *Morgn Frayhayt,* December 25, 1949.

75. Aaron Kurtz, "Di vant," *Morgn Frayhayt,* September 12, 1929, 5. The poem is dated September 9, 1929.

76. Kurtz, 5.

77. See Gennady Estraikh, *In Harness: Yiddish Writers' Romance with Communism* (Syracuse, NY: Syracuse University Press, 2005), 97.

78. Kurtz, "Di vant," 5.

79. Kurtz, 5.

80. For a good introduction to the relationship between Zionism and religion, see Shlomo Avineri, "Zionism and the Jewish Religious Tradition: The Dialectics of Redemption and Secularization," *Zionism and Religion,* ed. S. Almog, Jehuda Reinharz, and Anita Shapira (Hanover and London: Brandeis U.P., 1998) 1–9.

81. Karl Marx and Friedrich Engels, *The German Ideology, Part One,* ed. C. J. Arthur (New York: International, 2004), 121.

82. Menke Katz, "Tsu di antlofene," *Frayhayt,* October 2, 1929, 5.

83. Katz, 5.

84. M. Katz, "Tsu di antlofene," 5.

85. Menke Katz had a tumultuous relationship with the Party poets. He was expelled from Proletpen in 1932 due to a controversial book, rejoined the group, and began publishing poems about workers, and again broke with the group over his 1938 book *Brenendik shtetl* (Burning village). See Dovid Katz, "The Days of Proletpen," in *Proletpen: America's Rebel Yiddish Poets,* ed. Amelia Glaser and David Weintraub (Madison: University of Wisconsin Press, 2005), 23.

86. Harold Bloom, *The Anxiety of Influence: A Theory of Poetry,* 2nd ed. (Oxford: Oxford University Press, 1997), 11.

87. I thank Joshua Karlip for helping me to articulate this distinction.

88. Avrom Reyzen, "Groye teg" (in cycle "Lider un fantazyes") *Vokh* 1, no. 1 (October 4, 1929): 9.

89. Aaron Glantz-Leyeles, "Dem mufti's arbl" (The Mufti's sleeve), *Vokh* 1, no. 1 (October 4, 1929): 13.

90. Esther Shumiatcher, "Yung iz erd un royt iz blut," in *In shoen fun libshaft: Lider un poemes* (Vilne: Vilner farlag fun B. Kletskin, 1930), 276.

91. H. Leivick, "Farvos mir zaynen aroys fun der 'Frayhayt,'" *Vokh* 1, no. 1 (October 4, 1929): 4.

92. Spinoza became an important reference point among Jews in the 1930s. In a 1939 essay in the Paris journal *Oyfn Sheydveg* (At the crossroads), Charles Rappoport wrote, "It is difficult to be objective at such a dark time. It is even more difficult to follow the advice of the great Jewish thinker Spinoza: 'Neither to laugh nor to cry, but to understand.'" Rappoport, "On Several Aspects of the Jewish Question" (Vegn eynike aspektn fun der Yidisher problem), in *Oyfn Sheydveg*, ed. and trans. Joshua M. Karlip (Eugene, OR: Wipf and Stock, forthcoming in 2021), 112. I thank Dr. Karlip for sharing this anthology with me in advance of its publication.

93. Anna Shternshis, *Soviet and Kosher: Jewish Popular Culture in the Soviet Union, 1923–1939* (Bloomington: Indiana University Press, 2006), 94.

94. H. Leivick, "Royte tikhelekh," *Vokh*, October 18, 1929, 14.

95. Itche Goldberg, in a 2004 interview with *Jewish Currents*, discussed the importance of the Sacco-Vanzetti execution and the Yiddish poets, including H. Leivick, to his movement toward the Party. See "Itche Goldberg at 100: A Dynamic Figure of Yiddish Culture Talks about a Century of Letters and Activism," *Jewish Currents, A Secular, Progressive Bimonthly* 58, no. 3 (May–June, 2004): 16.

96. Leivick, "Royte tikhelekh," 14.

97. Leivick, 14.

98. Leivick, 14.

99. H. Leivick, "Farreter," *Vokh* 3 (October 18, 1929): 6.

100. Leivick, 6.

101. Shifre Vays, "Taynes" (Accusations), *Morgn Frayhayt*, November 3, 1929.

102. Nakhman Mayzel, "Nokhveyen," *Literarishe Bleter* 41, no. 284 (October 11, 1929): 800–801. On Mayzel's editorial, see also Katz, "Days of Proletpen," 10.

103. Hans-Georg Gadamer, "On the Contribution of Poetry to the Search for Truth" in *On the Relevance of the Beautiful*, trans. Nicholas Walker (Cambridge: Cambridge University Press, 1986) 113. James Risser has taken this "nearness" to be a form of homecoming, a return to language. Risser, *The Life of Understanding: A Contemporary Hermeneutics* (Bloomington: Indiana University Press, 2012), 35–36.

104. Speech of Shmuel Niger-Charney (Shmuel Niger), in *Der mishpet: Iber di Yidishe komunistn un zeyer hoyft-tsaytung "Di Morgn-frayhayt"* (New York: Farband-Labor Zionist Order, 1929), 17.

105. Leivick, "Farvos mir zaynen aroys fun der 'Frayhayt,'" 6.

106. Matthew Hoffman has observed that when new Arab revolts in Palestine broke out in the spring and summer of 1936, this renewed the conflicts among Jews in

the United States. "The *Forverts* and *Tog* accused the communists of being complicit in the anti-Jewish violence in Palestine, claiming that the Communist Party of Palestine had issued a proclamation calling for Arab attacks against Jews." The *Frayhayt* called William Randolph Hearst, as well as the socialist Yiddish press, "brutal fascist pogromists." Even with the increased collaboration under the Popular Front, the *Frayhayt* perpetually compared the right-wing US press to Nazis—especially Goebbels and Streicher. Hoffman, "Red Divide," 19–20.

107. Quoted in P. Novik, "Ven di literature dint nisht dem folk (Vegn an artikl fun Dr. A. Mukdoni un a vey-geshray fun H. Leivick—der muser haskel derfun)" (When literature doesn't serve the people [About an article by Dr. A. Mukdoni and H. Leivick's Cry of Pain—The Moral of the Story]), *Morgn Frayhayt*, August 11, 1944, 6. In this article, Novik attacks Mukdoni for insinuating that Soviet Jewish literature is bereft of Jewish culture. He considers Leivick's "cry of pain" an attack on Soviet Jewish culture.

108. Jacques Derrida, *Spectres of Marx*, trans. Peggy Kamuf (1993; New York: Routledge, 2012), 221.

3. SCOTTSBORO CROSS: TRANSLATING POGROMS TO LYNCHINGS

1. Malka Lee, "Gots shvartser lam," in *Lider* (New York: Idisher kultur gezelshaft tsvayg, 1932), 152; Berish Weinstein, "A Neger shtarbt," *Yidishe Kultur* 2 (December 1938): 67–68.

2. Menke Katz, "Di lintshndike kro," in *Der mentsh in togn* (New York: Signal, 1935), 120.

3. Lee, "Gots shvartser lam," 152.

4. In John 1:29, for example, we find, "The next day John saw Jesus coming toward him and said, 'Look, the Lamb of God, who takes away the sin of the world!'" (NIV).

5. Robin D. G. Kelley notes that "almost a year before Scottsboro, the Party launched a regional antilynching campaign that had been motivated by a multiple lynching in Emelle, Alabama." Kelley, *Hammer and Hoe: Alabama Communists during the Depression* (Chapel Hill: University of North Carolina Press, 1991), 81. Articles about the defendants appeared frequently in the USSR. For example, see S. Samet, "Negritianskaia intelligentsia i Amerikanskii kapital," in *Front nauki i tekhniki* 1 (January 1932): 90–96.

6. Hasia Diner, *In the Almost Promised Land: American Jews and Blacks, 1915–1935* (1977; repr., Baltimore: Johns Hopkins University Press, 1995), 31. For important discussions of portrayals of African Americans in the Yiddish and English-language Jewish press, see Diner, 28–117.

7. Langston Hughes, *Scottsboro Limited* (New York: Golden Stair, 1932). Robert Shulman, *The Power of Political Art: The 1930s Literary Left Reconsidered* (Chapel Hill:

University of North Carolina Press, 2000), 34. Rukeyser writes explicitly about Scottsboro in "The Trial," included in *Theory of Flight* (New Haven, CT: Yale University Press, 1935), which had won the Yale Younger Poets Prize.

8. The ILD existed from 1925 to 1947.

9. Kelley, *Hammer and Hoe*, xxi. Others have highlighted the potentially damaging role played by the Party. See, for example, Dan Carter, *Scottsboro: A Tragedy of the American South* (Baton Rouge: Louisiana State University Press, 2007).

10. Zishe Bagish, *Dos gezang fun Neger-folk iberdikhtungen* (Chicago: Farlag M. Tseshinski, 1936).

11. Yitshak Elhanan Rontsh notes that in Warsaw, in 1935, he came across a production of the play, under the direction of M. Vaykhert, who was later killed by the Nazis. See Rontsh, "The African American in Yiddish Literature," in *Amerike in der Yidisher literatur: An interpretatsye* (New York: Y. A. Rontsh bukh-komitet, 1945), 203.

12. Alyssa Quint, "Poland's Yiddish Theater as Utopian Space: Mikhl Vaykhtert's production of Leyb Malakh's *Mississippi*," in *World War I, Nationalism, and Jewish Culture*, ed. Joshua Karlip (Eugene, OR: Wipf and Stock, forthcoming in 2021). I am grateful to Dr. Quint for sharing her unpublished work with me.

13. Nikhil Pal Singh, *Black Is a Country: Race and the Unfinished Struggle for Democracy* (Cambridge, MA: Harvard University Press, 2004), 40.

14. Singh, 59. Singh notes that Du Bois "never explicitly referred to a black public sphere, but this concept helps illuminate the meaning behind his use of contemporary left-wing slogans describing black people in the United States as a nation within a nation."

15. Rontsh, "Der Neger in der Yidisher literatur" (The African American in Yiddish literature), in *Amerike in der Yidisher literatur* (New York: Y. A. Rontsh bukh-komitet, 1945), 204.

16. Acts 5:30 (KJV). We find additional references to the crucifixion as a hanging in the New Testament, for example, "And we are witnesses of all things which he [Jesus] did both in the land of the Jews, and in Jerusalem; whom they slew and hanged on a tree" (Acts 10:39); "And when they had fulfilled all that was written of him, they took him down from the tree, and laid him in a sepulchre" (Acts 13:29); "Who his own self bare our sins in his own body on the tree, that we, being dead to sins, should live unto righteousness" (Peter 2:24). In addition, the Babylonian Talmud describes the execution of Jesus as a hanging (*Sanhedrin* 43a). I thank Mira Balberg for these references and for helping me to understand the multiple interpretations of the crucifixion in Jewish and Christian antiquity.

17. Galatians 3:13 (NIV). Paul is quoting from Deuteronomy 21:23.

18. Lee, "Gots shvartser lam," 152.

19. Several scholars, including Hasia R. Diner, Merle Bachman, Milly Heyd, and Marc Caplan, have discussed Jews' writing and art about African Americans. Diner,

In the Almost Promised Land: American Jews and Blacks, 1915–1935 (Baltimore: Johns Hopkins University Press, 1995); Bachman, *Recovering "Yiddishland": Threshold Moments in American Literature* (Syracuse, NY: Syracuse University Press, 2008); Heyd, "Jews Mirroring African Americans: On Lynching," in *Mutual Reflections: Jews and Blacks in American Art* (New Brunswick, NJ: Rutgers University Press, 1999), 86–116; Caplan, "Yiddish Exceptionalism: Lynching, Race, and Racism in Opatoshu's Lintsheray," in *Joseph Opatoshu: A Yiddish Writer between Europe and America*, Studies in Yiddish 11 (Oxford, UK: Legenda, 2013), 173–187.

20. For discussions of Christian imagery in Jewish literature as it relates to anti-Jewish violence, see David Roskies, "Jews on the Cross," in *Against the Apocalypse: Responses to Catastrophe in Modern Jewish Culture* (Cambridge, MA: Harvard University Press, 1984), 258–312; Efraim Sicher, "Modernist Responses to War and Revolution: The Jewish Jesus," in *Jews in Russian Literature after the October Revolution: Writers and Artists between Hope and Apostasy* (Cambridge: Cambridge University Press, 1995), 40–70; Matthew B. Hoffman, *From Rebel to Rabbi: Reclaiming Jesus and the Making of Modern Jewish Culture* (Stanford, CA: Stanford University Press, 2007); Janet Hadda, "Christian Imagery and Dramatic Impulse in the Poetry of Itzik Manger," *Michigan Germanic Studies* 3, no. 2 (1977): 1–12; Neta Stahl, *Other and Brother: Jesus in the 20th-Century Jewish Literary Landscape* (New York: Oxford University Press, 2013); Avraham Nowersztern, *Kesem ha dimdumim: Apokalipsah umeshihiyut besifrut Yidish* (Jerusalem: Hotsaat sefarim a. sh. Y. L. Magnes ha-Universitah ha-Ivrit, 2003); Amelia Glaser, "The End of the Bazaar: Revolutionary Eschatology in Isaac Babel's *Konarmiia* and Peretz Markish's *Di Kupe*," *Jews in Russia and Eastern Europe* 2, no. 53 (Winter 2004): 5–32.

21. African Americans also wrote about the general connection between US racism and European antisemitism. In 1903, following the Kishinev pogrom in the Russian Empire, Booker T. Washington wrote, "Not only as a citizen of the American Republic, but as a member of a race which has, itself, been the victim of much wrong and oppression . . . my heart goes out to our Hebrew fellow-sufferers across the sea." Quoted in Louis R. Harlan, "Booker T. Washington's Discovery of Jews," in *Strangers and Neighbors: Relations between Blacks and Jews in the United States*, ed. John H. Bracey (Amherst: University of Massachusetts Press, 1999), 289. See also Arnold Shankman, "Brothers across the Sea: Afro-Americans on the Persecution of Russian Jews, 1881–1917," *Jewish Social Studies* 37 (1917): 114–121.

22. Sholem Asch's "In a karnival nakht" (On a carnival night) and Lamed Shapiro's "Der tseylem" (The cross) both appeared in 1909 in the American Yiddish journal *Dos Naye Lebn* and prompted a debate over Yiddish writers' use of the cross. For an excellent discussion of this debate and Asch's later Christological works, see Hoffman, *From Rebel to Rabbi*. See also Sicher, "Modernist Responses." I discuss the crucifixion motif, focusing on the work of Berish Weinstein, in my article, "From Jewish Jesus to

Black Christ: Race Violence in Leftist Yiddish Poetry," in *Studies in American Jewish Literature* 34, no. 1 (2015): 44–69.

23. Quoted in Sicher, "Modernist Responses," 45; Ziva Amishai-Maisels, *Depiction and Interpretation: The Influence of the Holocaust on the Visual Arts* (Oxford, UK: Pergamon, 1993).

24. Uri Tsvi Grinberg, "Uri Tsvi farn tseylem INRI," *Albatros* 1, no. 2 (1922): 3–4. Neta Stahl has discussed the shift in Grinberg's cross poetry toward nationalism in the early 1920s. See Stahl, "'Cut Off from All of His Brothers, from His Blood': The Figure of Jesus in the Poetry of Ur Zvi Greenberg," in *Other and Brother: Jesus in the Twentieth Century Jewish Literary Landscape* (Oxford: Oxford University Press, 2013), 50–82.

25. Grinberg, "Uri Tsvi farn tseylem," 3–4. My translation consults Stahl, "Cut Off," 60.

26. As Neta Stahl notes, "The poet's plea for Jesus to recall his Jewish past and to leave the aesthetic pleasure of the West—represented by the sounds of bells and Latin words—is then voicing Grinberg's inner struggle to leave European culture behind for the sake of reuniting with his people." Stahl, "Cut Off," 62.

27. Lee, "Gots shvartser lam," 152.

28. Moyshe Leyb Halpern, "A nakht," in *In Nyu-York* (New York: Farlag matones, 1954), 188.

29. Yehoash, "Lintshen," in *In Geveb,* vol. 2 (Farlag "Oyfgang," 1921), 66–67. Translation consults Yehoash, "Woven In," in *Sing, Stranger: A Century of American Yiddish Poetry, A Historical Anthology,* ed. Benjamin Harshav, trans. Benjamin Harshav and Barbara Harshav (Stanford, CA: Stanford University Press, 2006), 107.

30. Yehoash, "Lintshen," 66–67. Translation consults Yehoash, "Woven In," 107.

31. Bachman, *Recovering "Yiddishland,"* 153.

32. Reuben Ludwig, "Ver hot tseshosn dem kretikn niger," in *Gezamelte lider* (New York: I.L. Perets shrayber farayn, 1927), 64. Translation consults Ludvig, "Who Shot the Leprous Nigger?," in Harshav, *Sing, Stranger,* 548.

33. Malka Lee, "Der Neger in sobvey" (1933), in *Gezangen* (New York: Kooperetiver folks farlag fun di internatsionaln arbiter ordn in Nyu York, 1940), 34. First published in *Morgn Frayhayt,* November 23, 1933, 5.

34. Grinberg, "Uri Tsvi farn tseylem." Translation from Stahl, "Cut Off," 60–61.

35. Aaron Glantz-Leyeles, "In sobvey III," in *Rondos: Un andere lider* (New York: Inzikh, 1926), 45.

36. Lee, "Neger in sobvey," in *Gezangen,* 34.

37. Y. E. Rontsh, "Sotsiale dikhter" (Social poets) in *Amerike in der Yidisher literatur* (New York: Y. A. Rontsh bukh-komitet, 1945), 158.

38. Lee, "Gots shvartser lam," 152.

39. Katz, "Di lintshndike kro," 118. Translation consults Katz, "The Lynching Crow," in Harshav, *Sing, Stranger,* 594.

40. Katz, "Di lintshndike kro," 119–120. Translation consults Katz, "Lynching Crow," 596.

41. Derrida discusses the wound as a poetic password. Jacques Derrida, *Sovereignties in Question* (New York: Fordham University Press, 2005), 166.

42. The poem was first published as "Bitter Fruit." Lewis Allan (pseudonym for Abel Meeropol), "Bitter Fruit," *The New York Teacher*, January 1937, 17. I thank Dennis Childs for calling my attention to this connection, as well as Marcus Moseley, who discussed Meeropol's close connections to Yiddish literature at a conference at Stanford University, "From the Other Shore," January 24, 2016. For more on the history of Meeropol's poem, see David Margolick, *Strange Fruit: The Biography of a Song* (New York: HarperCollins, 2001).

43. Meeropol was a pallbearer at Ethel and Julius Rosenberg's funeral and later adopted their children. See Stephen J. Whitfield, *In Search of American Jewish Culture* (Hanover, NH: Brandeis University Press, 1999), 147.

44. The poem was originally published in *Opportunity*, December 1925. Frank Horne, "On Seeing Two Brown Boys in a Catholic Church," in *300 Years of Black Poetry*, ed. Alan Lomax and Raoul Abdul (New York: Dodd, Mead, 1984), 212.

45. Langston Hughes, "Christ in Alabama," in *Contempo* 1, no. 13 (December 1, 1931): 1. See Arnold Rampersad, *The Life of Langston Hughes: 1902–1941, I, Too, Sing America* (Oxford, UK: Oxford University Press, 2002), 218. Hughes here is referencing the abolitionist John Brown, who raided Harper's Ferry in 1859. Lewis Leary, an African American who joined John Brown in his attempt to free slaves and died in a naval conflict, was Langston Hughes's grandfather.

46. Cary Nelson, *Revolutionary Memory: Recovering the Poetry of the American Left* (New York: Routledge, 2011), 73.

47. Langston Hughes, "Scottsboro," *Opportunity*, December 1931, 379. A 1932 translation of Langston Hughes's play, *Scottsboro*, was published in the Soviet Union. Langston Hughes, A. Grevs, and A. Meier, *Scottsboro: Odnoaktnaia piesa* (TsK. MOPR, USSR, 1932).

48. Michael Thurston, "Black Christ, Red Flag: Langston Hughes on Scottsboro," *College Literature* 22, no. 3 (October 1995): 41.

49. Frank Marshall Davis, "Christ Is a Dixie Nigger," in *Black Moods: Collected Poems*, ed. John Edgar Tidwell (Urbana: University of Illinois Press, 2002), 67.

50. Stacy I. Morgan, *Rethinking Social Realism: African American Art and Literature, 1930–1953* (Athens: University of Georgia Press, 2004), 222.

51. Davis, "Christ Is a Dixie Nigger," 68.

52. Glenda Elizabeth Gilmore, *Defying Dixie: The Radical Roots of Civil Rights, 1919–1950* (New York: Norton, 2009), 173. For a discussion of the relationship between early Nazism and Jim Crow, see Gilmore's chapter "The Nazis and Dixie" (157–200). Milly Heyd has, moreover, demonstrated the visual conflation of the KKK and Nazism in

literary and popular culture. For example, a cartoon in the NAACP journal *Crisis*, founded and edited by W. E. B. Du Bois, shows a Klansman bearing a swastika, with the caption, "Nazi persecution of Jews and Negroes." Heyd, "Jews Mirroring African Americans: On Lynching," in *Mutual Reflections: Jews and Blacks in American Art* (New Brunswick, NJ: Rutgers University Press, 1999), 93–94.

53. "Scottsboro Death Ruling Upheld," *New York Times*, June 17, 1938; "Scottsboro Negro Is Saved from Death: Gov. Graves Commutes Sentence to Life," *New York Times*, July 6, 1938.

54. Langston Hughes, "August 19th . . . : A Poem for Clarence Norris," in *The Collected Poems of Langston Hughes*, ed. Arnold Rampersad and David Roessel (New York: Random House, 1994), 204.

55. Quoted in Joseph McLaren, *Langston Hughes: Folk Dramatist in the Protest Tradition, 1921–1943* (Westport, CT: Greenwood, 1997), 46. Hughes's play won a contest put forth by *New Theater* magazine for a dramatization of the Herndon case, to be judged by Herndon himself. See McLaren, 40.

56. Yuri Suhl, "Geblibn volt shoyn haynt fun zey," in *Dos likht af mayn gas* (New York: Signal, 1935), 56.

57. Suhl, "Andzhelo Hoyrndon krigt di post," in *Dos likht af mayn gas*, 61.

58. Suhl, 61.

59. Suhl, 58.

60. James Goodman, *Stories of Scottsboro* (New York: Vintage, 1994), 83.

61. Kwando M. Kinshasa, *The Scottsboro Boys in Their Own Words: Selected Letters, 1931–1950* (Jefferson, NC: McFarland, 2014), 88.

62. Betsalel Fridman, "Skotsboro (fragment)," in *Proletpen: America's Rebel Yiddish Poets*, ed. Amelia Glaser and David Weintraub, trans. Amelia Glaser (Madison: University of Wisconsin Press, 2005), 138–139.

63. Dan Carter calls *Contempo* "a journal of radical politics and modernist literature courageously published for a few years in Chapel Hill, North Carolina." Carter, *Scottsboro*, 68. According to Anne P. Rice, "When the editors of *Contempo* . . . asked Hughes for a contribution to their December 1931 issue, he responded with a blistering essay on the Scottsboro case, which was featured on the front cover of the magazine. 'Christ in Alabama' appeared inside." Rice, *Witnessing Lynching: American Writers Respond* (New Brunswick, NJ: Rutgers University Press, 2003), 268.

64. Y. E. Rontsh, "Scottsboro," in Glaser and Weintraub, eds., *Proletpen*, 142. Originally published in *Hungerike hent: Lider un poemes* (New York: Farlag "Signal" bam "Proletpen," 1936), 52.

65. Rontsh, 142 (translation revised).

66. Wright's "I Have Seen Black Hands" was anthologized in his *Uncle Tom's Children* in 1936. Another leftist Yiddish poet, Betsalel Fridman, references *Uncle Tom's Children* in his own poem "Skotsboro" (mentioned earlier). The National Negro

Congress was also held in 1936, and this event raised awareness about the state of race relations in the United States, particularly for those on the left.

67. Richard Wright, "I Have Seen Black Hands," in *Richard Wright Reader*, ed. Michel Fabre (New York: Da Capo, 1978), 245.

68. Wright, 246. For further analysis of this poem, see John M. Reilly, "Richard Wright's Apprenticeship," *Journal of Black Studies* 2, no. 4 (June 1, 1972): 446.

69. John Reilly demonstrates that Wright wrote this poem upon his return from his first John Reed Club meeting in 1933. Reilly, *Richard Wright: The Critical Reception* (New York: Burt Franklin, 1978), xi. Reilly cites Richard Wright, "I Tried to Be a Communist," *Atlantic Monthly*, August 1944, 61–70.

70. Y. E. Rontsh, "Done a Good Job," in Glaser and Weintraub, eds., *Proletpen*, 148–149; Yitshak Elhanan Rontsh, "In Alabama," in *Hungerike hent*, 53–57.

71. Y. E. Rontsh, "Neger-arbeter," in *Hungerike hent*, 51.

72. Rontsh, "African American in Yiddish Literature," 226.

73. Weinstein, "A Neger shtarbt," *Yidishe Kultur* 2 (December, 1938): 67. My translation, altered slightly here, first appeared in Glaser and Weintraub, eds., *Proletpen*, 167.

74. Caplan, "Yiddish Exceptionalism," 176.

75. Weinstein, "A Neger shtarbt," 67–68.

76. Weinstein, 68.

77. Bachman engages in an excellent reading of Weinstein's poems about African Americans. However, she does not discuss the language and imagery in these poems that borrow from Weinstein's poems about violence in Europe. Bachman, *Recovering "Yiddishland*,*"* 153.

78. The specific event that Weinstein is probably referencing took place in Pharus Hall, in the Wedding district in Berlin on February 11, 1927. This was a heavily communist-dominated region of Berlin. See Thomas Friedrich, *Hitler's Berlin: Abused City* (New Haven, CT: Yale University Press, 2012), 98.

79. Berish Weinstein, "Henkers," in *Brukhvarg* (New York: Farlag "Haveyrim-Komitet," 1936), 30.

80. Weinstein, 30.

81. Moishe Nadir, "Emets kumt . . ." in *Berish Vaynshteyn yoyvl bukh: tsu zayn zekht-sikstn geboyrn-tog,* ed. Moshe Starkman (Tel Aviv: ha-Menorah, 1967), 55.

82. Weinstein, "Henkers," 30. Translation alters Berish Weinstein, "Executioners," trans. Leonard Wolf, in *The Penguin Book of Modern Yiddish Verse*, ed. Irving Howe (New York: Penguin, 1987), 614.

83. Julia Fermentto-Tsaisler is researching Berish Weinstein's use of meat as a metaphor as part of her dissertation in comparative literature at the University of California, San Diego. I am grateful to her for many conversations about Weinstein's use of animal imagery.

84. Weinstein, "Henkers," 30. Translation alters Weinstein, "Executioners," 614.

85. Berish Weinstein also has a section called "Tregers un Negers" in *Amerike: Poeme* (New York: Tsiko, 1955), 71–82. The title literally means "Carriers/Porters and Negroes." The fortuitous rhyme allows Weinstein to draw attention to the connection between a subjugated people and the low-paid service profession they were often expected to fill in New York City. Weinstein's rejection letter from B. Goldberg, coeditor of the *Tog* is dated May 13, 1933. Berish Weinstein papers, YIVO Institute, New York, RG 626, Box 3.

86. Berish Weinstein, "Haknkreyts," in *Brukhvarg*, 33.

87. Berish Weinstein, "Yidn," in *Brukhvarg*, 35.

88. Weinstein, 36.

89. Weinstein, 35.

90. Berish Weinstein, "Lintshing," in *Brukhvarg*, 66. Translation revises Weinstein, "Lynching," in Harshav, *Sing, Stranger*, 340.

91. Weinstein, "Lintshing," 66. Translation revises Weinstein, "Lynching," 340.

92. *Mishnah Sanhedrin* 6:2. I am grateful to Mira Balberg for directing me to the Rabbinic and early Christian discourse surrounding confessions.

93. Weinstein, "Lintshing," 66. Translation revises Weinstein, "Lynching," in Harshav, *Sing, Stranger*, 340.

94. Berish Weinstein, "Negerish," in *Lider un poemes* (New York: Grenich, 1949), 181. Translation from Berish Vaynshteyn, "Harlem—A Negro Ghetto," in Harshav, *Sing, Stranger*, 349. Harshav adds the note, "'Ghetto' was not yet a common term for black slums in American cities. Weinstein uses a set of metaphors, projecting Jewish destiny onto the black experience."

95. Berish Weinstein, "Lintshing," in *Lider un poemes*, 57.

96. As Hasia R. Diner has explained, "An American Jewish culture, shaped, in part, by this Jewish tragedy and current political concerns, emerged in the immediate years after World War II, especially in the 1950s." Diner, "Before 'The Holocaust': American Jews Confront Catastrophe, 1945–62," in *American Jewish Identity Politics*, ed. Deborah Dash Moore (Ann Arbor: University of Michigan Press, 2009), 85–86. This movement away from internationalism would only grow more pronounced. Eric Sundquist suggests that "at key moments and in key arenas the post-civil rights era saw blacks and Jews become more deeply estranged than ever." Sundquist, *Strangers in the Land: Blacks, Jews, Post-Holocaust America* (Cambridge, MA: Harvard University Press, 2005), 84.

97. Steven Zipperstein, *Pogrom: Kishinev and the Tilt of History* (New York: Norton, 2018), 192–193.

98. Ta-Nehisi Coates, *We Were Eight Years in Power: An American Tragedy* (New York: Penguin Random House, 2017), 158.

99. Moyshe Leyb Halpern, "Salyut," in *Moyshe Leyb Halpern*, ed. Eliezer Greenberg, vol. 1 (New York: Moyshe Leyb Halpern Komitet, 1934), 49. The poem is undated in this posthumous collection but would have been written before 1932, when Halpern passed away.

100. Ruth Wisse, "Drowning in the Red Sea," *Jewish Review of Books*, Fall 2011, https://jewishreviewofbooks.com/articles/98/drowning-in-the-red-sea/.

101. Michael Denning, *The Cultural Front: The Laboring of American Culture in the Twentieth Century* (New York: Verso, 1997), xviii.

102. H. Leivick, "Negershes," in *Ale verk fun H. Leyvik*, vol. 1 (New York: H. Leyvik yubiley-komitet, 1940), 271. According to Hugh Denman, Leivick first published the poem in 1922, but likely wrote it earlier. Denman, "Blacks in American Yiddish Literature," *Report of the Oxford Center for Hebrew and Jewish Studies* (Oxford, UK: Oxford Centre for Hebrew and Jewish Studies, 2005), 37.

103. Leivick, "Negershes," 271.

104. H. Leivick, "A briv fun Amerike tsu a vaytn fraynt," in *Ale verk fun H. Leyvik*, 394; also published in *Royte Velt* 7 (July, 1929): 1–7.

105. Bruce Robbins, *The Beneficiary* (Durham, NC: Duke University Press, 2017). Robert Meister, too, discusses the "beneficiary" in *After Evil: A Politics of Human Rights* (New York: Columbia University Press, 2010).

106. Rontsh, *Amerike in dos Yidishe vort*, 234.

107. Michael Rothberg, *The Implicated Subject: Beyond Victims and Perpetrators* (Stanford, CA: Stanford University Press, 2019), 32. Rothberg cites Arendt, "Collective Responsibility," in *Responsibility and Judgment*, ed. Jerome Kohn (New York: Schocken, 2003), 157. (Rothberg cites Arendt on p. 1.)

4. *NO PASARÁN:* JEWISH COLLECTIVE MEMORY IN THE SPANISH CIVIL WAR

1. Irving Weissman, Diaries, 1938–1942, Folder 1, Box 1, MSS 528, Special Collections, University of California, San Diego Geisel Library. I thank Stephanie Weissman and Peter Carroll for sharing information about Irving Weissman's writing and time in Spain.

2. Irving Weissman, "The Return," *Massachusetts Review* 19, no. 3 (Autumn 1978): 619. Peter Carroll discusses Weissman and this essay in *The Odyssey of the Abraham Lincoln Brigade: Americans in the Spanish Civil War* (Stanford, CA: Stanford University Press, 1994), 1–2.

3. Wystan Hugh Auden, *Spain* (London: Faber and Faber, 1937). Quoted in Humphrey Carpenter, *W. H. Auden: A Biography* (London: Faber and Faber, 1981), 219.

4. Peretz Markish, "Shpanye," in *Lider vegn Shpanye* (Moscow: Farlag "Emes," 1938), 3.

5. Jacobo Glantz, "In vandervaytkayt fun mayn folk," in *Fonen in Blut* (1936), 17.

6. Aaron Kurtz, *"No Pasaran": Lider, balades un poemes fun Shpanishn folk in zayn kamf kegn fashizm* ("No Pasarán": Songs, ballads, and pomes of the Spanish people in its struggle against fascism) (New York: Yiddish Cooperative Book League of the Jewish Section of the International Workers Order, 1938). Hereafter cited as *NP*.

7. For a good overview of the Comintern's embrace of the Popular Front, see Helen Graham and Paul Preston, "The Popular Front and the Struggle against Fascism," in *The Popular Front in Europe,* ed. Graham and Preston (London: Macmillan, 1987), 1–19.

8. In a letter to Chaim Slovès of August 24, 1937, Leivick and Opatoshu expressed their strong concern that the Paris Yiddish Congress be as inclusive as possible, across the political spectrum, so as not to damage the common interests of defeating fascism. International Workers Order (IWO) and Jewish People's Fraternal Order (JPFO), Kheel Center for Labor-Management Documentation and Archives, Martin P. Catherwood Library, Cornell University, PDF available online: https://digital.library.cornell.edu/catalog/ss:19043860.

9. H. Leivick, "Di oyserlekhe un di inerlekhe konfliktn in der yiddisher kultur un literature," speech given at the first gathering of the Culture Congress, September 18, 1937, Paris. In *Literarishe Bleter* 41 (October, 1937): 650.

10. Gina Medem, "Jewish Fighters on the Battlefields of Spain," in *From a Ruined Garden: The Memorial Books of Polish Jewry,* 2nd ed., ed. and trans. Jack Kugelmass and Jonathan Boyarin (Bloomington: Indiana University Press, 1998), 166.

11. Melech Epstein, *Pages from a Colorful Life: An Autobiographical Sketch* (Detroit: Wayne State University Press, 1971), 123.

12. Gerben Zaagsma discusses these widely varying estimates and observes that "from a statistical point of view, the lumping together of Jewish volunteers is highly problematic, if not simply ahistorical." Zaagsma, *Jewish Volunteers, the International Brigades and the Spanish Civil War* (London: Bloomsbury, 2017), 22. On the Abraham Lincoln Brigade, see William Loren Katz and Marc Crawford, *The Lincoln Brigade: A Picture History* (Eugene, OR: Wipf and Stock, 1989), 22.

13. On the Botwin Company, see Gerben Zaagsma, "Propaganda or Fighting the Myth of *Pakhdones? Naye Prese,* the Popular Front, and the Spanish Civil War," in *Choosing Yiddish: New Frontiers of Language and Culture,* ed. Lara Rabinowich, Shiri Goren, and Hannah S. Pressman (Detroit: Wayne State University Press, 2013), 88–101.

14. On the involvement of Zionist volunteers in the International Brigades, see Zaagsma, *Jewish Volunteers,* 26–27.

15. Cary Nelson, "Introduction: The International Context for American Poetry about the Spanish Civil War," in *The Wound and the Dream: Sixty Years of American Poems about the Spanish Civil War,* ed. Cary Nelson (Urbana: University of Illinois Press, 2002), 23.

16. See Harry Ritter, *Dictionary of Concepts in History* (Westport, CT: Greenwood, 1986), 114. On Marx's interpretation of Hegelian dialectics, see H. P. Kainz, *Hegel's Philosophy of Right, with Marx's Commentary: A Handbook for Students* (The Hague: Martinus Nijhoff, 1974).

17. Georg Lukács, "The Historical Novel of Democratic Humanism," in *The Historical Novel* (Lincoln: University of Nebraska Press, 1983), 342–343.

18. Michael Löwy, *Redemption and Utopia: Jewish Libertarian Thought in Central Europe* (New York: Verso, 2017), 177.

19. The Comintern's financial and organizational support of the International Brigades in Spain alienated democratic governments, including the United States, whose noninterventionist policy may well have cost the Republic its victory. As Helen Graham has noted, for example, "The haemorrhaging of time and money that Non-Intervention inflicted at the start of the war, solely upon the Republic, was absolutely devastating." Graham, *The Spanish Republic at War, 1936–1939* (Cambridge: Cambridge University Press, 2002), 158.

20. Tim Kendall, *Modern English War Poetry* (Oxford: Oxford University Press, 2006), 108.

21. Hannah Arendt, *Men in Dark Times* (San Diego: Harcourt Brace, 1970), 216.

22. Marc Chagall, to Leo Kenig, 1948, quoted in Benjamin Harshav, *Marc Chagall and His Times: A Documentary Narrative* (Stanford, CA: Stanford University Press, 2004), 641. Chagall published his correspondence with Abraham Lisner, a Jewish fighter in Spain who suggested themes for Chagall to take up: "with your artistic rifle, your brush." Quoted in Harshav, 473–475.

23. Harsha Ram, "World Literature as World Revolution: Velimir Khlebnikov's *Zangezi* and the Utopian Geopoetics of the Russian Avant-Garde," in *Comintern Aesthetics,* ed. Amelia Glaser and Steven Lee (Toronto: University of Toronto Press, 2020), 34.

24. Kadye Molodowsky, "Tsu di volontyorn in Shpanye," in *In land fun mayn gebeyn* (Chicago: Shtayn, 1937), 17. The poem was also published in *Hamer* in 1938. Allison Schachter has written of Molodowsky that "her Yiddish poems in the 1930s had a decidedly brash style, referencing the Spanish Civil War and the Popular Front alongside New York City skyscrapers and Eastern European landscapes." Schachter, *Diasporic Modernisms: Hebrew and Yiddish Literature in the Twentieth Century* (Oxford: Oxford University Press, 2011), 178.

25. See Andrea Orzoff, "Interwar Democracy and the League of Nations," in *The Oxford Handbook of European History, 1914–45,* ed. Nicolas Doumanis (Oxford, UK: Oxford University Press, 2016), 269. Key Soviet literary figures debated ways of broadening literary policy to match the united political front. Ilya Ehrenburg, in a 1934 letter to Stalin, argued that a MORP (International Organization of Revolutionary

Writers) that was too closely aligned with Bolshevism would discredit the Soviet cause in the eyes of the West. Ehrenburg quoted in Anson Rabinbach, "Paris, Capital of Anti-Fascism," in *The Modernist Imagination: Intellectual History and Critical Theory,* ed. Warren Breckman, Peter E. Gordon, A. Dirk Moses, Samuel Moyn, and Elliot Neaman (New York: Berghahn Books, 2009), 199.

26. Nonetheless, as Pamela Radcliff and others have suggested, the Soviet focus of Comintern policy probably ultimately weakened the interwar Left. Radcliff, "The Political Left in Interwar Europe," in Doumanis, *Oxford Handbook of European History,* 294.

27. See, for example, Mario Revah, *Mexico and the Spanish Civil War: Political Repercussions for the Republican Cause* (Eastbourne, UK: Sussex Academic, 2015).

28. Edward Stankiewicz, remembering his meeting with Markish, would later compare him to a movie actor. Stankiewicz, *My War: Memoir of a Young Jewish Poet* (Syracuse, NY: Syracuse University Press, 2002), 27.

29. Markish, "Shpanye," 3.

30. See Yosef Haim Yerushalmi, "In the Wake of the Spanish Expulsion," in *Zakhor: Jewish History and Jewish Memory* (Seattle: University of Washington Press, 1982), 53-75.

31. Yerushalmi, 59-60.

32. Ismar Schorsch, "The Myth of Sephardic Supremacy," *Leo Beck Yearbook* 34 (1989): 47-66.

33. David Markish, personal correspondence, 2016.

34. Maurice Halbwachs, *On Collective Memory,* trans. Lewis A. Coser (Chicago: University of Chicago Press, 1992).

35. Peretz Markish, *Di kupe* (1921; Kyiv: Kultur-Lige, 1922). Translation consults David Roskies, *Against the Apocalypse: Responses to Catastrophe in Modern Jewish Culture* (Syracuse, NY: Syracuse University Press, 1984), 100.

36. Markish, "Shpanye," 7.

37. Maurice Halbwachs, *The Collective Memory,* trans. Francis J. Ditter, Jr., and Vida Yazdi Ditter (New York: Harper & Row, 1980), 52.

38. Harriet Murav has observed the similarity between Markish's 1921 *Di kupe* and his depiction of the spread of typhus in his 1929 "Brothers." Murav, *Music from a Speeding Train: Jewish Literature in Post-Revolution Russia* (Stanford, CA: Stanford University Press, 2011), 33.

39. Walter Benjamin, *Illuminations,* trans. Harry Zohn (New York: Schocken, 1968), 257. For a good discussion of Benjamin's approach to Marxism, see Michael Löwy, *Fire Alarm: Reading Walter Benjamin's "On the Concept of History"* (London: Verso, 2016).

40. As Eli Lederhendler has observed, "The Jewish ethnic press at large was consistent in identifying Franco with Fascism and, in addition, it signaled that a Spanish

Loyalist victory was vital for the free world and for the Jewish people, in particular." Lederhendler, *American Jewry: A New History* (Cambridge: Cambridge University Press, 2017), 205.

41. Peretz Markish, "Der baleidikter koved fun undzer folk fodert an entfer," in *Brider yidn fun der gantser velt* (Moscow: OGIZ, Der Emes farlag, 1941), 11. Cited in David Shneer, "Rivers of Blood: Peretz Markish, the Holocaust, and Jewish Vengeance," in *A Captive of the Dawn: The Life and Work of Peretz Markish (1895–1952),* ed. Joseph Sherman, Gennady Estraikh, David Shneer, and Jordan Finkin (Oxford, UK: Legenda, 2011), 142.

42. David Shneer, "Rivers of Blood: Peretz Markish, the Holocaust, and Jewish Vengeance," 142.

43. Sergei Narovchatov, "Perets Markish," in *Stikhotvoreniia i poemy* (Leningrad: Sovetskii pisatel', 1969), 29.

44. Harriet Murav has written of Markish's World War II works, "Perets Markish's poem 'Ho Lakhmo' (The bread of affliction) and his epic *Milkhome* (War) all respond to the killings of Jews." Murav, *Music from a Speeding Train,* 154.

45. Estraikh, "Anti-Nazi Rebellion in Peretz Markish's Drama and Prose," in Sherman et al., *Captive of the Dawn,* 173.

46. Lisa Kirschenbaum, *International Communism and the Spanish Civil War* (Cambridge: Cambridge University Press, 2015), 185.

47. As Karl Schlögel remarks, "From 16 July 1936, the first day of the revolt of the officers around General Franco against the Spanish Republic, to the capitulation of Republican Spain at the end of April 1938, Spain was a central topic of all reporting." Schlögel, *Moscow 1937,* trans. Rodney Livingstone (Cambridge, UK: Polity, 2013), 95.

48. Esther Markish, *The Long Return* (New York: Ballentine, 1978), 84–85.

49. Markish, "Shpanye," 4.

50. Estraikh sees the Spain cycle, along with Markish's 1935 *Dem balegufs toyt* (The kulak's death) and his 1940 *Poeme vegn Stalinen* (Poem about Stalin), as evidence of "Markish's readiness to be in effect an amanuensis for the regime." Estraikh, "Anti-Nazi Rebellion," 170. Including the Spain cycle in this list of Stalinist poems, however, denies its place in the continuity of Markish's antifascist writings.

51. Narovchatov, "Perets Markish," 27.

52. Markish, "Shpanye," 6.

53. Markish, 6.

54. Kurtz, "Kol Nidre," in *NP,* 56.

55. Kurtz, 56.

56. The first auto-da-fé is said to have taken place in 1481, leading to a mass exodus of Jews even before the Expulsion in 1492. See Manuel da Costa Fontes, *The Art of Subversion in Inquisitorial Spain: Rojas and Delicado* (West Lafayette, IN: Purdue University Press, 2005), 39.

57. Kurtz, "Kol Nidre," 58.

58. Kurtz, "Yosl," in *NP*, 73.

59. Kurtz, "Di letste levaye," in *NP*, 92.

60. Adina Cimet, *Ashkenazi Jews in Mexico* (Albany: SUNY Press, 1997), 79.

61. Adam Hochschild, *Spain in Our Hearts: Americans in the Spanish Civil War, 1936–1939* (Boston: Houghton Mifflin Harcourt, 2016), 45.

62. Rebecca Mina Schreiber, *Cold War Exiles in Mexico: U.S. Dissidents and the Culture of Critical Resistance* (Minneapolis: University of Minnesota Press, 2008), 14.

63. Cimet, *Ashkenazi Jews in Mexico*, 80.

64. Glantz, "In vandervaytkayt fun mayn folk," in *Fonen in blut*, 18 (emphasis in the original).

65. Glantz, "Nisht keyn araynfir—nor an oysfir" (Not an introduction—but a conclusion), in *Fonen in blut*, 7.

66. Todd Presner, *Muscular Judaism: The Jewish Body and the Politics of Regeneration* (London: Routledge, 2007), 4.

67. Esther Shumiatcher, "Ikh bin a Yid," in *Ale tog: Lider un poemes* (New York: Erd un heym, 1939), 109.

68. Shumiatcher, 111.

69. Paul Preston, *The Spanish Holocaust: Inquisition and Extermination in Twentieth-Century Spain* (New York, London: Norton, 2012), 10.

70. Melech Epstein, *Pages from a Colorful Life: An Autobiographical Sketch* (Detroit: Wayne State University Press, 1971), 123.

71. Glantz, "In vandervaytkayt fun mayn folk," 18.

72. Kurtz's seamless shift from trauma to politics falls into the trappings of what LaCapra has identified as "competitive victimology." Dominick LaCapra, *Writing History, Writing Trauma* (Baltimore: Johns Hopkins University Press, 2014), 217.

73. Glantz, "In vandervaytkayt fun mayn folk," 18.

74. For a good discussion of Baron and the "lachrymose conception" of history, see Robert Liberles, *Salo Wittmayer Baron: Architect of Jewish History* (New York: NYU Press, 1995), 338–359.

75. Glantz, "Di oygn fun Lina Odena," in *Fonen in blut*, 52.

76. Steven S. Lee, *The Ethnic Avant-Garde: Minority Cultures and World Revolution* (New York: Columbia University Press, 2015), 84. For his definition of factography, Lee cites Sergei Tret'iakov, "Happy New Year! Happy *New Left*!," in *Russian Futurism through Its Manifestos*, ed. Anna Lawton (Ithaca, NY: Cornell University Press, 1988), 267.

77. Glantz, "Di oygn fun Lina Odena," 52.

78. Tabea Alexa Linhard, *Fearless Women in the Mexican Revolution and the Spanish Civil War* (Columbia: University of Missouri Press, 2005), 125.

79. Dolores Ibárruri, Speech delivered at a People's Front Meeting in Madrid on October, 1936. See Dolores Ibárruri, *Speeches and Articles, 1936–1938* (London: Lawrence & Wishart, 1938), 38.

80. Klein views the Popular Front as an extension of Wilsonian interwar politics: "The popularity of the Front derived in part from its ability to tap into the reservoirs of Wilsonian internationalism that still existed and to create an institutional infrastructure in which a broad range of internationalists, from communists to liberals, could come together." Christina Klein, *Cold War Orientalism: Asia in the Middlebrow Imagination, 1945–1961* (Berkeley: University of California Press, 2003), 31.

81. Glantz, "Oyf farnakhtikn step fun La Mantsha," in *Fonen in blut,* 26.

82. Igal Halfin, *From Darkness to Light: Class, Consciousness, and Salvation in Revolutionary Russia* (Pittsburgh: University of Pittsburgh Press, 2000), 40.

83. Glantz, "Royter Kristus," in *Fonen in blut,* 27.

84. Aleksandr Blok, *Dvenadtsat* (St. Petersburg: Alkonost', 1918).

85. Glantz, "Royter Kristus," 28.

86. Seth Wolitz has discussed Markish's three long poems of the early 1920s, a triptych composed of *Volin* (Volhynia) as the past, *Di kupe* (The mound) as the present, and *Radyo* (Radio) as the future. Seth Wolitz, "Markish's *Radyo* (1922): Yiddish Modernism as Agitprop," in *Yiddish Modernism: Studies in Twentieth-Century Eastern European Jewish Culture* (Bloomington, IN: Slavica, 2014), 255.

87. Wolitz, 263.

88. Peretz Markish, "Veys ikh nit, tsi kh'bin in dr'heym" (I don't know if I'm at home), in *A shpigl af a shteyn: antologye: Poezye un proze fun tsvelf farshnitene yidishe shraybers in Ratn-Farband,* ed. Benjamin Hurshovski, Chone Shmuruk, and Mandel Piekarz (Tel-Aviv: Farlag di Goldene Keyt; Farlag Y. L., Perets, 1964), 376.

89. Markish, "Shpanye," 5.

90. Markish, "Balade vegn delegat," in *Lider vegn Shpanye,* 10.

91. Markish, "Toreador," in *Lider vegn Shpanye,* 28.

92. Markish, 29.

93. Hochschild, *Spain in Our Hearts,* 85.

94. Markish, "Shpanye," 6.

95. Markish, 6.

96. Hochschild, *Spain in Our Hearts,* 205.

97. Aaron Glantz-Leyeles, "Shpanishe balade," in *Opklayb lider poemes drames* (New York: Congress for Jewish Culture, 1968), 170. Translation from *A Century of Yiddish Poetry,* ed. and trans. Aaron Kramer (Cranbury, NJ: Cornwall Books, 1989), 151.

98. Aaron Glantz-Leyeles, "Oyfn Shpanishn front," *In Zikh* 36 (June 1937): 191.

99. In a review of the fifteenth-anniversary issue of the *Freiheit,* the editors of the Introspectivist journal *In Zikh,* which had published some of Kurtz's early experimental poems, accuse Kurtz of "conformism and Stalinist inertia." Citing Kurtz's open

appreciation of Stalin, the *In Zikh* editors write of Kurtz, "When the soul must answer to politics, to the Party-Cheka—this is already a great danger, death in the literal sense of the word, for the tiniest spark of artistry." "Reflektsies: Signal—epitaf oyf a bankrot," *In Zikh* 34 (April 1937) 126.

100. Kurtz, "Karmansita," in *NP*, 65.

101. Bertolt Brecht, *Die Gewehre der Frau Carrar: Text, Auffuhrung, Anmerkungen* (Dresden: Verlag der Kunst, 1952).

102. Kurtz, "Andaluzyer landshaft," in *NP*, 40. Translation revised from Kurtz, "Andalusian Landscape," in *Proletpen: America's Rebel Yiddish Poets,* ed. Amelia Glaser and David Weintraub, trans. Amelia Glaser (Madison: University of Wisconsin Press, 2005), 325.

103. Kurtz, *NP*, 3.

104. See, for example, Muriel Rukeyser, "Mediterranean: The Signs and Sounds of the First Days of the Spanish War Stamp on the Poet's Mind More than a Visual-Aural Impression," *New Masses,* September 14, 1937, 18. Rukeyser was evacuated from Spain, where she had been reporting on the 1936 antifascist Olympics, and the poem is written in the form of a report from one of the first Loyalists.

105. Kurtz, "A briv fun a kranknshvester," in *NP*, 36.

106. Kurtz, 37.

107. Langston Hughes, "Letter from Spain," in *The Collected Poems of Langston Hughes,* ed. Arnold Rampersad (New York: Vintage, 1994), 201–202.

108. Hughes later described visiting field hospitals where he met dark-skinned Moroccans fighting in Franco's army. Arnold Rampersad notes this in *Collected Poems of Langston Hughes,* 647n201.

109. Hughes, "Letter from Spain," 202.

110. Kurtz, "A briv fun a kranknshvester," 37.

111. Glantz, "A balade funem riter oyfn roytn ferd" (A ballad of the knight on a red horse), in *Fonen in blut,* 33.

112. Markish, "Agitprop Pontsho Vidio" in *Lider vegn Shpanye,* 30.

113. Nelson, "Introduction," 12.

114. Kurtz, "Der orkester" in *NP*, 59.

115. Kurtz, 59.

116. Aaron Kurtz, "Yunyon Skver," in *Plakatn* (New York: Yidish Leben, 1927), 10.

117. L. Khanukov, "Aaron Kurtz: Dikhter fun kreftikn vort," *Frayhayt,* March 20, 1938, 3.

118. Anthony Easthope, *Poetry as Discourse* (New York: Routledge, 1983), 15. Easthope cites Roman Jacobson, "The Dominant," in *Readings in Russian Poetics,* ed. L. Matejka and K. Pomorska (Cambridge, MA: MIT Press, 1960), 371.

119. Hannah Arendt, *Totalitarianism: Part Three of "The Origins of Totalitarianism"* (San Diego: Harcourt, 1968), 62.

120. Schlögel, *Moscow 1937,* 101. A purge of Trotskyists took place in Spain as well as in the Soviet Union. See Kirschenbaum, *International Communism,* 138.

121. Nelson, "Introduction," 30–31.

122. "The cipher," as Derrida writes, "like the date, is incorporated into the poem. They give access to the poem that they are, but a ciphered access." Jacques Derrida, *Sovereignties in Question: The Poetics of Paul Celan,* ed. Thomas Dutoit and Outi Pasanen (New York: Fordham University Press, 2005), 22.

123. Quoted in Derrida, 21.

124. Derrida, 29.

125. Glantz, *Fonen in blut,* 5.

126. Glantz, "Plakat" in *Fonen in blut,* 44.

127. Antony Beevor, *The Battle for Spain: The Spanish Civil War, 1936–1939* (New York: Penguin, 2006), 150.

128. Glantz, "A lid vegn bankir Khid in a shloflozer nakht fun Madrid (plakatish)" (A poem about banker Gid on a sleepless night in Madrid [placard-style]), in *Fonen in blut,* 47.

129. According to a description of winter campaign dress in the Spanish Civil War, "The *capote-manta,* a large, loose cape for winter, was used very widely by both Republicans and Nationalists." Patrick Turnbull, *The Spanish Civil War, 1936–39* (Oxford, UK: Osprey, 1978), 32–33.

130. Glantz, "A lid vegn bankir Khid," 49.

131. Derrida, *Sovereignties in Question,* 22.

132. Markish, "Komandir Diestro," in *Lider vegn Shpanye,* 36. The Vasilyev brothers' immensely popular 1934 film *Chapaev* was screened across Spain. Ilya Ehrenburg remarks that the Spanish anarchists were so upset by the death of the hero that the committee began cutting the end of the film: "They said: 'What's the point of fighting if the best men get killed?'" Ehrenburg, *Memoirs, 1921–1941,* trans. Tatania Shebunina in collaboration with Yvonne Kapp (Cleveland, OH: World, 1964), 370. As Lisa Kirschenbaum has put it, "Whereas in Spain Chapaev provided a model of Bolshevik masculinity, in the Soviet Union, coverage of the Spanish civil war offered influential and to some degree competing models of militarized and maternal communist womanhood." Kirschenbaum, *International Communism,* 127.

133. Markish, "Komandir Diestro," 37. Markish began publishing his Spain poems in journals in 1936. See, for example, Markish, "Shpanye," in *Naye Folkstsaytung,* November 28, 1936, 4.

134. Cited in Peter N. Carroll, *The Odyssey of the Abraham Lincoln Brigade: Americans in the Spanish Civil War,* 17. Carroll cites "If we sit by": Hyman Katz to mother, Nov. 25, 1937, box 8A, VALB MSS, BU.

135. Ehrenburg, *Memoirs,* 336.

136. David Lederman writes, for example, that it was forbidden to play anti-Nazi repertoire following the Hitler-Stalin pact. Lederman, *Fun yener zayt forhang* (From

the other side of the curtain) (Buenos Aires: Tsentral-farband fun Poylishe yidn in Argentine, 1960), 101–102. One of Markish's earliest poems about World War II, "The Dancer from the Ghetto," remained unpublished until after the war due to censorship. E. Markish, *Long Return,* 102–103.

137. See, for example, Estraikh, "Anti-Nazi Rebellion," 168–181; and Murav, *Music from a Speeding Train,* esp. chapter 5: "*Yeder zeyger a yortsayt:* The Past as Memory in Postwar Literature."

138. An excerpt of the novel was published in *Yidishe Kultur:* Peretz Markish, "In der varshever geto," *Yidishe Kultur* 4 (1957): 2.

139. Muriel Rukeyser, *Savage Coast* (New York: Feminist Press, 2013), 7.

5. MY SONGS, MY *DUMAS:* REWRITING UKRAINE

1. David Fishman notes, of this meeting, that Pasternak "still remembered some Yiddish from his childhood." Fishman, *The Book Smugglers: Partisans, Poets, and the Race to Save Jewish Treasures from the Nazis, The True Story of the Paper Brigade of Vilna* (Lebanon, NH: University Press of New England, 2017), 132.

2. Avrom Sutzkever, "Dermonung vegn Pasternak" (1976), in *Lider fun togbukh* (Tel Aviv: Di goldene keyt, 1977), 72.

3. Avrom Sutzkever, "A rege is gefaln" (April 7, 1943), in *Di festung lider un poemes: Geshribn in Vilner Geto un in vald 1941–1944* (New York: IKUF, 1945), 1949. Translation in Sutzkever, *Selected Poetry and Prose,* trans. Barbara Harshav and Benjamin Harshav (Berkeley: University of California Press, 1991), 158.

4. Jacques Derrida, *Sovereignties in Question: The Poetics of Paul Celan,* ed. Thomas Dutoit and Outi Pasanen (New York: Fordham University Press, 2005), 54.

5. Pasternak claimed, on multiple occasions, that the encounter never took place. Whether Sutzkever constructed the event or Pasternak wanted to avoid discussing his meeting with the Yiddish poet, who moved to Palestine soon after, is a matter of speculation. See Leonid Katsis, "Kogda razgulialos': Pis'ma Borisa Pasternaka 1945–1960 godov," *Lekhaim* 1, no. 189 (January 2008), https://lechaim.ru/ARHIV /189/kats.htm.

6. Sutzkever, "A rege is gefaln," 1949.

7. Hirsh Bloshteyn, "Tsvey bagegenishn mit Dovid Hofshteyn," *Folks-Shtime,* June 27, 1959, republished in *Briv fun Yidishe Sovetishe shraybers,* ed. Mordechai Altshuler (Jerusalem: Hebrew University in Jerusalem, Centre for Research and Documentation of East-European Jewry, 1979), 83.

8. Samantha Sherry has suggested that Pasternak managed in his translation of Hamlet "to make parallels between the past fictional events and the present state of cultural and political affairs." Sherry, *Discourses of Regulation and Resistance: Censoring Translation in the Stalin and Khrushchev Era Soviet Union* (Edinburgh: Edinburgh University Press, 2015), 143.

9. Pasternak, who was forced to stop publishing his own work in 1937, became, in Lazar Fleishman's words, the "translator of the poetry of national minorities" against his will. Fleishman, *Boris Pasternak: The Poet and His Politics* (Cambridge, MA: Harvard University Press, 1990), 210.

10. As Lital Levy and Allison Schachter have noted in their discussion of the significant Jewish contributions to world literature, "Writers throughout the Jewish world sought to develop modern Jewish-language literatures by translating contemporary European literature." Levy and Schachter, "Jewish Literature / World Literature: Between the Local and the Transnational," *PMLA* 130, no. 1 (2015): 96.

11. Yuri Slezkine has made the important point that even in the late 1930s the formal aspects of "nations" were prioritized, as long as those nations were geographically recognized as national republics. Although Jews were given the autonomous region of Birobidjan in 1934, Jews expressing national pride were seldom connected to this region and were therefore vulnerable to accusations of nationalism. Slezkine, "The USSR as Communal Apartment, or How a Socialist State Promoted Ethnic Particularism," *Slavic Review* 53, no. 2 (Summer 1994): 445–448.

12. Harriet Murav has made the important observation that Soviet Jewish writers indeed developed a Jewish World War II canon, which has not been adequately recognized by past scholars: "Yiddish and Russian literature from the Soviet Union does not emplot the destruction of the Jews in the same manner as Western readers might expect—with a story that describes the unique suffering of the Jews and the unique possibility of their restoration in the state of Israel." Murav, *Music from a Speeding Train: Jewish Literature in Post-Revolutionary Russia* (Stanford, CA: Stanford University Press, 2011), 194.

13. Taras Shevchenko, "Son (Komediia)" (St. Petersburg, 1844), in *Zibrannia tvoriv*, 6 vols. (Kyiv: Naukova dumka, 2003), 1:269.

14. Taras Shevchenko, "A kholem (Komedie)," in *Geklibene verk*, trans. Dovid Hofshteyn (Kyiv: Melukhe-farlag far di natsyonale minderhaytn in USSR, 1939), 63.

15. Dovid Hofshteyn, "In vinter farnakhtn," in *Lider un poemes*, 2 vols. (Tel Aviv: Yisroel-bukh, 1977), 1:28.

16. For Hofshteyn's translations of folksongs, see Dovid Hofshteyn and Itsik Fefer, ed. and trans., *Felker zingen* (Kyiv: Melukhe-farlag far di natsionale minderhaytn in USSR, 1939).

17. Katerina Clark, *Moscow, the Fourth Rome* (Cambridge, MA: Harvard University Press, 2011), 169.

18. Clark, 8.

19. Early Soviet writers were unified in their support of Yiddish. Seth Wolitz, "The Kiev-Grupe (1918–1920) Debate: The Function of Literature," *Studies in American Jewish Literature (1975–1979)* 4, no. 2 (Winter 1978): 100.

20. Kenneth B. Moss has identified 1920–1921 as the moment of transformation of Soviet Yiddish culture into a new, revolutionary mold. Moss, *Jewish Renaissance in the Russian Revolution* (Cambridge, MA: Harvard University Press, 2009), 255.

21. Murav, *Music from a Speeding Train,* 286.

22. Naomi Seidman, *Faithful Renderings: Jewish-Christian Difference and the Politics of Translation* (Chicago: University of Chicago Press, 2010), 154.

23. On Kyiv / Kiev as a Yiddish center after World War I, see Wolitz, "Kiev-Grupe," 97–106.

24. Kenneth B. Moss, "Not the Dybbuk but Don Quixote: Translation, Deparochialization, and Nationalism in Jewish Culture, 1917–1919," in *Culture Front: Representing Jews in Eastern Europe,* ed. Benjamin Nathans and Gabriella Safran (Philadelphia: University of Pennsylvania Press, 2008), 215. Litvakov, according to Moss, praised the group for getting rid of "Jewishy" associations. See Moss, *Jewish Renaissance,* 128.

25. Anthony Appiah, "Thick Translation," *Callaloo* 16, no. 4 (1993): 808–810, reprinted in *The Translation Studies Reader,* 3rd ed., ed. Lawrence Venuti (New York: Routledge, 2012), 341. Harriet Murav and Naomi Seidman have both discussed the relevance of recent postcolonial scholarship on translation to Jewish languages. See Murav, *Music from a Speeding Train,* 286; Seidman, *Faithful Renderings,* 195.

26. Jeffrey Veidlinger, *The Moscow State Yiddish Theater: Jewish Culture on the Soviet Stage* (Bloomington: Indiana University Press, 2000), 2–3.

27. See Moss, "Not the Dybbuk," 230.

28. Taras Shevchenko, "Shche iak buly my kozakamy," in *Zibrannia tvoriv,* 2:48; Shevchenko, "Az mir zaynen geveyn nokh kazakn," in *Geklibene verk,* 134.

29. Lawrence Venuti, "Local Contingencies: Translation and National Identities," in *Nation, Language, and the Ethics of Translation,* ed. Sandra Bermann and Michael Wood (Princeton, NJ: Princeton University Press, 2005), 180.

30. Venuti, 189.

31. Venuti, 196.

32. Venuti, 196.

33. Myroslav Shkandrij has written of the return of these themes of Ukrainian resentment against Jewish representatives of Bolshevism. See Shkandrij, "The Rising Tide of Resentment, 1929–1939," chapter 6 in *Jews in Ukrainian Literature: Representation and Identity* (New Haven, CT: Yale University Press, 2011), 137–165.

34. Clark, *Moscow,* 82.

35. Maksim Gorky to A. I. Yarlykin, January 1, 1929, trans. James McGavran, in *Russian Writers on Translation,* ed. Brian James Baer and Natalia Olshanskaya (Manchester, UK: St. Jerome, 2013), 67.

36. Dovid Hofshteyn to Daniel Charney, from Kyiv, 1927 (letter no. 30), in Altshuler, *Briv fun Yidishe Sovetishe shraybers,* 105. These proletarian writers groups were themselves disbanded in 1932 in favor of even more centralized government unions.

37. Hofshteyn to Charney, from Kharkiv, August 10, 1928 (letter no. 31), in Altshuler, *Briv fun Yidishe Sovetishe shraybers,* 107.

38. Slezkine, "USSR as Communal Apartment," 414.

39. Clark, *Moscow,* 308.

40. David Shneer writes that "by 1939 only 46 percent of Yiddish books were translations or by authors outside the Soviet Union, and the remaining 54 percent were original Soviet Yiddish publications." Shneer, "Who Owns the Means of Cultural Production? The Soviet Yiddish Publishing Industry of the 1920s," *Book History* 6 (2003): 200. Notwithstanding this rate of translation into national minority languages, according to Maurice Friedberg, overall "literary translation declined . . . in the 1930s." Friedberg, *Literary Translation in Russia: A Cultural History* (State College: Pennsylvania State University Press, 1997), 4.

41. Shneer, "Who Owns the Means of Cultural Production?," 209–210.

42. See Moss, "Not the Dybbuk," 218–219.

43. Murav, *Music from a Speeding Train,* 288. Murav cites *Druzhba Narodov* 1 (1939): 6.

44. Brian James Baer, "Literary Translation and the Construction of a Soviet Intelligentsia," *Massachusetts Review* 47, no. 3 (Fall 2006): 539.

45. For a comparison of Pasternak's and Marshak's translations of Shakespeare's sixty-sixth sonnet, see A. Yakobson, "Dva resheniia: Eshche raz o 66-om sonete," in *Masterstvo perevoda, 1966* (Moscow: Sovetskii Pisatel', 1966), 183–260. Tom Dolack discusses this translation in "Lyric Ventriloquism and the Dialogic Translations of Pasternak, Mandelstam and Celan," in *Poetry and Dialogism: Hearing Over,* ed. Mara Scanlon and Chad Engbers (New York: Palgrave Macmillan, 2014), 57–79.

46. Baer, "Literary Translation," 539.

47. Yohanan Petrovsky-Shtern has examined cases where Jews chose to identify with their "anti-imperial" Ukrainian neighbors by writing in Ukrainian. See Petrovsky-Shtern, *The Anti-Imperial Choice: The Making of the Ukrainian Jew* (New Haven, CT: Yale University Press, 2009).

48. Vladimir Jabotinsky, "Urok iubileia Shevchenko," in *Izbrannoe* (St. Petersburg: Gesharim, 1992), 153.

49. On Hofshteyn's Hebrew publications, see Altshuler, *Briv fun Yidishe Sovetishe shraybers,* 97n28; Feyge Hofshteyn, *Mit libe un veytik: Vegn Dovid Hofshteyn* (Tel Aviv: Reshafim, 1985), 17; and Eliezer Podriatshik, "A nakht fun has-goles," in *In profil fun tsaytn* (Tel Aviv: Y. L. Perets Farlag, 1979), 165.

50. *Der emes,* April 20, 1926, quoted in Altshuler, *Briv fun Yidishe Sovetishe shraybers,* 99. See also "Testimony by the Defendants: David Hofshteyn," in *Stalin's Secret Pogrom: The Postwar Inquisition of the Jewish Anti-Fascist Committee,* ed. Joshua Ru-

benstein and Vladimir P. Naumov, trans. Laura Esther Wolfson (New Haven, CT: Yale University Press, 2001), 187.

51. Dovid Hofshteyn, *Bay vegn,* in *Lider un poemes* 1:20.

52. Dobrushin, cited in Wolitz, "Kiev-Grupe," 103. According to Wolitz, "modern Yiddish verse received critical acclaim in direct proportion to the absence of Jewish consciousness." Years later, when Bergelson and Hofshteyn were both arrested as members of the Jewish Anti-Fascist Committee, Bergelson denounced Hofshteyn as a longtime nationalist and Zionist. See "Testimony of the Defendants: David Bergelson," in Naumov and Rubenstein, *Stalin's Secret Pogrom,* 163.

53. Eliezer Podriatshik, *Shmuesn mit andere un mit zikh* (Tel Aviv: Y. L. Perets Farlag, 1984), 61. Citing another of Podriatshik's written accounts, Feyge Hofshteyn writes, "Many years later, in 1940, in a conversation with Eliezer Podriatshik, Hofshteyn said: 'all in all I was in the land of Israel one year, from Pesach 1925 to Pesach 1926, but I will remember the flavor of that year forever. Spiritually I've never left." F. Hofshteyn, *Mit libe un veytik,* 17. F. Hofshteyn cites Podriatshik, *In profil fun tsaytn,* 165.

54. Hofshteyn, *Bay vegn,* 1:18.

55. Alexander Pomerantz, *Inzhenyern fun neshomes* (New York, 1943), 15–17.

56. Alexander Pomerantz, *Proletpen: Etyudn un materyaln tsu der geshikhte fun dem kamf far proletarisher literatur in Amerike* (Kyiv: All-Ukrainian Academy of Science, 1935).

57. Chana Kronfeld, *On the Margins of Modernism: Decentering Literary Dynamics* (Berkeley: University of California Press, 1996), 210.

58. Alexander Cheptsov, et al., "Court Record: The Sentence," in *Stalin's Secret Pogrom,* 489.

59. The current capital of Ukrainian is transliterated Kyiv (Ukrainian) and sometimes Kiev (Russian / Yiddish). I use the current Ukrainian spelling of the city, Kyiv, to refer to the city generally, and the Russian / Yiddish transliteration to refer to the title of Hofshteyn's book.

60. Dovid Hofshteyn, *Kiev (Poeme)* (Kyiv: Melukhe-farlag far di natsionale minderhaytn in USR"R, 1936). Hofshteyn cites the Ukrainian poet Mikhail Ivanovich Tereshchenko (1886–1956), who wrote about this Chinese Red Army soldier in his Ukrainian verse.

61. Hofshteyn, "Mikhaylover monastir," in *Kiev,* 34.

62. Vladimir Drunin, *Taras Shevchenko,* trans. Benyomen Rabinovich, poems and text trans. Dovid Hofshteyn (Kyiv: Kultur-Lige, 1927). On the fate of the Kultur-Lige press, see Moss, "Not the Dybbuk," 218–219. Gennady Estraikh has noted that "among Yiddish writers, Hofshteyn remained particularly committed to translating activities." Estraikh, "The Yiddish Kultur-Lige," in *Modernism in Kyiv: Jubilant Experimentation,* ed. Irene Roma Makaryk and Virlana Tkacz (Toronto: University of Toronto Press, 2010), 211.

63. A. A. Khvylia, *Taras Shevchenko: Der groyser demokrat, der dikhter-revolutsyoner,* trans. Dovid Hofshteyn (Kyiv: Farlag fun der Ukraynisher visnshaftlekher akademye, 1935).

64. Taras Shevchenko, *Zamlung far kinder,* trans. Dovid Hofshteyn (Kyiv: Melukhe-farlag far di natyonale minderhaytn in USSR, 1937).

65. Taras Shevchenko, *Lider,* trans. Dovid Hofshteyn (Kharkiv: Kinder farlag bam ts. K. l. k. Yu. F. u., 1939); Shevchenko, *A shaptsir mit fargenign un nit on moral,* trans. Dovid Hofshteyn (Kyiv: Melukhe-farlag far di natsyonale minderhaytn in USSR, 1939); Shevchenko, *Geklibene verk.*

66. New Soviet editions of Sholem Aleichem's work were published on the occasion of his centennial in 1959. Sholem Aleichem, *Oysgeveylte verk* (Moscow: Melukhe fun kinstlerisher literature, 1959); Sholem Aleichem, *Sobranie sochinenii* (Moscow: Gos. izd-vo. khudozh. lit-ry, 1959–1961).

67. Joshua First discusses the perceived risks of awakening nationalist sensibilities by Shevchenko in the Soviet Union. First, *Ukrainian Cinema: Belonging and Identity during the Soviet Thaw* (New York: Palgrave Macmillan, 2015), 72. Shevchenko embodied Gilles Deleuze and Félix Guattari's notion that, among the characteristics of minor literatures, "everything in them is political" and "everything takes on a collective value." Deleuze and Guattari, *Kafka: Toward a Minor Literature* (Minneapolis: University of Minnesota Press, 1986), 17.

68. N. S. Khrushchev, *The Great Mission of Literature and Art* (Moscow: Progress, 1964), 8. Mayhill Fowler has written of the Kharkiv statue of Shevchenko, which was erected in 1935 and reflected the aspirations and conflicts of the Soviet Ukrainian intelligentsia. See Fowler, *Beau Monde on Empire's Edge: State and Stage in Soviet Ukraine* (Toronto: University of Toronto Press, 2017), 169–171.

69. Shevchenko was a safe choice: Jeffrey Brooks has rightly pointed out that within the selective literary history under construction in Stalin's Russia, "Taras Shevchenko obscured artists more identified with Ukrainian nationalism and independence." Brooks, *Thank You, Comrade Stalin* (Princeton, NJ: Princeton University Press, 2000), 119.

70. For example, tributes to Shevchenko and translations of Shevchenko appeared in *Zaria Vostoka,* March 8, 1939, 1; *Zaria Vostoka,* March 9, 1939, 3; *Sovetskaia Abkhaziia,* March 9, 1939, 3; and *Sovetskaia Abkhaziia,* March 11, 1939, 3.

71. Kornei Chukovsky, *Vysokaia iskusstvo,* in *Sobranie sochinenii v 15 t.* (Moscow: Terra-Knizhnyi klub, 2001), 3:302. In Chukovsky's assessment, these new translations, generally speaking, were far superior in form and accuracy to their pre-Soviet counterparts. Chukovsky, 3:314.

72. Petro Al'tman, *T. G. Shevchenko: Biografishe fartsaykhenung* (Kyiv: Melukhe-farlag far di Natsionale minderhaytn in USSR, 1939), 5.

73. Dovid Hofshteyn, translator's introduction to Taras Shevchenko, *Lider* (Odessa: Kinder-farlag bam Ts. K. L. K. P. O., 1939), 13.

74. Gennady Estraikh, "Soviet Sholem Aleichem," in *Translating Sholem Aleichem: History, Politics and Art,* ed. Gennady Estraikh, Jordan Finkin, Kerstin Hoge, and Mikhail Krutikov (New York: Legenda, 2012), 69.

75. Volodimir Koriak, "Di Ukrainishe Sovetishe literature," *Prolit* 7–8 (July–August 1929): 139.

76. Kofsi, "Vegn hayntiker tematik (loyt D. Hofshteyn)," *Prolit* 5 (May 1929): 84.

77. Dovid Hofshteyn, "Ukrayne," in *Gezamlte verk* (Kyiv: Kultur-Lige, 1923), 158. In this 1923 collection, Hofshteyn renames his cycle "Troyer" with the Latin "Tristiia."

78. Hofshteyn, "Ukrayne," 159.

79. Taras Shevchenko, "Dumka" (1838, St. Petersburg), in *Kobzar,* ed. Mikhail Osipovich Mikeshin (St. Petersburg: P. A. Kulish 1860), 34–35.

80. Dovid Hofshteyn, "Ukrayne," in *Ikh gleyb* (Moscow: Emes, 1944), 29.

81. Susan Layton, *Russian Literature and Empire: Conquest of the Caucasus from Pushkin to Tolstoy* (Cambridge: Cambridge University Press, 1994), 175.

82. D. Hofshteyn, "Ukrayne," 29.

83. Hofshteyn, 29.

84. Party leadership in Ukraine included an overrepresentation of non-Ukrainians, with Russians making up the largest national group at 51.1 percent, followed by Jews at 18.4 percent. See George Liber, *Soviet Nationality Policy, Urban Growth, and Identity Change in the Ukrainian SSR 1923–1934* (Cambridge: Cambridge University Press, 1992), 92.

85. Ukraine played a leading role in developing a presence of national soviets in the 1920s. Terry Dean Martin, *The Affirmative Action Empire: Nations and Nationalism in the Soviet Union, 1923–1939* (Ithaca, NY: Cornell University Press, 2001), 33–37.

86. Shevchenko, "Kavkaz," in *Zibrannia tvoriv,* 1:344.

87. Mikhail Krutikov, *From Kabbalah to Class Struggle: Expressionism, Marxism, and Yiddish Literature in the Life and Work of Meir Wiener* (Stanford, CA: Stanford University Press, 2011), 111.

88. Dovid Hofshteyn, "In Armenie," in *Geklibene verk* (Moscow: Sovetskii Pisatel', 1968), 33. John Efron has discussed Jews' affinity for other colonial subjects, especially Muslims. Efron, "From Mitteleuropa to the Middle East: Orientalism through a Jewish Lens," *Jewish Quarterly Review* 94, no. 3 (Summer 2004): 491–492.

89. Hryhorii Danylovych Epik, "Taras Shevtshenko—der dikhter fun sotsialn kamf," *Royte Velt* 4 (March, 1925): 34.

90. In some cases, the sympathies of the diaspora community were enough to remove a Ukrainian writer from the Soviet canon. For example, Volodimir Koriak writes, "The fact that the foreign Ukrainian fascists showed their sympathy for Khviliovey, speaks for itself." Koriak, "Di hayntike Ukrainishe literature," *Royte Velt* 11 (November 1931): 105.

91. Taras Shevchenko, "Zapovit," in *Tvory*, 3 vols. (Kyiv: Derzh. Vydavnytstvo khudozh. Lit-ry URSR, 1961), 1:332.

92. Taras Shevchenko, "Lider mayne, dumes mayne," in *Geklibene verk*, 116.

93. Chukovsky lamented that even one of the best Soviet Russian-language translators of Shevchenko, Petr Semynin, sacrifices Shevchenko's internal rhymes. Chukovsky, *Vysokaia iskusstvo*, 3:309.

94. Shevchenko, "Dumy moi, dumy moi," in *Tvory*, 1:26.

95. Shevchenko, "Lider mayne, dumes mayne," 49.

96. A few translators have rendered Shevchenko's "Dumy moi" as "My thoughts." See Shevchenko, *Kobzar*, trans. Peter Fedynsky (London: Glagoslav, 2013); and Sergei Fatulov's Russian translations, at http://www.chitalnya.ru/work/340619/ (accessed August 4, 2015).

97. See Jacques Derrida, "Différance," in *Margins of Philosophy*, trans. Alan Bass (Chicago: University of Chicago Press, 1982); for a discussion of Derrida's "play of traces" as it relates to translation, see Edwin Gentzler, *Contemporary Translation Theories*, 2nd ed. (Clevedon, UK: Multilingual Matters, 2001), 157–164.

98. Derrida, *Sovereignties in Question*, 22.

99. Shevchenko, "Dumy moi, dumy moi," 1:28.

100. Shevchenko, "Lider mayne, dumes mayne," 52. Dmytro Chyzhevsky has called this poem "the most outstanding example of Shevchenko's 'secularization' of sacred history." Chyzhevsky, "Shevchenko and Religion," in *Shevchenko and the Critics*, ed. George S. N. Luckyj, trans. Dolly Ferguson and Sophia Yurkevich (Toronto: University of Toronto Press, 1980), 250–266, 258.

101. I thank Tetyana Batanova for calling my attention to the political implications of Hofshteyn's choice of preposition.

102. Dmytro Chyzhevsky, "Shevchenko and Religion," in *Shevchenko and the Critics*, ed. George S. N. Luckyj, trans. Dolly Ferguson and Sophia Yurkevich (Toronto: University of Toronto Press, 1980), 258.

103. Shkandrij, *Jews in Ukrainian Literature*, 30.

104. The theme of the illegitimate child appears across Shevchenko's poetry, particularly in his narratives of peasant women, such as his 1838 "Kateryna," an indictment of the unfair conditions under which serfs lived in the tsarist empire. See George Grabowicz, *The Poet as Mythmaker: A Study of Symbolic Meaning in Taras Ševčenko* (Cambridge, MA: Harvard Ukrainian Research Institute, 1982), 71–72.

105. Shevchenko, "Maria," *Povne zibrannia tvoriv*, 12 vols. (Kyiv: Naukova dumka, 1991), 2:252.

106. Shevchenko, "Maria," *Geklibene verk*, 198.

107. Fume Shames, "Der voylklang in David Hofshteyns lid," *Royte Velt* 6 (1930): 133–134. The article is dated 1927.

108. Leonid Fedorovych Khinkulov, *Taras Shevchenko* (Moscow: Molodaia Gvardiia, 1960), 321.

109. Murav, *Music from a Speeding Train,* 291.

110. Shevchenko, "Maria," translated by Boris Pasternak in *Stikhotvoreniia 1931–1959* (Moscow: Khudozhestvennaia literatura, 1989), 298.

111. Murav, *Music from a Speeding Train,* 291.

112. Shevchenko, "Maria," in *Povne zibrannia tvoriv,* 2:252.

113. Shevchenko, "Maria," in *Stikhotvoreniia,* 298.

114. Shevchenko, "Maria" in *Geklibene verk,* 198.

115. George Grabowicz has argued that these stereotypes are more complex in the work of Shevchenko than in most of his contemporaries' writings. Grabowicz, "The Jewish Theme in Nineteenth- and Early Twentieth-Century Ukrainian Literature," in *Ukrainian-Jewish Relations in Historical Perspective,* ed. Howard Aster and Peter J. Potichnyj (Edmonton: Canadian Institute, University of Alberta, 1988), 332.

116. Al'tman, *Shevchenko,* 44.

117. Khvylia, *Taras Shevtshenko,* 56.

118. Taras Shevchenko, *Progulka s udovol'stviem i ne bez morali* in *Tvory v p'iaty tomakh: Povisti,* 5 vols. (Kyiv: Vyd-vo khudozh. Lit-ry "Dnipro," 1978), 4:228.

119. Taras Shevchenko, *A shpatsir mit fargenign un nit on moral,* trans. Dovid Hofshteyn (Kyiv: Melukhe-farlag far di natsyonale minderhaytn in USSR, 1939), 11.

120. Semyon Lipkin, "Perevod i sovremmenost'," in *Masterstvo perevoda 1959* (Moscow: : Sovetskii Pisatel', 1959), 14.

121. Lipkin, 35.

122. Dovid Hofshteyn to Daniel Charney, 1926 (letter no. 27), in Altshuler, *Briv fun yidishe Sovetishe shraybers,* 101. Lipkin, in his own translations, was engaged in a similar specular process to Hofshteyn's. Harriet Murav, who has discussed Lipkin's translations and poetry in some detail, has written of Lipkin's translation from the Kirghiz, "Lipkin attempts, within the limits of Soviet national politics, to engage a hybrid translation of the other that is also a self-translation." Murav, *Music from a Speeding Train,* 305.

123. Dovid Hofshteyn, "Yo, ikh bin groys dermit . . . ," in Avrom Sutzkever, "Perets Markish un zayn svive," *Goldene Keyt* 43 (1962): 31.

124. Sutzkever, "Perets Markish un zayn svive," 31.

125. Sutzkever, 32. That Sutzkever writes of Jews returning from evacuation by 1944 calls his chronology into question. It is possible that the conversation took place on a subsequent visit, in 1946.

126. Dovid Hofshteyn, "Denkmol Khmelnitskin" (To the memory of Khmelnytsky), in *Kiev: Poeme* (Kyiv: Melukhe-farlag far di natsyonale minderhaytn in USR"R, 1936), 32.

127. Sutzkever, "Perets Markish un zayn svive," 32.

128. D. Hofshteyn, "Denkmol Khmelnitskin," 32. There is an apparent typographical error in the original: in the second line, Hofshteyn writes, "un gemeynt hot *der* tsar," as opposed to "*dem* tsar," making the tsar, inscrutably, a subject rather than a direct object. The error suggests that Hofshteyn wrote the poem quickly and took little time for editing. Sutzkever remembers the title as "Tsum denkmol fun Bogdan Khmelnitski."

129. Hofshteyn, 32.

130. Sutzkever, "Perets Markish un zayn svive," 33; translation: Benjamin Pinkus, *The Soviet Government and the Jews 1948–1967: A Documented Study* (Cambridge, UK: Cambridge University Press, 1984); "Document 100: Sutskever's meeting with Hofshteyn (1962)," 295.

131. Shevchenko, *Zibrannia tvoriv*, 6 vols. (Kyiv: Naukova dumka, 2003), 2:308. I have discussed modern Jewish literary interpretations of the Khmelnytsky uprising at length elsewhere. See Amelia Glaser, "The Heirs of Tul'chyn: A Modernist Reappraisal of Historical Narrative," in *Stories of Khmelnytsky: Competing Literary Legacies of the 1648 Ukrainian Cossack Uprising,* ed. Amelia Glaser (Stanford, CA: Stanford University Press, 2015), 127–138.

6. *TESHUVAH:* MOISHE NADIR'S RELOCATED PASSWORDS

1. Moishe Nadir, *Moyde ani,* ed. Leon Feinberg (New York: Narayev, 1944), 213.

2. J. Arch Getty, "*Samokritika* Rituals in the Stalinist Central Committee, 1933–38," *Russian Review* 58, no. 1 (January 1999): 52.

3. Elias Tcherikower and Yisroel Efroikin, "A Word to the Readers," in *Oyfn Sheydveg: At the Crossroads: Jewish Intellectuals and the Crisis of 1939,* ed. Joshua M. Karlip (Gottingen: Vandenhoeck and Ruprecht, forthcoming in 2021). I am grateful to Dr. Karlip for sharing an unpublished version of his translation with me.

4. *Moyde ani* contains an etching by Yitshokh Likhtenshteyn and a foreword by Leon Faynberg.

5. Translation: Macy Nulman, *The Encyclopedia of Jewish Prayer: The Ashkenazic and Sephardic Rites* (Lanham, MD: Rowman and Littlefield, 1996), 251–252.

6. Ehud Luz has discussed the double meaning of the word *teshuvah,* which can imply either "return" or "reply," with individual and collective implications. Luz notes, "The act of returning to one's original self is thus in and of itself a return to God and his teaching; and this is true on both the individual and the national levels." Luz, "Repentance," in *20th Century Jewish Religious Thought: Original Essays on Critical Concepts, Movements, and Beliefs,* ed. Arthur Allen Cohen and Paul Mendes-Flohr (Philadelphia: Jewish Publication Society, 2009), 785.

7. Moses Maimonides, "Hilchot Teshuvah," in *The Journey of the Soul: Traditional Sources on Teshuvah,* ed. and trans. Leonard S. Karavitz and Kerry M. Olitzky (Northvale, NJ: Jason Aronson, 1995), 229. In the context of Modern Hebrew, *teshuvah* is understood to mean "reply."

8. Alexander Mukdoni (Kappel), "Moyshe Nadir 'Post Mortem,'" *Der Morgen Zhurnal,* September 3, 1944, clipping in Nadir Archive, National Hebrew University Archives, Jerusalem (NHUAJ).

9. Oleg Kharkhordin, *The Collective and the Individual in Russia: A Study of Practices* (Berkeley: University of California Press, 1999), 63. See also Gina Herrmann, who equates Party conversion narratives during the Spanish Civil War to the confessions of Saint Augustine and Santa Teresa. Herrmann, "The Road to Consciousness: Youth and Conversion," in *Written in Red: The Communist Memoir in Spain* (Urbana: University of Illinois Press, 2009), 54–83.

10. Alan Wald warns that in discussing American communism, "The simplistic categories we've inherited of 'card-carrying member' or 'fellow-traveler' fail to accommodate the nuances and hybrids one can find among a range of possible responses." Wald, "From Old Left to New," in *Writing from the Left: New Essays on Radical Culture and Politics* (New York: Verso, 1994), 119. What I refer to as Nadir's "fellow traveler" status in the 1930s was an active support of Soviet communism, without formally joining the Party.

11. The critic Kalman Marmor wrote of Nadir's versatility and of the impossibility of categorizing him. Marmor, "Moyshe Nadirs 'A Lomp Afn Fenster,'" *Frayhayt,* February 18, 1929.

12. Nadir wrote under several pseudonyms, including Rinalde Rinaldini, Dr. Hotsikl, Ana Dona, Ida Shildkroyt, Ben-Meir, Dilenzi Mirkarosh, Y. Strier, R. Naldo, Der Royznkavalier, M. D'nardi, S. Fayerfoygl, and Yud-Ka Rish-zet. See Zalman Reyzen, *Leksikon fun der yiddisher literature, prese un filologie,* vol. 2 (Warsaw: Kletzkin, 1927), 505.

13. Nadir translated, among others, Anatole France, Peter Altenberg, Mark Twain, and Rudyard Kipling, as well as Sholem Aleichem from the Yiddish into English. Nadir edited *Der Groyser Kundes* (The great prankster) and *Der Yidisher Gazlon* (The Jewish bandit). According to Ruth Wisse, Nadir's humor writing was a liability when he joined the modernist Yunge. See Wisse, *A Little Love in Big Manhattan* (Cambridge, MA: Harvard University Press, 1988), 19.

14. See Gennady Estraikh, *In Harness: Yiddish Writers' Romance with Communism* (Syracuse, NY: Syracuse University Press, 2005), 99.

15. Alexander Pomerantz, *Proletpen: Etyudn un materyaln tsu der geshikhte fun dem kamf far proletarisher literature in Amerike* (Kiev: All-Ukrainian Academy of Science, 1935), 7.

16. Di Yunge emerged around 1912 with the journal *Shriftn*, and the Introspectivists formed in 1919 and conglomerated around the journal *In Zikh* (1920-1940).

17. The *In Zikh* editors, particularly Glatshteyn and Glantz-Leyeles, represented a range of Trotskyist beliefs. See Yankev Glatshteyn's discussion of Trotsky as an important critic of Stalin and Soviet communism, in "Mit Trotskin—Vuhin?," *In Zikh* 6, no. 2 (1937): 40-52. Glatshteyn advocates for a united antifascist front that excludes the communists in "Komintern versus idintern," *In Zikh* 19, no. 4 (December 1935): 3-11. In a 1937 editorial, the *In Zikh* editors characterize Aaron Kurtz, president of the Party-affiliated Proletpen group and former *In Zikh* contributor, as a Stalin apologist. See "Refleksies: *Signal*—epitaph oyf a bankrot," *In Zikh* 34 (April 1937): 123-126. Ruth Wisse notes that Leyeles remained closer to the Left until World War II. Wisse, "Language as Fate: Reflections on Jewish Literature in America," in *Literary Strategies: Jewish Texts and Contexts*, ed. Ezra Mendelsohn, Studies in Contemporary Jewry 12 (New York: Oxford University Press, 1996), 138.

18. Reyzen, *Leksikon*, 2:502. Reyzen notes that with Nadir's 1916 volume *Fun mentsh tsu mentsh*, he was recognized as a "stylist" of the Yiddish language.

19. Moishe Nadir, *Vilde royzn: Unshuldike aynfalen* (New York: Yiddish Literary Publishing, 1915), 48.

20. Nadir, 42.

21. Nadir, 3.

22. Moishe Nadir, *Peh-el-Peh*, trans. Joseph Kling, *Improvisations* (New York: Pagan, 1920). The book was published as two books bound into one, with the first half by Nadir and the second, in response, by Kling. Much of the material first appeared in the *Pagan*.

23. Moishe Nadir, "III," in *Fun mentsh tsu mentsh*, in *Zeks bikher*, vol. 2 (New York: Idisher farlag far literature un visenshaft, 1928), 9.

24. Shmuel Niger-Charney, "Vegn Moyshe Nadir," *Tsukunft* 12 (December 1920): 738.

25. For a good discussion of party organization in the early years of the American Communist Party and Jewish Federation, see Tony Michels, *A Fire in Their Hearts: Yiddish Socialists in New York* (Cambridge, MA: Harvard University Press, 2009). Michels deals with the messy permutations of American Jewish communism in particular in chapter 5, "'We Sought a Home for Our Souls': The Communist Gamble," 217-250.

26. See Estraikh, *In Harness*, 70. For Estraikh's reading of Nadir's Party affiliation, see Gennady Estraikh, "Di tragedye fun Moyshe Nadir," *Forverts*, February 3, 2012, https://yiddish2.forward.com/node/4190.html.

27. Photo labeled "Modjacot Shpeel," Nadir Archive, NHUAJ. The name "Modjacot" was used only in 1926 to incorporate Jack Tworkov's name into what was otherwise "Modicut." See John Bell, *Puppets, Masks, and Performing Objects* (Cambridge, MA: MIT Press, 2001), 109.

28. Noah Steinberg, *A bukh Moyshe Nadir* (Leben, 1926), 13. Zalman Reyzen, in his *Leksikon,* compared Nadir favorably to Heinrich Heine, Oscar Wilde, and Sholem Aleichem. Reyzen, *Leksikon,* 2:506–507

29. Reyzen, *Leksikon,* 2:505.

30. "Po Minsku," 1926, Nadir Archive, NHUAJ.

31. Kenneth Wishnia has similarly observed "Nadir's combination of badkhn-esque folk parody and transculturated cosmopolitan literacy." Peretz Markish, "Moyshe Nadir," *Literarishe Bleter,* July 16, 1926, 462, Moishe Nadir, Letters, National Library at Hebrew University, Jerusalem; Kenneth Wishnia, "At Home in Exile: The Living Para-doxes of Moishe Nadir's Early 20th-Century American Yiddish Satire (Discussion and Translation)," *MELUS* 25, no. 1 (April 1, 2000): 62, doi:10.2307 / 468151.

32. Melech Ravitch "Moyshe Nadir Un Zayn 'Heym,'" *Literarishe Bleter,* July 22, 1926, 117.

33. Moishe Nadir, "Moskve," *Der Emes,* November 23, 1926, quoted in Gennady Es-traikh, *Evreiskaia literaturnaia zhizn' Moskvy: 1917–1991* (St. Petersburg: Evropeiskii universitet v Sankt-Peterburge, 2015), 106.

34. Moishe Nadir, view of Moscow from the river, 1926 (?), unsigned, graphite on (onion skin) paper, 4*1523 VI 5, Nadir Archive, NHUAJ. Estraikh notes that Nadir ar-rived in Moscow on August 16, 1926, stayed on Sadovo-Samotechna Street, in the large home of the American businessman Armand Hammer—a stationery magnate. Major Moscow writers came to see Nadir: Kushnirov, Vev'orka, Daniel', and others. See Estraikh, *Evreiskaia literaturnaia zhizn' Moskvy,* 106.

35. Nadir, "M'ken zindikn," *Der Hamer,* September 1927, 28.

36. Nadir, 29.

37. Nadir, *Moyde ani,* 33.

38. Photos labeled "European trip," dated 1926, 4*1523, VI 15, Nadir Archive, NHUAJ.

39. Klara Jung to Moishe Nadir, Moscow, 1927, 4*1523, Nadir Archive, NHUAJ.

40. Moishe Nadir, *Fun mir tsu dir: Humoreskn* (Kiev: Kultur-Lige, 1927).

41. Wisse, *Little Love,* 155. Wisse cites Nadir's personal letter to Ravitch, signed Kovno, October 12, 1926, from the Ravitch Archive, NHUAJ.

42. Nadir, *Moyde ani,* 33.

43. In 1920, Nadir collaborated with Moyshe Leyb Halpern on a play, *Unter dem last fun tselem* (Under the burden of the cross), which was never staged. See Wisse, *Little Love,* 110–113. In Ruth Wisse's analysis, the play was too expressionist, too poetic and internal for the stage in 1920s America. Wisse, 112–113.

44. Joel Schechter, *Messiahs of 1933: How American Yiddish Theatre Survived Ad-versity through Satire* (Philadelphia: Temple University Press, 2008), 10.

45. Lamed Shapiro, "Vegn eynem vos iz nor vos avek," *Sviva,* August 1943, 6.

46. Shapiro, 7. Shapiro, it would seem, never liked Nadir's work. In *Vilde royzn,* Nadir includes a poem about Shapiro's dislike of the book. Nadir, "Vi in a tog bukh," in *Vilde royzn,* 25.

47. Moishe Nadir, "Driter period," in *Derlang aher di velt burzhoi* (New York: Farlag Morgn Frayhayt, 1930), 51

48. Robert Daniels observes that for many communists, the stock-market crash of 1929 vindicated the radical Third Period stance. Daniels, *Russia: The Roots of Confrontation* (Cambridge, MA: Harvard University Press, 1985), 198.

49. Moishe Nadir, "Di tsar-vakkhanalie," *Morgn Frayhayt,* September 14, 1929, 5. Alexander Pomerantz cites this in *Proletpen,* 87.

50. Nadir, "Di tsar-vakkhanalie," 5.

51. The editorial staff added a cautious footnote, noting their own departure from some of Nadir's beliefs, in particular the call for the "deserters" to return.

52. Nadir, "Di tsar-vakkhanalie," 5.

53. Pomerantz, *Proletpen,* 88.

54. Moishe Nadir, "Tsu a teyl Yidishe shrayber," in *Derlang aher di velt, burzhoy! Un andere lider* (New York: Morgn-frayhayt, 1930), 45.

55. Nadir, *Derlang aher di velt, burzshoy!,* 6.

56. Moishe Nadir and Lui Bunin, *Kind on keyt* (New York: Internatsyonaler arbeter ordn, 1936), 65.

57. Pomerantz, *Proletpen,* 101.

58. Brigitte Studer notes that "party members had to offer self-criticism in party and school meetings and evaluate their own work in 'self-reports' (*samootchety*)." Studer, *The Transnational World of the Cominternians* (New York; Palgrave Macmillan, 2015), 73. Sheila Fitzpatrick discusses the ways citizens could manipulate their "file selves" in *Tear Off the Masks! Identity and Imposture in Twentieth-Century Russia* (Princeton, NJ: Princeton University Press, 2005), 16–18.

59. Igal Halfin, *Red Autobiographies: Initiating the Bolshevik Self* (Seattle: University of Washington Press, 2011), 4.

60. This phrase is attributed to Stalin, who allegedly coined the term at a meeting at Maksim Gorky's home on October 26, 1932. See Irina Gutkin, *The Cultural Origins of the Socialist Realist Aesthetic, 1890–1934* (Evanston, IL: Northwestern University Press, 1999), 51. Gutkin cites Anthony Kemp-Welch, *Stalin and the Literary Intelligentsia, 1828–39* (New York: Palgrave-McMillan, 1991), 131.

61. Party members were not the first to translocate *teshuvah* into nonreligious terms. Marcus Moseley, in his analysis of Moshe Leyb Lilienblum's *Derekh teshuvah,* illuminates a case where secular interpretations for *teshuvah* could pattern a pre-Revolutionary Russian Jewish life narrative. Moseley discusses Lilienblum's changing conception of *teshuvah,* "which in 1877 he equated with secular studies, *Shtudium,*" to a more tradi-

tional "return to the [Jewish] people" by 1892. Moseley, *Being for Myself Alone: Origins of Jewish Autobiography* (Stanford, CA: Stanford University Press, 2006), 374.

62. Dovid Hofshteyn, "A briv in redaktsye," *Der Emes,* April 20, 1926, 3. Hofshteyn wrote in a subsequent letter to *Der Emes* on April 23, 1926, condemning English imperialism in Palestine. See Mordechai Altshuler, ed., *Briv fun Yidishe Sovetishe shrayber* (Jerusalem: Hebrew University in Jerusalem, Centre for Research and Documentation of East-European Jewry, 1979), 99–100. As Gennady Estraikh has found, even Bergelson's and Hofshteyn's self-critical letters in their bid to join the Party were not universally accepted. The Soviet writer David Volkenshteyn, for example, wrote to H. Leivick on June 19, 1926, "Bergelson and Hofshteyn are spiritually people of the *same* type. They always keep in mind one objective—fame and money. . . . This is how everyone here understands Bergelson's letter: as Bergelson's *maneuver.*" Quoted in Estraikh, "David Bergelson in and on America, 1927–1949," in *David Bergelson: From Modernism to Socialist Realism,* ed. Joseph Sherman and Gennady Estraikh (London: Legenda, 2007), 209.

63. Mordechai Altshuler cites this letter in *Briv fun Yidishe Sovetishe shrayber,* 80. Altshuler writes of Hofshteyn's April 20, 1926 open letter in *Der Emes* that a collective of Yiddish writers, on April 25, 1926, agreed that there was still a place for Hofshteyn to contribute to Soviet literature. (Altshuler cites *Der Emes,* April 28, 1926). Estraikh has discussed Bergelson's surprising popularity following his public "conversion" from the socialist *Forverts* to the communist *Frayhayt.* Estraikh, "Bergelson in and on America," 210.

64. Altshuler, *Briv fun Yidishe Sovetishe shrayber,* 100.

65. Dovid Bergelson, "A briv fun Dovid Bergelson," *Der Emes,* March 2, 1926, 3; Harriet Murav, *David Bergelson's Strange New World: Untimeliness and Futurity* (Bloomington: Indiana University Press, 2018), 209.

66. Bergelson, "A briv fun Dovid Bergelson," 3.

67. The American Yiddish writer Isaac Platner, for example, settled in the Soviet Union, where he was eventually arrested and sent to a gulag in 1949. See Estraikh, *In Harness,* 101.

68. Fitzpatrick, *Tear Off the Masks!,* 168.

69. "Di arbeter entfern di soynim fun der 'Morgn-Frayhayt,'" *Frayhayt,* September 16, 1929, 2.

70. Aaron Glantz-Leyeles, "Der kinstler in der gezelshaft" (The artist in society), *Vokh,* January 24, 1930, quoted in Pomerantz, *Proletpen,* 146.

71. Editorial notes, *Vokh* 1 (October 4, 1929): 1–2. Pomerantz discusses this article in *Proletpen,* 108–109.

72. Eitan Kensky, "Facing the Limits of Fiction: Self-Consciousness in Jewish American Literature" (PhD diss., Harvard University, 2013), 171. Kensky cites Moishe

Nadir, "The Writer in a Minority Language," in *American Writers' Congress,* ed. Henry Hart (New York: Jewish Book Company, 1929), 156.

73. After leaving the *Morgn Frayhayt,* Nadir wrote for *Der Tog* but complained that his salary of thirty dollars per week was too little to support him. In a letter of March 18, 1941, to the Y. L. Peretz Writers Union, he asks the union to intervene to raise his salary. See File 4*1523, Nadir Archive, NHUAJ. Estraikh discusses the café in *Evreiskaia literaturnaia zhizn' Moskvy,* 106.

74. On Halpern's death, see Wisse, *Little Love,* 193–204.

75. H. Leivick to Hirschbein and Shumiatcher, October 1, 1930, Peretz Hirschbein file, folder 23, YIVO Archive, New York. Leivick worked, for much of his life, as a wallpaper hanger.

76. Moishe Nadir, "A velt mit arbet," quoted in Pomerantz, *Proletpen,* 105.

77. Leivick to Hirschbein and Shumiatcher, October 1, 1930.

78. Vladimir V. Mayakovsky, "Kemp 'Nit Gedaige,'" in *Polnoe sobranie sochinenii v 13 tomakh,* vol. 7 (Moscow: Khudozh. lit., 1955–1961), 88–91. Mayakovsky dated the poem September 20, 1925 (91). Photo: 4*1523 VI 17, Nadir Archive, NHUAJ. For a description of the camp, which enjoyed frequent visits by poets and artists, see Norbert Evdaev, "Maiakovskii v N'iu-Iorke," in *David Burliuk v Amerike* (Moscow: Nauka, 2002), 122–123.

79. Yuri Slezkine and Bernard Wasserstein discuss the increased reliance on territories to define Soviet ethnicity: Slezkine, "The USSR as a Communal Apartment, or How a Socialist State Promoted Ethnic Particularism," *Slavic Review* 53, no. 2 (Summer 1994): 444; Wasserstein, *On the Eve: The Jews of Europe before the Second World War* (New York: Simon and Schuster, 2012), 52.

80. Dovid Katz attributes the exclusion of Soviet sympathizers from the Yiddish canon to the conservative strain in Cold War US literary studies: "Whoever left the Línke for the Rékhte after the Hebron riots of 1929 was completely kosher. Whoever left after the Ribbentrop-Molotov pact of 1939 was sufficiently kosher. But those who waited until confirmation of the Moscow murders of the writers in 1952 were banished from the canon." Katz, "The Days of Proletpen in American Yiddish Poetry," in *Proletpen: America's Rebel Yiddish Poets,* ed. Amelia Glaser and David Weintraub, trans. Amelia Glaser (Madison: University of Wisconsin Press, 2005), 13.

81. Alexander Pomerantz, *Di Sovetishe harugey-malkhus: Tsu zeyer 10tn yortsayt: Vegen dem tragishn goyrl fun di Yidishe shraybers un der Yidisher literatur in Sovetnland* (Buenos Aires: Yidisher Visnshaftlekher Institut-Yivo, 1962).

82. Moishe Nadir, untitled poem, *Signal,* November 1936, 5.

83. Nadir, *Moyde ani,* 10.

84. On the theme of "survivor guilt" in Jewish literature, see Sarika Talve-Goodman's dissertation, "Cultural Scars: The Poetics of Trauma and Disability in 20th Century Jewish Culture" (PhD diss., University of California–San Diego, 2016).

85. Nadir, *Moyde ani,* 25.

86. Nadir, 23.

87. Reyzen, *Leksikon,* 2:500.

88. Fitzpatrick, *Tear Off the Masks!,* 91.

89. Shakhne Epshteyn, a Comintern agent, together with Moyshe Olgin, founded the *Frayhayt* in 1922. It is likely that one of the two was colleague "X." See Gennady Estraikh, *Yiddish and the Cold War* (London: Legenda, 2008), 5.

90. Halfin, *Red Autobiographies,* 4.

91. Nadir, *Moyde ani,* 30.

92. Nadir, 30.

93. Nadir, 32.

94. Nadir, 32.

95. Nadir, 32.

96. Nadir, 33.

97. Arthur Koestler, in *The God That Failed,* rev. ed., ed. Richard Crossman (New York: Columbia University Press, 2001), 16.

98. Richard Wright, in Crossman, *The God That Failed,* 162.

99. Nadir, *Moyde ani,* 128–129.

100. Noakh Shteynberg, "Dos likht vos iz zekumen tsu shpet (vegn dem nayem bukh fun Moyshe Nadir, vos iz itst dershinen nokh zayn toyt in 1943) Part I," *Fraye Arbeter Shtime,* January 19, 1945, 7.

101. Shapiro, "Vegn eynem vos iz nor vos avek," 7.

102. Leonid Faynberg, foreword to Nadir, *Moyde ani,* 14.

103. Nadir, *Moyde ani,* 34.

104. Nadir, 24.

105. David Lederman, *Fun yener zayt forhang* (From the other side of the curtain) (Buenos Aires, 1960), 108. Joshua Rubenstein cites this passage in *Stalin's Secret Pogrom: The Postwar Inquisition of the Jewish Anti-Fascist Committee* (New Haven, CT: Yale University Press, 2001), 6.

106. Harriet Murav, *Music from a Speeding Train: Jewish Literature in Post-Revolution Russia* (Stanford, CA: Stanford University Press, 2011), 172.

107. David Hartman, *Maimonides: Torah and Philosophic Quest,* exp. ed. (New York: Jewish Publication Society, 2009), 151. Hartman cites *M.T., Hilkhot Teshuvah,* VII, 5, pp. 89a–89b.

108. Zvi Miller, *30 Days to Teshuvah: A Mussar Guide Based on Ohr Yisrael* (Southfield, MI: Targum, 2005), 20.

109. Nadir, *Moyde ani,* 215.

110. Nadir, 215.

111. Nadir, 216.

112. Nadir, 217.

113. Kensky, "Facing the Limits of Fiction," 210.

114. Ada Glazer to Moishe Nadir, September 21, 1941, 1, 4*1523 I-71, Nadir Archive, NHUAJ.

115. Aaron Glantz-Leyeles to Moishe Nadir, Rosh Hashanah Eve 1941, 1-2, 4*1523 Z-72, Nadir Archive, NHUAJ.

116. Glantz-Leyeles to Nadir.

117. Shmuel Leshtsinski, "Moyshe Nadir un zayn yerushe," *Fraye Arbeter Shtime,* April 20, 1945, Moishe Nadir Letters, National Library at Hebrew University, Jerusalem.

118. Hirsh Fugl (Vogel) to Moishe Nadir, c/o *Der Tog,* postmarked May 6, 1940, 4*1523. Nadir Archive, NHUAJ.

119. Moishe Nadir to Yankev Glatshteyn, November 15, 1941, 4*1523 I: 71-a, Nadir Archive, NHUAJ.

120. Melech Ravitch suggested in 1926 that Nadir's love of his former shtetl, Narayev, replaced God for him. "They say that the last and only word that Anatole France uttered a minute before his death was the word 'mother.' Believers say 'God.' . . . Every time Moishe Nadir says this word Galitsie, it sounds like Anatole-France's 'mother.'" Ravitch, "Moyshe Nadir un zayn 'Heym,'" 3. Narayev plays an important role in Nadir's last book: a section is devoted to the town.

121. Yankev Glatshteyn, "A gute nakht, velt," *In Zikh* 3, no. 8 (1938): 66-67.

122. Nadir to Glatshteyn, November 15, 1941, 4*1523, Nardir Archive, NHUAJ.

123. Moishe Nadir to H. Leivick, November 13, 1941, 1, 4*1523 I: 137, Nadir Archive, NHUAJ.

124. H. Leivick to Moishe Nadir, November 14, 1941, 4*1523 I: 137-a, Nadir Archive, NHUAJ.

125. Harry P. Nasuti, "Plumbing the Depths: Genre Ambiguity and Theological Creativity in the Interpretation of Psalm 130," in *The Idea of Biblical Interpretation: Essays in Honor of James L. Kugel,* ed. Hindy Najman and Newman (Leiden: Brill, 2004), 95.

126. It was also Martin Luther's favorite psalm, and Augustine believed "the voice in this psalm is that of one who is faithful and who prays with the heart." Nasuti, 110, 112.

127. Nasuti, 95.

128. Nadir, "Memameykim," *Moyde ani,* 41. This translation slightly alters my own earlier translation of this poem in Glaser and Weintraub, *Proletpen,* 311.

129. H. Leivick, "Lider tsu der baremhertsiker shvester," in *Ale verk fun H. Leyvik,* vol. 1, *Poems* (New York: Posy-Shoulson, 1940), 550-551.

130. Ira Eisenstein, "Kaplan as Liturgist," in *The American Judaism of Mordecai M. Kaplan,* ed. Emanuel Boldsmith, Mel Scult, and Robert Seltzer (New York: NYU Press, 1990), 320.

131. Nadir, *Moyde ani,* 213.

132. Nadir, 214.

133. Hans-Georg Gadamer, *Gadamer on Celan: "Who Am I and Who Are You?" and Other Essays,* ed. and trans. Richard Heinemann and Bruce Krajewski (Albany: SUNY Press, 1997), 171, 173.

134. Leon Faynberg, "Di legende Moyshe Nadir," *Der Tog,* June 9, 1943. Mukdoni explicitly disagrees with Faynberg, saying Nadir was merely a great writer, just as a virtuosic violinist cannot be considered a great Jew. Mukdoni, "Moyshe Nadir 'Post Mortem.'"

135. Ghenye Nadir later cited this passage in response to Niger-Charney's claim that Tabachnik wrote apologetically about Nadir. Avrom Tabachnik, "Vegn Moyshe Nadirn," *Tsukunft,* September 1943, 542; Nadir, "An open letter from Ghenya Nadir about Shmuel Niger," 1944, 4*1521 I 156-a, Nadir Archive, NHUAJ.

136. Shea Tenenboym, "Moyshe Nadir—Der farvunderter piero," *Proletarisher Gedank,* July 1, 1943, Nadir, Letters, National Library at Hebrew University, Jerusalem.

137. "Vegn Moyshe Nadirs lider-bukh 'Moyde Ani' (oykh vegen Moyshe Nadir mit politik—un politik mit Moyshe Nadir)," anonymous review, *Keneder Odler,* January 19, 1945, clipping in Nadir Archive, NHUAJ.

138. Shapiro, "Vegn eynem vos iz nor vos avek," 5. Shapiro is referencing a teaching of Maimonides from the *Mishnah Yoma Khet tet.*

139. Shapiro, 5.

140. Mukdoni, "Moyshe Nadir 'Post Mortem.'"

141. Mukdoni. Further, Mukdoni writes, "And here he is supposed to be a ba'al *teshuvah;* he begs forgiveness and pardon of everyone, whose drops of blood he spilled with his pen."

142. Shteynberg, "Dos likht vos iz gekumen tsu shpet," 5.

143. Shteynberg, 5. Shteynberg references what he considers to be narcissistic poems from *Moyde ani:* "To kiss one's own lips with desire— / and to kiss the mirror that kissed you. / To serve with oneself the self-full God / and following the traces of one's own steps." Nadir, *Moyde ani,* 46.

144. Faynberg, "Di legende Moyshe Nadir."

145. Elias Tcherikower, "The Tragedy of a Weak Generation," in *Oyfn Sheydveg.*

146. Tabachnik, "Vegn Moyshe Nadirn," 542.

147. Samuel Margoshes credits Nadir with leading the exodus from the Party. Margoshes, "Dialogue on Communism: Vincent Shean and Moyshe Nadir, the Road Back, a Piece of Advice," n.d., sec. News and Views. Nadir Archive, NHUAJ.

148. Moishe Nadir, "Ober mir vos zol ton? (A brivl tsu Khaim Grinbergn)," *Idisher Kempfer,* March 5, 1943, 7.

149. Hannah Arendt, "The Ex-Communists," in *Essays in Understanding, 1930–1954* (New York: Schocken, 1994), 393.

150. Faynberg, foreword to *Moyde ani,* 16.

151. Faynberg, 17–19.

AFTERWORD: KADDISH

1. Aaron Kurtz, "A milion por shikh," in *Lider* (New York: Aaron Kurtz Book Committee, 1966), 120.

2. Aaron Kurtz, "A Million Pairs of Shoes," trans. Olga Cabral, *New Currents* 2, no. 9 (1944): 29.

3. Moyshe Teyf, "Vilne, Zumer 1944," in *Oysderveylts: Lider, poemes, balades* (Moscow: Sovetskii pisatel', 1965), 17.

4. Teyf, 17.

5. In prison, Teyf wrote his "Tyurme-lider" (Prison poems), which remained unpublished in the Soviet Union. Teyf shifted to writing in Russian at the end of his life. "Moyshe Teyf," in *Kratkaia evreiskaia entsiklopediia*, ed. Iskhak Oren, vol. 8 (Jerusalem: Obshchestvo po issledovaniiu evreiskikh obshchin, 1998), 921–922.

6. Katie Trumpener, "Comintern Media Experiments, Leftist Exile, and World Literature from East Berlin," in *Comintern Aesthetics,* ed. Steven S. Lee and Amelia M. Glaser (Toronto: University of Toronto Press, 2020), 490. See also Jelena Subotić, *Yellow Star, Red Star: Holocaust Remembrance after Communism* (Ithaca, NY: Cornell University Press, 2019), 19; Zvi Gitelman, *Jewish Identities in Postcommunist Russia and Ukraine: An Uncertain Ethnicity* (Cambridge: Cambridge University Press, 2012), 227.

7. Judith Deutsch Kornblatt has written about the connections between dissident communities in the Soviet 1960s and Zionism. Kornblatt, *Doubly Chosen: Jewish Identity, the Soviet Intelligentsia, and the Russian Orthodox Church* (Madison: University of Wisconsin Press, 2004), 82.

8. Steven S. Lee, *"Borat,* Multiculturalism, *Mnogonatsional'nost',"* *Slavic Review* 67, no. 1 (Spring 2008): 19.

9. Steven S. Lee, *The Ethnic Avant-Garde: Minority Cultures and World Revolution* (New York: Columbia University Press, 2015), 152.

10. Harriet Murav, *Music from a Speeding Train: Jewish Literature in Post-Revolution Russia* (Stanford, CA: Stanford University Press, 2011), 203.

11. Peretz Markish, *Tsu a Yidisher tentserin* (Ramat Gan: Masada, 1976); Markish, Milkhome, 2 vols. (New York: Ikuf, 1956). For an excellent discussion of Markish's postwar writing, see Anna Elena Torres, "The Horizon Blossoms and the Borders Vanish: Peretz Markish's Poetry and Anarchist Diasporism," *Jewish Quarterly Review* 110, no. 3 (Summer 2020), 458–490.

12. Avrom Sutzkever, "Perets Markish un zayn svive," *Goldene Keyt* 43 (1962): 29.

13. Olga Gershenson has noted that, "At the time, Korczak's diary was one of the few Holocaust-related stories allowed to be discussed in the Soviet Union. That is because the events described by Korczak took place outside the USSR: in Warsaw ghetto and in Treblinka, one of the camps in Poland that the Soviets liberated." Gershenson,

The Phantom Holocaust: Soviet Cinema and Jewish Catastrophe (New Brunswick, NJ: Rutgers University Press, 2013), 115.

14. Alexander Galich, "Kadish" in *Pesni. Stikhi. Poemy. Kinopovest'. P'esa. Stat'i* (Ekaterinburg, Russia: U-Faktoriia, 1998), 328.

15. Alexander Galich, *Dress Rehearsal,* trans. Maria Bloshteyn (Bloomington, IN: Slavica, 2008) 121. Victoria Khiterer includes this exchange in her discussion of Soviet Jews in Galich's play *Matrosskaia tishina.* Khiterer, "Life and Fate of Soviet Jews in Aleksandr Galich's Play *Matrosskaia Tishina* and the Film *Papa,*" in *The Holocaust: Memories and History,* ed. Khiterer (Cambridge, UK: Cambridge Scholars, 2014), 214.

16. Grace Paley, "Conversations in Moscow," in *Just as I Thought* (New York: Farrar, Straus and Giroux, 1999), 101.

17. Alexander Galich "Poema o Staline," in *Pesni. Stikhi.,* 317.

18. Allen Ginsberg, "Kaddish," in *The Essential Ginsberg* (New York: HarperCollins, 2015), 47.

19. Leonard Bernstein, Symphony No. 3, "Kaddish," 1963.

20. David Shyovitz, "'You Have Saved Me from the Judgment of Gehenna': The Origins of the Mourner's Kaddish in Medieval Ashkenaz," *AJS Review* 39, no. 1 (April 2015): 49–73.

21. Allen R. Grossman, *The Long Schoolroom: Lessons in the Bitter Logic of the Poetic Principle* (Ann Arbor: University of Michigan Press, 1997), 158.

22. Olga Cabral, "At the Jewish Museum" in *Voice/Over: Selected Poems* (Albuquerque, NM: West End Press, 1993), 83.

23. Olga Cabral, "Shlusvort," in Kurtz, *Lider,* 369.

24. Aaron Kurtz, "Kadesh," in *Lider,* 307.

25. Kurtz, 308.

26. Kurtz, 308.

ACKNOWLEDGMENTS

This project began, in some sense, two decades ago when I was a masters student at the University of Oxford, and I am grateful to those advisors and cultural figures who were instrumental in my master's thesis on the Party-aligned American Proletpen poets, and in the publication in 2005 of a volume of my translations—*Proletpen, America's Rebel Yiddish Poets*. They include Joel Berkowitz, Dovid Katz, Dov-Ber Kerler, Miriam Trinh, Shoshana Volkovich, and the late Itche Goldberg. What became clear to me in translating the Proletpen poets was that they deserve to be discussed, explored, and engaged in all of their complexity. I therefore returned to the Party-aligned Yiddish poets over ten years (and a couple of projects) later, for by then I recognized that the story they have to tell us is not only a story of transnational Yiddish poetry, but of how identity is reassigned and reconsidered during times of struggle.

Many colleagues have helped me to tell this story. Steven Lee has, in addition to reading much of my work in draft form, led me to deepen my engagement with this moment by coediting with me a volume, *Comintern Aesthetics*. Harriet Murav, Marc Caplan, and Joshua Karlip read the entire manuscript at crucial stages. Daniel Kennedy carefully checked my Yiddish translations and transliterations, and Mira Balberg helped me understand several significant historical passwords. Many colleagues have read parts of this book, offered advice, or assisted me with sources: Zachary Baker, Elissa Bemporad, Peter Carroll, Katerina Clark, Hillel Cohen, Jeremy Dauber, Valera Dymshits, Gennady Estraikh, Kathryn Hellerstein, Dovid Katz, Sabine Koller, Mikhail Krutikov, Lital Levy, Serena Mayeri, David Mazower, Efim Melamed, Tony Michels, Kenneth Moss, Kevin Platt, Eddy Portnoy, Alyssa Quint, Harsha Ram, Ronald Robboy, Natalia Roudakova, Allison Schachter, Naomi Seidman, Sasha Senderovich, Marci Shore, Nariman Skakov, Sam Spinner, Sheera Talpaz, Kyla Wazana Tompkins, Anna Torres, Alan Wald, Stephanie Weissman, Ruth Wisse, Tetyana Yakovleva. I am especially grateful to have local friends and colleagues at UC San Diego who have read or discussed this project with me at various stages. Thanks in particular to Luis Martin Cabrera, Steven Cassedy, Dennis Childs, Michael Davidson, Robert Edelman, Marc Garallik, Deborah Hertz, Stephanie Jed, Scott Klemmer, Lisa Lampert-Weissig, Seth Lerer, Sal Nicolazzo, Bill Propp, Pamela Radcliffe, Erin Suzuki, and Elena Yulaeva. My graduate school mentors have, to my great fortune, continued to encourage me and to engage with my work in progress: Grisha Freidin, Monika Greenleaf, Dov-Ber Kerler, Gabriella Safran, and Steven Zipperstein. My graduate students have inspired me with their own work and are often the shrewdest of interlocutors. Special thanks go to Julia Fermentto-Tsaisler and Evelyn Vaquez, who worked with me as research assistants, as well as to Kevin Hart, Teresa Kuruc, Yuliya Ladygina, Olga Lazitsky, Maggie Levantovskaya, Stephen Mandiberg, Sarika Talve-Goodman, Adriana Tosun, Xiaojiao Wang, and Beatrice Waterhouse. These colleagues are in no way responsible for any shortcomings of this book, but I am grateful for their wisdom and generosity.

Thank you to the editorial team at Harvard University Press. In particular, I am grateful to Kathleen McDermott, Kathi Drummy, and Mihaela Pacurar for believing in the project, to Stephanie Vyce for her expertise and assistance in obtaining permissions, and to Andrew Katz and Karen Woerner for their editorial work, to Enid L. Zafran for the index, and to Mary Ribesky, who meticulously oversaw the production of the book. This is a work of salvage literary history, and as such, I have relied heavily on archival collections and interlibrary loans. I'd like to thank the Israel Library at Hebrew University in Jerusalem, the archivists and librarians at the YIVO institute, Harvard University's Widener Library, Stanford University's Green Library, the New York Public Library, the Howard Gottlieb Archival Research Center at Boston University, and UCSD's Geisel Library, with particular thanks to UCSD's interlibrary loan office and Special Collections. I am grateful to UCSD's Institute for Arts and Humanities, which awarded me a manuscript forum fellowship, and to UCSD's Academic Senate and Jewish Studies Program for helping to support research travel. I finished editing this manuscript in the Spring of 2020, when most of the world's libraries were on lock-down due to the global Covid-19 pandemic. Friends, colleagues, and librarians have helped me to track down needed sources, often from home libraries, and I am ever grateful for the wide network of scholars of the humanities. Thanks, in particular, to Ryan Beard, Ofer Dynes, Roe Grinwald, and Steven Schick.

Chapter 3 builds on ideas first discussed in "From Jewish Jesus to Black Christ: Race Violence in Leftist Yiddish Poetry," *Studies in American Jewish Literature* 34, no. 1 (2015): 44–69. Much of Chapter 4 was first published as "In the Shadow of the Inquisition" from *Comintern Aesthetics*, a work I edited with Steven Lee that was published in 2020 by the University of Toronto Press. Portions of Chapter 5 were first published as "Jewish Alienation through a Ukrainian Looking Glass," *Prooftexts* 36, nos. 1–2 (2017): 83–110. Chapter 6 reprints sections of text from "Mixed into Nothingness," *Modernism* 26, no. 1 (2019): 141–165. I thank these publications for permission to reprint these texts here. I am also grateful to Lea Dar, David Markish, Margo Glantz, Shula Shoenfeld, Pamela Lavitt, Jessica Hirschbein, the younger Peretz Hirschbein, Joel Leivick, and Yvette Marin for allowing me to reprint the text of poetry and my translations in this work. I thank Craig Gropper, Richard Steinberg, and the UCSD Library's Special Collections for their permission to use images in this book.

Finally, I thank my family. My parents, John and Carol Glaser, believe in compassionate communication, and I dedicate this book to them. My sister Bronwyn Glaser asks the right questions. Much of this book was drafted during my sleepless, but emotionally exuberant, parental leave and sabbatical, during the year after Lior Glaser Mukamel was born, in 2013, and I resumed work on it in 2015–16, during the miraculously generous naps of my second child, Mirah Glaser Mukamel. Both Lior and Mirah have taught me to read slowly, and to explain what I mean. Eran Mukamel has read, discussed, and occasionally questioned my ideas, and has lovingly made my passions his own.

INDEX

Aberbach, David, 273n56
Adorno, Theodor, 269n3
aestheticism, 92–93, 96, 130, 216
African Americans: crucifixion
  imagery and, 119–126; empathy
  with, 108, 109, 110–111, 245, 249–250;
  passwords and, 11, 126–134; Yiddish
  modernism and, 111–119. *See also*
  Scottsboro Nine
Agnew, Jeremy, 276n89
Agnon, S. Y., 283n63
al-Aqsa Mosque, 74
Albatros (journal), 25, 41, 113
al-Hussayni, Amin (Grand Mufti of
  Jerusalem), 74, 81, 130
Allan, Lewis. *See* Meeropol, Abel
All-Russian Association of Prole-
  tarian Writers (VAPP), 184
All-Ukrainian Union of Soviet
  Writers (VUSPP), 191
Altenberg, Peter, 321n13
Al'tman, Petro, 190–191, 205
Altshuler, Mordechai, 225, 325n63

American Jewish Joint Distribution
  Company, 63
American Writers' Congress, 215, 226
Appiah, Anthony, 181, 203
Arendt, Hannah, 36, 137–138, 143,
  168, 240
Asch, Sholem, 69, 103, 113; "In a
  karnival nakht" (On a carnival
  night), 296n22
Ashkenazi Jews, 15, 147; Ashkenazi
  pronunciation of Hebrew, 54, 213,
  283n60, 286n1
Auden, W. H.: *Spain, 1937*, 140, 143
avant-garde literature, 25, 33, 34, 49,
  55, 151, 247

Bachman, Merle, 115, 128, 295n19,
  300n77
Baer, Brian, 186
Bagish, Zishe: *Dos gezang fun
  neger-folk* (The song of the Negro
  people), 109–110
Bakhtin, Mikhail, 38, 166

Baron, Salo Wittmayer, 156, 307n74

Bartal, Israel, 288n29

Baudrillard, Jean, 10, 33

Bazhan, Mykola, 179

Beevor, Antony, 169

Benjamin, Walter, 14, 42, 68, 148–149, 305n39

Bergelson, Dovid: arrest of and execution of, 9, 229; Communist Party and, 34–35, 225; Crimea and, 64; *Frayhayt* and, 97, 325n63; on Hofshteyn, 187; Jewish Anti-Fascist Committee and, 315n52; Kiev-grupe and, 25, 181; Teyf and, 85, 289n38

Berkman, Alexander, 12

Bernstein, Leonard, 247–248

Bhabha, Homi, 13, 16, 271n27

Bialik, Chaim Nachman, 14, 35, 52, 56, 69, 77, 181–182, 285n101; "B'ir haHaregah" (In the city of slaughter), 21, 54–55, 66, 72, 76, 83, 85–86, 244, 250, 273n56, 289n34, 290n43

Blok, Alexander, 24, 46, 158

Bloom, Harold, 96

Bloomgarden, Solomon. *See* Yehoash

Bloshteyn, Hirsh, 175, 200, 210

Blum, Leon, 172

Bolshevik Revolution, 5, 19, 22, 24, 50, 59, 62, 79, 83, 146, 159; image of the Bolshevik, 35, 67–68, 154, 160, 219, 281n34, 310n132, 171–172; Jewish culture after, 22, 180, 187; and messianism, 86; Perekop battle in, 68, 159; world revolution and, 61, 282n50;

Boreysho, Menachem, 78, 91, 98, 103, 135, 216, 218, 222, 287n9

Brandenberger, David, 274n76

Brecht, Bertolt, 1, 4, 36, 142, 143, 162

Brooks, Jeffrey, 316n68

Brotherhood of Saints Cyril and Methodius, 178

Brown, John, 121, 298n45

Bukh, Alexander, 47, 281n30, 282n46, 282n50

Bukharin, Nikolai, 28, 276n89

Cabral, Olga, 243–244, 249, 272n38; "At the Jewish Museum," 248

Caplan, Marc, 127, 269n3, 271n30, 295n19

Carner, Josep: "Castillian Cat," 182–183

Carroll, Lewis: *Alice in Wonderland*, 182

Carroll, Peter, 302n2

Carter, Dan, 299n63

Caruth, Cathy, 52

Celan, Paul, 175, 198; "As One," 168–169

Chagall, Marc, 113, 119, 143, 144, 304n22

Chapaev, Vasily, 171, 310n132

Charney, Daniel, 184, 207, 225

Chernikhovsky, Saul, 87

Chikovani, Simon, 176

Childs, Dennis, 298n42

China: Hirschbein on, 51; internationalism in, 46–52, 185; Shumiatcher in, 45–46, 52–60, 66; Yangtze River in, 48, 49–50, 59–60; Soviet interest in, 34, 68

Chukovsky, Kornei, 190, 316n71, 318n93

Chyzhevsky, Dmytro, 200, 318n100

Cimet, Adina, 152

Clark, Katerina, 30, 47, 53–54, 86, 179, 184–185, 270n12, 282n49

Coates, Ta-Nehisi, 135
Cohen, Hillel, 76, 79
colonialism (and anticolonialism), 38, 74–75, 79, 164, 280n22, 290n48, 313n25
Communist International, 42, 110, 229, 245, 289n40, 290n47, 290n48, 305n26; African Americans and, 32, 111; Arab uprising and, 7, 73, 75–77, 86, 91, 95, 97, 104, 136; East Asia and, 45; founding and dissolution of, 6, 28, 215, 218, 228, 245; *Frayhayt* and, 34–35, 94; Spain and, 140–141, 143, 145, 154, 159, 165, 172–173, 304n19; Russia as center of, 40, 179, 184, 186, 219; Sixth Comintern Congress, 5, 28, 87, 221, 276n89;
Communist Party: Soviet Union, 2, 4–10, 11, 27, 28, 189–190, 218–221; Communist Party USA, 32, 78, 92, 108, 110, 121, 139, 152, 218, 322n25; Hitler and, 131; Palestinian Communist Party, Palestinian Communist Party (PCP), 86–87, 289n40, 293–294n106; Jewish revolutionary movements and, 19, 69; ILD and, 7, 109, 123; Party confessions, 213, 222. *See also* Communist International; Poale Tzion
Communist University of the Toilers of the East (KUTV), 31–32, 289n40
competitive victimology, 155, 307n72
Contempo (magazine), 124
Crenshaw, Kimberlé, 26
Crimea: history and demographics of, 62, 284n83; Jewish territorial project in, 5, 62–64, 188; Shumiatcher's poems about, 7, 44, 60–69; Soviet writers on, 64–65,

67–68; Hirschbein's writings about, 40. *See also* Ukrainian literature
Crimean War (1853–1856), 62
crucifixion imagery, 12, 107–115, 119–126, 132–133
Culler, Jonathan, 15
cultural pluralism, 29
Cutler, Yosl, 218

Daniels, Robert, 324n48
Davis, Frank Marshall: "Christ Is a Dixie Nigger," 121
Dekel-Chen, Jonathan, 63, 284n83, 285n93
Deleuze, Gilles, 316n67
Denman, Hugh, 302n102
Denning, Michael, 9, 33, 136
deparochialization, 24, 110
Der Nister (Pinchas Kahanovitch), 30, 97, 181
Derrida, Jacques, 16, 198, 275n86, 310n122, 318n97; *Sovereignties in Question*, 10, 18, 168–171, 175; *Spectres of Marx*, 106
Der Tog (daily), 51, 79–80, 89, 131, 235, 240, 326n73
Diner, Hasia, 108, 295n19, 301n96
Dirlik, Arif, 283n58
Di Yunge (poet group), 8, 78, 100, 216–218, 221, 236, 321n13, 322n16
Djagalov, Rossen, 37, 277n103
Dobroliubov, Nikolay, 190
Dobrushin, Yehezkel, 85, 187
Dreiser, Theodore, 42
Drunin, Vladimir, 189
Druzhba Narodov (literary journal), 185
Dryden, John, 14
Du Bois, W. E. B., 110, 295n14

Easthope, Anthony, 168
Edelshtadt, Dovid, 20
Efroikin, Yisroel, 212
Efron, John, 317n88
Ehrenburg, Ilya, 172, 304n25, 310n132
Eisenstein, Sergei, 46, 47
Der Emes (daily), 30, 34, 100, 187, 219, 224–225, 277n109, 287n9, 325n62
empathy: with African Americans, 108, 109, 110–111; communism and, 6, 36, 214; Jewish trauma and, 9; with Palestinian Arabs, 106; proletarian culture and, 24; in Shumiatcher's works, 44–45, 56; translocation and, 33, 37–38
Engdahl, J. Louis, 124
Engelhardt, Paul, 178
Engels, Friedrich, 95, 142
Epik, Hryhorii, 195–196
Epshteyn, Shakhne, 34, 98, 100, 277n106, 327n89
Epstein, Melech, 98, 141, 155
Epstein, Shakhne, 327n89
Estraikh, Gennady, 25, 30, 77, 149, 191, 218, 276nn93–94, 277n109, 279nn12–13, 285n89, 291n60, 306n50, 315n62, 323n34, 325n62, 325n63
exoticism, 107, 116, 146, 282n49; self-exoticism, 7, 43, 54, 71, 195

factography, 47, 156, 159, 307n76
Faynberg, Leon, 212, 233, 239, 240, 241, 329n134
Fefer, Itzik, 9, 188, 195, 276n93
Fermentto-Tsaisler, Julia, 300n83
Fichte, Johann Gottlieb, 142
Finkin, Jordan, 13, 270n9

First, Joshua, 316n67
Fishman, David, 20, 273n47, 311n1
Fitzpatrick, Sheila, 76–77, 225–226, 230–231, 324n58
Fleishman, Lazar, 312n9
Foa, Eugénie, 44, 280n21
Fogel, Joshua A., 280n24
Ford, Henry, 27
Forverts (daily), 34, 76, 89, 286n3, 293n106, 325n63
Foshko, Joseph, 80, 81, 82
Foucault, Michel, 213
Fowler, Mayhill, 316n68
France, Anatole, 321n13
Frankel, Jonathan, 19, 290n51
Frayhayt. See Morgn Frayhayt (daily)
Frayhayt Writers' Union, 94
Fridman, Betsalel: "Palestine," 86–87, "Skotsboro" (Scottsboro), 124, 299n66
Fugl, Hirsh, 235–236
Fuller, Alvin, 2–3, 6

Gadamer, Hans-Georg, 104, 238
Galich, Alexander, 246–247; *Mattroskaia tishina*, 331n15; "Poema o Staline" (Poem about Stalin), 247
Gandhi, Mahatma, 121
García Lorca, Federico, 165
Garvey, Marcus, 110
Gellner, Ernst, 23
Genette, Gerard, 76
Gershenson, Olga, 330n13
Getty, J. Arch, 212
Gildin, Chaim, 100, 276n93
Gilmore, Glenda, 121–122
Ginsberg, Allen, 247–248
Gitelman, Zvi, 285n93

Glantz, Jacobo: Communist Party and, 42; "Di oygn fun Lina Odena" (Lina Odena's eyes), 156–157; *Fonen in blut* (Flags in blood), 140, 152–153; "In vandervaytkayt fun mayn folk" (In the wide wanderings of my people), 153; "A lid vegn banker Khid in a shloflozer nakht fun Madrid" (A poem about Gid the banker on a sleepless Madrid night), 170; "Oyf farnakhtikn step fun La Mancha" (On the evening steppe of La Mancha), 157–158; "Plakat" (Placard), 169–170; "Royter kristus" (Red Christ), 158–159; Spanish Civil War and, 8, 142, 145, 152–156, 162, 165, 169

Glantz-Leyeles, Aaron, 23, 78, 97, 216, 226, 235, 322n17; "Dem Muftis arbl" (The Mufti's sleeve), 81; "In sobvey" (In the subway), 117; "Shpanishe balade" (Ballad of Spain), 161

Glatshteyn, Yankev, 216, 236, 322n17; "A gute nakht, velt" (Good night, world), 236

Glazer, Ada, 235

Glik, Hirsh: "Zog nit keymmol" (Never say), 250

Goebbels, Joseph, 129

Goethe, Johann Wolfgang von, 176

Gold, Mike, 124, 228

Goldberg, Itche, x, 293n95

Goldman, Emma, 12

Gordon, Yehudah Leib: "Awake, my people," 65

Gorky, Maxim, 184, 324n60

Grabowicz, George, 201, 319n115

Graham, Helen, 7–8, 304n19

Great Appropriation (Soviet Union), 179, 210

Grinberg, Uri Tzvi, 22, 25, 52, 113, 119; "Uri Tsvi farn tseylem INRI" (Uri Tsvi before the cross INRI), 113–114, 116, 132

Gropper, William, 79, 152

Grossman, Allen, 248

Guattari, Félix, 316n67

Hadda, Janet, 113

Halbwachs, Maurice, 21, 147–148

Halfin, Igal, 158, 224, 231

Halpern, Moyshe Leyb, 34, 135, 137, 216, 227, 302n99, 323n43, 326n74; *Frayhayt* and, 218, 231; "Salyut" (Salute), 135; Moyshe Leyb Halpern Prize, 127

Der Hamer (journal), 12, 41, 48, 50, 218, 219

Harshav, Benjamin, 22, 301n94

Haynt (daily), 104

Hearst, William Randolph, 294n106

Hebrew Writers' Union, 69

Hegelian model of transubstantiation. *See* transubstantiation

Heine, Heinrich, 323n28

Hemingway, Ernest: *For Whom the Bell Tolls*, 172

Herndon, Angelo, 111, 122, 123, 126, 299n55

Herrmann, Gina, 321n9

Herzl, Theodor: *Der Judenstadt* (The Jewish state), 88

Heyd, Milly, 295n19, 298n52

Hirschbein, Peretz, 7, 40, 42–43, 46–48, 51, 56, 97, 227, 279n3, 279n4, 280n14; *Royte felder* (Red fields), 40; relationship to Palestine, 69–70, 286n101

Hitler, Adolph, 131, 141, 142, 149, 172–173, 177, 229, 233. *See also* Molotov-Ribbentrop pact; Nazism.

Hitler-Stalin pact. *See* Molotov-Ribbentrop pact (1939)

Hochschild, Adam, 152

Hoffman, Matthew, 76, 78, 113, 292n71, 293n106

Hofshteyn, Dovid, 14, 175–192; arrest of and execution of, 9, 188, 229; *Bay vegn* (On roads), 187, 195, 197; Communist Party and, 189–190; Communist press and, 34, 184, 185, 187, 191–192, 224–225, 325n62, 325n63; "Crimea Cycle," 64; "Denkmol Khmelnytskin" (Monument to Khmelnytsky), 208–209, 320n128; "Dnieper," 188; *Felker zingen* (Peoples sing), 195; "In Armenie" (In Armenia), 195; internationalism and, 186–192; Kiev-grupe and, 42, 85, 146, 181; Jewish Anti-Fascist Committee and, 315n52; *Kiev*, 188–189, 210; "Kiev-hoyptshtot" (Kyiv-capital city), 188–189; *Kultur-Lige* and, 181, 315n62; "Mikhaylover monastir" (Mikhailov monastery), 189; Nadir and, 220; "October," 188; Palestine and, 42, 85, 188, 314n49, 315n53; "Protsesye," 188; Shevchenko translated by, 8–9, 177–186, 189, 200–206; move to the Soviet Union, 30, 64; Teyf influenced by, 85; translocation by, 14, 200–205; *Troyer* (Sorrow), 192; "Ukrayne" (1944), 193–194; "Ukrayne" (1922), 192–193

Hofshteyn, Feyge, 315n53

Holiday, Billie, 119

Holocaust, x, 1, 26, 134, 173, 234, 245, 248, 301n96; Kurtz on, 248–250;

Markish on, 149, 173; Sutzkever on 174–175, 208–209; Teyf and, 243. *See also* Vilna Ghetto; Warsaw Ghetto

Homel pogrom (1903), 57–58

Hood, Thomas: "Song of the Shirt," 20

Horkheimer, Max, 269n3

Horne, Frank: "On Seeing Two Brown Boys in a Catholic Church," 119

Horowitz, Aron, 286n101

Hughes, Langston, 25, 109, 110, 163, 298n45, 309n108; *Angelo Herndon Jones*, 122, 299n55; "August 19th . . . : A Poem for Clarence Norris," 122; "Christ in Alabama," 109, 119–120, 299n63; "Letter from Spain," 164; "Scottsboro," 109, 120–121; *Scottsboro Limited*, 120–121, 133, 298n47

Hutchings, Stephen C., 273n61

Ibárruri, Dolores (La Pasionaria), 157, 160

IKOR (organization), 104

In Shpan (journal), 25

International Brigades, 140–142, 143, 146, 154, 167, 170, 171, 173, 304n19

internationalism: in China, 46–52; Hofshteyn and, 30, 34, 186–192; Shumiatcher and, 60–69; Soviet Third Period and, 28–29; Yiddish literature influenced by, 4, 27–38

International Labor Defense (ILD), 109, 123–124

International Organization of Revolutionary Writers (MORP), 305n25

International Workers Order (IWO), 141, 303n8

In Zikh (group), 23, 216, 269n2

In Zikh (journal), 13, 23, 161, 308n99, 322nn16–17

Jabotinsky, Vladimir (Ze'ev), 186, 289n34
Jakobson, Roman, 275n79
Jensen, Peter Alberg, 281n34
Jewish Anti-Fascist Committee, 315n52
Jewish Enlightenment (Haskalah), 19–20, 65
Jews on the Land (film), 64
Jones, Faith, 41, 44, 279n4, 280nn19–20
Jung, Klara, 220

Kalinin, Mikhail, 64, 285n89
Kallen, Horace, 29, 42
Kaplan, Mordecai, 238
Karlip, Joshua, 36, 292n87, 293n92
Katz, Dovid, xi, 271n19, 278n113, 283n60, 286n1, 293n102, 326n80
Katz, Hyman, 172
Katz, Menke, 292n85; *Der mentsh in togn* (The dawning man), 118; "Di lintshndike kro" (The lynching crow), 107, 118; "Tsu di antlofene" (To the runaways), 95–96
Kelley, Robin, 7, 32, 109, 294n5
Kensky, Eitan, 227, 235
Kiev-grupe (group), 25, 42, 55, 85, 100, 146, 181
Khalyastre (group), 22, 41
Khanukov, L., 167
Kharkhordin, Oleg, 213
Khinkulov, Leonid, 202
Khiterer, Victoria, 331n15
Khlebnikov, Velimir, 46, 281n27
Khmelnytsky, Bohdan, 208–209, 210, 288n29, 320n131
Khrushchev, Nikita, 190
Khvylia, Andrii, 189, 206
Kinshasa, Kwando, 124

Kipling, Rudyard, 321n13
Kirschenbaum, Lisa, 150, 310n132
Kishinev pogrom (1903), 14, 21, 54, 58, 72–73, 76, 83, 134, 296n21
Klausner, Joseph, 21
Klein, Christina, 157, 308n80
Kling, Joseph, 217
Knight, Nathanial, 280n22
Koestler, Arthur, 232
Kofsi (satirist), 192
Korczak, Janusz, 246, 330n13
Koriak, Volodymyr, 191, 317n90
Kornblatt, Judith Deutsch, 330n7
Kronfeld, Chana, 23, 188
Krutikov, Mikhail, 195
Kultur-Lige, 24, 181, 185, 189, 220, 274n74, 315n62
Kurtz, Aaron: ix, 93, 248; "Andaluzyer landshaft" (Andalusian landscape), 162–163; "A briv fun a kranknshvester" (A letter from a nurse), 163–164, 170; Cabral and, 248, 272n38; Communist Party and, 218, 243; "Der orkester" (The orchestra), 166–167; "Di letste levaye" (The last funeral), 152; "Di vant" (The wall), 93–96; *In Zikh* and, 308n99, 322n17; "Kaddish," 249–250, 264–267; "Kol Nidre," 150–151, 155, 261–264; "A milion por shikh" (A Million Pairs of Shoes), 243–244; "Mishpet" (Trial), 92–93; *No Pasaran*, 140, 162, 163, 166, 167–168, 171–172, 250; Palestine and, 92–95, 101, 243; *Plakatn* (Placards), 167, 169; Pomerantz on, 292n73; Proletpen and, 94, 244; Spanish Civil War and, 8, 142, 145–146, 150–152, 155–156, 161–165; "Yosl," 152; "Yunyon Skver" (Union Square), 167

KUTV (Communist University of the Toilers of the East), 31–32, 289n40

Kuznitz, Cecile, 23–24

Kvitko, Leyb, 9, 42, 85, 100, 146, 181, 188, 190, 220, 229, 276n93

Labor Zionism, 11. *See also* Poale Zion

LaCapra, Dominick, 155, 307n72

Layton, Susan, 194

League of Nations, 28

Leary, Lewis, 298n45

Lederhendler, Eli, 277n106, 305n40

Lederman, David, 233–234, 310n136

Lee, Malka, 108, 111, 114; *Gezangen* (Songs), 114; "Gots shvartser lam" (God's black lamb), 107, 111–113, 117–118, 128, 130, 256–257; "In Yezus's nomen" (In Jesus's name), 114; "Niger in sobvey" (Nigger in the subway), 116, 117; "Zangen un tslomim" (Corn and crosses), 114–115

Lee, Steven, 29, 47, 156, 245, 281n29, 307n76

Leivick, H.: "A briv fun Amerike tsu a vaytn fraynt" (A letter from America to a distant friend), 42, 137; anti-Stalinism and, 5; Communist Party and, 37, 100–101, 141, 293n95; in Di Yunge, 216, 218; on financial difficulties, 227; "Farreter" (Traitors) 101–102; *Frayhayt* and, 34, 78, 89–92, 99–103, 104–105, 136, 218, 222, 226, 294n107; Hirschbeins and, 51, 227; "Memameykim" (Out of the depths), 236–238; Nadir and, 219, 222, 227, 236; *Naye Lider,* 137; "Negershes,"

136–137; Palestine and, 7, 42, 70, 78; password usage by, 11–13, 99; Popular Front and, 70, 105, 136, 141, 303n8; "Royte tikhelekh" (Red kerchiefs), 99–101; as "runaway" poet, 89–91, 99–102, 104–105; on Sacco and Vanzetti, 2–4, 6, 18, 27–28, 251–252, 275n86; "Sacco un Vanzettis Mitvokh" (Sacco and Vanzetti's Wednesday), 13, 275n86; Revolutionary activity of, 12, 103, 236; in Soviet Union, 7, 30–31, 42, 90, 279n10, 291n60; translocation by, 18–19, 30–31, 37–38; "Vider geshtorbn a shokhn" (Again a neighbor died), 37–38, 137; *Vokh* and, 70, 98–99, 104, 135, 226; "A yor Sako Vanzeti" (A Sacco-Vanzetti year), 2–4, 6, 11–13, 18, 27–28, 251–252

Lenin, Vladimir, 5, 19, 27, 28, 30, 31, 121, 191, 277n97; and the Bund, 271 n46, 273n52. *See also* Marxist-Leninist Ideology

Leshtsinski, Shmuel, 235

Levin, Khane, 64; "Krime motivn" (Crimean motifs), 64–66

Levy, Lital, 312n10

Levy, Naomi, 247

Lewis, Pericles, 274n68, 275n88

Lilienblum, Moshe Leyb: *Derekh tshuvah,* 324n61

Linhard, Tabea Alexa, 157

Lipkin, Semyon, 206–207, 319n122

Lisner, Abraham, 304n22

Literarishe Bleter (journal), 25, 78, 90, 103, 146, 219

Litvakov, Moyshe, 34, 277n109, 313n24

Löwy, Michael, 143

Ludwig, Reuben: "Ver hot tseshosn dem krekhtikn niger" (Who shot the leprous nigger), 116

Lukács, Georg, 142

Luz, Ehud, 320n6

lynchings, 13, 32, 107–109, 111, 115–119, 121–123, 125–127, 133, 135–138, 294n5, 295n19; comparisons to Nazism, 111, 122, 129–134, 298n52. *See also* Scottsboro Nine

Macdonald, James Ramsay, 79

Maimonides, Moses, 213, 234

Malakh, Leyb: *Mississippi,* 110

Mandestam, Osip, 41

Manjapra, Kris, 270n12

MAPP (Moscow Association of Proletarian Writers), 84, 92, 184

Margolin, Anna, 113

Margoshes, Samuel, 329n147

Marinetti, Filippo Tomaso, 21–22

Markish, Esther, 150

Markish, Lorenzo, 147; "Brothers," 148

Markish, Peretz: "Agitprop Pancho Video," 165; arrest and execution of, 9, 188, 229, 247; "Balade vegn delegat" (Ballad of a delegate), 159–160; *Brider* (Brothers), 67–68, 148, 305n38; Communist Party and, 97, 100, 190, 247; Crimea and, 64, 67–68; *Dem balegufs toyt* (The kulak's death), 306n50; *Di kupe* (The mound), 22, 49, 54, 55–57, 66, 148, 246, 282n44, 305n38, 308n86; *Frayhayt* and, 34, 97; Galich and, 247; Hofshteyn and, 181; Khalyastre group and, 22; Kiev-grupe and, 25, 42, 55, 100, 181; "Komandir Diestro" (Commander Diestro), 171–172; *Lider vegn Shpanye* (Poems about Spain), 140, 310n133; *Literarishe Bleter,* 219; "Mayn nomen iz atsind" (My name is now), 159; Nadir and, 219, 220, 233–234; Palestine and, 97, 100; *Poeme vegn Stalinen* (Poem about Stalin), 306n50; *Radyo,* 159, 308n86; Shumiatcher and, 55–56; in Soviet Union, 22, 30, 42, 160, 219, 276n94; "Shpanye" (Spain), 140, 146–148, 150, 155, 159–161, 257–261, 306n50; religion and, 151; Revolutionary themes of, 159, 181–182; Spanish Civil War and, 8, 140, 142, 145, 146–152, 156, 163, 165; Stankiewicz and 305n28; Sutzkever and, 207; "Toreador," 160; translocation by, 22–23, 25, 26–27, 30; *Trot fun doyres* (Footsteps of a generation), 173; *Tsu a yidishe tentserin* (To a Jewish dancer; Russian translation: Dancer from the Ghetto), 177, 246, 311n136; "Veys ikh nit, tsi kh'bin in der'heym" (I don't know if I'm at home" 308n88; *Volin* (Volhynia), 308n86; WWII and Jewish themes of, 26, 149, 173, 177, 233–234, 306n44

Marmor, Kalman, 89, 321n11

Marranos, 140, 150, 209–210

Martin, Terry, 277n97, 277n99; *The Affirmative Action Empire,* 31

martyrdom, 111, 114, 115, 131, 165, 173

Marx, Karl, 46, 95, 142

Marxist-Leninist ideology: Hofshteyn and, 182, 185, 191; Nadir and, 221, 231–232; Palestine and, 105; religion and, 99; Shumiatcher and, 53; Spanish Civil War and, 158, 173; Yiddish literature influenced by, 31–32, 180, 182, 185, 191

Maud, Zuni, 218

Mayakovsky, Vladimir, 24, 25, 42, 49, 64, 228, 247; *Jews on the Land*, 64; "Kemp 'Nit Gedaige," 228, 326n78; *Mystery Bouffe*, 51

Mayzel, Nakhman, 25, 69–70, 103, 146

McCarthyism, 9

McDermott, Kevin, 276n89

Medem, Gina, 141

Medem, Vladimir, 91; "Social Democracy and the National Question," 272n47

Meeropol, Abel (pseudonym for Lewis Allan), 298nn42–43; "Strange Fruit," 118–119

Mendelson, Ezra, 274n71

messianism, 68, 86, 95, 143, 220, 249

Mexico, 5, 42, 145, 152

Michels, Tony, 34, 322n25

Mikhoels, Solomon, 9

Mintz, Alan, 283n63

Miron, Dan, 21

Molodowsky, Kadye: "Tsu di volontyorn in Shpanye" (To the volunteers in Spain), 144, 304n24

Molotov-Ribbentrop pact (1939), 8, 9, 33, 36, 105, 149, 172, 177, 214, 228, 229, 246, 231, 310n136

Morgan, Stacy, 121

Morgn Frayhayt (daily): Bergelson and, 34–35, 97, 325n63; Communist International and 15, 34–35; founding of, 231, 327n89; *Frayhayt* Writers' Union, 94; Halpern and, 218; In Zikh and 216; Lee and, 108, 116; Leivick and, 12, 34, 89–91, 99–102, 104–105, 136, 218, 222, 226; Markish and, 34; Nadir and, 8, 15, 34, 215, 218–221, 224, 227, 233, 235, 326n73; Nazism and 131; Palestine

and, 34–35, 75–77, 78, 79, 88–104, 221–222; "runaway" poets and, 8, 78, 88–105, 108, 223, 227; Popular Front and 135–136; race-violence and, 108, 116, 125; self-criticism published in, 226; Yiddish literature influenced by, 34–35

Morgn Zhurnal (daily), 89

Moscow Association of Proletarian Writers (MAPP), 84, 92, 184

Moseley, Marcus, 298n42, 324n61

Moss, Kenneth, 22, 24, 181, 272n45, 274n74, 313n20

Mukdoni, Alexander, 89, 213, 239, 294n107, 329n134, 329n141

multiculturalism, 29, 245, 248

multidirectional memory, 26, 38

Murav, Harriet, 26–27, 67, 180, 185, 203, 225, 234, 246, 285n88, 305n38, 306n44, 312n12, 313n25, 319n122

Nadir, Ghenia, 212, 329n135

Nadir, Moishe, 211–241; "Amol gevolt zikh shmadn" (I once wanted to be baptized), 216; "Arbeter vig-lid" (Workers' lullaby), 223–224; Communist Party and, 8–9, 218–221; *Derlang aher di velt, burzhoy!* (We want the world; literally "Hand over the world, bourgeois!"), 223; "Der Rebbe Elimelekh," 214; "Di tsar-vakkhanalie" (The sorrow-orgy), 222; Di Yunge and, 8, 78; "Driter period" (Third period), 221–222; "Far vemen" (For whom), 232–233; *Frayhayt* and, 8, 15, 34, 215, 218–221, 224, 227; *Fun mentsh tsu mentsh* (From man to man), 217–218; *Fun mir tsu dir* (From me to you), 220; "Memameykim" (Out of the depths), 236–238; *Messiah in America,* 220; modernism and, 216–218; *Moyde ani,* 212, 230, 239, 240, 329n143; "Moyde-ani: Oytobiografish" (Confession: Autobiographical), 230; "Neenter" (Closer), 211–212, 213, 238, 240; "Pen un biks" (Pen and rifle), 224, 233; post-Party *teshuva* of, 229–241; pseudonyms used by, 321n12; in Soviet Union, 30, 42; "A Tfilah" (A prayer), 234–235; translations by, 15–16; "Tsion vakkhanalia" (Zion bacchanalia), 78; "Tsu a teyl Yidishe shrayber" (To some Yiddish writers), 223; "A velt mit arbet" (A world with work), 227; *Vilde royzn* (Wild roses), 216, 220; Weinstein and, 130

Naftali Botwin Company, 141–142

Narovchatov, Sergei, 149

National Workers Alliance, 89

Nation of Islam, 110

Naye Folkstsaytung (newspaper), 150

Naye Presse (newspaper), 141. 303n13

Nazism, 105, 111, 133–134, 173; Nadir on, 233; Spanish Civil War and, 140, 141–142, 144, 145, 149, 161. *See also* Holocaust

Nelson, Cary, 119–120, 142, 168

New Masses (journal), 124, 125

Niger-Charney, Shmuel (critic also known as Shmuel Charney and Shmuel Niger), 30, 44, 71, 89, 104, 105, 218, 279n3, 329n135; name of, 276n95

Nit Gedayget (Yiddish summer camp), 42, 228, 247, 326n78

Norich, Anita, 4

Norris, Clarence, 122

Novershtern, Avraham, 113, 296n20

Novik, P., 294n107

Novogrudsky, Lipa, 291n53

Odena, Lina, 156–157, 160, 163

Olgin, Moyshe, 34, 76, 98, 226, 277n106, 279n10, 327n89

Opatoshu, Joseph, 303n8

Opportunity (magazine), 124

Orwell, George: *Homage to Catalonia,* 143

Ottoman Empire, 62, 64

Oyfn sheydveg (journal), 212, 240, 293n92

OZET (Soviet Jewish colonization aid organization), 7, 69

Palestine, 7, 72–106; 1929 violence, 7, 32, 34, 42, 73–75, 136, 141, 178, 224, 286n3, 293n106; Cossack metaphors for, 79, 81, 288n29; Crimea and 63, 285n93; *Frayhayt* and, 34–36, 75, 77, 78, 88–104, 287n9; Hirschbein and, 45, 63, 69–71, 286n101; Hofshteyn and, 42, 85, 186, 188, 192, 207–208, 224; imperialism and, 26, 29, 73, 95, 287n13, 287–288n17, 325n62; Kurtz and, 92–95, 101, 151; Leivick and, 7, 42, 70, 78; Markish and, 97, 100; Nadir and, 15–16, 78; 221–222; "runaway" poets and, 88–104, 105, 226; Shumiatcher and, 75, 78, 97–98; Soviet Third Period and, 87, 93; Temple Mount, 74; Trotsky on 288n22; Western Wall, 74, 96. *See also* Zionism

Paley, Grace, 247

Pan-Africanism, 110

Paris, Harold Persico: *Kaddish for the Little Children*, 248

parrhesia, 76

passwords: African American, 11, 110, 126–134; "black-eyed," 195; "brider" (brothers), 59, 68, 97, 116–117; "Chapaev," 171; empathy and, 9; "ergets" (somewhere), 207–208; "Ganeydn" (Garden of Eden), 204–205; *halef* (slaughtering knife), 131; Hofshteyn's use of, 176, 183, 200–205; "hulyet" (carouse), 88, 102, 178; inclusive / exclusive nature of, 11; "Inquisition," 8, 147–148, 151, 153, 154; internationalist, 121, 127; "Kaddish," 244–245, 247–248; "kamf" (struggle), 92, 97, 125, 126; *kateyger,* 3–4, 6, 11–12, 269n3, 270n4; *kherem,* 98–100; *kupe* (mound), 49, 54–55, 148; "lynch law," 111; "lynch tree," 117, 118, 122–123; "makhnes" (squadrons), 97, 103; "Marrano," 209–210; "memameykim," 236–237; "mistbarg" (trash heap), 53–54, 56, 66; "moyde zayn" (to admit or confess), 224–225; Nadir's use of, 211–241; "¡No pasarán!," 7–8, 11, 140, 168–169; "pogrom," 17–27, 52–60, 66, 75–76, 79–87, 98, 104, 110; "pritsim," 196; proletarian, 41–42; *rege* (moment), 174–175; "Sacco-Vanzetti," 11, 12–13; "Scottsboro," 7, 11, 111; for Scottsboro Nine, 11, 110, 126–134; *sharf* (sharp), 129, 131; *shibboleth,* 10; *shkhite* (ritual slaughter), 131; *shkiye* (sunset), 131; Shumiatcher's use of, 43, 45, 71; Soviet-identified, 30; for Spanish Civil War, 11, 151, 160–161, 168, 173; "Tammuz," 127; *teshuvah,* 8–9, 211–215, 221–241, 320n6, 324n61; translocation of, 13–17, 211–241; *tseylem* (cross), 107–108, 113–115, 130; Ukrainian, 197–198; "uprising," 79–87, 104; use of term, 3–4; "vant" (wall), 93–95; *vide* (confession), 133; *vund* (wound), 18, 24, 52, 129, 131, 162, 243; Yangtze River, 59–60; Yiddish literature's use of, 10–13

Pasternak, Boris, 174–176, 186, 200, 202–204, 311n1, 311n5, 312n9

PCP (Palestinian Communist Party), 87

Peretz, Y. L., 14, 19, 35, 78, 83, 289n34; "Bontshe Shvayg" (Bontshe Silent), 3–4

Petliura, Simon, 80

Petrovsky-Shtern, Yohanan, 314n47

pietà imagery, 107, 112, 128

Pilniak, Boris, 47–48, 49–50, 51, 61, 280n23, 281n30, 281n34, 282nn49–50, 284n79; *Chinese Diary,* 47; "Chinese Story," 48

Pinsker, Shachar, 280n15

Platner, Ayzik (Isaac), 101, 325n67; "Tsu di antlofene" (To the runaways), 91–92

Poale Tsion (Workers of Zion), 87, 92

Podriatshik, Eliezer, 187, 315n53

pogrom poetry, 14, 17–18, 44, 52, 55, 57, 75–76, 128

Pomerantz, Alexander, 25, 187–188, 218, 223–225, 229, 277n101, 292n73

Popular Front (Spain), 7–8, 9, 70, 93, 105, 136, 139, 141, 144, 153–154, 156, 163, 165, 168, 170, 172, 177, 214, 229, 277n103, 293–294n106, 303n7, 308n80

Pound, Ezra, 47
Presner, Todd, 153
Preston, Paul, 7–8, 154, 303n7
proletarian culture, x, 4–6, 15, 24–25, 31, 32, 33–35, 84, 92, 94, 104, 124, 169, 184, 188, 191, 224, 228–229, 274n76, 314
Proletkult, 24, 274n74
Proletpen (writers' union), x, 35, 94, 126, 188, 244, 277n101, 278n113, 292n85, 322n17
Prolit (journal), 24–25, 191–192
Pushkin, Alexander, 190

Quint, Alyssa, 110

Raboy, Isaac, 78, 222
Radcliff, Pamela, 305n26
Radt, Jula, 42
Ram, Harsha, 144
Rampersad, Arnold, 309n108
Rancière, Jacques, 14–15
RAPP (Russian Association of Proletarian Writers), 92
Rappoport, Charles, 293n92
Ravitch, Melech, 25, 44, 61, 71, 146, 219–220, 280nn19–20, 328n120
Reilly, John, 300n69
Reiss, Isaac. *See* Nadir, Moishe
Revolutionary Jewish Bund, 12, 19, 20, 23, 34, 77–78, 88, 91, 103, 178, 272n, 273n52, 277n106, 290n49, 290n50, 290–291n53
Reyzen, Avrom, 19–20, 30, 42, 77–78, 88–92, 97, 100, 102, 103, 178, 222, 227, 290n49, 290n53; "Groye teg" (Gray days), 97; "Hulyet, hulyet beyze vintn" (Revel, revel angry winds), 19, 178; "Vinter-lid"

(Winter song), 88, 91, 279n10, 290n49, 290n53
Reyzen, Zalman, 323n28
Rice, Anne P., 299n63
Rich, Adrienne, 83
Risser, James, 293n103
Robbins, Bruce, 137
Robeson, Paul, 250
Rodríguez, Melchor, 160
Rogger, Hans, 58
Rontsh, Y. E., 111, 117, 124–126, 133, 137, 295n11; "Bluegrass," 126; "A gut dzhab gemakht" (Done a good job), 125; "In Alabama," 125, 126; "Neger-arbeter" (Negro-worker), 126; "Shvarts un royt" (Black and red), 126; "Skotsboro" (Scottsboro), 124, 126, 133
Room, Abram, 64
Roosevelt, Eleanor, 161
Roosevelt, Franklin, 27
Rosenberg, Ethel and Julius, 9, 298n43
Rosenfeld, Morris, 20, 273n49
Roskies, David, 21, 113, 273n53, 283n61
Rothberg, Michael, *Multidirectional Memory*, 26, 38; *The Implicated Subject*, 137
Royte Velt (literary journal), 12, 15, 24–25, 39, 41–42, 52, 56, 58, 64, 67, 191, 196
Rubenstein, Joshua, 276n94, 327n105
Rukeyser, Muriel, 163, 295n7; "The Lynchings of Jesus," 109; *Savage Coast*, 173, 309n104
"runaway" poets, 8, 88–104, 108. *See also specific individuals*
Russian Association of Proletarian Writers (RAPP), 92
Russian Orthodox Church, 86
Russo-Japanese War (1904–1905), 50

Sacco and Vanzetti, 2–4, 6, 11–13, 18–19, 27–28, 32, 100, 109, 113, 163, 272n43, 275n86, 293n95

Sacco, Nicola. See Sacco and Vanzetti

Said, Edward, 280n17, 288n17

samokritika. See self-criticism

Samuels, Maurice, 44, 280n21

Saussure, Ferdinand de, 22

Schachter, Allison, 274n69, 304n24, 312n10

Schechter, Joel, 220

Schlögel, Karl, 306n47

Schorsch, Ismar, 147

Scottsboro Nine, 7, 34, 107–138; Communist Party and 32, 36, 105, 141, 294n5, 295n9; crucifixion imagery and, 107, 109, 111–114, 119–126; Grinberg and, 113, 114, 116, 119, 132; Halpern and, 135, 137; Herndon and, 111, 122, 123, 126; Katz and, 107, 118; Lee and, 107–108, 111–117, 128, 130; Leivick and, 136–137; martyrdom poems and, 111, 114, 115, 131; modernism and, 111–119, 163, 295n7, 298n47, 299n63; passwords and, 11, 33, 110–118, 121–123, 126–134, 249; pietà imagery and, 107, 112, 128; Rontsh and, 111, 117, 124–126, 133, 137; Weinstein and, 107, 111, 127–134

secularism, 11, 19, 23, 143, 152, 154, 158, 200, 205, 217, 231, 238, 248, 218n100

Seidman, Naomi, 17, 180, 313n25

self-criticism (samokritika), 212, 215, 224, 225–226, 324n58

Seligman, Adam, 11–12

Sephardic Jews, 147

Sergeevna, Olga, 56

Shafir, Gershon, 270n10

Shakespeare, William, 84, 176, 186, 314n45

Shames, Fume (Fayvl), 202

Shapiro, Lamed, 78, 113, 220–221, 233, 239, 324n46; "Der tseylem" (The cross), 57, 296n22

Sherry, Samantha, 311n8

Shevchenko, Taras, 8, 14, 176, 177–186, 194, 316n67; "Dumy moi" (My songs), 197; "Haidamaki," 206; Hofshteyn's translations of, 8–9, 177–186, 189, 200–205; "Kateryna," 318n104; "Kavkaz" (The Caucasus), 195; Kobzar, 190; "Maria," 200–205; A shpatsir mit fargenign un nit on moral (A walk with pleasure and not without a moral), 189; "Son" (A Dream), 177; "Zapovit" (Testament), 196

Shkandrij, Myroslav, 200–201, 313n33

Shklovsky, Viktor, 64

Shneer, David, 41, 149, 314n40

Sholem, Aleichem (pseudonym for Sholem Rabinovich), 30, 83, 190, 196, 316n66, 321n13, 323n28

Shternshis, Anna, 99

Shteynberg, Noakh, 233, 239–240, 329n143; A bukh Moyshe Nadir (A Moishe Nadir book), 219, 239

Shumiatcher, Esther, 6–7, 39–71; "Albatros" (Albatross), 41; Ale Tog (All day), 70; "Baym rand fun Khine" (At the border of China), 52–53, 56, 66, 252–253; "A betler" (A beggar), 50; in China, 45, 52–60; Crimea and, 7, 60–69; empathy in works of, 44–45, 56;

"Homel, 1928," 60–61; "Honik fun birebidzhan" (Honey from Birobidjan), 70; "Ikh bin a yid" (I am a Jew), 154; *In shoen fun libshaft* (In the hours of love), 41, 68; internationalism and, 60–69; Markish and, 55–56; Marxist-Leninist ideology and, 53; "May lid" (May song), 39, 44, 52, 61, 68; "Nito a freyd aza" (No happiness like this), 58–59; Palestine and, 75, 78, 97–98; password usage by, 43, 45, 71; "Saygon" (Saigon), 48–49, 50; Spanish Civil War and, 154; translocation by, 45, 52–60; "Tsigeyner" (Gypsies), 61–62; "Yung iz erd un royt iz blut" (Young is the earth and red is blood), 63, 98; Zionism and, 63–64, 69–70

Shyovitz, David, 247

Sicher, Efraim, 113

Signal (journal), 229

Singer, Israel Joshua, 25, 146, 220

Singh, Nikhil Pal, 295n14; *Black Is a Country*, 110

Skakov, Nariman, x, 269n3

Slezkine, Yuri, 5, 185, 274n76, 312n11, 326n79

Socialist Realism, x, 190–191, 203, 228

Sosiura, Volodymyr, 179

Soviet Union: Communist Party in, 4–6, 11, 27, 28, 218–221; Great Appropriation in, 179, 210; internationalism and, 28–29; Palestine and, 87, 93; passwords and, 30; Spanish Civil War and, 141, 144; State Publishing House for National Minorities, 185;

Third Period in, 5, 28–29, 32, 87, 93, 141, 144, 213, 221–222, 276n89, 290n48; Yiddish authors in, 30, 42, 291n60. See also Crimea; *specific individuals*

Spanish Civil War, 7–8, 139–173; Glantz and, 8, 142, 145, 152–156, 162, 165, 169; Hofshteyn and, 146; Kurtz and, 8, 142, 145, 150–152, 161–162, 165; Leivick and, 141, 303n8; Markish and, 8, 142, 145, 146–150, 165; Marxist-Leninist ideology and, 158, 173; passwords for, 11, 151, 160–161, 168, 173; Shumiatcher and, 154; Soviet Third Period and, 141, 144; Zionism and, 142

Spanish Inquisition, 8, 147–148, 151, 153, 154

Spartak (journal), 25

specular translation process, 182, 183, 194–195, 319n122

Spinoza, Baruch, 99, 293n92

Stahl, Neta, 113, 116–117, 297n24, 297n26

Stalin, Joseph, 5, 28–29, 31, 33, 272n43, 324n60

Stankiewicz, Edward, 305n28

State Publishing House for National Minorities (Soviet Union), 185

Steffin, Margarete, 162

stereotypes, 17, 128, 135, 153–154, 205, 209–210, 319n115

Studer, Brigitte, 324n58

Suhl, Yuri: *Dos likht af mayn gas* (The light on my street), 122–123

Sundquist, Eric, 301n96

Suny, Ronald, 37

Sutzkever, Avrom, 174–175, 207–209, 246, 311n5, 319n125

Tabachnick, Avrom, 239, 329n135
Tanievitsh, Dovid, 89, 90
Taylor, Prentiss, 120
Tcherikover, Elias, 212, 240
Temkin, Moshik, 272n43
Temple Mount (Palestine), 74
Tenenboym, Shea, 239
Tereshchenko, Mikhail Ivanovich, 315n60
Teyf, Moyshe, 14, 72–73, 76, 83–86, 89, 244, 246; *Milkhome lider* (War poems), 244; "Tiurme-lider" (Prison poems), 330n5; "Vilne, Zumer 1944" (Vilnius, Summer 1944), 244; "Zing, vint fun midber!" (Sing, desert wind!), 73, 83, 85, 87, 88, 90–91, 253–255
Third Period (Soviet Union): anticolonialism and, 32, 290n48; internationalism and, 28–29; Nadir and, 213, 221–222; Palestine and, 87, 93; Spanish Civil War and, 141, 144; start of, 5, 276n89
Thurston, Michael, 121
translocation: of culture, 13–17; empathy and, 33, 37–38; Hofshteyn's use of, 14, 200–205; Leivick's use of, 18–19, 30–31, 37–38; Markish's use of, 22–23, 25, 26–27, 30; of modernist pogrom poems, 17–27; Nadir's use of, 15–16; of passwords, 13–17, 211–241; Shumiatcher's use of, 45, 52–60; by Weinstein, 131, 132
transubstantiation, 60, 71, 284n76
Tretiakov, Sergei, 46–47, 54; *Roar China*, 46
tribalism, 96, 186
Trivaks, Avrom-Yizkhak, 11
Trotsky, Leon, 5, 53, 54, 288n22, 322n17

Trumpener, Katie, 245
Tsvetaeva, Marina: "Poema kontsa" (Poem of the end), 17–18
Turner, Nat, 121
Twain, Mark, 321n13
Tworkov, Jack, 218, 322n27
Tychyna, Pavlo, 179
Tzara, Tristan, 22

Ukrainian Civil War (1918–1920), 55, 80, 148, 193–194, 196. *See also* Bolshevik Revolution
Ukrainian literature, 8, 174–210; Hofshteyn's translations of Shevchenko, 8–9, 177–186, 189, 200–205; internationalism and, 186–192; Marxist-Leninist ideology and, 180, 182, 185, 191; nationalist vs. internationalist, 186–192; passwords in, 174–176, 178, 183, 195–198, 200–205, 207–210. *See also specific authors*
Union Square (journal), 25
Usen'ko, Pavlo, 179

Vanzetti, Bartolomeo. *See* Sacco and Vanzetti
VAPP (All-Russian Association of Proletarian Writers), 184
Vaykhert, Mikhl, 110, 295n11
Vays, Shifre, 102; "Accusations," 255–256
Veidlinger, Jeffrey, 181
Venuti, Lawrence, 182, 183
Vergelis, Aaron, 289n38
Vilna Ghetto, 174, 175, 207, 244
Vokh (literary journal), 78–79, 81, 97, 98, 104, 108, 135, 226, 288n22
VOKS (Soviet Society for Cultural Relations with Foreign Countries), 47

Volkenshteyn, David, 325n62
Vsemirnaia Literatura (publishing house), 184
Vujacic, Valijko, 281n34
VUSPP (All-Ukrainian Union of Soviet Writers), 191

Wald, Alan, 36, 321n10
Walker, Jimmy, 89
Warsaw Ghetto, 208, 246, 250, 330n13
Washington, Booker T., 296n21
Wasserstein, Bernard, 326n79
Weinstein, Berish, 111, 300nn77–78, 300n83; "Apostoln" (Apostles), 130; Brukhvarg, 131; "Haknkreyts" (Swastika), 131; "Henkers" (Executioners), 129–131; "Idn" (Jews), 132, 133; "Lintshing" (Lynching), 132–134; "A Neger shtarbt" (A Negro dies), 107, 127–131, 132; "Nones" (Nuns), 130; Reyshe: Poema (Rzeszow: A poem), 127; "Tregers un negers" (Carriers/Porters and Negroes), 301n85; "Tslomim" (Crosses), 129, 130
Weissman, Irving, 139–140
Weller, Robert, 11–12
Western Wall (Palestine), 74, 93–94, 96, 250
Wexler, Paul, 285n91
Wiggins, Ella May, 92, 93
Wilde, Oscar, 323n28
Williams, Raymond: Keywords, 11
Winchevsky, Morris, 20, 30, 42, 279n10; "To the Worker," 20; "Unfurl the Red Flag," 20
Wishnia, Kenneth, 323n31
Wisse, Ruth, 77, 135, 220, 270n7, 321n13, 322n17, 323n43
Wolitz, Seth, 22, 159, 308n86, 315n52

Workers Party of America, 32
World Yiddish Cultural Congress (1937), 141
Wright, Ada, 124
Wright, Andrew, 124
Wright, Richard, 124, 232; "I Have Seen Black Hands," 125, 299n66
Wright, Roy, 124

Yangtze River (China), 48, 49–50, 59–60
Yehoash (Solomon Bloomgarden): "Lintshen" (Lynching), 115, 128
Yerushalmi, Yosef Hayim: Zakhor, 147
Yiddish Writers' Union, 78, 94
Yidishe kultur (journal), x, 127
Young Communist League, 139
Yung Kuznye (journal), 25, 218

Zaagsma, Gerben, 303nn12–14
Zamenhof, Ludwik, 20
Zhdanov, Andrei, 228
Zhitlowsky, Chaim, 24
Zionism, 5–6, 11, 20, 88, 270n10; Bialik and, 21, 52, 54, 69, 73, 77, 83, 181, 244; British and 22, 69, 73, 76, 80, 89, 91; Crimea and, 62–65, 69, 285n93; Grinberg and, 52, 113–114; Hirschbein and, 69–70; Hofshteyn and 188, 192, 196, 208, 315n52; Jabotinsky and, 186; Modern Hebrew and, 22, 54–55, 274n69; rejection of, 14–16, 20, 26, 69–70, 75, 83–85, 87, 89–90, 93–94, 96, 97, 213, 222; Shumiatcher and, 63–64, 69–70; Soviet dissidents and, 330n7; Spanish Civil War and, 141–142, 155. See also Palestine
Zipperstein, Steven, 21, 134
Žižek, Slavoj, 284n76